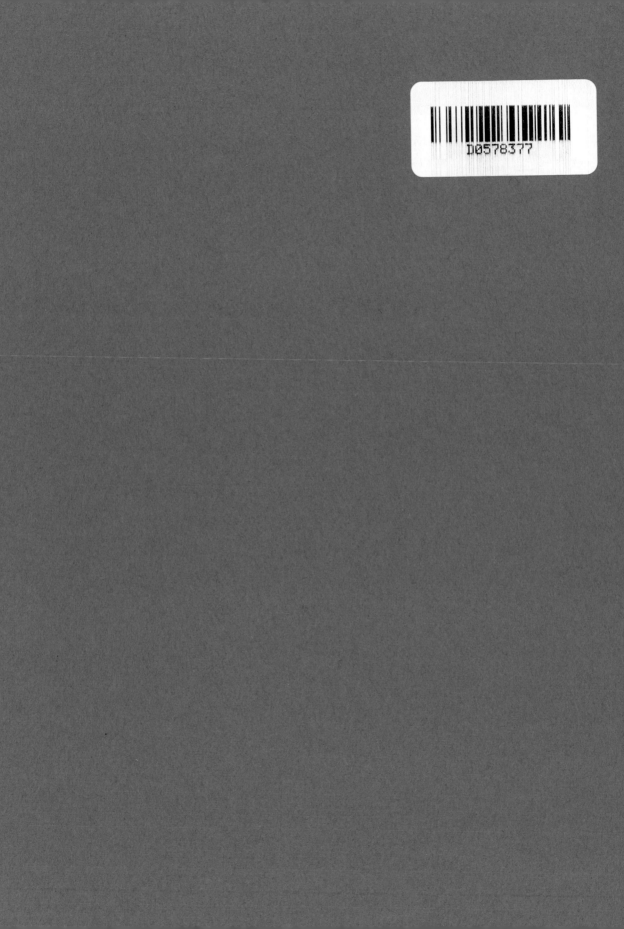

The Southern Hospitality Cookbook

The Southern Hospitality Cookbook

by Winifred Green Cheney

Acknowledgments

Acknowledgements are gratefully made to Miss Eudora Welty for her inspirational help, Mrs. Seymour Gordon for her fine editing, to Mrs. Frank Hagaman, Mrs. Charles Hughes, Mrs. Sallie Jorgensen, and Mrs. Hugh Luckett for their valuable assistance, and to the friends and restaurants around the world who shared their prize recipes with me.

Copyright ©1976 by Oxmoor House, Inc.
Book division of the Progressive Farmer Company
P.O. Box 2463, Birmingham, Alabama 35202

ISBN: 0-8487-0417-7
Library of Congress Catalog Card Number: 75-42943

Manufactured in the United States of America

First Printing 1976
Second Printing 1976

Southern Hospitality Cookbook

Editor: Candace C. Franklin
Photographers: Taylor Lewis, Burt O'Neal, Phil
    Kretchmar and Kent Kirkley
Illustrations: Carol Hanna

Contents

To My
Beloved Reynolds

Preface

by Eudora Welty

A NOTE ON THE COOK

Winifred Green Cheney is an old friend and near neighbor of mine in Jackson, Mississippi, and although I am not a cook, I am well equipped to testify to her cooking—from the dining room if not the kitchen. Her cooking is superb. But knowing there are further qualifications for a good cookbook, Mrs. Cheney has seen to those admirably too.

Winifred Cheney has not only collected and thoroughly tested and wisely chosen her dishes, she has learned all about them. She has traveled and tasted all over our part of the world with an alert, investigative interest in the background and provenance of the recipes she works from. The variety of Southern dishes is wide: indeed, the South is a big place—bigger than France, as has been pointed out—and it has had a long history. Its dishes, distinctively Southern as they have become, may go back in origin to the French, Spanish, English, German, Mexican, Greek, Dalmatian, African, Creole, or Caribbean comers to the land. Mrs. Cheney sets value on this ingredient of flavor. Her respect for the local dish and for the time-honored style of preparing it forms the *roux*, you might say, on which her own creations are based.

The recipes here come to us by way of long experience in the kitchen and out of the patience of the perfectionist. The zest Mrs. Cheney takes in her cooking comes through in the zest with which she writes down her recipes for us. She makes us acquainted, altogether, with the essence and character as well as the proper substance of the dish at hand.

The cook who can make a dream of a dish isn't necessarily able thereby to set down for others the exact way to prepare it. I can testify that one of the hardest things in the language to write is a set of clear directions. Mrs. Cheney has the gift, and the conscience, for doing it.

Winifred at home cooks for her family, for her friends, of course. She cooks to honor the visitor, and also she cooks for a varying but ever-present list of neighbors or friends who are convalescing from illness, who are in trouble of some kind, who are alone or confined to their homes. (And for some reason known only to her kindness, she includes in her list writers. Let me be confined to my typewriter with a deadline, and, as though it were a fate I didn't deserve, Winifred appears with something on a tray to sustain me.) The original Lady Bountiful was the invention of an Irish dramatist in 1707. Winifred exists as her own version. She makes her rounds with baskets and trays as a simple extension of her natural hospitality. In good weather but especially in bad, splashing forth in raincoat and tennis shoes, carrying a warm cake straight from her oven, she sympathizes with you or celebrates with you by sharing her table with you.

I hope Winifred does not mind my coming out in print about her character—after all, it is no secret in her hometown—for my reason is that I believe it has something positive to do with how good the food is. All of Mrs. Cheney's dishes came about through the explicit idea of giving pleasure to particular people—with real people, and a real occasion, in mind. I think that may be a very good secret of the best cooking.

When Jane Austen's Miss Bates, attending Mr. Weston's ball, is seated at the supper, she surveys the table with a cry, "How shall we ever recollect half of the dishes?" When I sit down to Sunday dinner at Winifred's I feel just like Miss Bates. What guest could not? But it now becomes possible for us to recollect the dishes we've dined on there. The cook herself has recollected—and here presented—the recipes for them. They are here to study and follow in her own cookbook.

It's a gracious cookbook. It's like another extension of Winifred Cheney's hospitality; she has added another leaf to her table.

Introduction

We Southerners live at a leisurely pace and sharing our hospitality with our family, friends, and the stranger within our gate is one of our greatest joys. I hope my book will inspire you to cook an unforgettable meal and to take the time to savor it.

From the mountains of Virginia to the Texas Plains there is a Southern way of life and it begins with hospitality and a proper emphasis on good cooking. Hospitality assumes varied forms in each locale, for our forefathers came from many different countries.

Here in the South we call it "the home flavor." We like to honor a visitor at our own dinner table, to prepare our favorite food to please his palate. It may be piping hot, fluffy spoonbread served with broiled quail for an exciting breakfast treat. Or, like the Natchez belle of the early 1800s, we may finish our dinner with Love's Delight Cake and trust that our guest will recall its memorable flavor long after he has returned home.

In the Low Country of South Carolina we may savor the rich delicacy of Charleston's favorite She-Crab Soup. Or, while attending a holiday open house along Virginia's Tidewater section, we may enjoy for the first time hot, beaten biscuits filled with delectable Spiced Round and cups of creamy eggnog.

Down Mobile way there is nothing more elegant than the bay's fresh crabmeat served with tasty homemade mayonnaise or lightly sautéed in butter and served with tomato wedges. mushrooms, and sherry.

Louisiana offers its visitors two cuisines different from the plantation fare of some of the other Southern states: the Creole of the New Orleans area with herbs, seasonings, and spices blended to enhance, not drown, the taste of the natural food; and the robust, zesty, country cooking of the Cajun country with its crawfish étouffée, jambalaya, and boudin.

Texans delight in the many different cuisines of its early settlers. Years ago I dined in a stately home on King William Street, part of San Antonio's old German section known as Sauerkraut Bend. We enjoyed flavorful split pea soup, rabbit stew with rich dumplings, fresh garden salad served in a tomato cup, and luscious almond torte. At a ranch near Center Point, celebrating a family gathering, we feasted on savory barbecued beef, chicken, and an unusually fine potato salad. A visitor in the state during the hunting season might enjoy a gourmet dish of doves or quail sautéed in butter with shallots, mushrooms, and seasonings, then baked in vermouth. Where else can you find such an abundance of authentic Mexican food such as chili con queso, chicken chalupas, enchiladas verdes, beef tacos with native beers, and refreshing Sangria?

I want you to sample the full range of Southern cookery as well as that of other sections and other lands. My recipes are time-tested and as foolproof as possible. I learn through experience. My interest began during a seven-year-long engagement. I wished to keep my sweetheart's interest and to meet the competition—my prospective mother-in-law was the best cook in town and my fiancé was accustomed to fine food.

There was a procession of great cooks through my own mother's kitchen, and they all cooked with a pinch of this and a dash of that, using no definite recipes. Watching Maria Mitchell, one of the Mississippi Coast's finest cooks, make Crab Gumbo I took notes of what and how much she put into the soup kettle by measuring each ingredient before she dumped it in. The next day, under her supervision, I made the gumbo, carefully following the directions. Consequently, I am able to give you one of the most delectable seafood recipes.

The most important lesson I learned those hot summer mornings over the wood burning stove was "to taste." No matter whose recipe you are following, taste the dish while cooking to be sure the seasonings are correct. That often makes the difference between an ordinary dish and a masterpiece. I even sample my cake batter before baking. I enjoy dreaming up new creations and unusual combinations of foods; at least 40 percent of my recipes are my own brain children. For your utmost enjoyment I often suggest the proper accompaniments.

Good food around a common table welds a family together with strong bonds of affection and camaraderie. My appreciation for its blessings dates from earliest childhood recollections. I remember the Easter the bishop came to dinner. Mama's immense Chinese platters were piled high with golden fried chicken—all breasts, short thighs, and drumsticks, not a back or neck in sight. Gabe Vaughn, our cook and butler, had outdone himself. He had surrounded my favorite food with brightly stuffed tomatoes and for dessert he served luscious strawberry shortcake.

The year's most important event was the annual family Christmas tree held on Christmas Eve. All sixty clan members gathered at my mother's home to exchange gifts and to enjoy Aunt Winnie's homemade raspberry ice cream and rocks. In later years I found that appetite is bred by variety, and change is often beneficial. The housewife who is truly imaginative adapts and rectifies, consulting her own and her family's tastes and those of frequent guests. The table is indeed the center of a happy home, the lure and sustainer of loving hearts. If I mentioned at breakfast that I was having stuffed sirloin steak and Waldorf scalloped potatoes for dinner, do you think I would have an empty seat at the table no matter what activity was going on that night?

Join me in my kitchen. I know I can add more zest to your everyday meal and give you a taste of sparkling Southern Hospitality.

Eudora's Niche

AT HOME WITH EUDORA WELTY

"This is a *real* home, isn't it, Grandmother? Every time I come here it makes me feel so nice and easy." The parting remark of my young granddaughter as we walked down the front steps of Eudora Welty's house describes its mistress also.

Our first lady of American letters, whose latest book, *Losing Battles*, is on the national best-seller list, has the remarkable ability to make even the very young feel at home. She comes down to their level naturally and without offense. This to me is a mark of the truly great. Eudora is just that.

"I like that famous lady," my granddaughter continued.

Antoinette had overwhelmed my favorite author with many questions. "Do you stack your papers to the ceiling in the room where you work? How long did it take you to write *Losing Battles*?"

Eudora had smiled quietly. "How old are you, Antoinette?"

"I'll be ten in October, M'am."

"Well, it took me that many years to complete my book, but I was not writing on it all the time."

"Gee." Antoinette's eyes flew wide open.

My granddaughter and I had gone over to take a serving of my new creation, Avocado Mousse, to Eudora. On many occasions she has been gracious enough to help me with the proper seasoning. Among Eudora's own specialties are old-fashioned fig preserves and fruit cake. These delights she often shares with friends all over the world. She is an excellent cook, and her discriminating taste in foods is almost as choice as her use of words.

CHESTINA WELTY'S GREEN TOMATO MINCEMEAT

Eudora's mother's recipe and a great favorite of Eudora's. She enjoys it as a conserve on a sandwich. It is delicious with ham or pork. I find it makes a delightful mince pie by using 3 cups mincemeat, dotting with butter, adding ¼ cup sherry and baking in an unbaked 9-inch pie crust for 30 minutes at 450°.

 1 gallon ground green tomatoes
½ gallon ground tart apples
   Juice and grated rind of 2 lemons
 2 pounds seedless raisins
 5 pounds sugar
 1 pint cider vinegar
 1 teaspoon freshly ground nutmeg
 1 teaspoon freshly ground allspice
 2 teaspoons ground cinnamon
 2 tablespoons salt
¼ pound butter
 1 pound shelled pecans, finely sliced

Wash and grind tomatoes and apples, reserving juice. In a large dishpan heat tomatoes, apples, and juices. Drain, bring to a boil, and drain again. Add raisins, sugar, vinegar, seasonings, butter, and pecans and boil for 30 minutes, stirring constantly. Seal hot in sterilized jars. Yield: 10 to 12 pints.

FIG PRESERVES

Select figs that are ripe but firm enough to hold their shape when skinned. Make only a small amount of preserves at one time—not more than 6 cups.

Peel and measure the figs, and then measure an equal amount of sugar. Place the figs and the sugar gently in a bowl in layers and leave in the refrigerator overnight. By morning the sugar will have drawn the juice from the figs, and it will be unnecessary to add any liquid. Thinly slice a lemon and add to the fig and juice mixture, putting all into a deep kettle on a slow burner. Gradually bring to a boil and cook gently until figs are transparent; taste to tell when done. Skim off foam, lift out fruit, and pack into jars. Pour juice over figs, and seal. Chill before serving.

APPLES EUDORA

An elegant dessert created especially for my dear friend Eudora in honor of Eudora Welty Day. Governor Bill Waller proclaimed a state-wide celebration to pay homage to Mississippi's illustrious daughter. The recipe combines Eudora's favorites: tart apples cooked in a delicious syrup, drained and baked in a rich custard, then filled with an apricot rum filling and topped with a dollop of whipped cream.

**8 medium-size to large tart apples, Jonathan,
    Winesap, Rome Beauty**
1 cup water
2 cups sugar
2 tablespoons freshly strained lemon juice
¼ teaspoon red food coloring
1 teaspoon ground cinnamon
⅛ teaspoon ground nutmeg
**   Custard**
**   Apricot Rum Filling**

Wash, core, and peel apples, reserving some of the peel. Be sure the center of apple is open from bottom to top. Combine water, sugar, lemon juice, red food coloring, spices, and reserved apple peel in a large skillet and bring to rapid boil over high heat. Stir until sugar is dissolved. Place apples in skillet, reduce heat to medium, and cook about 20 minutes or until a straw pierces apple easily. Turn apples over carefully once or twice during cooking process. Remove apples to a large platter to drain while preparing custard.

Custard:

** 4 large eggs**
½ cup sugar
2½ cups milk
**½ cup whipping cream or undiluted
    evaporated milk**
⅛ teaspoon salt
2 teaspoons vanilla extract
1 teaspoon butter

Break eggs into a large bowl; add sugar, milk, cream, salt, and vanilla. Beat mixture lightly with a wire whisk—just enough to mix well. Gently place apples in a buttered, oblong 2-quart casserole and pour custard around them. Place casserole in a pan and surround with hot water at least half-way up its side (about 1 inch in depth). Bake in a preheated 300° oven for 45 to 50 minutes. Insert knife into custard at center of casserole; it should come out clean. Remove casserole from pan of water and fill with Apricot Rum filling.

Apricot Rum Filling:

** 1 cup dried apricots**
**   Water to cover**
1⅓ cups sugar
** 2 tablespoons dark rum**
** 1 cup whipping cream,
    whipped**
** 2 tablespoons powdered sugar**

In a saucepan cover apricots with water and bring to boil over medium heat. Keep on a simmering boil for 35 to 40 minutes; apricots must be tender. Add sugar the last 10 minutes of cooking. Drain apricots and puree in blender or put through food mill or ricer; add rum. Fill center of apples with puree and mound some on top. Chill casserole 2 hours before serving. Cut into square wedges and top with a dollop of whipped cream sweetened with powdered sugar. Yield: 6 servings.

Note: Any remaining puree will keep refrigerated for several weeks sealed in pint jar; it will also freeze. Delicious on toast or ice cream.

SQUASH EUDORA

A tribute in the field of cookery is called a "signature recipe." *Squash Eudora* is just such a tribute—a toast to my friend and neighbor Eudora Welty for her perfection in expressing the written word both in the novel and the short story.

"In these dark days," writes Martha Graham, the great dancer, in the 1969 Spring issue of the Washington and Lee University's *Shenandoah,* "it is all the clearer that Miss Welty's novels and stories are a national treasure. We must guard it zealously for such a glory as Eudora does not often come to look at us, study us, and sing about us."

For those who would enjoy an unforgettable meal using Squash Eudora as an entrée, serve a chilled garden tomato, peeled and stuffed with cottage cheese mixed with well-seasoned mayonnaise; tender Kentucky Wonder pole beans cooked with ham nubbins; a pickled peach; hot buttered biscuits; and your own blackberry jelly.

2 pounds tender yellow squash
3 tablespoons butter
½ teaspoon salt
1 teaspoon dried green onion
¼ teaspoon freshly ground black pepper
¼ teaspoon paprika
¾ pound chicken livers
3 tablespoons butter
4 teaspoons Worcestershire sauce
½ teaspoon salt
¼ teaspoon freshly ground black pepper
¼ teaspoon celery seeds
⅛ teaspoon curry powder
1 egg, lightly beaten
Grated Parmesan cheese

Wash squash but do not peel. Slice as thinly as possible, and place slices in a saucepan with 3 tablespoons butter, ½ teaspoon salt, dried green onion, ¼ teaspoon freshly ground black pepper, and paprika. Simmer over low heat about 25 minutes or until squash is tender when tested with a fork.

Wash chicken livers and cut in halves. Melt 3 tablespoons butter; put in a 2-quart baking dish and add Worcestershire sauce, ½ teaspoon salt, and ¼ teaspoon freshly ground black pepper. Marinate livers in this mixture for 20 minutes. Bake, uncovered, in a preheated 350° oven for 20 minutes. Turn livers after 10 minutes.

Add cooked chicken livers to cooked squash, celery seeds, curry powder, and lightly beaten egg. Mix lightly and taste to see if more salt is needed. Place mixture in the same baking dish. Sprinkle top with grated Parmesan cheese, and bake in a preheated 350° oven about 25 minutes. Yield: 6 to 8 servings.

Variation: You may substitute 1 pound lump crabmeat for the chicken livers. Carefully pick through crabmeat for bits of shell. Delete marinating ingredients and add crabmeat directly to cooked squash. Proceed as directed above.

SAVORING MISS WELTY'S WIT AT A SPECIAL SEAFOOD LUNCH

By David W. Hacker

The rarest of all persons are those for whom fame is no more important than the permanence of a single beam of sunshine, a lone raindrop, or a quiet cough. Such a person is Eudora Welty. For more years than she cares to remember she has been quietly turning out, from her large, old, comfortable house on Pinehurst Street in Jackson, Mississippi, the wryly wrought, incredibly detailed, pointillist portraits of her much-loved rural Mississippi. She is a Jackson girl who never much cared to be anything other than a Jackson girl and a Mississippian.

I have dipped only occasionally into Miss Welty's work, enough to know that she is among the first five or so living American novelists, and certainly, the South's leading lady writer.

So I felt flattered and full of appreciation when Winifred Green Cheney, a frequent contributor to this column (*The National Observer*), invited me to lunch in Jackson with Miss Welty, her old and close friend. This was not to be a literary luncheon, so I left behind my tape recorder. It was an intimate luncheon for four. For two hours, as it turned out, Eudora and I did talk of literature, writing, the state of *our* craft and of *her* art.

I made desultory notes afterward on the plane (my pause in Jackson was, literally, a luncheon stop between St. Louis and Atlanta), but so overwhelmed was I by Eudora's charm, wit, twinkle, humor, and calm good sense that I abandoned my notes.

Character, like the sunbeam, the splashing raindrop, the stoicism of death, the ecstasy of love, is not something easily written about. So I chose merely to savor (I promised myself to return with a tape recorder someday) that interlude, a savoring made all the sharper when, a few days later, I received from Mrs. Cheney the recipe for the main course that she had created just for the luncheon. She calls it *Les Merveilles de la Mer*—marvels of the sea.

Miss Welty found it to her taste, and so did I.

LES MERVEILLES DE LA MER

A superb seafood casserole I created for David W. Hacker, my foods editor from *The National Observer,* who flew down from Washington, D.C., to have lunch at my home with Eudora Welty and me.

½ cup plus 1 tablespoon butter
4 tablespoons all-purpose flour
1 pint half-and-half, heated
⅛ teaspoon ground mace
¼ teaspoon salt
¼ teaspoon Tabasco
⅛ teaspoon freshly ground white pepper
1 (14-ounce) can artichoke hearts
1 (6-ounce) can buttered whole crown mushrooms or ½ pound fresh mushrooms, sautéed in ½ stick butter
½ pound fresh lump crabmeat or frozen Alaskan king crabmeat, thawed and drained
½ pound cooked, peeled, and deveined shrimp
4 tablespoons good dry sauterne

Melt ½ cup butter in top of a double boiler over rapidly boiling water or in a teflon skillet over low heat. Blend in flour with a wire whisk; slowly stir in hot cream. Add mace, salt, Tabasco, and white pepper. Cook and stir until sauce is smooth and thickened. Taste to see if more salt is needed.

Rinse artichoke hearts in cold water, drain, and dry on paper towel; cut in halves. In another saucepan over low heat warm mushrooms and artichoke hearts. Arrange these in a large flat-bottomed casserole buttered with remaining 1 tablespoon butter and crabmeat and shrimp. Cover with white sauce to which you have added the sauterne. Cover with foil and bake in a preheated 325° oven for 20 to 30 minutes or until sauce is bubbly. Do not overcook for that destroys the marvelous flavor of the fresh crabmeat; only heat thoroughly. Serve with saffron rice, broccoli with lemon butter sauce, tossed green salad and hot biscuits or French bread. This dish reheats well. I would not recommend freezing. Yield: 8 to 10 servings.

RASPBERRY RAPTURE

Created and served at a dinner party honoring my dear friend Eudora Welty who had just returned home after receiving the Gold Medal for fiction. (The highest award given by the National Academy of Arts and Letters, it is bestowed once every 10 years.)

On tasting the dessert Eudora asked, "What are you going to call it, *Raspberry Rapture?* It's so divine, I am not sure that title is adequate." I thought it was.

2 (9-inch) pie shells, baked and frozen
1 (10-ounce) package frozen red raspberries
2 large egg whites
1 cup sifted sugar
1 tablespoon strained lemon juice
2 teaspoons crème d' almond, divided
½ pint very cold whipping cream
1 teaspoon vanilla extract
1 tablespoon sugar
1 tablespoon brandy—Framboise, if available
¼ cup sliced butter-toasted almonds

If you make your own pastry, add ½ teaspoon almond extract to the dough. Place partially thawed berries, egg whites, sugar, lemon juice, and 1 teaspoon crème d' almond in a large mixing bowl and beat at high speed of electric mixer for 15 minutes. Constantly cut down mixture from sides with spatula during process. This makes a very buoyant mixture.

Whip chilled cream in a cold narrow bowl. When it stands in peaks add remaining 1 teaspoon crème d' almond, vanilla, sugar, and brandy. Fold whipped cream and toasted almonds into raspberry mixture. Spoon into frozen baked shells and freeze. Take out of freezer at least 30 minutes before serving. Yield: 12 servings.

Appetizers and Hors d'Oeuvres

FRESH PICKLED MUSHROOMS

A superb and zesty hors d'oeuvre! A joy to fix and to eat. Make plenty; they vanish like the wind. Use as a gourmet touch for a green salad.

1½ quarts large, fresh white mushrooms with
    short stems (cut off tip of stem)
    Cold water to cover
2½ teaspoons salt
  8 tablespoons rice wine or white wine
    vinegar
  4 teaspoons grated onion
  2 teaspoons dried green onion
  1 cup olive oil
  4 cloves garlic, thinly sliced
12 peppercorns

Cover mushrooms with cold water and soak for 20 minutes. Rinse thoroughly in cold water and drain in a colander. Place mushrooms in saucepan, sprinkle with salt, cover, and cook for 12 minutes over medium heat. Do not add water; when mushrooms begin to boil, lower heat to a simmer. In a large bowl combine rice wine, grated onion, dried green onion, and olive oil; blend well. Add mushrooms and mix well. Sterilize three 8-ounce jars, placing equal amounts of garlic and peppercorns in each. Pack mushrooms into jars with button ends down. Pour vinegar and oil mixture over them and seal. These will keep for a week or two in a cool place and ten months to a year if refrigerated. Always allow mushrooms to sit for at least a few days before using. Serve on a toothpick. The mushrooms look most attractive studding a grapefruit or cabbage head. These make a wonderful gift for your drinking friends and those who watch their calories. Yield: 1½ pints.

PARTY MUSHROOM SANDWICHES

Delicious in place of rolls for luncheon or coffee, tea or cocktail party. Sandwiches may be completely prepared, baked, and frozen; just reheat to serve.

6 tablespoons butter, divided
3 tablespoons all-purpose flour
1 cup milk, hot
1 chicken bouillon cube
¼ teaspoon salt
⅛ teaspoon paprika
⅛ teaspoon ground mace
½ teaspoon grated lemon rind or lemon bits
 3 or 4 dashes Tabasco
¾ cup fresh mushrooms
23 slices very fresh sandwich bread, crusts
    removed

In a saucepan melt 3 tablespoons butter; add and blend in flour. Slowly stir in hot milk that has dissolved bouillon cube in it. Add seasonings and Tabasco. Wash mushrooms under cold running water and dry on paper towels. Sauté mushrooms in 2 tablespoons butter over medium heat for 5 to 7 minutes. Cool; chop mushrooms and add to hot cream sauce. Allow mixture to cool. Spread on bread slices; roll and secure with a toothpick. Brush rolls with remaining 1 tablespoon melted butter; refrigerate. Place on greased cookie sheet and toast at 350° for about 20 minutes or until nicely browned. Cut in half with kitchen scissors and serve hot. Yield: 23 whole sandwich rolls or 46 halves.

HOT MUSHROOM DIP

A superb dip for a chafing dish, this recipe is easy to prepare and a quickie.

1 pound fresh white mushrooms
4 tablespoons butter
1 tablespoon grated onion or onion puree
1 tablespoon prepared Dijon mustard
½ teaspoon salt
⅛ teaspoon ground nutmeg
1 clove garlic, minced, or ⅛ teaspoon garlic
**   powder**
2 tablespoons finely chopped dried, frozen, or
**   fresh parsley**
¼ teaspoon Tabasco
1 cup commercial sour cream
**   Melba rounds**

Wash mushrooms under cold running water; dry and slice lengthwise. Melt butter in chafing dish, add remaining ingredients except sour cream and cook over medium heat for 7 to 10 minutes or until mushrooms are tender. Fold in sour cream; taste to see if more salt is needed. Serve hot on melba rounds. Yield: about 6 cups—72 servings.

ELLY LAUNIUS' RIPE OLIVE DIP

A great dip, this can be served hot or cold.

1 cup ripe olives, coarsely chopped
8 ounces sharp cheese, finely shredded
¼ cup mayonnaise
2 tablespoons finely chopped onion
1 teaspoon curry powder
½ teaspoon garlic salt
**   Toast rounds**

Combine all ingredients in a large bowl; mix well. To use hot, spread mixture on toast rounds and broil until cheese melts. Yield: about 2 cups—24 servings.

Variations: To serve chilled, form balls from a teaspoonful of mixture; roll in chopped parsley, sesame seeds, or chili powder. Chill and serve with melba toast. To use as a dip, mix equal parts of mixture with sour cream. Serve with crackers or chips. For a festive holiday scheme, use green olives stuffed with pimiento.

BEER CHEESE

A delicious cheese spread for snacks, parties, or for Christmas gifts.

1 pound sharp cheddar cheese
1 pound Swiss cheese
1 teaspoon dry mustard
1 small clove garlic, minced, or ⅛ teaspoon
**   garlic powder**
1 teaspoon Worcestershire sauce
1 cup beer
**   Crackers, rye bread, or celery**

Shred cheeses and blend with remaining ingredients. Pack into 6-ounce containers. Age four or five days in refrigerator. Allow mixture to reach room temperature before serving with crackers or rye bread. Beer Cheese also makes a tangy spread to stuff 2- to 3-inch strips of celery for use at a cocktail party. Yield: 5 (6-ounce) containers.

BRANDIED CHEESE

A full-bodied cheese with the bouquet of a fine brandy. This is ideal for home use, a party, a bazaar, or for Christmas gifts.

1 pound sharp cheddar cheese
2 tablespoons butter or margarine
1 teaspoon sugar
⅛ teaspoon cayenne pepper
½ cup brandy
    Salted crackers, rye or French bread, or
      fresh fruit

Shred cheese. Allow cheese and butter to reach room temperature. Add sugar and cayenne pepper; blend until smooth. Gradually beat in brandy. (A blender does a marvelous job.) Pack into 6-ounce containers and cover tightly with foil or jar tops. Age four or five days in the refrigerator. Allow mixture to reach room temperature before serving with salted crackers or rye or French bread. It is also very tasty with fresh pears, apples, and a dessert wine. Yield: 3 (6-ounce) containers.

PEGGY COLLINS' CHEESE-OLIVE PUFFS

Delightfully different! A tasty morsel for a morning coffee, a tea, or a cocktail party. Make ahead of time; they must freeze for one or two hours before baking and will keep from four to six weeks in the freezer.

½ pound sharp cheddar cheese, shredded
½ cup butter, softened
1 cup all-purpose flour, sifted
½ teaspoon salt
1 teaspoon paprika
48 small stuffed olives

In large bowl, blend cheese and butter; add flour, salt, and paprika. Wrap each pimiento-stuffed olive in 1 teaspoon of dough. Arrange

balls in an ungreased shallow pan and freeze 1 to 2 hours. Take out of freezer a few minutes before baking. Bake in a preheated 425° oven for 12 to 15 minutes; serve hot. Keep unused frozen balls in plastic bags in freezer. Freezing the balls keeps the dough from spreading during the cooking process. Yield: 4 dozen.

FRANCES ELISE REMBERT'S HOT CHEESE STRAWS

Marvelous at a cocktail party.

½ pound extra sharp cheddar cheese, grated
1 cup butter or margarine, softened
2 cups all-purpose flour
1 teaspoon salt
½ teaspoon cayenne pepper
1 teaspoon Tabasco

Blend cheese and butter in a bowl. Sift flour, salt, and cayenne pepper into cheese mixture; add Tabasco and blend thoroughly with pastry blender or forks. Squeeze through cookie press or shape into balls and chill 2 hours. Roll out dough ⅛ inch thick. Cut into strips 3 x ¼ inches. Bake in a preheated 425° oven for 8 minutes. Yield: 6 dozen.

SESAME CHEESE STRAWS

A gourmet treat! These are excellent with alcoholic beverages.

½ pound very sharp cheddar cheese, shredded
1 (2¼-ounce) jar sesame seeds
½ cup butter or margarine, softened
1¼ cups all-purpose flour
1 teaspoon salt
⅛ teaspoon cayenne pepper

Allow shredded cheese to reach room temperature. Toast sesame seeds in a heavy skillet, stirring constantly over low heat about 20 minutes or until golden brown; cool. Combine cheese, butter, flour, salt, and cayenne pepper; work dough until mixture is thoroughly blended. Add sesame seeds. Roll dough to ⅛ inch thickness; cut into 4- x ½-inch strips. Bake in a preheated 400° oven for 12 to 15 minutes until golden brown; cool on wire rack. Place in an airtight container. These keep fresh for several weeks. Yield: 5 dozen.

GOLDEN CHEESE DELIGHTS

This is a delicious and colorful tidbit to serve for a morning coffee, afternoon tea, or cocktail party. Ideal for a group of young people after a football game with colas or hot chocolate. The recipe must be prepared at least four hours ahead of time—preferably a day in advance—and kept refrigerated.

1 large loaf white pullman bread, unsliced
1 pound sharp Wisconsin or New York State cheddar cheese, finely grated
1 cup homemade mayonnaise or 1 cup commercial mayonnaise made with lemon juice
3 tablespoons whipping cream
¼ teaspoon Tabasco
1 tablespoon Worcestershire sauce
1 tablespoon finely grated onion or 3 teaspoons onion puree
½ teaspoon Beau Monde seasoning

Keep bread one day and remove crust; slice 1 inch thick and cut each slice into fourths. In a large bowl, combine grated cheese, mayonnaise, and cream. Mixture should be easy to spread. Add remaining ingredients. Taste to see if more salt is needed.

Spread cheese mixture on all sides of bread cubes except bottom—icing as you would a cake. Place cubes on a large ungreased cookie sheet and cover with waxed paper. Refrigerate until ready to serve. Bake in a preheated 400° oven for 5 minutes, watching carefully. To keep warm, hold delights at 200° for 30 min-

utes to 1 hour after baking. Cooked and uncooked, these freeze well. If you like, put a dozen on several foil trays and bring out when needed. Yield: 2½ dozen.

Note: By cutting each 1-inch thick slice of bread into eighths instead of into fourths, you increase the yield to 60 delights and have an excellent size for cocktail parties.

FROZEN CHIVE CHEESE CANAPES

Serve these tasty and tempting appetizers when unexpected guests stop in. After freezing on cookie sheet, package them in containers.

2 cups grated sharp cheddar cheese
1 egg, beaten
10 dashes Tabasco
¼ teaspoon Worcestershire sauce
¼ teaspoon salt
8 slices white bread
2 tablespoons chopped frozen or freeze-dried chives
3 sweet pickles, sliced
4 slices bacon, fried crisp and drained

Combine grated cheese, egg, Tabasco, Worcestershire sauce, and salt; mix well. Trim crusts from bread and cut each slice into four squares, triangles, or strips. Toast at 350° for 20 minutes. Mound a teaspoonful of cheese mixture on each piece of bread, covering to the edge. Press chopped chives around the bread's edges. Garnish the center of some with a pickle slice, others with crumbled bacon. Bake at 450° for about 3 minutes, until cheese begins to puff and is slightly melted. Yield: about 3 dozen.

CRUNCHY CHEESE ROUNDS

Crisp and zesty—ideal to serve at a cocktail party; delicious as a snack with colas or with coffee for a morning party.

2 cups grated sharp cheddar cheese
1 cup margarine, softened
2 cups all-purpose flour
⅛ teaspoon sugar
¼ teaspoon cayenne pepper
¾ teaspoon salt
1 teaspoon Worcestershire sauce
¼ teaspoon Tabasco
2 cups crispy rice cereal

Blend cheese and margarine in large bowl. Sift flour, sugar, cayenne pepper, and salt into mixture; add remaining ingredients. Work dough with pastry blender or hands. Pinch dough into small balls, 1 inch in diameter. Place balls on ungreased cookie sheet and press down with palm of hand into small circle. Bake in a preheated 350° oven for 12 minutes until golden brown. Cool on wire rack and store in sealed container. Handle gently; they are very crisp. Yield: 11 dozen.

MARINATED CRAB CLAWS

A zesty taste thrill.

12 crab claws, boiled
1 (16-ounce) bottle fine Italian dressing
1 cup virgin olive oil
3 tablespoons wine or rice vinegar
2 tablespoons lemon juice
3 garlic cloves, minced
2 tablespoons red or white wine
½ cup dried parsley flakes
½ teaspoon salt
1 teaspoon freshly ground black pepper
1 teaspoon ground oregano
2 tablespoons Worcestershire sauce
½ cup grated Parmesan cheese

Place crab claws in 13- x 9- x 2-inch glass casserole. In large bowl blend remaining ingredients and pour over crab claws; cover with foil and refrigerate at least 8 hours or overnight. Yield: 12 marinated crab claws—6 servings.

SNOW RING CRAB MOLD

This makes an elegant party mold to serve with cocktails or a tart fruit punch of the nonalcoholic variety. It serves 20 to 25—or more if other party food is served. It may be prepared a day in advance and kept refrigerated. The Rémoulade Sauce must be made at least one day before using and is also delicious on boiled shrimp or fresh crabmeat.

2 (7¼-ounce) cans white Alaskan or
**   Japanese crabmeat or 1 pound fresh**
**   white crabmeat**
1½ tablespoons unflavored gelatin
⅓ cup cold water
½ cup boiling water
** Rémoulade Sauce**
** Salt to taste**
** Crackers**
** Parsley**

Wash hands and pick through crabmeat carefully for bits of shell and cartilage. To perk up canned crabmeat, pour ice water over crabmeat in a colander and gently press out excess water. Soften gelatin in cold water, and dissolve in boiling water; cool. Lightly grease 8-inch ring mold with oil or mayonnaise. In large bowl blend Rémoulade Sauce and dissolved cooled gelatin; add crabmeat and salt (canned crabmeat already has salt in it). The mold sets very quickly—in about 1 hour. To unmold ring, run small sharp knife around sides to loosen, and then place lower half of mold in hot water for a minute, tap gently on top and place platter upside down on top of mold and turn over together. Use large flat platter or silver tray lined with clear plastic. Surround with crackers and decorate with sprigs of parsley. Yield: 1 (8½-inch) ring mold—20 to 25 servings.

Rémoulade Sauce:

3 teaspoons finely chopped anchovies
1 cup commercial mayonnaise made with
    lemon juice
1 tablespoon tarragon vinegar
1 tablespoon white wine vinegar
2 tablespoons dry sherry
¼ teaspoon garlic powder
½ cup chopped parsley, fresh or frozen
4 tablespoons small capers, well-drained
1 tablespoon onion juice or onion puree
½ teaspoon Tabasco

Combine all ingredients and blend well. Refrigerate. Yield: 1½ cups.

SMOKED OYSTERS

A rare and piquant recipe for oysters, this makes a delicious hors d'oeuvre.

2 quarts oysters
3 tablespoons liquid smoke
2 tablespoons strained lemon juice
1 teaspoon Accént
1 teaspoon garlic salt
1 cup corn or olive oil
2 tablespoons soy sauce
2 tablespoons Worcestershire sauce
1 teaspoon celery salt
1 teaspoon chili powder
  Bread
  Wheat crackers

Drain oysters. Combine remaining ingredients thoroughly in large mixing bowl. Marinate oysters in this mixture for 3 hours in refrigerator. Place oysters close together in shallow pan, and bake in a preheated 350° oven for 15 minutes on each side. Baste several times. To use smoked oysters at a later time, pack tightly in pint jars within an inch of top, add 2 tablespoons oil, and pressure cook 35 minutes at 10 pounds. For immediate use, serve on buttered bread, white or rye, or your favorite wheat crackers. Sliced dill pickle makes an excellent accompaniment. Yield: 4 pints.

CAROLINE LEGARE'S HOT CRAB DIP

A South Carolina taste delight. Excellent with a Bloody Mary or Screwdriver or a tart non-alcoholic punch. The dip will serve 25 to 30 guests when accompanied by other hors d'oeuvres.

2 (7-ounce) cans crabmeat or 12 ounces
    frozen crabmeat, thawed
2 (8-ounce) packages cream cheese
¼ teaspoon garlic salt
½ cup homemade mayonnaise or ½ cup
    commercial mayonnaise made with
    lemon juice
2 teaspoons dry mustard
2 teaspoons powdered sugar
1 teaspoon onion powder
  Salt to taste
¼ cup dry sherry
  Crackers or melba rounds

Place crabmeat in a colander and rinse with ice water; drain thoroughly. Check crabmeat for particles of shell or cartilage. Combine all ingredients except sherry in top of a double boiler and heat over rapidly boiling water. Add sherry and transfer mixture to heated chafing dish. Serve with crackers or melba rounds. Yield: about 4 cups—48 servings.

SHRIMP DELIGHT MOLD

Excellent as an entreé for a luncheon or as a spread for a cocktail party. Serves 30 to 35 guests as a spread, 8 to 10 guests for a luncheon entrée.

 4 teaspoons unflavored gelatin
¾ cup cold water
 1 cup mayonnaise
 2 (3-ounce) packages cream cheese,
    softened
⅓ cup strained lemon juice
 1 teaspoon Worcestershire sauce
 1 tablespoon small capers
 1 teaspoon salt
¼ teaspoon Tabasco
½ teaspoon paprika, divided
 1 teaspoon onion puree or juice of
    1 onion
½ teaspoon dried green onion
 1 hard-boiled egg, grated
    Mashed Shrimp
    Assorted crackers
    Parsley sprigs

Soak gelatin in cold water (place in pan of hot water to aid dissolving). When gelatin has dissolved, put aside to cool. Add mayonnaise and remaining ingredients except crackers and parsley, reserving ¼ teaspoon paprika for garnish; blend well. Grease a 9-inch ring mold or small loaf pan with mayonnaise and sprinkle with ¼ teaspoon paprika. Pour shrimp mixture into mold and chill; this will keep several days refrigerated or it may be frozen. To unmold ring, run small sharp knife around sides to loosen and then place lower half of mold into hot water for a minute. Tap gently on top, and place platter upside down on top of mold and turn over together. Use large flat platter or silver tray lined with clear plastic. Surround with assorted crackers and garnish with sprigs of parsley. Yield: 1 (9-inch) ring mold—30 to 35 servings as a spread or 7 to 10 servings as a luncheon entrée.

Mashed Shrimp:

1¼ pounds raw or frozen shrimp or 2
    (5-ounce) cans shrimp
 3 quarts water
½ lemon, juice and peel
 1 tablespoon Worcestershire sauce
½ teaspoon paprika
½ teaspoon dried green onion
 3 teaspoons salt
½ teaspoon Tabasco

Cook frozen shrimp according to package directions. Drain and rinse canned shrimp, and sprinkle with juice of ½ lemon. To cook raw shrimp, combine all ingredients including shrimp in a large saucepan and bring to a boil over high heat; turn down to a simmering boil and boil for 5 to 8 minutes (depending on size of shrimp) or until shells turn pink. From cooked shrimp remove shells and dark sand vein running along the back. Mash shrimp finely with fork or blender.

FESTIVE OYSTER DIP

Tasty and easy to prepare. Add more bread crumbs to the dip and have an entrée.

 1 quart oysters, drained
 1 cup butter or margarine
 1 bunch green onions, tops and all finely
    chopped
1½ cups finely chopped celery
⅓ cup chopped parsley
½ teaspoon dry mustard
 1 teaspoon freshly ground black pepper
 1 teaspoon salt
 4 eggs, slightly beaten
    About ½ cup toasted bread crumbs
    Assorted crackers

Cut oysters into small pieces. In large iron skillet melt butter and cook onions, celery, and parsley over medium heat until onions are golden and clear. Add oysters, mustard, pepper, salt, and eggs. When oysters plump up, add enough bread crumbs to thicken the mixture slightly. Transfer mixture to a hot chafing dish and serve with assorted crackers. Yield: about 2 quarts—108 servings.

Variation: To serve this as an entrée, increase the amount of bread crumbs to give the mixture substance, and place in 8 to 10 scallop or crab shells. Sprinkle with paprika and dot with a sprig of fresh parsley. Boiled new potatoes and fresh green asparagus make a marvelous accompaniment for a luncheon.

MILDRED REYNOLDS' MISSISSIPPI CAVIAR

2 (15¼-ounce) cans cooked black-eyed peas
1 cup salad oil
½ cup wine or rice vinegar
1 clove garlic, minced
¼ cup thinly sliced onions
½ teaspoon salt
⅛ teaspoon freshly ground black pepper
4 or 5 dashes Tabasco
  Crackers

Drain liquid from peas and place peas in a glass or stainless steel bowl. Add remaining ingredients and mix thoroughly. Place mixture in sealed glass jar in refrigerator for at least three days. Remove garlic after the first day. Serve on small party crackers. Yield: about 6 cups.

ADELE WEAVER'S CAVIAR MOUSSE

Marvelous!

1 envelope (1 tablespoon) unflavored
  gelatin
2 tablespoons cold water
½ cup boiling water
1 tablespoon strained lemon juice
1 tablespoon Worcestershire sauce
2 tablespoons mayonnaise
2 cups commercial sour cream
½ teaspoon dry mustard
1 tablespoon grated onion
¼ teaspoon Beau Monde seasoning
1 (4½-ounce) jar red caviar
2 hard-boiled eggs, finely chopped
  Lemon slices
  Paprika
  Melba rounds

Soften gelatin in cold water, then dissolve in boiling water. Add lemon juice and Worcestershire sauce; allow to cool. Combine mayonnaise with sour cream and add mustard, onion, and Beau Monde seasoning. Add to liquid mixture and blend well. Stir in caviar and chopped eggs.

Grease a 4-cup ring mold with a little vegetable oil, and pour in mousse. Refrigerate about 1 hour until set. To unmold, place lower half of mold in hot water for a minute or two, and gently cut around the edges of mold with a sharp knife. Place platter upside down on top of mold; then turn plate and mold over together. Be sure mold is squarely on plate before removing. Serve on crystal platter or silver platter lined with plastic. Garnish with lemon slices and paprika; surround mold with melba rounds. It is best to make the mousse the morning you plan to use it; do not make a day ahead of time. If there should be any leftovers, discard, for it becomes bitter if stored. Yield: 1 (4-cup) ring mold—30 to 35 servings.

CLAM PUFFS

Exotic morsels!

 2 (3-ounce) packages cream cheese, softened
⅛ teaspoon garlic powder
 1 (8-ounce) can minced clams, drained
 1 egg, slightly beaten
½ teaspoon seasoned salt
 4 drops Tabasco
 1 teaspoon Worcestershire sauce
40 rye bread rounds or melba toast

In mixing bowl, blend cheese until smooth and fluffy; add remaining ingredients except bread rounds and mix well. Toast bread rounds on one side and spread uncooked side with a heaping teaspoon of cheese and clam mixture. Place in broiler 4 inches from heat until puffy and lightly browned. Watch carefully to prevent burning. Yield: about 3½ dozen.

TANGY PICKLED SHRIMP

Boiled shrimp in a zippy sauce which keeps them fresh and tasty in the refrigerator for two weeks. Ideal for cocktail parties, buffet suppers, or as a pleasant surprise for your sweetheart with his predinner drink. The sauce is adequate for 1½ to 2½ pounds of fresh or frozen shrimp, deveined. Five pounds will serve 20 guests generously. Cook the desired amount of frozen shrimp according to package directions in the following mixture:

1½ quarts water
 1 tablespoon plus 1 teaspoon salt
¼ teaspoon dried green onion
 1 slice lemon
½ cup celery tops
 1 tablespoon Worcestershire sauce
¼ teaspoon instant crab and shrimp boil or
¼ teaspoon Tabasco and ¼ teaspoon
    paprika

If using fresh shrimp, bring water with all ingredients to a boil, add shrimp and return to a boil for 1 minute. Allow shrimp to cool in water 2 to 3 minutes after removing from heat. Drain at once in colander, and place in glass bowl or large jar and fill with:

1¼ cups salad oil
 ¾ cup vinegar
 3 tablespoons capers with juice
2½ teaspoons celery seeds
1½ teaspoons salt
 ¼ teaspoon Tabasco
 ¼ teaspoon dried green onion
 1 tablespoon pickling spices
 ½ cup chopped celery tops

Keep the shrimp tightly covered, and store in coldest part of refrigerator. Do not freeze. Yield: sauce for 1½ to 2½ pounds shrimp.

STEAK TARTARE

Easily prepared, it can be made a day in advance.

 2 pounds ground sirloin or round steak
½ cup finely chopped onion
 2 cloves garlic, minced
 1 teaspoon salt
 1 teaspoon freshly ground black pepper
 2 tablespoons Worcestershire sauce
¼ cup chopped parsley
⅓ cup cognac
   Pumpernickel bread slices, assorted
     crackers, or melba rounds

Place beef in a large glass or stainless steel bowl; add remaining ingredients. Mix well and refrigerate until serving time. Spread 1 heaping tablespoonful mixture on pumpernickel bread slices, crackers, or melba rounds. Yield: about 4 cups—48 servings.

ZESTY COCKTAIL WEINERS

A simple and superb cocktail food for a chafing dish.

 1 pound skinless, all-meat weiners
½ cup bourbon
½ cup catsup
¼ cup firmly packed dark brown sugar
 1 tablespoon grated onion
⅛ teaspoon ground oregano
⅛ teaspoon powdered rosemary
     (optional)

Cut weiners into 1-inch pieces. Combine bourbon, catsup, brown sugar, onion, oregano, and rosemary, if desired, in saucepan. Bring to a simmering boil and add weiners. Simmer in sauce until weiners are tender. If possible, refrigerate overnight in sauce. Serve in chafing

dish in hot sauce. Next to chafing dish, place an attractive container filled with toothpicks for spearing. Yield: 4 dozen (1-inch) pieces.

CHICKEN WINGS

24 chicken wings
¾ cup melted butter
½ (15-ounce) can Italian bread crumbs
½ cup grated Parmesan cheese
 2 tablespoons chopped parsley
 2 teaspoons garlic salt
 1 teaspoon pepper
¼ teaspoon cayenne pepper

Remove two wing joints and leave the large plump section that resembles a drumstick. Dip this into melted butter, then into bread crumbs that have been blended with cheese, parsley, and seasonings. Coat well and arrange in oblong baking pan. Pour remaining butter over chicken. Bake in a preheated 350° oven for about 40 minutes or until tender without turning. Baste often with drippings. Serve hot. Yield: 2 dozen.

HOT CORNED BEEF
HORS D'OEUVRES

1 (12-ounce) can corned beef
1 pound sharp cheddar cheese,
     shredded
1 (6-ounce) jar mustard
    About 4 tablespoons mayonnaise
1 small onion, grated
24 thin slices white bread

In large bowl, combine all ingredients except bread until blended. Remove crust from bread and spread lightly with mixture; roll up and insert toothpick into rolled sandwiches to hold firmly. Place on an ungreased cookie sheet. Bake in a preheated 400° oven for 10 minutes or until golden brown. Yield: 2 dozen.

BROILED GRAPEFRUIT

A lovely first course for a holiday dinner.

1 grapefruit
2 tablespoons firmly packed brown sugar
2 tablespoons sherry
  Maraschino or crème de menthe cherries

Cut grapefruit in half, separate sections, and core. To each grapefruit half, add 1 tablespoon brown sugar and 1 tablespoon sherry. Place on cookie sheet on center rack about 4 inches from heat. Broil; watch closely. As soon as sugar is melted, garnish with cherries and serve. You may bake in a preheated 350° oven for 15 minutes and attain the same result. This is also delicious when served cold. Yield: 2 servings.

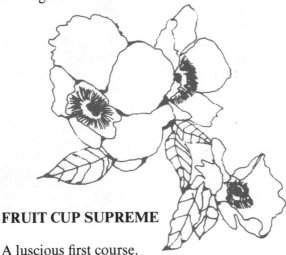

FRUIT CUP SUPREME

A luscious first course.

  1 medium-size, fully ripe cantaloupe, seeds
    removed
  1 medium-size, fully ripe honeydew melon,
    seeds removed
  1 large ripe peach, peeled
  1 large nectarine, peeled
  1 large navel orange, peeled and sectioned
  ¼ pound white seedless grapes, halved
  8 large strawberries or 8 ripe cherries
  16 tablespoons cointreau, divided

Scoop small balls from the cantaloupe, melon, and peach; place in separate bowls. Cut nectarine into bite-size pieces. Cut orange sections and grapes in half. In sherbet cups place orange sections first, then pieces of nectarine, peach balls, cantaloupe balls, and honeydew balls. Top with grapes, and place a single strawberry or cherry in center. Pour 2 tablespoons cointreau over each cup. Cover with plastic wrap and chill for at least 4 hours. Yield: 8 servings.

DELICIOUS COCKTAIL FINGERS

This recipe makes enough ½-inch thick fingerlike loaves to serve 30 guests if you are serving some other canapé or dip. Inexpensive, these are excellent with punch and alcoholic beverages. You may make weeks in advance, freeze, and bake as needed.

½ pound hot sausage
 1 cup finely chopped onion
½ cup finely chopped celery
 4 cups chicken broth
   Corn Bread, crumbled
 8 slices white bread, toasted and finely rolled
     or 1 cup commercial bread crumbs
 1 teaspoon salt
⅛ teaspoon white pepper
 1 teaspoon Worcestershire sauce

Cook sausage in skillet over medium heat until crisp; drain well. Boil onions and celery in chicken broth until tender; drain broth and reserve. In large bowl, add cooked onion and celery to crumbled corn bread and bread crumbs. Add salt, white pepper, Worcestershire sauce, and about 3 cups reserved broth (enough to moisten mixture so that you can shape the fingers). Add sausage. Shape into fingerlike loaves about ½ inch thick. Bake in a preheated 350° oven until golden brown and crisp. Watch fingers carefully to keep from burning. Serve hot. Yield: 7 to 7½ dozen.

Corn Bread:

1 cup cornmeal
1 teaspoon salt
1½ teaspoons baking powder
1 teaspoon sugar
⅛ teaspoon soda
½ to 1 cup buttermilk
1 egg, well beaten
2 tablespoons bacon drippings,
    divided

In a large bowl, combine cornmeal, salt, baking powder, and sugar. Add soda to buttermilk in a separate bowl. Add egg to dry ingredients and blend well. Add enough buttermilk to make batter runny, and beat thoroughly. Melt bacon drippings in a 9-inch skillet. Add 1 tablespoon drippings to cornmeal mixture and swirl the remainder around to grease the skillet. Pour batter into hot skillet and bake in a preheated 450° oven for 15 to 30 minutes, until golden. Set aside to cool.

COCKTAIL PARTY MEXICAN CORN BREAD

Colorful and zesty, this quickie corn bread is a fit companion for an old fashioned cocktail or a dry martini. Baked in miniature muffin tins, these freeze well. Serve in regular-size muffin tins for a vegetable dinner or with roast beef or ham.

2½ medium-size canned jalapeño peppers
1 cup white cream-style corn
2 large eggs, well beaten
1 cup milk
⅓ cup vegetable oil
1 cup shredded very sharp cheddar cheese
½ (4-ounce) can pimientos, finely mashed

Remove seed from peppers, peel if necessary, and mash with a fork. (Use jalapeños for a very hot dish; use green chilies for a milder muffin.) Mash corn with a fork, and discard any hull that clings. In large bowl, mix all ingredients, and spoon into greased muffin tins or a 9-inch skillet. Miniature muffin tins hold 1 level tablespoon. If you plan to freeze, bake this size in a preheated 400° oven for 15 minutes until set. Reheat frozen muffins at 350° for 10 minutes.

Bake regular-size muffins at 350° for 25 to 30 minutes. The muffins must be served hot to be at their best. Yield: 5 dozen miniature muffins or about 2 dozen regular-size muffins.

TOASTED PECANS

Delicious to serve with any type of drink at any party. This recipe will suffice for a tea or reception for 45 to 50 guests. More nuts will be needed if served with alcoholic beverages.

4 cups pecan halves
¼ cup butter
3 teaspoons salt

Place pecans on cookie sheet or large pan; avoid stacking. Bake in a preheated 325° oven for 10 minutes. Add butter and stir until pecans are coated. Sprinkle salt over all, lower heat to 250°, and bake for 20 to 30 minutes longer or until golden brown. Stir twice during that period. Taste one and see if it is crunchy, not soft. Cool in pan. When cold, place nuts in a sealed glass jar or lined, metal container. Nuts will keep 10 to 12 weeks. Yield: about 2 pints—45 to 50 servings.

DRY ROASTED NUTS

Marvelous for a party and for those watching their weight.

1 teaspoon sugar
1 teaspoon salt
1 teaspoon milk
1 teaspoon water
1 egg white, stiffly beaten
1 quart pecan halves

Add sugar, salt, milk, and water to stiffly beaten egg white in bowl. Coat pecan halves thoroughly with mixture, using rubber spatula. Place layer of foil on cookie sheet; arrange pecans in single layer on cookie sheet. Bake in a preheated 275° oven for 15 minutes. Remove pan from oven and stir carefully, lifting pecans from foil. Return to oven and bake an additional 15 minutes; stir. Repeat this process twice more, cooking pecans a total of 1 hour. Remove from oven and cool. Store in sealed jar. Yield: 1 quart pecans.

WINIFRED C. BARRON'S SPICED NUTS

An unusual treatment for nuts that is simply delicious. Easy to do, they will keep well if stored in a tightly covered jar or can.

¼ pound walnut or pecan halves
1 cup sugar
1 teaspoon salt
1 teaspoon ground ginger
½ teaspoon ground nutmeg
¼ teaspoon ground cloves
1 tablespoon cold water
1 large egg white, room
  temperature

Place nuts on large cookie sheet and bake in a preheated 350° oven for 4 to 5 minutes; remove from oven. Combine sugar, salt, and spices; sift three times, the last time into a bowl. Add water to egg white in another bowl and beat until frothy but not too stiff. Dip nuts in egg white mixture, then roll in sugar mixture. Cover bottom of cookie sheet with some of sugar mixture; spread nuts on this so that they do not touch each other. Sift remaining sugar over nuts. Bake at 275° about 1 hour. Remove nuts from cookie sheet at once and shake off excess sugar. Cool and store. These nuts are most attractive and lend a great deal to any kind of party. Yield: ¼ pound.

PECAN TEASERS

12 strips thinly sliced bacon
½ cup chopped pecans
1 cup grated sharp cheddar cheese
1 teaspoon grated onion
½ cup mayonnaise
½ teaspoon salt
12 thin slices white bread

In large skillet, cook bacon over medium heat until crisp, turning often; drain, then crumble. Blend with nuts and remaining ingredients except bread. Remove crusts from bread, cut bread into squares, and spread mixture on top of squares. Place on large cookie sheet and toast at 350° until squares are lightly browned. Serve hot. Yield: 48 squares.

GOURMET BLACK-EYED PEA DIP

Celebrate New Year's Day with this tasty dip and—according to Southern tradition—have good luck throughout the coming year.

  1 pound dried black-eyed peas
  4 cups water
2½ teaspoons salt
⅓ cup lean ham, diced, or 2 tablespoons
     bacon drippings
  1 teaspoon red food coloring
  1 (10-ounce) can tomatoes with green
     chilies
  2 tablespoons liquid from 1 (4-ounce) can
     green chilies
  ½ cup finely chopped onion
  ⅛ teaspoon garlic powder
  ½ (8-ounce) jar pasteurized process cheese
     spread, American, Brick, or Muenster
  ¼ teaspoon Tabasco
     Crackers or corn chips

Cover peas with water and allow to soak overnight; drain and cover with 4 cups fresh water. In a large saucepan bring peas to a boil; simmer, covered, for 30 minutes. Remove 2 cups peas with at least 1 cup liquid and place in another saucepan to use for Good Luck Torte (see Cakes). Add salt and diced ham to remaining peas in large saucepan, and cook at simmering boil for 25 to 30 minutes. Add red food coloring. Drain liquid from peas, and reserve, if needed, to thin puree. Place 3 cups cooked peas, tomatoes, green chilies liquid, onion, and garlic powder into a blender and puree, or put mixture through a food mill or ricer. Add a little of the juice or potlicker if mixture is too stiff. Pour this into the top of a double boiler over medium heat; add cheese spread and Tabasco. When cheese has melted, blend ingredients thoroughly. This is delicious

warm but also good at room temperature. Serve in a chafing dish with crackers or corn chips. This will keep for days refrigerated, or you can freeze it. Yield: about 4 cups—48 servings.

MARIE ELLIOT'S HOT BROCCOLI DIP

A marvous cocktail dip to serve from a chafing dish. This may be prepared ahead of time and will keep several days in the refrigerator. Ideal for a Saint Patrick's Day party.

  ½ cup finely chopped onion
  ¼ cup finely chopped celery
  2 tablespoons butter
  1 (3-ounce) can sliced buttered mushrooms
  1 (10-ounce) package frozen chopped broccoli
  ¼ teaspoon lemon bits or grated lemon rind
  1 (6-ounce) roll commercial garlic cheese
  1 (10¾-ounce) can condensed cream of
     mushroom soup
  1 teaspoon Worcestershire sauce
  5 drops Tabasco
  2 drops green food coloring
     Crackers or corn chips

Sauté onion and celery in butter over medium heat. Cook until onions are clear, then stir in mushrooms. Cook broccoli with lemon bits according to package directions; drain. Add garlic cheese and undiluted soup, stirring until well blended. Add drained broccoli, Worcestershire, Tabasco, and food coloring. Lower heat; keep warm until serving time. If you prefer, use a double boiler. You may prepare sautéed onion, celery, and cooked broccoli ahead of time and combine ingredients just before serving. The completed dip may be refrigerated and reheated. Serve with crackers or corn chips. Yield: about 6½ cups—75 servings.

Beverages

BAJAN BENTLEY

This delightful, nonalcoholic drink is a great favorite of the Bajans. It is served in the Bajan home for a morning party or luncheon in the same manner in which we might serve colas or Bloody Marys.

¾ cup fresh lime juice, strained
1½ ounces Simple Syrup
2 dashes aromatic bitters
1 maraschino cherry

Pour all ingredients except cherry over crushed ice in a highball glass. Stir and add maraschino cherry on a pick. Yield: 1 drink.

Simple Syrup:

1 cup cold water
2 cups sugar

Combine water and sugar and bring to a boil over high heat, stirring until sugar dissolves. Boil for 4 minutes. Pour into a clean jar or bottle; seal and refrigerate. Yield: 2 cups.

CHI CHI

A well-known Hawaiian drink.

½ ounce Coconut Syrup
1¼ ounces vodka
1 ounce lemon juice
1 teaspoon sugar
2 wedges fresh pineapple
2 ounces pineapple juice

Mix all ingredients in blender with shaved ice. Serve in a tall frosted glass. Yield: 1 serving.

Coconut Syrup:

1¾ cups coconut milk drained from coconut
before cracking, divided
3 cups firmly packed, grated fresh coconut
1½ cups sugar
¼ teaspoon cream of tartar

If the coconut does not yield 1¾ cups milk, add water. Heat coconut milk and pour over grated coconut in a large bowl; strain through cheesecloth. Add sugar and cream of tartar to 1¼ cups coconut milk, stirring well until sugar dissolves. Bring mixture to 224°, stirring constantly; add ¼ cup more coconut milk and heat again to 224°. Repeat, adding remaining ¼ cup liquid and cooking to 224° until all the coconut milk has been used. Remove from heat, pour into sterilized jars, and seal.

Note: A commercial, sweetened coconut juice is available in a 7¾-ounce can should you wish to substitute for the homemade syrup.

CARDINAL BOWL

A very potent punch, this is excellent for a debutante or wedding party.

1 medium-size grapefruit
2 small or 1 large orange
1 lemon
1 lime (optional)
½ cup cold water
½ cup sugar
2 (⁴/₅-quart) bottles well-chilled dry white wine (sauterne or Rhine)
1 (⁴/₅-quart) bottle well-chilled champagne, either dry or extra dry

Wash fruit and peel thinly; cover peelings with cold water and refrigerate for at least four hours, preferably twelve. Squeeze juice from the fruit; strain and add sugar. Drain the peelings (the liquid should be a deep orange color), and add liquid to the fruit juice. Pour into a prechilled punch bowl. Be sure sugar is thoroughly dissolved. Add white wine and champagne. If you wish to serve in quantity, the base can be prepared in advance and refrigerated either in single or double portions. Yield: 3 quarts—24 punch-cup servings.

RUSSIAN TEA

This exotic tea is excellent for party use and will keep well in the refrigerator in sealed glass jars or milk bottles.

4 quarts cold water, divided
5 tablespoons tea
3 cups orange juice (about 6 oranges)
8 tablespoons lemon juice (about 4 lemons)
1½ cups sugar
3 sticks cinnamon
1½ tablespoons whole cloves
1 (18-ounce) can unsweetened pineapple juice

Place 2 quarts of cold water in a large enameled or stainless steel saucepan; add tea and bring to a boil. Strain off the tea and add the remaining 2 quarts water, orange juice, lemon juice, and sugar. Tie cinnamon sticks and whole cloves together in a cheesecloth bag and add to the tea mixture. Bring to a quick boil and simmer gently for 1 hour. Add pineapple juice the last 10 minutes of cooking. Yield: About 5½ quarts—40 to 42 punch-cup servings.

SANGRÍA

A delightfully refreshing Spanish beverage, it is ideal served with spicy Mexican food. It is a particular favorite of the Spanish-speaking people in and around San Antonio, Texas.

½ gallon Burgundy
1 quart fresh orange juice, or frozen concentrate, properly mixed
1 quart club soda, chilled
Juice of 3 lemons, strained
Juice of 5 limes, strained
3 dashes aromatic bitters
1 to 1½ cups sugar
Orange, lemon, or lime slivers for garnish

In a large enameled pan or punch bowl, combine all ingredients except sugar. Add 1 cup sugar, stirring well, and taste. This drink needs to be sweet rather than tart. If you get it too sweet, add more club soda. Garnish punch bowl or individual cups with orange, lemon, or lime slices. Always stir your beverage between servings. Yield: About 5 quarts—40 punch-cup servings.

ICED TEA SUPERB

**3 tablespoons tea (choice blend of Indian and
    Ceylon)**
1 small bundle of fresh mint leaves
3 teacups cold water, brought to a boil
¾ cup sugar
    Juice of 2 medium-size limes, strained

Scald the teapot. (Use a china or earthenware
pot; metal spoils the flavor.) Place tea and mint
leaves in pot and add boiling water. Allow to
stand 5 minutes; strain tea into a pitcher with
sugar. (Use glass, enamel or stainless steel
pitcher, never a metal one such as aluminum
or tin.) When the tea is slightly cooled, add
lime juice and serve over crushed ice. Yield:
4 to 5 glasses.

ICED TEA PUNCH

**2 teaspoons tea (for stronger tea, use 2 dessert
    spoons)**
4 cups cold water, brought to a boil
1 cup sugar
    Juice and rind of 2 lemons

Scald teapot. (Use a china or earthenware pot;
metal spoils the flavor.) Place tea in pot and
pour in boiling water. Add sugar, strained
lemon juice, and lemon rinds. Remove rinds
after 10 minutes. Allow tea mixture to stand
for an additional 2½ hours; strain. This may
be kept in glass jars in refrigerator for several
days. Serve punch over ice; do not dilute.
Yield: 6 to 8 punch-cup servings.

PLANTATION COFFEE PUNCH

Try a new and delightful punch for a morning
coffee, brunch, or summer afternoon party.

**⅓ cup instant coffee dissolved in ½ cup
    boiling water**
¼ cup sugar
1 teaspoon vanilla
5 cups milk
2 cups vanilla ice cream
1 cup whipping cream, whipped

Mix the dissolved instant coffee with sugar,
vanilla and milk; refrigerate. (This may be
made the day before using.) Before serving,
chill punch bowl with crushed ice; drain and
dry thoroughly. Pour in coffee mixture, spoon
in hunks of ice cream. If using block ice cream,
cut into thin slices. Add blobs of whipped
cream. Yield: 2 quarts—15 punch-cup servings.

CAFÉ AU LAIT

The delicious New Orleans way of preparing
coffee with milk.

1 cup fresh boiling water
**1 heaping tablespoon drip or finely ground
    coffee (either pure or with chicory)**
1 cup milk
    Sugar (optional)

Use a French drip pot if possible. Pour boiling
water a few spoonfuls at a time over coffee.
Heat milk to boiling point and add hot coffee.
Add sugar, if desired, and serve at once. Yield:
about 2 cups.

---

*Beat the summer heat with a colorful, refreshing
beverage served icy-cold and garnished with fresh
fruit. An array of favorites, both potent and nonalcoholic, hot and cold, is found in the Beverages
chapter.*

CAFÉ AU LAIT WITH INSTANT COFFEE

1 cup milk
1 cup water
2 teaspoons instant coffee with chicory

Place ingredients in a medium-size saucepan and heat to boiling point. Use a dover egg beater and beat until mixture comes to a boil. Yield: 2 cups.

HOT SPICED PERCOLATOR PUNCH
(Large Group)

An invigorating punch to serve after a football game or sleigh ride on a cold winter's night. This is festive enough for a holiday gathering. The punch may be served cold.

2 quarts unsweetened pineapple juice
2 quarts cranberry juice cocktail
1 quart cold water
⅔ cup firmly packed dark brown sugar
1 tablespoon whole allspice
1 tablespoon whole cloves
4 (2-inch) sticks cinnamon, broken into small pieces
2 large lemons, washed and sliced

Pour pineapple and cranberry juices and water into bottom part of a 30-cup percolator. Place sugar, allspice, cloves, cinnamon, and sliced lemon in the basket at the top. Allow mixture to percolate for 30 to 35 minutes. Serve hot. If you do not have a percolator, tie the allspice, cloves, and cinnamon into a cheesecloth bag; place with all other ingredients in a large

enamel or stainless steel pan, and cook over a medium heat until the mixture begins to boil. Lower heat and allow punch to simmer for at least 30 minutes. Taste to see if the punch has a good spicy flavor; if not, cook a few minutes longer. Yield: 1¼ gallons—28 to 30 punch-cup servings.

HOT SPICED PERCOLATOR PUNCH
(Small Group)

A delicious hot punch for a small group.

2¼ cups pineapple juice
2 cups cranberry juice
1¾ cups cold water
½ cup firmly packed dark brown sugar
1 tablespoon whole allspice
1 tablespoon whole cloves
3 sticks cinnamon, broken into small pieces
¼ teaspoon salt

Pour fruit juices and water into bottom part of an 8-cup percolator. Place the remaining ingredients in the basket at top. Perk for 10 minutes or until spices permeate; taste. Serve hot. If you do not have a percolator, tie allspice, cloves, and cinnamon into a cheesecloth bag; place with all other ingredients in a 4-quart enamel or stainless steel pan and bring to a simmering boil. Simmer for 12 to 15 minutes with pan covered. Taste to see if the punch has a strong spicy flavor. It not, cook a few minutes longer. Yield: About 1½ quarts—12 punch-cup servings.

Few perfumes are as enticing as the aroma of fresh, hot breads straight from the oven. Winifred's Breads chapter is full of such favorites as nut and fruit breads, innumerable muffin and roll specialties, and a variety of sourdough creations.

FRESH FRUIT PUNCH

This is an ideal tart punch for any occasion.

3 cups boiling water
4 tablespoons tea
3½ cups sugar, divided
3 cups sliced strawberries
1½ quarts cold water
1½ cups lemon juice
3 cups orange juice
1½ quarts ginger ale
    Orange and lemon slices
    Fresh mint (optional)

Pour boiling water over tea; steep 5 minutes and strain. (Make tea only in enameled, pyrex, or stainless steel bowl to avoid a chemical reaction.) While tea is hot, add 3 cups sugar and stir until dissolved; cool. Sprinkle sliced strawberries with remaining ½ cup sugar. Add cold water, lemon and orange juices and strawberries to tea mixture. Pour over ice in a chilled punch bowl. Just before serving add ginger ale. Garnish with thin slices of orange and lemon and fresh mint, if desired. Yield: About 1½ gallons—38 punch-cup servings.

PINK RUM WINE PUNCH

A beautiful and delightfully refreshing punch, ideal for a graduation, debutante, or bridal party. The alcoholic beverages lend a flavor and exhilarating quality to the punch without making it intoxicating. The punch base may be made a day or two in advance and kept refrigerated; add the ginger ale and soda water just before serving.

26 ounces simple syrup
26 ounces fresh lemon juice (about 40 lemons)
2 quarts fresh orange juice (frozen will do if kept tart and not diluted too much)
1 (46-ounce) can unsweetened pineapple juice
1 quart white port
1 fifth good light rum
1 quart ginger ale
1 quart soda water
6 tablespoons or more of grenadine (enough to color punch a soft pink)

To make simple syrup, bring to a boil 2 parts sugar to 1 part water and boil briskly 1 minute. The syrup may be made well in advance as it will keep almost indefinitely in a sealed bottle or container in a cool place.

In a 2-gallon enamel or stainless steel kettle, combine simple syrup, lemon, orange, and pineapple juices, white port, and rum; mix well and keep chilled until time to pour into a chilled punch bowl. Just before serving, add ginger ale, soda water, and just enough grenadine to color punch a soft pink. Yield: 2¼ gallons—70 punch-cup servings.

HOLIDAY WASSAIL BOWL (Puritan)

An old family recipe and one of the best.

1 cup fresh lemon juice
2 cups fresh orange juice or frozen concentrate, properly mixed
2 cups unsweetened pineapple juice
½ gallon apple cider
1 teaspoon whole cloves
1 stick cinnamon
¼ cup sugar

Pour all juices into a large enamel or stainless steel pan; tie cloves and cinnamon in a small cotton or cheesecloth bag, and add to the fruit juices. Bring to a simmering boil over medium heat. Cover pan and allow mixture to simmer for 1 hour. Dissolve sugar in hot wassail before removing from heat. Serve hot in mugs or punch cups. Yield: About 3¼ quarts—26 punch-cup servings.

Variation: For extra kick, add 1 pint apple brandy or hard cider to the cooked wassail. Heat, but do not boil.

HOLIDAY WASSAIL BOWL (Potent)

Let's revive the custom of hot punches, a delightful way to occupy oneself on Christmas Eve. Here is the recipe for the brew; you supply the other kind of spirits.

3 quarts beer, divided
1 pound sugar
1 teaspoon freshly grated nutmeg
1 teaspoon ground ginger
4 slices lemon
2 cups dry sherry
10 to 12 spiced whole crab apples, studded
  with whole cloves

In a large enamel dishpan or soup kettle, combine 1 quart of beer, sugar, spices, and lemon slices; cook over medium heat, stirring until sugar dissolves. Add remaining beer, sherry, and crab apples. Heat for 15 minutes, but do not boil. To serve, pour mixture into warmed punch bowl and float studded apples on top. Yield: 3½ quarts—33 punch-cup servings.

QUICK AS A WINK PUNCH

A colorful, tart, fruit punch for any occasion. A real quickie—the only preparation involved is opening cans and stirring. Chill the juices in the cans and pour over ice right into the punch bowl. You can easily cut the recipe in half for less punch or double for more. If you wish an alcoholic one, substitute wine or liquor for club soda.

2 (46-ounce) cans commercial orange juice or
  the same amount of fresh
2 (46-ounce) cans unsweetened pineapple
  juice
2 (18-ounce) cans unsweetened grapefruit
  juice
2 (6-ounce) cans frozen lemonade
  concentrate, thawed
1 (46-ounce) can Hawaiian fancy red berry
  juice
1 quart club soda, chilled

Pour all fruit juices into a large dishpan and stir well. Store in glass or plastic gallon jars under refrigeration until ready to serve; then add club soda. Yield: 2¼ gallons—75 punch-cup servings.

Note: For a holiday punch, make an ice mold of red and green maraschino cherries. The number of jars of cherries will depend on size of mold used. Drain juice from cherries and arrange on bottom of mold and barely cover with water. Freeze, then continue the same process until mold is filled with layers of frozen cherries. A circular salad mold makes a festive wreath. A heart-shaped mold with all red cherries is lovely for St. Valentine's Day.

Breads

APPLE BREAD

Plan a simple supper, add to it spicy apple bread, and your family will leave the table wearing a satisfied smile.

½ cup butter or margarine, softened
¾ cup sugar, sifted
2 large eggs, well beaten
3 tablespoons buttermilk or soured sweet
   milk
2 cups all-purpose flour, sifted
1 teaspoon baking soda
1 teaspoon salt
1 teaspoon ground cinnamon
1 teaspoon ground nutmeg
1 cup sliced pecans or walnuts (optional)
1 cup sweetened applesauce

In a large bowl cream butter by hand or with electric mixer on medium speed until light and fluffy. Add sifted sugar and beaten eggs and continue beating. Add milk alternately with sifted flour, soda, salt, and spices, starting and ending with flour mixture. To substitute sweet milk for buttermilk, pour 1 tablespoon lemon juice or vinegar into 1 cup measure; fill cup with milk and allow to stand while assembling other ingredients. If you wish to use nuts, reserve 1 tablespoon flour to sprinkle over them. Add nuts and applesauce to mixture. Pour batter into well-greased loaf pan lined with waxed paper. Bake in a preheated 350° oven for 45 to 55 minutes or until bread tests done. Straw should come out clean. Remove immediately from pan and cool on wire rack, or eat with butter. Yield: 1 (9- x 5- x 3-inch) loaf.

NANNIE L. JEFFERSON'S BISCUITS

Irresistible! These are good enough to eat without butter—with butter they are perfect.

2⅓ cups sifted flour, spooned into cup, divided
  6 teaspoons double acting baking powder
  1 teaspoon salt
½ cup plus 2 tablespoons shortening
¾ cup cold milk

Sift together 2 cups flour, baking powder, and salt into a large bowl; cut in shortening with a pastry blender or two knives until mixture is consistency of coarse cornmeal. Make a well in center of batter and gradually pour in milk: stir slowly until there is no danger of spilling it, then stir vigorously. Turn dough onto board dusted with some of the remaining ⅓ cup flour. Knead the dough gently for a minute or two until it feels smooth and pliable. Roll dough with lightly floured rolling pin until it is about ¼ inch thick; cut with biscuit cutter or rim of orange juice glass. Place on a lightly greased cookie sheet and bake in a preheated 450° oven for 12 to 15 minutes or until biscuits are light golden brown top and bottom. To hold biscuits for 15 to 20 minutes, remove from oven and cover with clean dish towel. When cold, keep in plastic bag; to reheat the next day pat top of each biscuit lightly with a little water, and bake at 350° for about 10 minutes. These will freeze well after cooked. Yield: about 3 dozen (1½-inch) biscuits.

MINI APPLE-CHEESE PIZZAS

A wintertime special for unexpected guests. A teenager's favorite, this snappy and quickly prepared grilled sandwich will disappear in a wink. Be prepared to whip up a second batch.

      2 tablespoons butter or margarine
      4 English muffins, split and toasted
      8 slices boiled ham
   1½ cups canned applesauce
      2 cups shredded cheddar cheese

Spread butter on English muffins. Top each half with a ham slice. Combine applesauce and cheese. Spread ⅓ cup of this mixture on each ham slice. Place under broiler until cheese melts, about 3 minutes. Serve at once. Yield: 8 mini pizzas.

MARGUERITE MELVIN'S CORN BREAD

Excellent and foolproof.

    1 cup cornmeal
   ⅓ cup all-purpose flour
   ½ teaspoon salt
    1 teaspoon baking powder
    1 teaspoon sugar
   ½ teaspoon soda
    1 egg, well beaten
    1 cup buttermilk
    2 tablespoons bacon drippings

Sift dry ingredients into a large bowl. Add egg and buttermilk; stir just enough to blend. Heat bacon drippings in 9-inch skillet, swish grease around sides and then pour into mixture. Heat skillet in 400° oven and pour corn bread mixture into it. Bake in a preheated 400° oven for 25 minutes or until browned on top. Yield: 1 (9-inch) round loaf—10 to 12 servings.

BLUEBERRY BREAD

Luscious! A treat for breakfast served buttered, hot with coffee, delicious for lunch with hot tea, and equally good cold with a glass of milk for supper or a bedtime snack.

      1 cup blueberries, fresh or frozen, divided
   ½ cup butter or margarine
      2 large eggs, room temperature
      1 cup sugar
   ½ teaspoon salt
      2 teaspoons baking powder
   2¼ cups all-purpose flour, measured after
         sifting
   ½ cup milk
   1½ teaspoons lemon extract
      2 teaspoons grated lemon rind
      1 tablespoon wheat germ
      1 teaspoon cinnamon sugar

Wash and dry fresh berries on a paper towel; thaw completely frozen blueberries, and dry on a paper towel. Allow butter or margarine to soften in large mixing bowl. Add eggs and sugar, and beat for 4 minutes with electric beater on high speed until mixture is light and fluffy. Put salt, baking powder, and measured flour into sifter. At low speed, add flour mixture in fourths alternating in thirds with milk. Start and finish with flour mixture. Beat just until smooth; light handling of mixture is important. Add lemon extract, lemon rind, and wheat germ; fold in blueberries gently with rubber spatula, withholding 1 tablespoon of berries. Spoon batter into well-greased and floured loaf pan lined with waxed paper. Before adding the last bit of batter, sprinkle with remaining berries to insure an even distribution. Generously sprinkle top of batter with cinnamon sugar. Bake in a preheated 350° oven on middle rack for 45 to 50 minutes until golden brown and bread tests done. Remove from oven and allow to cool for 10 minutes before taking from pan. Continue cooling on wire rack. Yield: 1 (9- x 5- x 3-inch) loaf.

MYRTLE LAIR'S CAJUN BRIOCHE ROLLS

These rolls are as delicious as any you will find in Paris. They freeze beautifully. It is worth every minute of the seven hours it takes for them to reach perfection. You are not working all that time, but you have to be around when it is ready to be kneaded.

　1 cup milk
⅓ cup vegetable shortening
½ cup sugar (reserve 1 teaspoon for yeast)
½ teaspoon salt
　1 package active dry yeast
　2 tablespoons lukewarm water
4½ to 5 cups all-purpose flour, divided
　3 large eggs
　1 teaspoon lemon extract
　1 tablespoon melted butter
　2 cups powdered sugar
　5 tablespoons milk
　1 teaspoon vanilla extract

In a saucepan cook milk, shortening, sugar, and salt over medium heat until shortening is melted. Remove from stove and cool to luke-warm. Dissolve yeast in warm water to which reserved sugar has been added. In large bowl add dissolved yeast to milk mixture; add 1 cup flour, and beat well. Cover bowl with waxed paper and a clean dish towel, and place in a cold oven beside a large bowl of very hot water. Let dough rise for 1 hour. Add beaten eggs and lemon extract; mix well. Add enough flour to make a firm dough (about 4 cups), beating well with a spoon.

On a floured board knead dough until smooth and elastic. To knead, press dough flat with heels of hands folding dough to center. Repeat process of pressing and folding dough in a rhythmic motion. When the dough begins to feel smooth and elastic, roll out into ¼-inch thick rectangle. Spread lightly with melted butter, cover, and move to a warm place to rise for 3 hours. Cut dough into pieces ½ inch wide; twist ends in opposite directions, bring ends together and press in center with thumb. Place rolls on a greased cookie sheet and let rise another 3 hours uncovered.

Bake in a preheated 400° oven for 15 to 20 minutes or until golden brown. Make an icing by blending powdered sugar, 5 tablespoons milk, and vanilla. Spread icing on Brioche while hot. If you plan to freeze rolls, bake for 10 minutes and do not let brown. Do not add icing until after you brown rolls at a later time. Yield: 2 dozen.

APRICOT BREAD

Plan a simple meal such as broiled chicken or ham and spice it up with a special treat in the form of a quick hot bread made with tart apricots, apples, mellow bananas, tangy lemons, oranges, or sour cherries. In a little more than an hour you can easily prepare any number of tasty breads.

1 cup dried apricots
　Warm water to cover
1 cup sugar
2 cups all-purpose flour, measured after
　　sifting
3 teaspoons baking powder
¼ teaspoon baking soda
1 large egg, well beaten
2 teaspoons melted butter
1 cup chopped pecans or walnuts
1 tablespoon all-purpose flour

Cover apricots with warm water and soak for 30 minutes; drain and reserve ½ cup liquid. Cut apricots into fine pieces. In a large bowl sift dry ingredients. In another bowl combine beaten egg, melted butter, ½ cup liquid from apricots; add gradually to dry ingredients. Mix well. Stir in chopped nuts that have been sprinkled with 1 tablespoon flour and well-drained apricot pieces. Spoon batter into well-greased loaf pans lined with wax paper. Bake in a preheated 350° oven: large loaf for 1 hour, small loaves for 45 minutes or until straw inserted into loaf comes out clean. Cool on wire rack for 10 minutes and remove from pan. This bread freezes well. Yield: 1 (9- x 5- x 3-inch) loaf or 2 (7- x 3- x 2-inch) loaves.

BANANA NUT BREAD

Distinctive and mellow!

¼ cup butter
½ cup sugar
1 large egg, well beaten
1 cup all-bran cereal
1½ cups mashed bananas (4 medium-size bananas)
2 tablespoons water
1½ cups all-purpose flour, measured before sifting
2 teaspoons baking powder
½ teaspoon salt
½ teaspoon soda
1 teaspoon vanilla extract
1 cup chopped pecans or walnuts (optional)
1 tablespoon flour

Cream butter and sugar until light and fluffy. Add beaten egg and stir in all-bran cereal. Remove white stringy covering before mashing bananas. Combine thoroughly mashed bananas and water; add to creamed mixture. Sift measured flour, baking powder, salt, and soda and add to banana mixture gradually. Do not beat, stir gently only until blended. Add

vanilla. Fold in chopped nuts that have been coated with 1 tablespoon flour. Spoon batter into a greased loaf pan lined with waxed paper. Bake in a preheated 350° oven for 50 minutes or until bread tests done. Cool on rack for 10 minutes and remove from pan. This bread freezes well and slices nicely when frozen. Keep in refrigerator for best taste results. Yield: 1 (8- x 4- x 2-inch) loaf.

STEAMED BOSTON BROWN BREAD

3 cups whole wheat or graham flour (reserve 2 tablespoons for nuts)
1 cup all-purpose white flour
1 tablespoon sugar
1 teaspoon salt
3 teaspoons soda
1 cup dark corn syrup or molasses
1 egg, well beaten
2½ cups buttermilk
2 cups raisins
1 cup nuts, sliced

Combine dry ingredients except 2 tablespoons whole wheat flour in a large bowl; sift. Add molasses, egg, and buttermilk; stir until well mixed. Sprinkle reserved flour on raisins and nuts, and fold into batter. Grease three (16-ounce) baking powder cans; spoon in batter not more than ⅔ full. Cover tightly and place cans on trivet in kettle containing boiling water, allowing water to come halfway up around cans. Cover kettle tightly and steam 2½ to 3 hours, keeping water at boiling point. Add more boiling water as needed. Yield: 3 loaves.

CINNAMON RAISIN BREAD

The best!

  2 packages active dry yeast
½ cup warm water
  1 teaspoon sugar
  3 cups warm water
¾ cup sugar
¾ cup corn or vegetable oil
  3 large eggs
  2 tablespoons salt
12 cups all-purpose flour, divided
  2 teaspoons ground cinnamon, divided
1¾ cup raisins
  3 tablespoons wheat germ
  2 cups firmly packed light brown sugar

Dissolve yeast in ½ cup warm water to which you add 1 teaspoon sugar. When this begins to rise, pour into a very large bowl which has 3 cups of warm water in it. Add ¾ cup sugar, oil, and eggs; beat well. Sift in salt, 8 cups flour, and 1 teaspoon cinnamon; blend well. Cover bowl with plastic wrap and a clean dish towel, and place in a cold oven beside a large bowl of very hot water. Allow batter to rise until doubled in bulk, from 1½ to 2 hours. In a separate bowl, sift ½ cup flour onto raisins and toss to coat. Sift 2 cups flour into batter. Add wheat germ and floured raisins to batter, and turn out on floured board. Wash hands thoroughly to remove any odors; then knead dough by pressing mass of dough flat, then folding over onto itself toward you. Sift the remainder of flour gradually as you need it. When the dough begins to feel elastic after about 5 minutes, shape into a long roll and cut into four equal parts. (Each loaf should weigh about 1½ pounds.)

Slap dough hard to press out gas bubbles, then stretch into an oblong piece. Blend brown sugar and 1 teaspoon cinnamon, and divide into four equal parts, ½ cup each, on waxed paper. Spread one part on each oblong piece, and fold over the long side tightly as you would a jelly roll, tuck ends under. Place folded sides down in four buttered loaf pans; sprinkle top with a little of reserved cinnamon sugar. Cover with waxed paper and clean dish towel, and allow loaves to rise until they completely fill the pans and rise above sides, about 1½ to 2 hours. Bake in a preheated 375° oven for 10 minutes, then lower heat to 350° and cook for 15 to 20 minutes longer. Cool on wire rack about 10 minutes, and remove from pans and continue cooling. The bread will cut better if completely cold, but tastes heavenly when warm. Yield: 4 (9- x 5- x 3-inch) loaves.

MARIE BARRON'S BLUEBERRY MUFFINS

There are none better. These are ideal for serving at any meal or for a morning brunch.

  1 cup fresh blueberries or 1 (10-ounce)
     package frozen blueberries
½ cup butter or margarine, room
     temperature
  2 large eggs, room temperature
  1 cup sugar
1½ teaspoons baking powder
¼ teaspoon salt
  2 cups all-purpose flour, measured after
     sifting
½ cup milk
  1 teaspoon lemon extract
  1 teaspoon cinnamon sugar

Wash fresh blueberries, and dry on paper towel. Allow frozen berries to thaw completely; dry. Allow butter to soften in large mixing bowl; add eggs, and sugar, then cream until light and fluffy for about 4 minutes with electric beater on high speed. Put baking powder and salt with measured flour into sifter. At low speed, add flour mixture in fourths alternating in thirds with milk. Begin and end with flour mixture. Beat just until smooth; light handling of mixture is important. Add lemon extract and gently fold in blueberries with rubber spatula. Grease muffin tins or use paper liners. Fill about ⅔ full after sprinkling with cinnamon sugar. Bake in a preheated 375° oven for 15 to 18 minutes until golden brown. Remove to wire rack and let cool slightly. Yield: about 2 dozen.

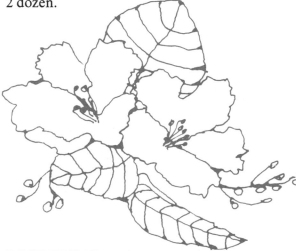

LOST BREAD—*PAIN PERDU*

For breakfast with coffee, *pain perdu* replaces the humdrum toast and eggs. Served with honey, jelly, or powdered sugar this is a light and lovely dessert. For supper it is an ideal side dish with broiled hamburgers or sausage.

 2 large eggs, separated
 ⅛ teaspoon salt
 2 tablespoons sugar
 ½ cup cold milk
 ¼ teaspoon vanilla extract or brandy
 ⅛ teaspoon ground nutmeg
 ½ cup butter
 2 tablespoons vegetable oil
 6 to 8 slices stale white or French bread
   Sugar, jelly, cinnamon sugar, or honey

In a deep mixing bowl, beat the egg whites with the salt until stiff. Add yolks and 2 tablespoons sugar and continue beating. Pour in milk, vanilla and nutmeg; mix well. Place butter and oil in a large heavy skillet over medium heat (have the mixture hot enough to brown a cube of bread in 60 seconds). Quickly dip each slice of bread into the egg-milk mixture, coat on both sides, and drop into skillet. The bread will brown rapidly. With a broad spatula turn to other side to brown. Remove and drain on absorbent paper. You can usually fry three slices at the same time, depending on the size of skillet. You may also use a hot griddle. Serve *pain perdu* with sugar lightly sprinkled on top and jelly on the other side or with cinnamon sugar or with honey. Yield: 6 to 8 slices.

CRANBERRY BREAD

Superb! A good bazaar bread.

 2 cups sifted all-purpose flour
 1 cup sugar
1½ teaspoons baking powder
 ½ teaspoon soda
 1 teaspoon salt
 ¼ cup vegetable oil or shortening or softened margarine
 ¾ cup orange juice
 1 tablespoon grated orange rind
 1 large egg, well beaten
 ½ cup chopped pecans or walnuts
 2 cups chopped fresh cranberries

Sift all dry ingredients into a large mixing bowl. Cut in shortening with pastry blender. Combine orange juice, orange rind, and well-beaten egg. Pour into flour mixture; stir just enough to moisten well. Fold in nuts and cranberries. Spoon into well-greased loaf pans lined with waxed paper. When spreading batter in pan, spread corners and sides higher than center. Bake in a preheated 350° oven for 1 hour or until bread tests done. Cool for 10 minutes; remove from pan. Return bread to oven and invert on rack for 10 minutes to insure a crusty bottom. This bread freezes well. To make it out of season, keep packaged cranberries in freezer. Yield: 1 (9- x 5- x 3-inch) loaf or 2 (8- x 4- x 2-inch) loaves.

FAVORITE CHRISTMAS BREAD

During the Christmas season I like to delight my friends with this beautiful and delicious bread. From year to year I bake it as a gift of love. The bread may be used hot for breakfast with butter or cold for lunch or supper with a glass of sherry and a piece of cheese. Slice it and cover it with cream cheese to serve with hot tea for an afternoon party. It is ideal for gifts or bazaars. The bread will freeze but it keeps well wrapped in foil for a week or two.

3¼ cups all-purpose flour (reserve ¼ cup for
    nuts and fruit)
 1 cup sugar
 1 teaspoon salt
3½ teaspoons baking powder
1½ teaspoons ground cinnamon
 2 large eggs, room temperature
1½ cups milk
 3 tablespoons cottonseed or vegetable oil
 1 teaspoon vanilla extract
1¼ cups chopped pecans or walnuts
1¼ cup black or white raisins
1¼ cups chopped candied fruit (cherries,
    pineapple, citron, orange and lemon
    peel)
    Candied cherry halves
    Pecans

Sift 3 cups flour and other dry ingredients into a large bowl. Beat eggs in another small bowl until light; add milk to eggs. Stir liquid mixture into dry ingredients and mix well. If using an electric beater, place on medium speed. Add oil gradually, add vanilla, then stir in nuts, raisins, and chopped candied fruit, all of which have been dusted with the reserved flour. Spoon batter into greased loaf pans lined with waxed paper. Before baking, allow pans to stand for 30 minutes; decorate top of bread with candied cherry halves and pecans to form an attractive pattern. Bake in a preheated 350° oven: medium-size loaves for 1 hour or more,

large loaf for 1 hour 15 to 30 minutes, or until bread tests done. Cool on wire rack for 10 minutes. Remove from pans and continue cooling. If you are not sure of your oven's temperature accuracy, get an oven thermometer; this bread browns easily because of the dark batter. The finished product should be a beautiful golden color. Yield: 1 (11- x 5- x 3-inch) loaf or 2 (8- x 4- x 2-inch) loaves.

ANNE McKEOWN'S FRENCH BREAD

Excellent texture and crust.

 ½ cup milk
 ¾ cup boiling water
 1 package active dry yeast
 ¼ cup warm water
 ¼ teaspoon sugar
1½ tablespoons vegetable oil
 1 tablespoon sugar
 4 to 5 cups all-purpose flour
 2 teaspoons sugar
 2 teaspoons salt
 2 teaspoons cornmeal
 1 egg white, beaten
 1 tablespoon cold water

Scald milk in a saucepan over low heat. Add boiling water and set aside to cool. In small bowl dissolve yeast in warm water; add ¼ teaspoon sugar and allow to rest 10 minutes. When drop of milk feels lukewarm to the inside of wrist, add the risen dissolved yeast mixture, vegetable oil, and 1 tablespoon sugar to the milk mixture and stir well. Measure into large mixing bowl 4 cups flour, 2 teaspoons sugar, and 2 teaspoons salt. Make a hole in center and pour in liquid mixture. Stir thoroughly, but do not knead. This will be a soft dough. Cover with waxed paper or clean damp cloth, and place in cold oven beside a large bowl of very hot water. Allow 2 hours for rising or until dough doubles in bulk.

Remove from oven and break down dough with spoon; place on lightly floured board and cut into two equal parts. (Each loaf should weigh about 1 pound.) Form into a loaf by patting dough gently into an even thick rectangle about 6 x 8 inches. Start with upper end of rectangle, and fold and roll toward you as you would a jelly roll. Place hands on dough, side by side, and roll back and forth pressing outward with the hands until a long thin loaf is formed about 2½ inches in diameter and 15 inches long.

Place loaves on buttered cookie sheet sprinkled with cornmeal. Cut diagonal slits across the top of loaves with sharp-pointed scissors to form indentations. Set again in cold oven beside bowl of hot water until bread rises to more than double in bulk. Place a pie tin filled with boiling water on bottom rack of oven. Bake loaves in a preheated 400° oven for 15 minutes. Using a fine mist, spray bread with cold water. Lower heat to 350° and bake for 30 minutes; continue to spray bread every 5 minutes. Five minutes before bread is finished, brush loaves with a glaze of beaten egg white and 1 tablespoon cold water. Cool bread on wire rack. Yield: 2 loaves.

PEANUT BUTTER BREAD

    2 cups all-purpose flour
    2 teaspoons baking powder
    ½ teaspoon salt
    ½ cup sugar
    3½ tablespoons vegetable shortening
    1 (6¼-ounce) jar smooth peanut butter
    2 eggs, lightly beaten
    1 cup milk

Sift together flour, baking powder, salt, and sugar. Rub vegetable shortening and peanut butter into dry mixture with fingers or mixer until blended. Combine eggs with milk; add to dry mixture and mix well. Turn into greased loaf pan. Bake in a preheated 325° oven for 1¼ hours or until bread tests done. Yield: 1 (8- x 4- x 2-inch) loaf.

LEMON BREAD

A taste delight, this is ideal sliced thin for a coffee party or brunch. Top with butter or softened cream cheese.

    ½ cup margarine, room temperature
    2 large eggs, room temperature, divided
    1 cup sugar
    1¼ teaspoons baking powder
    ¼ teaspoon salt
    1½ cups all-purpose flour, measured after
        sifting
    ½ cup milk
    1 teaspoon lemon extract
    2 tablespoons plus 1 teaspoon grated lemon
        rind
    ½ cup chopped pecans or walnuts
        Cinnamon sugar

Combine softened margarine, 1 egg, and sugar in a large mixing bowl; cream until light and fluffy, about 4 minutes with electric beater at high speed. Add remaining egg and beat well. Put baking powder, salt, and flour into sifter. At low speed, add flour mixture in fourths alternating in thirds with milk. Begin and end with flour mixture. Beat just until smooth; light handling of mixture is important. Add lemon extract and fold in lemon rind and chopped nuts with spatula. Spoon batter into greased loaf pan lined with waxed paper. Sprinkle top lightly with cinnamon sugar, and bake in a preheated 350° oven for 50 to 60 minutes or until bread tests done. Cool on rack 10 minutes; then remove from pan. Yield: 1 (9- x 5- x 3-inch) loaf.

LUSSECAKE OR LUCIA BUN

Following an ancient custom the holiday season begins in Sweden on December 13th with the birthday of Saint Lucia, the saint of light. "To banish the darkness due to winter solstice," writes Anna Greta, my friend in Sweden, "a bright maiden—the eldest daughter in the family—rises very early in the morning. She dresses in a flowing white gown with a red sash and wears a crown of whortleberry leaves with lighted candles rising from it. Bearing a tray of coffee and freshly baked Lussecake, she enters her parents' bedroom singing the old Venetian song, 'Santa Lucia.' Her song gives hope of light and happiness: tomorrow the days will be longer and the sun will be reborn."

  1 cup milk, scalded
  ½ cup butter or margarine
  ½ cup sugar
  ½ teaspoon salt
  1 teaspoon saffron threads
  2 tablespoons boiling water
  1 package active dry yeast
  ¼ cup warm water
  5 cups sifted all-purpose flour, divided
  2 egg yolks, beaten
  ⅓ cup seedless raisins
  ½ cup chopped pecans
   Seedless raisins
   Melted butter
  1 egg, beaten
  1 tablespoon cold water

In a large mixing bowl, add scalded milk to butter, sugar, and salt; stir until butter is melted. Allow to cool. Place saffron threads in boiling water and set aside. Dissolve yeast in warm water, stirring until blended; add to milk and butter mixture. Add 1 cup flour to milk and butter mixture, and beat with mixer on medium speed until smooth. Add cool saffron mixture, beaten egg yolks, ⅓ cup raisins, and pecans. Add enough of the remaining flour to make a soft dough. Turn onto a marble or floured board, cover with fresh towel, and let stand for 10 minutes. Knead dough until smooth and elastic. Place in large greased bowl. Touch top of dough lightly with melted butter; cover, and let rise in warm place for 1½ hours until doubled in bulk. Punch down with spoon. Cut into 32 equal pieces, roll dough pieces into very thin strips about 12 to 14 inches long; roll strips at each end on the same side toward the middle leaving about one inch unrolled. Form each bun by placing two rolled strips back to back on lightly greased cookie sheets. Sprinkle raisins on top of each coil. Cover and let rise again until doubled in bulk, about 45 minutes. Brush top of each bun with 1 beaten egg blended with 1 tablespoon cold water. Bake in a preheated 375° oven for 12 to 15 minutes or until golden brown. Cool on wire rack. Yield: 16 very large buns.

HUSH PUPPIES

This name originated when hunters or fishermen around the bayou's campfires threw these tasty morsels to their howling dogs to keep them quiet. Today, hush puppies are served at fish fries, barbecues, pig pickin' parties, and on most menus at catfish houses. They are easy to prepare and are great with fish.

  2 cups white cornmeal
   Scant ½ teaspoon soda
  1 teaspoon salt
  ⅛ teaspoon pepper
  1 tablespoon all-purpose flour
  1 teaspoon baking powder
  3 tablespoons finely chopped onion
  1 cup buttermilk
  1 egg, well beaten
  2 dashes Tabasco
   Enough vegetable oil for deep fat frying

Combine dry ingredients in a large bowl. Add onion, buttermilk, beaten egg, and Tabasco; blend well. Make a rounded roll of batter on an iced-tea spoon, and drop into large iron skillet of deep fat heated to 400°. These small balls will puff up and turn golden brown in a minute or two; turn once with fork as they brown. Drain on paper towels. Place on cookie sheet, cover with another paper towel, and keep them warm in oven. (I usually cook 2 fish and 4 hush puppies simultaneously. The fish flavor the hush puppies and everything is ready at the same time.) Yield: about 2 dozen.

QUICK MARMALADE BREAD

An excellent accompaniment for coffee at a brunch or club group. Delicious served hot with butter or served cold with cream cheese.

3 cups all-purpose flour, unsifted, spooned into cup (reserve ¼ cup for nuts)
3½ teaspoons baking powder
1 teaspoon salt
½ cup sugar
1 teaspoon ground cinnamon
1 egg, well beaten
¾ cup milk
2 tablespoons vegetable oil
1 cup broken pecans or other nuts
¾ cup homemade or commercial marmalade

Sift flour, baking powder, salt, sugar, cinnamon into a large bowl. Beat egg and add milk to it. Pour egg mixture into dry ingredients and mix well. Add oil, nuts that have been dusted with reserved flour, and marmalade. Spoon into greased loaf pan, and let stand for 30 minutes. Bake in a preheated 350° oven for

1 hour or until bread tests done. Cool in pan for 10 minutes; remove from pan and continue cooling on wire rack. Yield: 1 (9- x 5- x 3-inch) loaf.

ERNESTINE GREEN'S MONKEY BREAD

Serve as pièce de résistance for a luncheon, or place a bowl of seasoned chili (no beans) in the center of the ring and use bread as a dip for a cocktail party.

1 package active dry yeast
½ cup lukewarm water
1 cup milk, scalded
1 cup mashed potatoes
⅔ cup shortening
⅔ cup sugar
1 teaspoon salt
2 eggs, well beaten
5 to 6 cups all-purpose flour, divided
½ cup butter, melted

Dissolve yeast in ½ cup lukewarm water. Combine milk, potatoes, shortening, sugar, and salt in a greased mixing bowl. Let stand until mixture is lukewarm, then add dissolved yeast. Add eggs and 1½ cups flour; beat well. Add enough additional flour to make a stiff dough. Turn out on a floured board and knead until elastic. Return to the greased mixing bowl; brush top of dough with some of the melted butter. Cover and let rise for 2 hours; refrigerate.

About 1½ hours before serving, roll out dough ½ inch thick and cut into 2-inch diamond shapes. Pull diamonds at opposite ends to elongate. Dip in remaining melted butter. Arrange in alternate order around a buttered ring mold; do not let diamond points fall on top of each other. Repeat until dough is used. Bake in a preheated 400° oven for 20 to 25 minutes. Yield: 1 to 2 ring molds, depending on size of molds—8 servings for luncheon, 20 to 25 servings as a dip.

CATHERINE HAGAMAN'S POPOVERS

Delightful and easy to make!

2 cups self-rising flour
3 tablespoons mayonnaise
1 cup milk
1 teaspoon sugar

Combine all ingredients in small bowl and mix thoroughly. Spoon into well-greased muffin tins; bake in a preheated 350° oven for about 20 minutes. Yield: 1 dozen large muffins or 2 dozen small muffins.

MIRIAM MAYO'S MORAVIAN SUGAR BREAD

This is a real delicacy with superb texture and flavor. May be served as a dessert when it comes fresh from the oven. Warmed, it's a breakfast treat.

  2 medium-size potatoes
2½ cups water
  ⅔ cup vegetable shortening
  ⅔ cup sugar
1½ teaspoons salt
1½ cups warm potato water
  1 package active dry yeast
  2 eggs, well beaten
6½ to 7 cups unbleached all-purpose flour
  ½ cup butter, softened
  1 pound light brown sugar
  3 teaspoons ground cinnamon
  ½ teaspoon ground nutmeg

Peel and slice potatoes. Place in a saucepan; add water, cover, and cook over medium high heat about 20 minutes or until tender. Drain, reserve liquid, and mash potatoes measuring one cup. In large bowl place potatoes, shortening, sugar, salt, and reserved warm potato water, at least 130°. Mix well with pastry blender. Allow mixture to cool until a drop against inside wrist is lukewarm, about 105°. Sprinkle yeast over mixture and add well-beaten eggs; blend thoroughly. Sift in flour gradually, and work with spatula until thick enough to knead on floured board. Knead 8 to 10 minutes. Cut batter into three equal parts. (Each piece should weigh about 1½ pounds.) With greased hands mash or press down dough into three greased pans. In another bowl, blend softened butter, sugar, and spices. Sprinkle mixture evenly over three pans of dough. Allow to rise, uncovered, in warm spot for 2 hours. Refrigerate overnight. May be refrigerated up to three days. Uncooked dough will freeze successfully. Remove from refrigerator or freezer, and allow to rise until dough reaches top of pan. Punch dough at 1½-inch intervals with a rounded handle or your thumb so that when butter and spices melt the mixture will flow into holes. Bake in a preheated 350° oven for 20 minutes or until bread tests done. Yield: 3 (13- x 9- x 2-inch) loaves.

BEST EVER MUFFINS

A treat for any occasion.

  ½ cup butter
  ¼ cup sugar
  1 large egg, well beaten
2⅓ cups all-purpose flour
  5 teaspoons baking powder
  ½ teaspoon salt
  1 cup milk

Allow butter to soften in a large mixing bowl; add sugar, and cream until light and fluffy with electric mixer on high speed for 4 minutes. Add egg and beat well. Sift flour and measure. Put baking powder and salt with measured flour into sifter. At low speed, add flour mixture in fourths alternating in thirds with milk. Begin and end with flour mixture. Blend just until smooth; light handling of mixture is important. Fill greased muffin tins or paper baking cups ½ full. Bake in a preheated 400° oven for 15 to 20 minutes until golden brown. Serve hot. Yield: 2 dozen (2-inch) muffins.

BECKY VOGHT'S OATMEAL BREAD

　2 packages active dry yeast
　1 cup very warm water
　2 teaspoons sugar
　⅓ cup butter
　1 cup boiling water
　1 cup regular oats
　½ cup molasses
　1 tablespoon salt
　2¼ cups unbleached white flour, divided
　2¼ cups whole wheat flour
　1 large egg

In a two-cup measure or pint bowl dissolve yeast in very warm water (at least 130°) to which sugar has been added; let stand 10 minutes and stir well. In large bowl cut butter into small pieces, add boiling water, and stir until completely dissolved. Add oats, molasses and salt; blend well and cool to lukewarm. Add dissolved yeast mixture and work in with spatula or spoon. Reserve ½ cup white flour for board. Sift remaining measured flour into yeast mixture and work in with wooden spoon or spatula. Add egg and beat well. Turn dough out on board that has been dusted with reserved ½ cup flour; knead until thoroughly blended. Put dough into large greased bowl, turn upside down to grease top. Chill for 2 to 4 hours. Remove and halve dough, place in well-greased loaf pans, and let rise in warm place until doubled in bulk, about 2 hours. Bake in a preheated 350° oven for 45 minutes to 1 hour or until loaves are nicely browned

and test done. If at end of 45 minutes bread is browned but not done, cover with foil to prevent burning and continue to bake. When done, remove from oven and cool on rack. Makes good sandwiches. Slice thinly. Yield: 2 (9- x 5- x 3-inch) loaves.

ZUCCHINI NUT BREAD

Serve this marvelous bread in many different ways: hot with coffee for breakfast or a brunch, cold with cheese as a snack, at mealtime to children as a vegetable.

　2 cups coarsely grated zucchini
　4 large eggs, room temperature
　2 cups sugar
　1 cup vegetable oil
3½ cups unsifted all-purpose flour (reserve ¼
　　　cup for nuts and raisins)
　4 teaspoons baking powder
1½ teaspoons salt
　2 teaspoons ground cinnamon
　2 teaspoons wheat germ
　1 cup sliced pecans or walnuts
　1 cup raisins
1½ teaspoons vanilla extract

Soak zucchini for an hour in ice water; dry and grate unpeeled. In a large bowl beat eggs on high speed of electric mixer until thick and lemon colored. Gradually beat in sugar and oil. Spoon flour into cup for measuring. Sift into another bowl 3¼ cups flour, baking powder, salt, and cinnamon. On low speed add dry ingredients to egg mixture along with wheat germ alternately with zucchini. Fold in nuts and raisins that have been dusted with reserved flour. Stir in vanilla. Spoon batter into two greased and lightly floured loaf pans lined with waxed paper. Bake in a preheated 350° oven on lowest shelf for 55 to 60 minutes or until bread tests done. Cool in pans for 10 minutes, and turn out on wire racks. Serve hot or cold. This bread keeps well both refrigerated and frozen. Yield: 2 (9- x 5- x 3-inch) loaves.

WHOLE WHEAT BREAD

   1 cup milk
   ½ cup vegetable shortening
   ½ cup firmly packed dark brown sugar
   1 cup cold water
   1 package active dry yeast dissolved in ¼
      cup warm water
   1 egg, well beaten
   3 cups all-purpose white flour, spooned into
      cup
2½ teaspoons salt
   2 tablespoons wheat germ
   4 to 5 cups whole wheat flour
   1 tablespoon butter or margarine, melted

Combine milk and shortening in saucepan and let come almost to a boil. Stir constantly over medium heat. When mixture shows signs of boiling around the edges, remove from heat and add brown sugar. Stir until dissolved. Add cold water and pour into large mixing bowl. When a drop of mixture on the wrist is warm but not hot, add dissolved yeast. Add beaten egg and sift in white flour; beat by hand as you would cake batter or use an electric mixer on medium speed. Cover bowl with waxed paper and a clean dish towel, and place in oven beside a bowl of very hot water. The batter should double in bulk in 1 to 1½ hours.

Sift in salt and stir in wheat germ. Gradually add in sifted whole wheat flour until mixture holds together enough to work with the hands. Turn out on lightly floured board and knead. To knead dough, press mass of dough flat with heel of hands, then fold to center. Repeat process of pressing and folding in a rhythmic motion. Knead about 7 minutes until dough begins to feel elastic and pliable. Press dough into a long roll and cut in two parts. Roll each half into a 12- x 9-inch rectangle; pat dough gently to press out gas bubbles. Start with upper end of rectangle and roll it toward you. Roll tightly, and after each turn press roll at bottom edge with thumbs to seal. Fold sealed ends under and place folded side down in two greased loaf pans.

Brush top of loaves with melted butter or margarine. Let loaves rise in pans in warm place covered with clean dish towels until sides come to tops of pans and loaf tops are rounded, about 1 to 1½ hours. Place pans on middle rack of oven. Bake in a preheated 350° oven for 25 to 30 minutes or until crust is deep golden brown and bread tests done. Turn out onto wire racks; brush tops with remaining melted butter. Serve slightly warm or let cool completely. Yield: 2 (9- x 5- x 3-inch) loaves.

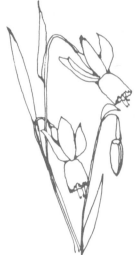

ORANGE NUT BREAD

Mellow, golden, and delicious, a wholesome taste treat that's hard to beat.

   ¾ cup sugar, sifted
   2 tablespoons butter, margarine, or
      vegetable shortening
   1 large egg, well beaten
   ¾ cup milk
   ¾ cup orange juice
   4 teaspoons grated orange rind
   3 cups all-purpose flour, unsifted (reserve 1
      tablespoon for nuts)
3½ teaspoons baking powder
   1 teaspoon salt
   1 cup sliced pecans, peanuts, or walnuts

In a large bowl, cream sugar and shortening by hand or electric mixer on medium speed until light and fluffy. Add beaten egg. Blend milk and orange juice; add orange rind. Reserve 1 tablespoon flour to sprinkle over nuts. Sift flour, baking powder, and salt onto plate and add alternately with milk-orange juice mixture to creamed batter, starting and ending with flour. Fold in nuts that have been dusted with reserved flour; blend well. Pour batter into well-greased loaf pan lined with waxed paper. Bake in a preheated 350° oven for 50 to 60 minutes or until bread tests done. Remove immediately from pan and cool on wire rack. Yield: 1 (9- x 5- x 3-inch) loaf.

SWISS MERINGUE ROLLS

A delicious pastry from the Swiss Booth at Milwaukee's Annual Fair. This is ideal for an unusual dessert.

4 cups all-purpose flour, measured after
    sifting
½ teaspoon salt
1 package active dry yeast
1¼ cups butter
3 egg yolks, slightly beaten
½ cup commercial sour cream
1 teaspoon vanilla extract
    Meringue Filling
    Powdered sugar
½ cup chopped walnuts or pecans
    Powdered Sugar Icing

In a large mixing bowl, combine flour, salt, and undissolved yeast; stir thoroughly. With pastry blender cut in butter until particles are fine. Add beaten egg yolks, sour cream, and vanilla. Mix well with hands. Divide into six equal portions, forming each into a ball. Chill while preparing Meringue Filling.

Sprinkle board with powdered sugar. Roll out one ball at a time into a 10- x 5-inch rectangle, about ⅛ inch thick. Keep remaining dough chilled. Spread rectangle with one-sixth of Meringue Filling and sprinkle with nuts. Roll up from long side neither too tightly nor too loosely. Follow same process with remaining dough. Place rolls seam side down three inches apart on lightly greased cookie sheets. Bake in a preheated 350° oven about 35 to 40 minutes, until lightly browned and meringue showing at end of rolls is firm. (The meringue dissolves in center of pastries but stays crisp at ends.) With a wide spatula, remove at once to wire rack to cool. Frost with Powdered Sugar Icing. Yield: 6 large rolls.

Meringue Filling:

3 egg whites
1 cup sugar
1 teaspoon vanilla extract

Beat egg whites until stiff with electric mixer on high speed. Gradually beat in sugar. Continue beating until meringue holds stiff straight peaks; add vanilla. Gently level meringue and mark off top into six equal portions.

Powdered Sugar Icing:

1½ tablespoons butter, room temperature
  1 cup sifted powdered sugar
⅛ teaspoon salt
½ teaspoon almond extract
  1 teaspoon vanilla extract or 1 tablespoon
    brandy, sherry, or rum

Beat butter until soft and creamy. Gradually add sugar. Add salt, almond extract and your favorite flavoring.

PUMPKIN BREAD

Spicy and light!

**3½ cups all-purpose flour, spoon into cup
    (reserve 1 tablespoon for nuts)
  3 cups sugar
1½ teaspoons salt
  2 teaspoons soda
  1 teaspoon ground cinnamon
  1 teaspoon ground nutmeg
  1 cup buttery vegetable oil
  4 large eggs, room temperature
⅔ cup water
  2 cups canned pumpkin
  1 cup chopped pecans or walnuts**

Blend dry ingredients in bowl until well mixed.
Combine oil, eggs, water and pumpkin and
beat until well blended. Add dry ingredients
slowly and beat well. Stir in pecans that have
been dusted with reserved flour and pour batter into greased loaf pans. Bake in a preheated
350° oven: large loaves for 1 hour 15 minutes,
small loaves for 60 to 65 minutes. Cool 10
minutes before removing from pans and continue cooling on wire racks. Wrap in foil and
keep in refrigerator, or freeze. Yield: 2 (9- x
5- x 3-inch) loaves or 3 (8- x 4- x 2-inch) loaves.

SOURDOUGH BREAD

A delicious bread with a delightful fragrance.

Sourdough Starter:

**½ teaspoon sugar
  1 package active dry yeast
2½ cups fully warm water (105° to 115°)
  1 cup instant nonfat dry milk powder
  2 tablespoons sugar
  4 cups all-purpose flour**

In a small bowl dissolve ½ teaspoon sugar,
yeast, and fully warm water. When yeast begins
to bubble up and rise, pour mixture into a
2½-quart glass, enamel, or stainless steel bowl,
and gradually stir in milk powder, 2 tablespoons sugar, and flour until batter is smooth.
Cover loosely and let stand in a warm place
for 3 or 4 days. When batter rises up to top
of bowl, stir down. The first day watch carefully so that it does not overflow. Place a large
plastic piece or newspaper beneath the bowl
to prevent unnecessary cleaning up. Cover
bowl loosely and store in refrigerator.

To keep the starter alive, once or twice a
week add:

**1 cup all-purpose flour
1 cup milk
¼ cup sugar**

Mix well and keep refrigerated. If you have
a small family, use only half of the measurements. Always add these ingredients on the
same day of the week or the day before or the
day after.

Bread:

**2 slightly rounded cups Sourdough Starter
  2 teaspoons baking powder
½ teaspoon soda
  1 teaspoon salt
¼ cup vegetable oil
2½ cups all-purpose flour, divided
    Butter**

Place Sourdough Starter in large bowl. Sift in
baking powder, soda, and salt. Add vegetable
oil and mix well. Flour board with ½ cup flour
and put remaining flour into sifter. Gradually
add flour from sifter, and blend after each
addition. When mixture begins to hold
together well, grease hands and turn mixture
out onto board. As you add remaining flour,
knead it in a rhythmic fashion. To knead, press
mass of dough flat with the heels of your

hands; fold to center. Then repeat process of pressing and folding dough rhythmically. When dough begins to feel elastic after about 5 minutes, slap dough with the full palms of the hands to press out gas bubbles, then stretch it into an oblong piece. Fold long sides under first, and tuck ends under. Place dough folded sides down in a greased loaf pan. Brush top of loaf with melted butter or dot with butter in several places. Cover with waxed paper and a clean dish towel, and place on stove top where it is warm. Let rise in pan until doubled in bulk; the dough should completely fill the pan and be rising above it. This takes 2½ to 3 hours depending on the warmth of the kitchen. Bake in a preheated 400° oven for 20 to 25 minutes or until golden brown. Cool on a wire rack. Yield: 1 (9- x 5- x 3-inch) loaf.

Note: If you prefer the rounded loaf, shape the mass of dough into a dome rounding it with your hands. Place on a greased cookie sheet with cornmeal sprinkled on the bottom. Brush tops and sides of dough with melted butter and sprinkle with cornmeal. Allow to rise until doubled in bulk and bake in same manner as above.

SOUR CHERRY BREAD

This bread has a unique flavor—you will relish every mouthful.

    ½ cup butter or margarine
    1½ cups sugar
    1 (16-ounce) can sour red cherries, well drained
    1 teaspoon soda
    1 teaspoon salt
    2 cups sifted all-purpose flour (reserve 1 tablespoon for nuts)
    3 tablespoons buttermilk or sour milk
    2 large eggs, well beaten, room temperature
    1 teaspoon almond extract
    1 cup chopped pecans or walnuts

Cream butter and sugar. Make pulp out of cherries either in blender or mixer. Combine soda, salt, and flour and sift into creamed mixture alternating with buttermilk; beat well. Add cherry pulp and beaten eggs and almond extract. Fold in chopped nuts that have been dusted with reserved flour. Spoon batter into greased loaf pan lined with waxed paper. Bake in a preheated 350° oven for 50 to 60 minutes or until bread tests done. Cool on wire rack for 10 minutes before removing from pan. This freezes well and slices better when cold. Yield: 1 (9- x 5- x 3-inch) loaf.

Note: If buttermilk is not available, substitute sour milk. Warm 1 cup milk; add 1⅓ tablespoons vinegar. Allow to sit for 5 minutes.

SOURDOUGH ROLLS

    1 cup Sourdough Starter
    ½ cup all-purpose flour
    1 teaspoon baking powder
    ¼ teaspoon soda
    ¼ cup salad oil
    ½ teaspoon salt

Combine all ingredients and mix thoroughly. Fill greased muffin tins about ⅔ full. Bake in a preheated 400° oven for 15 minutes. By adding a little grated cheddar cheese you may make delicious cheese rolls. Yield: 10 or 11 medium-size rolls.

SOURDOUGH PANCAKES

  1 cup Sourdough Starter
  ½ cup all-purpose flour
  2 teaspoons baking powder
  1 egg
  ¼ teaspoon soda
  ¼ cup melted shortening
  ½ teaspoon salt

Combine all ingredients and mix thoroughly. Using ¼ cup batter for each pancake, pour onto a well-greased griddle. Yield: 10 to 12 pancakes.

NEVER FAIL ROLLS

These light and delicious rolls are easy to make, economical, and require no kneading. To freeze, I put them up in foil trays of a dozen each. They will keep frozen two months or more and retain flavor.

  2 cups milk, divided
  ½ cup plus 2 tablespoons vegetable
     shortening
  1 package active dry yeast
  ¼ cup warm water
  ½ cup plus 2 tablespoons sugar
  4 cups all-purpose flour
  1 teaspoon baking powder
  1 teaspoon soda
  1½ teaspoons salt
  1½ cups all-purpose flour
  ½ cup margarine, melted

Place 1 cup milk with shortening in a saucepan. Stir constantly over medium heat until shortening melts; do not allow to boil. If it begins to boil, remove from heat and let shortening melt in hot milk. Add remaining 1 cup milk and yeast that has been dissolved in warm water. Combine sugar, 4 cups flour, baking powder, soda, and salt in sifter. In a very large bowl, gradually add these dry ingredients to milk mixture, using a wire whisk or electric mixer. Place uncovered bowl on stove. Allow dough to rise 2 to 2½ hours until doubled in bulk. Lightly flour board and stir in 1½ cups flour; mix well. Divide dough in half, roll out until ⅛ inch thick. Brush with melted margarine and cut with biscuit cutter. Fold each roll over and dip into melted margarine, place on greased cookie sheets or six individual foil trays. (I save those in which bakery products are packaged.) For immediate use, continue to let rolls rise 2 hours or until doubled in bulk. Refrigerate or freeze rolls you do not plan to use at once. Bake in a preheated 425° oven for 15 to 20 minutes until golden brown. When using frozen rolls, remove from freezer at least 4 hours before serving. Allow 3 hours for those in refrigerator. Yield: 6 dozen.

CINNAMON ROLLS

  ⅔ cup seedless raisins, white or black
  1½ pounds kneaded Enriched White Bread
     dough
  ¾ stick melted butter or margarine
  ¾ cup sugar
  3 tablespoons firmly packed dark brown
     sugar
  2 teaspoons ground cinnamon

Plump raisins in bowl by pouring 2 cups of hot water over them. Let stand 15 minutes, then drain on paper towel. This prevents over-browning. Take kneaded white bread dough, roll out into a ¼-inch thick 18- x 8-inch rectangle. Brush with melted butter. Blend sugars and cinnamon and sprinkle generously over surface. Place raisins in line down center. Roll up as for jelly roll, cut into ¾-inch slices and place cut side down in greased pan. Cover with clean dish towel and let rise until doubled in bulk. Bake in a preheated 400° oven for 15 to 20 minutes. Remove at once to wire rack to cool or serve hot. These will keep fresh ten days or two weeks in sealed can and will also freeze beautifully. Yield: about 2 dozen.

RAISIN NUT BREAD

For breakfast this tasty bread is delicious served hot with butter or cold. Spread with cream cheese and serve with a glass of milk or a cup of hot tea or coffee.

3¼ cups all-purpose flour (reserve ¼ cup for nuts)
1 cup sugar
1 teaspoon salt
3 teaspoons baking powder
1 rounded teaspoon ground cinnamon
1 large egg, room temperature
1½ cups milk
3 tablespoons vegetable oil
1 teaspoon vanilla extract
1 cup chopped pecans or walnuts
1 cup dark or white seedless raisins
Candied cherry halves
Pecans

Mix and sift together 3 cups flour, sugar, salt, baking powder, and cinnamon into a large bowl. Beat egg until light in another small bowl. Add milk to beaten egg. Stir liquid mixture into dry ingredients and mix well. (If using an electric beater, place on medium speed.) Add oil gradually; add vanilla, then stir in nuts and raisins that have been dusted with reserved flour. Spoon batter into greased loaf pans lined with waxed paper. Let pans stand for ½ hour before baking; decorate top of bread with candied cherry halves and pecans to form an attractive pattern. Bake in a preheated 350° oven until bread tests done: large loaf for 1 hour 15 to 30 minutes, medium-size loaves about 1 hour. If you are not sure of your oven temperature, use an oven thermometer. This bread browns easily because of the dark batter, and you want the finished product to be a beautiful golden color. Cool on wire rack for 10 minutes. Remove from pans and allow to continue cooling. Yield: 1 (11- x 5- x 3-inch) loaf or 2 (8- x 4- x 2-inch) loaves.

SPOON BREAD

Fluffy spoonbread is that favorite dish we serve from the plains of Texas to the mountains of Virginia when welcoming the stranger within our gates. The recipe is easy, economical, and excellent with a bonus thrown in: you can assemble it in the morning, and put it aside while you go about your business. Just pop it into the oven 50 minutes before you plan to serve. With fried chicken or country fried ham and red-eye gravy, the combination is unbeatable. It is equally good with a beef or pork roast. Without gravy, a generous supply of butter is a must.

3 cups milk, divided
1 cup cornmeal
2 rounded tablespoons vegetable shortening
1 teaspoon salt
1 teaspoon baking powder
4 egg yolks, well beaten
4 egg whites, stiffly beaten

Pour 1 cup milk over cornmeal in a medium-size bowl. Scald 2 cups milk over medium heat. When milk begins to boil, add meal mixture and cook 10 minutes, stirring constantly. The mixture should become very thick. Add shortening, salt, and baking powder. Remove from heat, add well-beaten egg yolks and fold in stiffly beaten egg whites. Pour into greased 1½-quart casserole and allow to sit on back of stove until ready to be cooked. Bake in a preheated 375° oven for 50 minutes. Serve piping hot. Spoon Bread should be eaten as soon as it comes from oven; you can turn the heat off and hold for 10 minutes, no longer. Yield: 6 servings.

The variations: For fancy Spoon Bread, and a complete meal when accompanied by a salad and dessert, add ½ pound finely ground chuck or round steak to the batter. Gently stir in immediately before baking since this batter should not be refrigerated after meat is added. Yield: 6 servings.

ENRICHED WHITE BREAD

Today the ancient art of baking bread at home is coming back into its proper place. Nothing is more tantalizing than the aroma of fresh hot bread. The manufacturer who can bottle that fragrance will make a fortune. Let me give you my foolproof recipe for a delicious bread. It has more flavor and substance because of its enrichment with high quality proteins.

    1 package active dry yeast
¼ cup fully warm water
½ teaspoon sugar
  2 cups milk
½ cup sugar
½ cup shortening, butter, or vegetable oil
3 tablespoons nonfat dry milk powder
3 tablespoons wheat germ
6½ cups all-purpose flour, divided
  2 teaspoons salt
½ teaspoon baking powder
½ teaspoon soda
    Melted butter or margarine

In a small bowl dissolve yeast in ¼ cup very warm water; add ½ teaspoon sugar. Heat milk, ½ cup sugar, and shortening in large saucepan over medium heat stirring constantly until milk bubbles at the edges. Do not let milk boil. Remove and cool pan in bowl of ice. When a drop of milk feels lukewarm to the wrist, add the risen dissolved yeast. Pour mixture into large bowl; add nonfat dry milk and wheat germ. Beat with mixer on low speed until thoroughly blended. Gradually add 2½ cups sifted flour to mixture and continue beating. Cut down from sides with spatula. Cover bowl with waxed paper and a clean dish towel, and place in cold oven beside large bowl of very hot water until dough doubles in bulk, about 1½ hours. Sift in 2 cups flour, salt, baking powder, and soda, stirring well. Turn out on floured board and knead using both hands. To knead, press dough flat with heels of hands folding to center. Repeat process of pressing and folding dough in a rhythmic motion. Gradually use remainder of flour.

When dough begins to feel elastic and smooth, shape into a long roll and cut into two equal parts. (Each loaf should weigh about 1½ pounds.) Roll the dough into an even, thick, 14- x 9-inch rectangle. Pat the dough gently to press out air bubbles. Start with upper end of rectangle and roll it toward you. Roll tightly and after each turn, press roll at bottom edge with thumbs to seal. Turn seam side down, and seal ends by pressing sides of hands down on each end. Fold sealed ends under and place folded side down in two well-greased loaf pans. Brush top of loaves with melted butter. Cover loaves with clean dishtowel and let rise in pans until doubled in bulk. Bake in a preheated 375° oven for 20 to 25 minutes or until bread tests done. Remove and cool on wire rack. Better still, slice and serve immediately with butter and wild blackberry jam, and enjoy food fit for the gods on Mount Olympus. Yield: 2 (9- x 5- x 3-inch) loaves.

Note: If you wish to prepare cinnamon rolls, divide the dough before baking. Use 1 pound dough in a greased 8- x 4- x 2-inch loaf pan and ¾ pound in a greased 7- x 3- x 2-inch loaf pan. Bake in a preheated 375° oven for 20 minutes. This division leaves 1½ pounds dough for cinnamon rolls.

SOURDOUGH COFFEE CAKE

Unusual and tasty.

¾ cup all-purpose flour, measured after
    sifting
½ cup sugar
  1 teaspoon salt
½ teaspoon soda
2½ teaspoons baking powder
1½ cups Sourdough Starter
  ¼ cup vegetable oil
  1 egg, slightly beaten
    Spicy Topping
  2 teaspoons butter or margarine

Sift flour, sugar, salt, soda, and baking powder into a large bowl. Add Sourdough Starter, oil, and lightly beaten egg. Grease a 9-inch square pan and pour part of the batter into it. Sprinkle half of the Spicy Topping over batter, pour remaining batter into pan, and top with remaining Topping. Insert slivers of butter into dough, and bake in a preheated 375° oven for 25 to 30 minutes or until cake tests done. Yield: 1 (9-inch) square cake.

Spicy Topping:

¼ cup firmly packed light brown sugar
2 teaspoons cinnamon
1 tablespoon melted butter
¼ cup pecans or walnuts, finely sliced

Blend all ingredients in a small bowl.

CARNIVAL SPOON BREAD

Colorful as a carnival parade and a meal in itself with salad and dessert.

2 cups yellow cornmeal
2½ cups boiling water
2 tablespoons vinegar
1 teaspoon dried green onion
1 (13-ounce) can evaporated milk
1½ teaspoons melted margarine
1½ teaspoons salt
2 egg yolks, slightly beaten
¾ cup shredded cheddar cheese
1 teaspoon soda
1 (4-ounce) can mushrooms, drained and dried
1 (2-ounce) can pimientos, drained and dried
2 egg whites, stiffly beaten

Put cornmeal into a large mixing bowl. Pour boiling water over cornmeal and stir well. Let stand until mixture has cooled. (If pressed for time, cool in pan of ice.) Combine remaining ingredients except egg whites and add to cooled mixture. Fold in egg whites and pour mixture into well-greased, 2-quart casserole. Bake in a preheated 425° oven for 40 to 45 minutes. Serve piping hot. Yield: 10 servings.

LA VERNE HESTER'S ONION-RYE BREAD

1 cup milk
2 tablespoons sugar
2 teaspoons salt
2 tablespoons shortening
2 packages active dry yeast
½ cup lukewarm water
1 teaspoon sugar
3 cups sifted all-purpose flour
5 teaspoons caraway seeds
3 tablespoons grated onion
   About 1½ cups unsifted rye flour
   Salad oil

Scald milk. In a large mixing bowl add 2 tablespoons sugar, salt, and shortening to scalded milk, and stir until mixture is lukewarm. Dissolve yeast in lukewarm water to which 1 teaspoon sugar has been added; stir until mixture softens and begins to bubble. Add to milk mixture along with flour; mix until smooth. Sprinkle caraway seeds on dough. Add grated onion and enough rye flour to make dough firm. On rye-floured board, knead dough until elastic. Place in greased bowl, brush top with salad oil, and place in cold oven beside a large bowl of very hot water. Allow to rise until doubled in bulk. Knead again and shape into loaf; place in greased loaf pan, brush top with salad oil, cover, and let rise again until doubled in bulk. Bake in a preheated 350° oven for 45 to 50 minutes. Yield: 1 (9- x 5- x 3-inch) loaf.

Cakes and Icings

NEVER FAIL WHITE ICING

  3 medium-size or large egg whites
  ¼ teaspoon cream of tartar
1½ cups sifted sugar
  5 tablespoons cold water
1½ teaspoons light corn syrup
  1 teaspoon vanilla extract

Place all ingredients with exception of vanilla in top of a double boiler over rapidly boiling water. Beat mixture with electric mixer at high speed. You may use a rotary beater or wire whisk; but the electric mixer makes it easier. Cut down mixture from sides of pan with spatula as it cooks. Beat constantly about 7 minutes or until icing will stand in peaks and has attained a high gloss. Remove icing from heat and add vanilla. Center a layer of cake on cake plate and put 5 heaping tablespoons icing in a circle on top and gently spread toward the sides. Use a dinner knife or a 1-inch wide spatula for spreading. Position top cake layer and repeat icing method. To ice the sides apply a tablespoon of icing at top of side working it down as you go around the cake. Repeat until cake is completely covered. Yield: icing for sides and tops of 2 (9-inch) layers.

LIGHT CHOCOLATE ICING

2 (1-ounce) squares unsweetened chocolate
  Never Fail White Icing

Melt unsweetened chocolate in top of a double boiler over hot water and stir with a wooden spoon. Cool and fold into Never Fail White Icing. Icing should stiffen quickly. If it does not, allow time before spreading. Yield: icing for sides and tops of 2 (9-inch) layers.

COCONUT ICING

  Never Fail White Icing
1½ cups freshly grated coconut

Ice bottom cake layer with Never Fail White Icing. Sprinkle top heavily with some of the coconut. Repeat process on top layer and sides. Frozen or canned coconut may be substituted but the flavor of fresh is preferable. Yield: icing for sides and tops of 2 (9-inch) layers.

LEMON ICING

The best!

¾ cup sugar
¼ cup cornstarch or all-purpose flour
½ teaspoon salt
1 cup cold water
2 large egg yolks
2 tablespoons lemon rind
½ cup lemon juice
2 tablespoons butter

Combine sugar, cornstarch, salt, and water in top of a double boiler over rapidly boiling water. Stir until mixture boils; boil for 2 minutes. Beat egg yolks in deep bowl until thick and creamy, add lemon rind and juice; blend thoroughly. Add cooked cornstarch mixture slowly to egg mixture; beat well. Return to stove and boil for 1 minute, stirring constantly. Remove from heat, add butter. Cool before icing cake. Yield: icing for sides and top of 2 (9-inch) layers.

QUICKIE CHOCOLATE FUDGE ICING

Easy and excellent.

¼ cup powdered cocoa
1 cup sugar
½ cup milk
2 teaspoons light corn syrup
1½ to 2 cups powdered sugar, sifted
1 teaspoon vanilla extract

Combine all ingredients except vanilla extract and powdered sugar in a heavy saucepan. Bring to boil over medium heat, stirring constantly for 2 minutes. Cool and add powdered sugar and vanilla; spread on cake. If icing seems too firm, add a few drops of hot water. Yield: icing for sides and tops of 2 (8-inch) layers or a Bundt cake.

PECAN ICING

A fabulous icing to complete a three-layer white cake. This recipe comes from historical Beau Fort, the home of Mrs. C. Vernon Cloutier. The cake was served on festive occasions such as Thanksgiving and Christmas.

2½ cups sugar
11 tablespoons cold water
4 tablespoons light corn syrup
3 egg whites, well beaten, using 2 large eggs and 1 small egg
3½ cups ground pecans
1 cup pecan meal
1 teaspoon vanilla extract

In a large, flat-bottomed saucepan combine sugar, water, and corn syrup. Bring mixture to a boil over medium high heat; stir until sugar is dissolved. Cook until candy thermometer reaches 240°. Remove from heat and pour gradually over beaten egg whites. Add ground pecans, pecan meal, and vanilla extract. If mixture gets too thick before you can spread it on the cake, add 1 teaspoon hot water on spatula. Spread icing quickly. Yield: icing for sides and tops of 3 (9-inch) layers.

BROWNED BUTTER FROSTING

Delectable!

4 tablespoons butter
1¾ cups powdered sugar, sifted
2 tablespoons or more whipping cream
⅛ teaspoon salt
1 teaspoon vanilla extract

Brown butter in an iron skillet over low heat; cool. Blend sifted sugar, cream, and salt into butter. (It may take more than 2 tablespoons cream for a spreading consistency.) Add vanilla. Remove frosting from skillet and spread at once. Yield: frosting for sides and tops of 2 (8-inch) layers.

BECKY VOGHT'S CARAMEL ICING

Easy to make and a delight to eat.

  1 cup buttermilk
  2 cups sugar
  ½ cup firmly packed dark brown sugar
  ½ teaspoon soda
  ½ cup butter
  1 teaspoon vanilla extract
    Whipping cream

Combine buttermilk, sugars, and soda in a large saucepan. Stir over medium heat until sugars are dissolved; then allow to boil without stirring to soft ball stage (238°). If you do not have a candy thermometer, have a cup of cold water handy; drop a tiny bit of boiling syrup into water. When syrup can be gathered up in fingers into a soft ball that will almost hold its shape, it has reached the soft ball stage. Add butter; remove from heat and cool 5 minutes. Add vanilla and beat until thick and creamy. If mixture becomes too heavy, thin it with a little cream until it is the right consistency to spread. If icing gets too firm while spreading, dip knife into very hot water and it will help considerably. Yield: icing for sides and top of 2 (9-inch) layers.

FABULOUS FOOLPROOF CHOCOLATE ICING

The easiest icing to make, it becomes firm enough to wrap and it freezes successfully. For a luscious thick icing, double recipe. Be sure cake layers are completely cool before icing. Use the milk chocolate pieces for a sweeter icing.

  2 cups semisweet chocolate pieces or milk
      chocolate pieces
  1 cup commercial sour cream
  ⅛ teaspoon salt
  2 tablespoons powdered sugar
  1 teaspoon vanilla extract

Melt chocolate pieces in top of a double boiler over *very hot water. Do not allow to boil.* Blend in sour cream, salt, and sugar with wooden spoon or spatula. Stir until smooth; remove from heat. Add vanilla and spread icing on cake. It lends itself to swirls and designs; they will stay put. To use as a sauce add a small amount of hot water. Yield: icing for sides and tops of 2 (9-inch) layers.

ANGEL QUICKIE CHOCOLATE ICING

Marvelous for that unexpected company. Pick up cake at the bakery, and ice in ten minutes. This recipe also does a beautiful job of topping a 10-inch meringue, making a chocolate angel pie. Place icing on meringue the night before using. Grate sweetened chocolate over top of pie before serving.

  1 large egg white, room temperature
  5 tablespoons sugar, divided
  1 (5½-ounce) can commercial chocolate
      syrup
  1 teaspoon vanilla extract, divided
  ½ pint whipping cream
  1 (10-inch) angel food cake, commercial or
      homemade

Beat egg white until light and frothy. Gradually add 3 tablespoons sugar. Use high speed of electric mixer or dover egg beater. Fold in chocolate syrup and ½ teaspoon vanilla. Whip cream, adding remaining 2 tablespoons sugar and ½ teaspoon vanilla. Fold chocolate mixture into whipped cream. Ice cake and chill at once; refrigerate until ready to serve. Yield: icing for 1 (10-inch) tube cake.

ALMOND TORTE

A marvelous cake to complete an elegant meal.

  6 large eggs, separated, room temperature
  1 cup sifted sugar, divided
1½ tablespoons strained lemon juice
1½ cups (about 9 ounces) ground blanched
      almonds
1½ cups toasted fine bread crumbs
  ½ teaspoon almond extract
  1 teaspoon baking powder
3½ tablespoons grated lemon rind
  ⅛ teaspoon salt
  ⅛ teaspoon cream of tartar
      Lemon Syrup Glaze

In small narrow bowl beat yolks at high speed of electric mixer. When they are thick and light, gradually add ½ cup sugar. With mixer on low speed, add lemon juice, 1 cup ground almonds, fine bread crumbs, almond extract, and baking powder. Stir in lemon rind and blend well; set mixture aside. At high speed beat egg whites, salt, and cream of tartar until they begin to stand in soft peaks; add remaining ½ cup sugar gradually and remaining ground almonds. Fold egg white mixture into egg yolk batter; blend gently with up and out motion.

Pour batter into two 8-inch layer pans or one 13- x 9- x 2-inch pan, greased, floured, and lined with waxed paper. This cake is very light and difficult to remove from pan. Pans with removable rims are most helpful. Bake in a preheated 350° oven for 25 to 30 minutes or until cake tests done. Cool 9- x 13-inch cake in pan. Remove bottoms of 8-inch cake pans, cool for 10 minutes and remove layers; allow to finish cooling on rack. Serve the oblong cake with Lemon Syrup Glaze, the layer cake with your favorite lemon or chocolate butter filling. Yield: 2 (8-inch) layers or 1 (13- x 9- x 2-inch) cake—20 to 22 servings.

Lemon Syrup Glaze:

  4 tablespoons strained lemon juice
  ¼ cup water
  ¾ cup sugar

Combine all ingredients and bring to a boil in saucepan over medium heat. Stir constantly until sugar is dissolved; cook until thickened. Spoon hot syrup over torte while torte is still in pan. When syrup is cold, cut torte into 2-inch squares. The torte is even more delicious if allowed to sit overnight before cutting.

BLUEBERRY DRIP CAKE

It's so easy to make it's almost unbelievable.

  1 (15-ounce) can blueberries
  ¼ teaspoon ground cinnamon
  2 cups commercial cake mix, white or yellow
  4 tablespoons butter

Remove ½ cup juice from berries. Spread berries with remaining juice in buttered baking dish. Sprinkle with cinnamon and spread the dry cake mix evenly over top of berries. Do not add anything to cake mix. Top with thinly sliced butter. Bake in a preheated 350° oven for 50 minutes. Serve warm and plain or with a dollop of ice cream or whipped cream. Almost any fruit will respond to this treatment. Apricots and cherries are particularly delicious used in this fashion. Yield: 1 (13- x 9- x 2-inch) cake—8 to 10 servings.

BAJAN SPONGE CAKE

Ideal to use as a base for any dessert, this sponge cake from Barbados is the easiest and cheapest to make.

 2 large eggs, room temperature
½ teaspoon salt
 1 cup sifted sugar
½ cup milk
 1 tablespoon butter
 1 cup sifted all-purpose flour
 1 teaspoon baking powder
 1 teaspoon vanilla extract

Beat eggs until light in a large bowl, using high speed of electric mixer. Add salt and sugar and continue beating. Put milk and butter in saucepan over very low heat until milk bubbles at the edges. Cool until a drop on the wrist is warm to the touch; add to egg mixture. Sift flour and baking powder and add gradually to mixture, using medium speed. Add vanilla and beat well. Pour batter into a greased tube or Bundt pan. Bake in a preheated 350° oven for 30 minutes or until cake tests done. Allow to cool upside down on wire rack, then remove from pan. Yield: 1 (10-inch) tube or Bundt cake—12 servings.

WHITE FRUIT CAKE

1½ cups butter, softened
  2 cups sugar
  6 large eggs
  4 cups sifted all-purpose flour (reserve ½ cup for fruit and nuts)
  2 teaspoons baking powder
½ cup whiskey
  2 teaspoons vanilla extract
  1 pound candied cherries, chopped
  1 pound candied pineapple, cut into small pieces
  4 cups pecans, chopped

In a large bowl cream butter and sugar until light and fluffy. Add eggs, beating in one at a time. Sift 3½ cups flour and baking powder into creamed mixture gradually, alternating with whiskey. Add vanilla. Stir in fruits and nuts that have been dusted with reserved flour and spoon into a 10-inch tube pan lined with greased brown or waxed paper. Grease only bottom of paper. Spoon batter into pan and bake in a preheated 300° oven for 2 hours. Allow cake to cool on rack before removing from pan. Yield: 1 (10-inch) tube cake—20 to 22 servings.

MY BEST DARK FRUIT CAKE

  6 (16-ounce) boxes seedless raisins
1¼ pounds pecans, lightly toasted
1¼ pounds candied cherries
1¼ pounds candied pineapple
  1 pound butter
  1 pound sugar
  1 cup maple syrup
  1 dozen eggs, beaten
  1 cup sherry or coffee
1½ tablespoons ground nutmeg
  1 tablespoon ground cloves
  1 tablespoon ground cinnamon
1¼ pounds all-purpose flour, sifted, divided
    Sherry or bourbon

Wash raisins and dry. Cut pecans in half and cut cherries and pineapple into very small pieces. Cream butter and sugar; add syrup, then beaten eggs. Add sherry or coffee, spices, and half the sifted flour; sprinkle remaining flour over pecans, raisins, cherries, and pineapple. Stir fruit and pecans into creamed mixture with clean hands.

Grease and line with brown paper or four layers of thin waxed paper several large loaf pans or smaller attractive fruit cake pans with spouts. Fill spouts with waxed paper. Divide cake batter into the pans.

There are two ways to steam a cake: Cover the bottom of the oven with shallow pans filled 1 inch deep with very hot water and bake large loaf pans in preheated 300° oven for 2 to 3 hours or until cake tests done. Place fruit cake pans with spouts in a large covered turkey roaster or roasting pan and fill bottom 1 inch deep with very hot water. Cook on top of stove or in a preheated 250° oven.

Steam a 2- to 5-pound cake for 1 to 1½ hours, then dry in a 250° oven for 1 hour. Steam a 1- to 1½-pound cake for ½ hour, then dry in a 250° oven for 1 hour. Allow cakes to cool. When cakes are cold and have been removed from pan, dribble sherry or, preferably, bourbon over the top. Yield: 13 to 14 pounds.

FRESH APPLE OR PEAR CAKE

This tasty cake stays moist and fresh for days and is very good served with coffee.

1⅓ cups vegetable oil
2 cups sugar
3 eggs, well beaten
1 teaspoon salt
1 teaspoon soda
2 teaspoons baking powder
2 teaspoons ground cinnamon
2½ cups all-purpose flour, measured after sifting (reserve 2 tablespoons for fruit and nuts)
3 cups fresh apples or pears, peeled and chopped
1 cup chopped pecans
1 teaspoon vanilla extract

Combine oil and sugar in a large bowl; add well-beaten eggs and beat until creamy using medium speed of electric mixer or by hand. Sift together salt, soda, baking powder, and cinnamon; add small amount to creamed mixture, beating well. Add flour by same method. Fold in apples and pecans that have been dusted with reserved flour; add vanilla. Pour batter into a well-greased and floured 13- x 9- x 2-inch pan. Bake in a preheated 300° oven for 1 hour. Ripe sand or sickle pears may be used in place of apples. A tart apple such as Jonathan, Winesap, or Rome Beauty does the best job. Yield: 1 (13- x 9- x 2-inch) cake—20 servings.

VOLA HOLLEMAN'S FRUIT COCKTAIL CAKE

2 cups all-purpose flour
2 cups sugar
2 eggs
2 teaspoons soda
¼ teaspoon salt
1 (17-ounce) can fruit cocktail, undrained
Topping

Combine all ingredients in a large bowl and beat by hand or with electric mixer on medium speed for 5 minutes. Pour into greased and floured 13- x 9- x 2-inch pan. Bake in a preheated 375° oven for 45 minutes. Pour Topping on cake. Allow cake to cool for 2 hours before cutting. Yield: 1 (13- x 9- x 2-inch) cake—24 servings.

Topping:

1 cup margarine
1 cup sugar
1 cup evaporated milk
½ cup chopped pecans
1 cup shredded coconut
1 teaspoon vanilla extract

Combine margarine, sugar, and evaporated milk in a large saucepan; boil for 10 minutes. (Be careful or mixture will overflow.) Remove from heat; add pecans, coconut, and vanilla and pour on cake while Topping is hot.

ALMA SHAND'S ANGEL FOOD CAKE

A prize angel food cake! This recipe resembles my mother-in-law's—the best ever. An electric mixer and proper directions simplify its creation.

1⅛ cups sifted cake flour
 ¾ cup sugar
1½ cups egg whites, room temperature
 ½ teaspoon salt
1½ teaspoons cream of tartar
 1 cup sugar
 1 teaspoon vanilla extract
 1 teaspoon almond extract

Sift together five times flour and ¾ cup sugar; put aside on a large platter. In a large mixing bowl beat egg whites and salt on medium-high speed until foamy; add cream of tartar and continue beating on same speed until whites are stiff and stand in peaks, about 2½ to 3 minutes. *Do not beat until dry.* Using slightly slower speed, gradually sprinkle in 1 cup sugar. Beat only until sugar is blended, about 1½ minutes. On lowest speed, add flavorings. Sprinkle in flour mixture evenly and quickly. Beat only enough to blend, about 1½ minutes, scraping bowl to blend in quickly. Pour into an ungreased tube pan; cut through batter with knife or spatula going around in circular motion three times to release large air bubbles. Bake in a preheated 375° oven for 30 to 35 minutes until golden brown. Invert on cake rack and let cool for 2 hours. Run knife around pan and tube to loosen, turn out, and run knife around bottom of pan to release cake. Yield: 1 (10-inch) tube cake—20 to 22 servings.

LINDY'S CHEESE CAKE

An outstanding cheese cake from the famous New York restaurant. A 9-inch springform pan is necessary to make this cake. There are two easy steps plus a topping.

 1 cup all-purpose flour, measured after sifting
½ cup sugar
 1 teaspoon grated lemon rind
 1 large egg yolk, room temperature
 ¼ cup melted butter
 ¼ teaspoon vanilla extract
   Cream Cheese Mixture
   Topping

Combine flour, sugar, and lemon rind in a large bowl. Make a well in center. Add egg yolk, butter, and vanilla and work together quickly until blended. Add a little cold water if necessary to make it hold together. Wrap in waxed paper and chill 1 hour. Roll out dough ⅛ inch thick and place over greased bottom of springform pan with sides removed. Trim off extra dough. Bake in a preheated 400° oven for 20 minutes or until light golden color. Cool. Replace sides of pan and grease. Roll remaining dough ⅛ inch thick and line sides of pan. Fill with Cream Cheese Mixture.

Cream Cheese Mixture:

 5 (8-ounce) packages cream cheese
1¾ cups sugar
 3 tablespoons all-purpose flour
 ⅛ cup whipping cream
1½ teaspoons grated lemon rind
1½ teaspoons grated orange rind
 ½ teaspoon vanilla extract
 5 large eggs
 2 egg yolks

In a large bowl beat cream cheese on medium speed of electric mixer. Add sugar gradually, then add flour, cream, lemon and orange rinds, and vanilla. Add eggs and yolks one at a time, beating lightly after each addition. When well blended and smooth, pour into pastry lined pan. Bake in a preheated 500° oven for 12 to 15 minutes. If possible, check oven heat with an extra thermometer. Reduce heat to 200° and continue baking for 1 hour. Cool thoroughly on wire rack before removing from pan. Serve plain, with a topping, or with a faint sprinkling of cinnamon. Yield: 1 (9-inch) cheese cake—18 to 20 servings.

Cherry Topping:

My favorite and the easiest.

**1 (16-ounce) can cherry pie filling
Red food coloring**

Combine cherry pie filling with several drops red food coloring. Spread on top of cooled cheese cake.

Cranberry Topping:

Great for a bright Christmas dessert.

**1 (16-ounce) can whole cranberry sauce
1 tablespoon cornstarch
2 tablespoons sugar
1 teaspoon lemon juice, strained**

In a saucepan over low heat cook cranberry sauce, cornstarch, and sugar until clear and thickened, stirring constantly. Add lemon juice and blend well. Cool and spread on top of cheese cake.

Strawberry Topping:

Pretty as a picture and very tasty.

**3 cups firm ripe strawberries
1 cup water
1 cup sugar
3 tablespoons cornstarch
⅓ cup water
1 cup whole strawberries**

Combine 3 cups strawberries, 1 cup water, and sugar in medium-size saucepan; bring to a boil over a moderately high heat. Reduce heat and keep at a simmering boil for 15 minutes. Blend cornstarch and ⅓ cup water, add to cooked berries, stirring constantly until clear and thick. Strain and cool mixture. Place cup of whole berries on top of cake and pour glaze over all, covering each berry.

LORENE COVINGTON'S COCONUT PECAN CAKE

This cake has a delicious flavor and ages well. Preparation is simple.

**1 cup butter or margarine, room
     temperature
2 cups sifted sugar
6 large eggs, room temperature
1 (12-ounce) package vanilla wafers, finely
     rolled
1 (7-ounce) package extra moist, sweetened,
     thin coconut flakes
1 cup chopped pecans**

Cream butter and sugar in a very large mixing bowl using medium speed on electric beater. Separate eggs. Beat yolks until thick and add to creamed mixture. With clean hands add finely rolled vanilla wafers, coconut, and chopped pecans. Beat egg whites on high speed until stiff but not dry; fold into batter. Spoon batter into a 9-inch tube pan or two 5-inch tube pans, greased and lined with waxed paper. Bake in a preheated 300° oven: large tube pan for 1 hour 10 minutes, small tube pans for 1 hour or until cake tests done. Cool on wire rack 15 minutes, remove from pan. This cake will stay moist for two weeks and does not require refrigeration. Keep in tin can or under cake cover for best results. Yield: 1 (9-inch) tube cake or 2 (5-inch) tube cakes—22 to 24 servings.

STRAWBERRY CAKE

Beautiful to behold and to taste, this cake is ideal for Christmas dinner or for a Valentine party.

1 (10-ounce) package frozen strawberries
3 tablespoons all-purpose flour
1 (20-ounce) package white cake mix
1 (3-ounce) package strawberry gelatin
1 cup cottonseed or corn oil
4 large eggs, room temperature
  Strawberry Icing

Thaw frozen strawberries completely. Blend juice and berries, divide in half, using one-half for cake and reserving the other half for icing. Take 1 tablespoon juice reserved for icing, and put into a measuring cup; then fill with water, making ½ cup liquid. Sift flour into large bowl containing cake mix and strawberry gelatin; blend with electric mixer on low speed. Add ½ cup liquid, oil, and eggs, 1 at a time; blend at medium speed. Beat for specified time on cake package (usually 4 minutes). Fold in half of berries and juice reserved for cake. If mixer does not have a folding speed, use lowest speed or fold by hand. Divide batter between two 9-inch layer pans, lined with waxed paper and sides greased and floured. Bake in a preheated 350° oven on middle rack for 25 minutes until layers are golden brown and cake tests done. Cool on wire rack. Frost with Strawberry Icing. Yield: 2 (9-inch) layers—16 to 18 servings.

Strawberry Icing:

1 (16-ounce) package powdered sugar
½ cup butter, softened
½ package frozen strawberries

Pour sugar into mixing bowl with softened butter. Take reserved berries and juice from which 1 tablespoon juice was removed, and separate. Add all berries and half of juice to sugar mixture; blend well on low speed. Add remaining juice, teaspoon by teaspoon, to attain desired consistency for spreading. Use great care; a drop too much can make icing runny.

PFLAUMEN KUCHEN

Monica Feldman's German plum cake is deliciously different. Apples may be substituted for plums.

2 pounds plums, any variety, or 7 small to
  medium-size apples
½ cup butter, softened
1 cup sugar
2 large eggs, room temperature
1 teaspoon vanilla extract
2 cups all-purpose flour, measured after
  sifting
3 teaspoons baking powder
½ cup milk
  Powdered sugar

Wash plums, cut in half, and remove seeds. If using apples, peel and slice thinly so that they can be arranged flat on top of batter. Cream butter; add sugar gradually, continuing to cream well. Add eggs one at a time, beat well; add vanilla. Combine flour and baking powder in sifter and gradually beat into creamed batter, alternating with milk. Spoon batter into a greased and floured 13- x 9- x 2-inch pan. Arrange cut up plums or thinly sliced apples on top. Bake in a preheated 375° oven for 50 minutes to 1 hour or until cake tests done. Sprinkle with powdered sugar when hot. Allow cake to cool in pan, and then cut into squares. Yield: 1 (13- x 9- x 2-inch) cake— 12 to 14 servings.

Don't wait for a birthday to serve layer cake iced with creamy chocolate fudge frosting—what a scrumptious dessert for any occasion. The Cakes and Icings chapter as well as the Dazzling Desserts chapter is bursting with spectacular creations.

BEST-COOK-IN-TOWN BLACKBERRY JAM CAKE

I inherited this jam cake recipe from my mother-in-law whose cooking footsteps I tried to follow. You will never eat a better cake.

1 cup butter, softened
2 cups sifted sugar
4 large eggs, room temperature
3 cups cake flour, measured after sifting
3 teaspoons baking powder
1 teaspoon ground cinnamon
⅛ teaspoon salt
1 teaspoon ground cloves
1 cup milk
1 teaspoon lemon extract
1 teaspoon grated lemon rind
1 cup fairly firm blackberry jam, preferably seedless

Cream butter and sugar until light and fluffy in a large bowl. Add eggs one at a time; beat well. If using an electric mixer, place butter, sugar and 2 eggs in a large, deep bowl and beat 4 minutes at high speed. Add remaining 2 eggs, one at a time, and beat well. Sift flour, baking powder, cinnamon, salt, and cloves together three times. Add flour mixture to creamed mixture alternately with milk, a small amount each time, ending with flour mixture; beat well. Add lemon extract and rind; then add jam. Spoon batter into three greased and floured layer pans. Bake in a preheated 350° oven for 20 to 25 minutes or until cake tests done. Cool on wire rack for 15 minutes. Great with Never Fail White Icing. If making cake for a party, use two batches of icing—one for putting between the layers, the other for top and sides of cake. Yield: 3 (9-inch) layers—14 to 16 servings.

Honor a bride-to-be or welcome a new neighbor to the community by serving an elegant array of party favorites from the Candies and Cookies chapter along with the coffee.

FRESH APPLE POUND CAKE

Luscious apple all the way and easy to make.

3 cups all-purpose flour, spooned into cup
1 teaspoon soda
1 teaspoon salt
1½ cups corn oil
2 cups sugar
3 large eggs, room temperature
2 teaspoons vanilla extract
1¼ cups medium-fine chopped pecans
2 cups finely chopped pared apples
Brown Sugar Topping

Sift flour, soda, and salt onto a platter or waxed paper. In large bowl beat oil, sugar, eggs, and vanilla at medium speed of electric mixer for 3 or 4 minutes until well blended. Gradually add flour mixture and beat until smooth. Fold in pecans and apples. Pour batter into a greased and floured Bundt pan. Bake in a preheated 325° oven about 1 hour 20 minutes or until cake tests done. Cool on wire rack 20 minutes.

For a festive occasion dribble Brown Sugar Topping over warm cake. For an elegant dessert, slice cake and top each serving with a baked custard. This cake is marvelous plain. Serve warm or cold. Store cake in foil or tin can for a day or two. To keep longer, refrigerate and bring to room temperature before serving. Fresh apples tend to mold easily. Yield: 1 (10-inch) Bundt cake—22 to 24 servings.

Brown Sugar Topping:

½ cup butter or margarine
½ cup firmly packed light brown sugar
2 teaspoons milk

Combine all ingredients and bring to a boil over medium heat; cook 2 minutes, stirring constantly. Spoon hot sugar mixture over warm cake.

FIG CAKE

A light and luscious cake with the subtle and delicate flavor of the Celeste fig. This would make a fitting dessert for Thanksgiving or other holiday dinners.

  1 cup whole fig preserves
  2 cups all-purpose flour, measured after
     sifting
1½ cups sugar
  1 teaspoon soda
  1 teaspoon ground cinnamon
  1 teaspoon freshly ground nutmeg
  ½ teaspoon ground cloves
  1 teaspoon salt
  1 cup buttery vegetable oil
  3 large eggs, room temperature
  1 tablespoon vanilla extract
  1 cup buttermilk
    Topping

Remove stems of figs and cut each into 4 pieces. Sift dry ingredients into a large bowl; blend well with a spoon. Add oil, eggs, and vanilla; beat for 2 or 3 minutes at medium speed of electric mixer. Add buttermilk and figs and beat 2 minutes more on same speed. Pour batter into an ungreased 13- x 9- x 2-inch pan. Bake in a preheated 325° oven for 45 minutes or until cake tests done. Place on wire rack while you prepare Topping to pour over hot cake. Yield: 1 (13- x 9- x 2-inch) cake—24 servings.

Topping:

1 cup margarine
1 cup buttermilk
2 cups sugar
2 tablespoons light corn syrup
1 teaspoon soda
2 tablespoons vanilla extract

Combine all ingredients except vanilla, and bring to a boil over medium heat in a very large and deep saucepan. Boil for 3 minutes; add vanilla and pour over cake enough hot sauce, about ¼ of it, to cover top of cake. Serve cake warm and cover each slice with more sauce. The cake is delicious cold, but warm the sauce. Allow cake to remain in pan and serve from it for best results.

PLUM SPICE CAKE (A Dump Cake)

Scrumptious, economical, and easy to prepare.

2 (4¾-ounce) jars strained plums with tapioca
    (baby food)
2 cups self-rising flour, measured after sifting
2 cups sugar
1 teaspoon ground cloves
1 teaspoon cinnamon
2 tablespoons wheat germ
1 cup vegetable oil
3 large eggs, room temperature
    Sugar Glaze

Combine plums, flour, sugar, spices, and wheat germ in a large bowl. Add oil and blend well. Add eggs, beat 1 minute at medium speed of electric mixer, then 2 minutes on high speed. Spoon batter into a 10-inch tube pan, greased, floured and lined with waxed paper. Bake in a preheated 325° oven for 1 hour or until cake tests done. Cool 15 minutes on wire rack and remove from pan. Top with Sugar or Lemon Glaze. (See Catherine Moore's Pound Cake for Lemon Glaze.) The cake is also delectable with a thin film of Vermont maple cream spread over it. Yield: 1 (10-inch) tube cake—24 to 26 servings.

Sugar Glaze:

½ cup butter
2 tablespoons milk
½ cup firmly packed dark brown sugar
½ teaspoon vanilla extract

Bring all ingredients except vanilla to a slow boil in a saucepan over medium heat. Boil for 3 minutes, stirring constantly. Remove from heat, add vanilla, and drizzle glaze over cake.

QUICKIE BANANA SUPREME CAKE

Banana all the way! Moist until the last bite and freezes like a dream.

2 large ripe bananas
1 (18½-ounce) package commercial banana
    cake mix
1 (3¾-ounce) package instant banana cream
    pudding
½ cup buttery vegetable oil
4 large eggs, room temperature
1 teaspoon lemon extract
½ cup water
    Glaze

Peel bananas, scrape off stringy white part and liquefy in blender or mash and whip with a fork. Blend all ingredients in a large bowl with electric mixer; beat at medium speed 3 minutes. Spoon batter into a tube pan or two medium-size loaf pans, greased, floured, and lined with waxed paper, or into a greased and floured Bundt pan. Tap pan very hard on counter. Bake in a preheated 350° oven for 45 to 55 minutes or until cake tests done. Cool cake right side up 25 minutes and carefully remove from tube or Bundt pan. Remove cake from loaf pans after 10 minutes. Drizzle Glaze over warm cake. This cake freezes nicely. When frozen, allow to thaw uncovered at room temperature. Yield: 1 (10-inch) tube cake, 2 (9- x 5- x 3-inch) loaf cakes, or 1 (10-inch) Bundt cake—20 to 22 servings.

Glaze:

1 cup powdered sugar
2 tablespoons freshly squeezed lemon juice

Blend ingredients well and drizzle over warm cake.

JAN POSEY'S BLACKBERRY CAKE

This is a truly great cake. Its fragrance and deep rich color will delight your family and friends.

1 cup blackberries
6 tablespoons reserved blackberry juice
1 (18½-ounce) package white cake mix
½ cup milk
¼ cup water
¾ cup vegetable oil
1 (3-ounce) package black raspberry flavored
    gelatin
4 large eggs, room temperature
    Icing

Puree 1 cup blackberries in blender; strain and reserve juice; use 6 tablespoons juice in cake and reserve 6 tablespoons for icing. In a large bowl combine all ingredients except eggs and Icing. Add eggs one at a time, and beat well for 2 minutes on high speed of electric mixer. Spoon batter into a greased and floured tube pan. Bake in a preheated 350° oven for 50 minutes or until cake tests done. Allow to cool on rack 15 minutes and ice. Yield: 1 (10-inch) tube cake—20 to 22 servings.

Icing:

1 cup powdered sugar
½ cup butter, softened
6 tablespoons reserved blackberry juice

Blend all ingredients in an ovenproof bowl. Place in a preheated 300° oven for 2 minutes; then spread on cake.

COCONUT POUND CAKE

Delightful with the refreshing flavor of coconut.

2½ cups sugar
  1 cup vegetable shortening
½ cup margarine
  5 large eggs, room temperature
1½ tablespoons coconut flavoring
  3 cups cake flour, measured after sifting
  1 teaspoon baking powder
¼ teaspoon salt
  1 cup milk
  1 (6-ounce) package frozen coconut or
      freshly grated coconut

Cream sugar and shortenings well; beat 4 minutes on high speed of electric mixer. Add eggs one at a time, beating well after each addition. Add coconut flavoring. Sift together flour, baking powder, and salt. Add flour mixture and milk alternately, beginning and ending with flour and beating after each addition until smooth. Fold in coconut. Pour batter into a greased and floured 10-inch tube pan or 3 small loaf pans. Bake in a preheated 300° oven: tube pan for 1 hour 30 minutes, loaf pans for 45 to 60 minutes or until cake tests done. Cool 15 minutes on wire rack, remove, and allow to cool completely on rack. Yield: 1 (10-inch) tube cake or 3 (7- x 3- x 2-inch) loaf cakes—22 to 24 servings.

CHOCOLATE SHEATH CAKE

A chocolate lover's dream cake!

Step 1:

  2 cups all-purpose flour
  2 cups sugar
½ teaspoon salt
  1 teaspoon ground cinnamon

Sift dry ingredients into large bowl; set aside.

Step 2:

½ cup cold water
½ cup margarine
  4 tablespoons powdered cocoa
½ cup vegetable
  2 large eggs
½ cup buttermilk
  1 teaspoon vanilla extract
  1 teaspoon soda

Combine water, margarine, cocoa, and vegetable oil in a saucepan over medium heat and bring to boil. Stir constantly until mixture is smooth and all margarine has melted; then stir occasionally. Mixture is boiling when bubbles rise to surface and break. Remove from heat and pour over dry ingredients. Blend with mixer on low speed for 2 minutes. Cool about 4 minutes until batter is barely warm to the touch.

Combine remaining ingredients, add to batter, and beat on medium speed for 2 minutes. Pour batter into a greased and floured 13- x 9- x 2-inch pan. Bake in a preheated 400° oven for 20 to 25 minutes or until cake tests done. During last five minutes of baking prepare icing.

Step 3:

½ cup butter or margarine
  4 tablespoons powdered cocoa
  6 tablespoons evaporated milk
  1 (16-ounce) package powdered sugar
  1 teaspoon vanilla extract
  1 cup chopped pecans (optional)

Combine butter, cocoa, and milk in a saucepan and bring to a boil over medium heat, stirring constantly. When boiling begins, remove and add powdered sugar, vanilla, and pecans, if desired. Put cake on wire rack to cool. After 5 minutes, spread icing over hot cake. Cake should be cold before cutting into 1½-inch squares. For a festive touch add a dollop of whipped cream or non-dairy topping. However, the cake is so delicious, it needs no embellishments. Yield: 1 (13- x 9- x 2-inch) cake—28 servings.

COLA CAKE

This cake is a delightful surprise; its flavor is marvelous.

    2 cups all-purpose flour
    2 cups sugar
    1 cup margarine
    3 tablespoons powdered cocoa
    1 cup cola
    ½ cup buttermilk
    ¼ teaspoon salt
    1 teaspoon soda
    2 large eggs, well-beaten
    1 teaspoon vanilla extract
    1½ cup miniature marshmallows or chopped
        regular-size marshmallows
        Cola Icing

Sift flour and sugar into a large bowl. Combine margarine, cocoa, and cola in saucepan and bring to a boil; boil just until margarine melts. Remove from heat and pour over flour mixture. Add buttermilk, salt, soda, and eggs; blend well. Stir in vanilla and marshmallows. This will be a thin batter and marshmallows will float on top. Pour batter into a 13- x 9- x 2-inch pan lined with brown paper and oiled or a greased tube pan. Bake in a preheated 350° oven: large pan for 30 to 35 minutes, tube pan for 45 minutes or until cake tests done. Cool in pan and ice while hot. Yield: 1 (13- x 9- x 2-inch) cake or 1 (10-inch) tube cake—18 to 20 servings.

Cola Icing:

½ cup margarine
3 tablespoons cocoa
6 tablespoons cola
1 (16-ounce) package powdered sugar
1 cup chopped nuts
1 teaspoon vanilla extract

Combine margarine, cocoa, and cola in a saucepan; bring to a boil. When margarine has melted, remove from heat and add sugar, nuts, and vanilla. Mix well and spread on hot cake while still in pan.

SPONGE CAKE

    6 large eggs, room temperature
    1½ cups sugar, divided
    ½ teaspoon salt
    1½ cups all-purpose flour
    4½ tablespoons cold water
    1 teaspoon vanilla extract
    1½ teaspoons baking powder

Separate eggs. Beat egg yolks until light and add gradually ¾ cup sifted sugar; continue beating until yolks are thick and creamy yellow. If using electric beater, set on high speed. Beat egg whites in another bowl at same speed until light and stand in soft peaks. Gradually add ¾ cup sifted sugar, beating until whites are stiff but not dry. Fold egg white mixture into yolk mixture. Add salt to measured flour in sifter. Fold flour and water alternately into egg mixture. Start and end with flour. Add vanilla and baking powder. Pour cake batter into an ungreased 10-inch tube pan. Bake in a preheated 350° oven on lowest rack in oven for 25 to 30 minutes or until cake tests done. Remove from oven and invert on rack until cold. Slide spatula gently around the cake. If cake clings to bottom of pan, return to oven just long enough to fully heat the pan, and the cake will come out with ease. Yield: 1 (10-inch) tube cake—18 to 20 servings.

WHITE CAKE SUPREME

The best in taste, texture, and fragrance. The cake may be made in a tube pan, three layers, as cupcakes, or party squares. It is an ideal birthday cake.

  1 **cup butter, softened**
2¼ **cups sifted sugar**
  4 **cups minus 1 tablespoon cake flour,**
     measured after sifting
  1 **tablespoon cornstarch**
  ⅛ **teaspoon salt**
  4 **teaspoons baking powder**
1½ **cups milk**
  8 **large egg whites, room temperature**
1½ **teaspoons vanilla extract**

Cream butter and sugar until perfectly smooth, light, and fluffy, about 15 minutes with electric mixer on medium speed. Sift flour, cornstarch, salt, and baking powder four times. Add ½ cup flour mixture alternately with small amount of milk to creamed mixture until all has been used; end with flour.

Beat egg whites on high speed until stiff but not dry, fold into batter. Add vanilla and fold several times to blend well. Spoon batter into a greased and floured 10-inch tube pan. Bake in a preheated 375° oven for 1 hour or until cake tests done. Cool on wire rack 15 minutes; remove from pan. Cake must be cold before icing. Yield: 1 (10-inch) tube cake—20 to 22 servings.

Variations: To bake in layers, pour batter into three well-greased and floured 9-inch layer pans. Bake in a preheated 375° oven for 25 to 30 minutes or until cake tests done. Cool 10 minutes and remove from pan. Cool thoroughly before icing. Yield: 3 (9-inch) layers.

To bake cupcakes, fill fluted paper cups half-full and bake in a preheated 375° oven for 25 to 30 minutes. Cool and ice. Yield: 3½ to 4 dozen (2-inch) cupcakes.

As birthday squares, pour batter into a large greased and floured sheet pan and bake in a preheated 375° oven for 25 to 30 minutes or until cake tests done. Cool 20 minutes before turning out of pan onto a flat surface. Trim side and end crusts. Ice top, score in squares, and decorate to suit the occasion. Cut just before serving to prevent drying. Yield: 3½ to 4 dozen squares.

WHITE MOON GLOW CAKE

A delicate creamy cake, ideal for those who have cholesterol problems. The batter contains only egg whites, and you may use polyunsaturated shortening. This poundlike cake retains its freshness and tenderness for a week or more if properly wrapped in plastic or kept in a tin. It will freeze.

⅔ **cup butter or corn margarine, room**
    temperature
⅓ **cup vegetable shortening**
 2 **cups sugar, sifted**
 1 **teaspoon vanilla extract**
 1 **teaspoon artificial butter flavoring (use only**
    with margarine)
 3 **cups all-purpose flour, measured after**
    sifting
 ½ **teaspoon salt**
 3 **teaspoons baking powder**
 1 **cup milk**
 1 **tablespoon brandy**
 6 **large egg whites, room temperature**

Cream margarine and shortening for 10 minutes or until very light and fluffy, using electric mixer on medium speed. Slowly dribble in sugar, 1 tablespoon at a time, beating well after all sugar is added. Blend in flavorings. Sift flour, salt, and baking powder together, and add to creamed mixture alternately with milk, beating after each addition until smooth. Start and end with flour. Add brandy. In separate bowl beat egg whites until stiff but not dry, and fold into batter. Spoon into a greased and floured 10-inch tube or Bundt pan, or three 8-inch layer pans. Bake in a preheated 325° oven on lowest rack: tube pan for 1 hour, layer pans for 25 to 30 minutes. Remove and invert for 10 minutes, loosen from sides with spatula, and allow to cool on wire rack. Yield: 1 (10-inch) tube or Bundt cake or 3 (8-inch) layers—18 to 20 servings.

CATHERINE MOORE'S POUND CAKE

Exotic flavor! Great with alcoholic beverages and spiced tea.

   1 cup butter
1⅔ cups sifted sugar
   5 large eggs, room temperature
   2 cups all-purpose flour, spooned into cup
   1 tablespoon ground mace
   2 tablespoon vanilla extract
      Lemon Glaze

Cream butter and sugar. Add eggs one at a time, beating thoroughly after each addition. Fold in sifted flour and mace. Add vanilla extract. Spoon into a floured and buttered 10-inch tube pan. Bake in a preheated 300° oven for 1 hour or until cake tests done. Cool for 10 minutes and remove from pan. Ice with Lemon Glaze while still hot. Yield: 1 (10-inch) tube cake—18 to 20 servings.

Lemon Glaze:

¼ **cup butter**
⅔ **cup sugar**
⅓ **cup lemon juice**

Warm all ingredients in a saucepan over medium heat until sugar is dissolved. Pour over hot cake. Allow to cool before cutting.

RIVERS YERGER POUND CAKE SUPREME

Delectable!

   1 cup softened butter
   3 cups sifted sugar
   3 cups sifted cake flour, measured after
      sifting
   6 large eggs, room temperature
½ pint whipping cream
   1 teaspoon vanilla extract
½ teaspoon almond extract
   2 teaspoons good brandy
      Toasted bread crumbs

Cream butter 10 minutes or until very fluffy, using an electric mixer on medium speed. Add sugar, 2 tablespoons at a time, creaming thoroughly after each addition. Add ½ cup flour alternately with 1 egg at a time, beginning and ending with flour and beating after each addition until smooth. Add cream (do not whip) gradually with flavorings and brandy and beat well. Grease thoroughly a 10-inch tube pan with a solid vegetable shortening; flour the pan's sides but sprinkle commercial toasted bread crumbs on bottom. Place in cold oven and turn heat to 325°. Bake for 1 hour and 25 minutes. *Do not open door.* Cake should test done. I have always found the cake completely done, but ovens vary in heating. Cool in pan on rack for 15 minutes, remove and cool completely on rack. Yield: 1 (10-inch) tube cake—20 to 22 servings.

APPLE CAKE SUPREME

A luscious cake with full-bodied apple flavor and easy to prepare.

  1 cup corn oil
  2 cups sifted sugar
  3 large eggs, well beaten
  2 cups self-rising flour, spooned into cup
  ⅛ teaspoon salt
  2 heaping tablespoons ground cinnamon
  2 teaspoons vanilla extract
  3 cups chopped raw tart apples
  1 cup pecan pieces
  ¼ cup powdered sugar
    Lemon Sauce

Blend oil and sugar in a large bowl; add well-beaten eggs and beat until creamy, using medium speed of electric mixer or by hand. Sift flour, salt, and cinnamon into creamed mixture and beat well. Stir in vanilla and apples. Fold in nuts. Spread batter evenly into a greased and floured 13- x 9- x 2-inch pan. Bake in a preheated 350° oven on middle shelf for 25 to 30 minutes or until cake tests done. Cool in pan on wire rack; sprinkle with powdered sugar while hot. This cake stays moist for days. Serve plain, warm or cold, for a morning coffee or brunch. Serve hot as a dessert with Lemon Sauce. Yield: 1 (13- x 9- x 2-inch) cake—20 to 22 servings.

Lemon Sauce:

  1 cup sugar
  1 cup hot water
  3 tablespoons lemon juice
    Grated rind of ½ lemon
  ⅛ teaspoon salt
  1 tablespoon butter
  2 tablespoons all-purpose flour
  1 egg

Combine all ingredients in top of a double boiler over rapidly boiling water, and cook until mixture begins to thicken, stirring constantly. Make sauce ahead of time and keep refrigerated. Reheat to use.

SOUR CREAM POUND CAKE

With no exceptions, this is the best pound cake I have ever tasted.

1½ cups butter, room temperature
  3 cups sugar
  6 large eggs, room temperature
  1 cup commercial sour cream
  3 cups all-purpose flour, measured after sifting
  ½ teaspoon soda
  ⅛ teaspoon salt
  1 teaspoon flavoring (vanilla, lemon, or ½ teaspoon vanilla and ½ teaspoon almond)
    Powdered sugar

Cream butter by hand or an electric mixer until it has reached the consistency of whipped cream. When you think you have creamed it enough, cream some more. Slowly dribble in sugar a tablespoon at a time; beat well. Add eggs one at a time, beating well after each addition. Stir in sour cream. Put measured flour into sifter with soda and salt, and resift three times. Add flour ½ cup at a time to creamed butter, blending well with mixer on lowest speed. Add flavoring. (I use vanilla and almond along with 2 tablespoons brandy.) Pour batter into one Bundt pan and one small loaf pan or two large pans, greased and lined with heavy waxed paper. Bake in a preheated 325° oven: Bundt cake for 1¼ to 1½ hours, small loaf for about 55 minutes, large loaves for 65 minutes or until cake tests done. Cool on rack 15 minutes and sprinkle with powdered sugar. Remove from pan and allow to continue cooling to prevent sweating. Yield: 1 (10-inch) Bundt cake and 1 (7- x 3- x 2-inch) loaf cake or 2 (9- x 5- x 3-inch) cakes—40 to 44 servings.

RASPBERRY NUT POUND CAKE

A delicately flavored loaf cake, ideal for bazaars or for holiday giving. Blueberry or strawberry preserves may be substituted for raspberry.

    1 cup butter or margarine, softened
1½ cups sifted sugar
    4 large eggs, room temperature, divided
3¼ cups all-purpose flour, measured after
        sifting (reserve 1 tablespoon for nuts)
    1 teaspoon salt
    ½ teaspoon soda
    1 teaspoon cream of tartar
    1 (12-ounce) jar seedless black or red
        raspberry preserves
    2 tablespoons strained lemon juice
    1 cup commercial sour cream
    ½ teaspoon lemon extract
    1 teaspoon vanilla extract
1½ tablespoons wheat germ
1½ cups sliced pecans or walnuts

In a large mixing bowl combine softened butter, sugar, and two eggs; beat on high speed of electric beater for 4 minutes. Add remaining eggs one at a time, beating well after each addition. Sift flour, salt, soda, and cream of tartar into another bowl. Blend raspberry preserves with lemon juice in another bowl; add sour cream and stir until thoroughly blended. Add 2 heaping tablespoons jam mixture to creamed mixture alternately with same amount of flour mixture until both are used, ending with flour. Add flavorings and wheat germ; beat well. Sprinkle reserved flour over nuts and fold into batter. Spoon batter into well-greased loaf pans with double thickness of brown paper lining. Place pan of warm water on top shelf of oven. Bake in a preheated 325° oven: medium-size loaves for 45 to 50 minutes, small loaves for 40 to 45 minutes, and large loaves about 1 hour. Remove pan of water after 30 minutes and raise oven temperature to 350°. Cakes should test done. Cool 10 minutes on wire rack then remove from pans. Yield: 2 (8- x 4- x 2-inch) and 1 (7- x 3- x 2-inch) loaf cakes or 2 (9- x 5- x 3-inch) cakes—40 to 44 servings.

BETTY SCOTT'S SOUR CREAM COFFEE CAKE

    1 cup softened butter or
        margarine
    2 cups sugar
    2 large eggs
    2 cups sifted cake flour
    ¼ teaspoon salt
    1 teaspoon baking powder
    1 teaspoon vanilla extract
    1 cup commercial sour cream
    ½ cup finely chopped nuts
    2 teaspoons ground cinnamon
    2 teaspoons sugar
        Powdered sugar

Preheat oven to 300°. Cream butter, sugar, and eggs until light and fluffy. Sift flour, salt, and baking powder together, and add to creamed mixture; beat well. Add vanilla and fold in sour cream. Mix nuts, cinnamon, and sugar together and set aside. Pour one-half batter into a lightly greased 10-inch Bundt pan. Sprinkle half the nut mixture over this. Add remaining batter, then remaining nut mixture on top. Increase oven temperature to 350°, and bake for 1 hour and 20 minutes or until cake tests done. Invert onto dish and wrap two wet dish towels around pan for 10 minutes. Cake will come out easily. Sprinkle top with powdered sugar. Yield: 1 (10-inch) Bundt cake—20 servings.

SOUR CREAM SURPRISE CAKE

 3 tablespoons firmly packed light brown sugar
 3 teaspoons ground cinnamon
½ cup chopped nuts
½ cup sugar
 1 (19-ounce) box yellow butter cake mix
 1 cup commercial sour cream
¾ cup buttery vegetable oil
 4 large eggs
 1 teaspoon vanilla extract

Blend brown sugar, cinnamon, and nuts together in a cup. In a large bowl, add sugar to cake mix. Add sour cream and oil, blending well. Add eggs, one at a time, beating well after each addition. Add vanilla. Pour one half batter into a greased and floured 10-inch tube or Bundt pan. Sprinkle with cinnamon-sugar mixture. Cover with remaining batter. Put in a cold oven; then turn heat to 350°, and bake for 1 hour. Do not preheat oven. Cake requires no frosting. Yield: 1 (10-inch) tube or Bundt cake—20 servings.

WINE CAKE

An elegant party cake! Make in tube or Bundt pan or create 45 to 48 individual cupcakes 2½ inches in diameter. Do not use fine sherry in this recipe, it will not work as well as the inexpensive brands.

 1 (18½-ounce) package commercial yellow
    cake mix
 1 (4½-ounce) package instant vanilla
    pudding
1¼ cups inexpensive sherry, divided
 ¾ cup vegetable oil
 4 large eggs, room temperature
2½ cups powdered sugar

In a large mixing bowl, combine cake mix, instant pudding, ¾ cup sherry, and oil; blend for 1 minute with electric mixer on low speed. Add eggs, one at a time, and beat on high speed

for 5 minutes. Pour batter into a greased and floured 10-inch tube or Bundt pan. Bake in a preheated 325° oven for 45 to 55 minutes. For individual cupcakes, use a rounded measuring tablespoonful of batter and bake in a preheated 350° oven for 20 minutes or until cake tests done. Cool on wire rack 10 minutes. With a fine straw or slender toothpick punch holes in bottom of cake. Make a glaze with remaining ½ cup sherry and powdered sugar and dribble half over cake. Invert cake on serving platter and punch holes in top and sides of cake; dribble remaining glaze over cake. In cupcakes put only two or three holes; dribble glaze over each. Yield: 1 (10-inch) tube or Bundt cake or cupcakes—18 to 20 servings.

MY BEST YELLOW CAKE

This recipe of my great-grandmother's came from Lonestar Plantation in the Mississippi Delta. She had written down the ingredients in her fine Spencerian hand, but there were no directions. I found this to be true with most of the old "receipts" in her walnut *escritoire papeterie*.

11 egg yolks, room temperature
 2 cups sifted sugar
 1 cup scalded milk
 2 teaspoons baking powder
¼ teaspoon salt
2¼ cups all-purpose flour, measured after
    sifting
½ cup butter, melted
 2 teaspoons vanilla extract or 1 teaspoon
    vanilla extract and 1 teaspoon brandy

Beat yolks well with dover beater and add sugar gradually. If using an electric mixer, put on high speed. Add hot milk slowly and continue beating. Gradually sift baking powder, salt, and flour into batter using low speed on mixer. Fold in melted butter and vanilla. Pour batter into a 10-inch tube pan, greased, floured, and lined with waxed paper. Place a large pan of water directly over cake in oven; remove as soon as cake begins to brown. Bake in a preheated 325° oven for 1 hour 15 minutes or until cake tests done. For a cake as large as this it is wise to place another piece of waxed paper over top of pan; remove when cake rises to reach it. Yield: 1 (10-inch) tube cake—20 to 22 servings.

LADY BALTIMORE CAKE

Aunt Sally's best white cake with Lady Baltimore Filling has no equal for texture and flavor. The recipe comes from Old Virginia.

 3 cups cake flour, measured after sifting
 3 teaspoons baking powder
 ⅛ teaspoon salt
 1 cup butter or ½ cup butter plus ½ cup
    vegetable shortening, room temperature
1¾ cups sugar, measured after sifting, divided
 5 large egg whites, room temperature,
    divided
 1 cup milk
 1 teaspoon vanilla or almond extract
    Lady Baltimore Filling

Sift together three times the flour, baking powder, and salt. Cream butter; gradually add 1½ cups sugar. Beat until light and fluffy. Place each egg white in a separate cup; add one egg white to creamed mixture and continue beating. Drop in second egg white and beat well. Add flour mixture alternately with milk, about 2 tablespoons flour at a time. Start and end with flour and beat well after each addition. Add vanilla.

Make a meringue of the remaining 3 egg whites by beating until light and frothy and gradually adding remaining ¼ cup sugar. Add meringue to cake batter. Spread batter into three 8-inch layer pans, greased, floured, and lined with waxed paper. Bake in a preheated 350° oven for 20 to 25 minutes or until cake tests done. Cool on a wire rack for 15 minutes. Insert a sharp knife around rim of cake layers and remove from pan. Cool completely before icing. If you prefer, use your own favorite icing or try this Lady Baltimore Filling. Yield: 3 (8-inch) layers—12 to 14 servings.

Lady Baltimore Filling:

 3 unbeaten egg whites
 ¼ teaspoon cream of tartar
 5 tablespoons cold water
1½ cups sugar
1½ teaspoons light corn syrup
 1 teaspoon vanilla extract
 1 cup puffed seedless raisins or ½ cup
    seedless and ½ cup golden seedless
    raisins
 ¾ cup candied cherries, finely chopped,
    divided
 ¾ cup candied pineapple, finely chopped,
    divided
 ¾ cup chopped pecans, blanched almonds, or
    English walnuts

Place egg whites, cream of tartar, cold water, sugar, and corn syrup in top of a double boiler over rapidly boiling water. Beat with electric mixer on top speed or dover beater for 7 minutes until icing stands in peaks: remove from heat and add vanilla.

Pour hot water over raisins and allow to set for 5 minutes or until plump; dry on paper towel. Reserve ¼ cup each raisins, candied fruit, and nuts to use as garnish. Put half of icing into another bowl and quickly add remaining raisins, fruits, and nuts. Spread the tops of two layers with this icing, making as level as possible. Each layer takes about 4 rounded tablespoonfuls.

Ice the top and sides of the third layer with the remaining plain frosting and sprinkle the reserved raisins, candied fruits, and nuts as artistically as possible for a beautiful cake.

ELTA POSEY'S UPSIDE-DOWN LEMON CUSTARD CAKES

A light and piquant taste treat.

1 tablespoon melted butter
1 cup milk
  Juice and rind of 1 lemon
2 large egg yolks
3 tablespoons all-purpose flour
1 cup sugar
  Pinch salt
2 large egg whites, stiffly beaten
  Whipped cream

Melt butter over low heat in a saucepan. In a large bowl add butter to milk, lemon juice and rind, and unbeaten egg yolks; mix well. Sift in dry ingredients and beat until blended. Fold in stiffly beaten egg whites. Spoon into well-greased custard cups and place cups in pan with about ¼ inch of water. Bake in a preheated 350° oven about 20 minutes. Cool and store in refrigerator. When ready to serve, run a knife around cake and serve upside down, topped with whipped cream. Yield: 4 to 6 cupcakes.

GOOD LUCK TORTE

Serve this torte on New Year's Day and according to Southern custom you will have good luck the whole year through. It's inexpensive and delightful.

Step 1:

1½ cups dried black-eyed peas
  3 cups water

Cover peas with water and allow to soak overnight. Drain and cover with 3 cups fresh water. In a large saucepan bring peas to a boil, cover, and simmer for 1 hour. Drain peas in colander and reserve ½ cup potlikker or pea liquid.

Puree peas in blender or put through food mill and reserve 1¼ cups puree.

Step 2:

1½ cups sugar, divided
1¾ cups all-purpose flour, measured after
    sifting
  1 teaspoon soda
  ¾ teaspoon salt
  ¼ teaspoon baking powder
  ⅓ cup buttery vegetable oil
  1 cup reserved black-eyed pea puree
  ¼ cup reserved potlikker
  2 large eggs, separated, room temperature
  2 (1-ounce) squares German's sweet
    chocolate
  Lemon Filling
  Chocolate Filling

Sift together 1 cup sugar, flour, soda, salt, and baking powder into a large mixing bowl. Add oil, 1 cup pea puree, ¼ cup potlikker, and 2 beaten egg yolks. Melt chocolate in top of a double boiler and add to batter. Beat on low speed of electric mixer until well blended, then beat 1 minute on high speed. With a wire whisk or electric mixer beat 2 egg whites until frothy. Gradually add remaining ½ cup sugar and continue beating until whites are stiff and stand in peaks but are not dry. Fold beaten egg whites into flour mixture. Measure batter evenly into two 8-inch layer pans, greased, floured, and lined with waxed paper. Bake in a preheated 350° oven for 30 to 35 minutes. Cool on a wire rack 10 minutes and remove from pans.

When cake layers are completely cold, slice each horizontally into halves. Spread bottom half with Lemon Filling; second layer with Chocolate Filling, and repeat, ending with chocolate on top. In applying filling, bring it out and cover the sides of each layer. The completed torte will be most attractive with its chocolate top and lemon middle section. Yield: 2 (8-inch) layers—20 servings.

Lemon Filling:

 2 cups powdered sugar
¼ cup butter or margarine, softened
  Juice and grated rind of 1 lemon
¼ cup reserved black-eyed pea potlikker
  Whipping cream (optional)

Combine sugar and butter in top of a double boiler and blend well. Beat in grated rind and juice and potlikker. If consistency is too thick for spreading, add 1 or more teaspoons whipping cream. Allow to stand over hot, not boiling, water for 10 to 15 minutes; this removes the raw sugar taste.

Variation: You may prefer to use 1 can commercial lemon frosting mix, 1 teaspoon lemon extract, and ¼ cup black-eyed pea potlikker and follow directions on frosting can.

Chocolate Filling:

 3 (1-ounce) squares unsweetened chocolate
 2 tablespoons butter or margarine
 1 teaspoon vanilla extract
¼ cup reserved black-eyed pea puree,
   warmed
⅛ teaspoon salt
1½ to 2 cups powdered sugar

Melt chocolate and butter in top of a double boiler over hot water and allow to cool. Add vanilla and warmed puree. Sift and gradually add salt and powdered sugar. Add only enough sugar for spreading consistency: I find 1½ cups work best for me.

BUTTERMILK CAKE

A company dessert—beautiful and versatile! Who could ask for more?

1½ cups butter, softened
½ cup vegetable shortening
 3 cups sugar
 5 large eggs, room temperature
 3 tablespoons sugar
½ teaspoon soda
 1 tablespoon boiling water
 3 cups cake flour, measured after sifting,
   divided
 1 cup buttermilk, divided
 1 tablespoon vanilla extract
 1 teaspoon good brandy

Cream butter and shortening until light. Gradually add 3 cups sugar and continue beating until fluffy, about 10 minutes on medium high speed of electric mixer. Cut down batter often from sides with spatula.

Separate whites from egg yolks; make a meringue by beating egg whites until foamy on high speed of mixer. Slowly add 3 tablespoons sugar; continue beating until stiff but not dry. Set aside.

Dissolve soda in boiling water. Beat egg yolks until light, add to creamed mixture along with 1 cup flour. Add soda water with ½ cup buttermilk; beat well. Add remaining flour and buttermilk alternately, beating after each addition. Continue beating 2 minutes at medium-high speed of mixer. Add vanilla and brandy and blend well. Gently fold in egg white meringue and pour batter into greased and floured tube pan. Bake in a preheated 325° oven on lowest rack in oven for 1 hour 35 minutes or until cake tests done. Cool in pan on wire rack; do not invert. Serve plain, hot or cold, or with almost any icing. The cake retains its superb flavor longer than most if wrapped properly in plastic or foil. This will freeze. Yield: 1 (10-inch) tube cake—20 to 24 servings.

GENOISE CAKE

Catherine de Medici brought this famous cake to the French court when she came from Italy in 1533. It is often called "un objet d'art de la patisserie."

  1 cup eggs (about 5 medium-size), room temperature
  1 cup sifted sugar
  ½ teaspoon salt
  1 teaspoon vanilla extract
  1¼ cups cake flour, measured after sifting
    Butter Cream
    Chocolate Icing

In a large bowl beat eggs until light and fluffy using medium speed of electric mixer. Gradually add sugar, salt, and vanilla. Beat until thick and lemon colored. Fold in flour, 2 tablespoons at a time. Pour batter into two 8-inch round layer pans, greased and lined with waxed paper. Bake in a preheated 350° oven for 25 to 30 minutes or until cake tests done. Cool in pan on wire rack. Remove and slice horizontally through center of each layer with sharp, thin knife blade. Spread the four layers with Butter Cream and top with Chocolate Icing. Yield: 2 (8-inch) layers—20 to 22 servings.

Butter Cream—*Crème au Beurre:*

  ¾ cup sugar
  2 tablespoons cornstarch
  3 large eggs
1½ cups milk
  1 teaspoon vanilla extract
  ½ cup softened butter, creamed

Blend sugar and cornstarch in a saucepan over medium heat; add eggs and beat until light and fluffy. Stir in milk and cook until thickened, stirring constantly. Remove pan from heat and add vanilla; cool. Blend in creamed butter.

Chocolate Icing:

  1 cup sifted powdered sugar
  1 small egg, well beaten
  2 tablespoons butter or margarine
  1 (1-ounce) square unsweetened chocolate
  ½ teaspoon vanilla extract

Blend powdered sugar with well-beaten egg. Melt butter and chocolate in a saucepan over very hot water; cool a minute, then add to sugar and egg mixture. Add vanilla and beat until icing is smooth.

CHOCOLATE POUND CAKE

A superb cake! Rich enough without frosting. Serve with a dollop of sweetened whipped cream for a festive occasion. Delicious toasted and topped with scoop of vanilla or pistachio ice cream. For a chocolate lover's birthday party use chocolate icing.

1 cup butter, softened
½ cup margarine or vegetable shortening
5 large eggs, room temperature, divided
3 cups sugar, measured after sifting
3 cups all-purpose flour, measured after
    sifting
½ teaspoon salt
1 teaspoon baking powder
½ cup powdered cocoa
1 cup milk
2 teaspoons vanilla extract
    Chocolate Icing

In a large bowl cream butter and margarine at medium speed of electric mixer for 3 minutes. Add one egg and gradually add sugar. When mixture is fluffy and creamy after 4 or 5 minutes of beating, add remaining 4 eggs one at a time. Beat well on high speed. Sift dry ingredients into small bowl. Add flour mixture, a rounded ¼ cup at a time alternately with small amount of milk to creamed mixture; mix on low speed. Add vanilla and beat well. Spoon batter into a tube pan, greased, floured, and lined with waxed paper. Place pan of warm water on upper oven shelf and place cakepan on lowest rack. Bake in a preheated 325° oven for 1 hour 20 minutes or until cake tests done. Remove water pan after 1 hour. Cool on rack 15 minutes; then run knife around sides of tube; remove and allow cake to finish cooling on rack. The Chocolate Icing adds extra richness to cake but is not necessary. Yield: 1 (10-inch) tube cake—20 to 22 servings.

Chocolate Icing:

½ cup butter or margarine
2 tablespoons powdered cocoa
    Pinch salt
¾ cup sugar
¼ cup firmly packed light brown sugar
¾ cup evaporated milk
1 egg yolk
1 teaspoon vanilla extract
2 cups powdered sugar

In a saucepan cook butter, cocoa, salt, sugars and evaporated milk over medium heat until mixture begins to bubble. Cook for 5 minutes at a bubbling boil, stirring constantly from the time you put icing on stove. Remove from heat and allow to set 5 minutes. Add unbeaten egg yolk and vanilla and beat well. Gradually beat in powdered sugar until mixture reaches a spreading consistency. Ice cake.

RED NICHOLSON'S PECAN CAKE

Marvelous!

1 cup butter
2 cups sugar
6 large eggs, room temperature
1 tablespoon ground cinnamon
1 teaspoon ground nutmeg
½ cup bourbon
3½ cups all-purpose flour, spooned into cup
    (reserve ½ cup for raisins and nuts)
1½ pounds seedless raisins
4 cups pecans, finely chopped
2 teaspoons baking powder
½ cup firmly packed dark brown sugar
¼ cup bourbon

Cream butter and sugar until light and fluffy; add eggs, one at a time, beating well after each addition. Add spices and ½ cup bourbon and blend well. Sprinkle reserved flour over raisins and chopped pecans in another bowl and mix well; add to creamed mixture. Sift in flour and baking powder and beat well. Spoon batter into a 10-inch tube pan, greased, floured, and lined with brown paper. Bake in a preheated 250° oven on lowest rack for 1½ hours or until cake tests done. Remove from oven to wire rack. After 15 minutes sprinkle top of cake with brown sugar and pour ¼ cup bourbon over all; this creates a crust that seals moisture in cake. Allow cake to finish cooling in pan. Yield: 1 (10-inch) tube cake—20 to 22 servings.

CHOCOLATE CAKE COUPERY

A very rich and luscious all-chocolate cake created for Dr. Coupery Shands. It needs no icing; you may serve with a dollop of whipped cream or scoop of vanilla ice cream for extra special guests.

  2 (1½-ounce) milk chocolate bars or 5
     (¾-ounce) milk chocolate bars
  2 (5½-ounce) cans commercial chocolate
     syrup
2½ cups all-purpose flour, measured after
     sifting
  ½ teaspoon soda
  2 cups sifted sugar
  1 cup margarine, softened
  4 large eggs, room temperature, divided
  1 cup buttermilk
  1 teaspoon vanilla extract

Melt chocolate bars in chocolate syrup in top of a double boiler over simmering water, Cool. Sift flour and soda together three times. Beat sugar, margarine, and 2 eggs until light and fluffy using electric beater on medium speed for 4 minutes. Add remaining 2 eggs, one at a time; beat well. On low speed add flour mixture and buttermilk alternately, ending with flour. Blend in cooled chocolate mixture and vanilla. Pour into a 9-inch tube or Bundt pan, greased and lined with waxed paper. Bake in a preheated 350° oven for 1 hour 15 minutes or until cake tests done. Cool in pan 10 minutes and finish cooling on rack. This may be iced with Never Fail White Icing or a light chocolate frosting, but it is not necessary. Yield: 1 (9-inch) tube or Bundt cake—20 servings.

EMERALD VELVET CAKE

For Saint Patrick's Day this easily prepared and delicious cake has the vivid green beauty of Connemara's countryside and provides a special treat for the wearer of the shamrock.

  ½ cup butter or margarine
1½ cups sugar
  2 large eggs, room temperature
  2 tablespoons powdered cocoa
  2 (½-ounce) bottles green food coloring
  1 teaspoon salt
2¼ cups all-purpose flour, measured after
     sifting
  1 cup buttermilk
  2 teaspoons vanilla extract
  1 tablespoon vinegar
  1 teaspoon soda
  Butter Frosting

Cream butter and sugar until fluffy using medium speed of electric mixer for 4 minutes. Add eggs and beat 2 minutes on high speed. In a deep bowl put cocoa into green coloring and make into a paste; add slowly to batter. Add salt to flour, then add dry ingredients alternately with buttermilk with mixer on low speed. Add vanilla, vinegar, and soda; blend well. Pour batter into two 9-inch or three 8-inch layer pans, greased and lined with waxed paper. Bake in a preheated 350° oven for 25 to 30 minutes or until cake tests done. Cool on wire racks for 15 minutes and remove from pans for further cooling. Ice with Butter Frosting. Yield: 2 (9-inch) layers or 3 (8-inch) layers—20 servings.

Butter Frosting:

  ½ cup butter
  ½ cup vegetable shortening
  3 tablespoons all-purpose flour
  1 (16-ounce) package powdered sugar, sifted
  ⅛ teaspoon salt
  1 teaspoon vanilla extract
  ¼ teaspoon almond extract
  3 or 4 tablespoons milk
  3 or 4 drops green food coloring

Cream butter and shortening; blend in flour, 1 tablespoon at a time, beating thoroughly after each addition. Add sifted sugar and salt, a small amount at a time, beating constantly. Add flavorings. Add milk as needed for desired spreading consistency. Add green food coloring. Spread on cake.

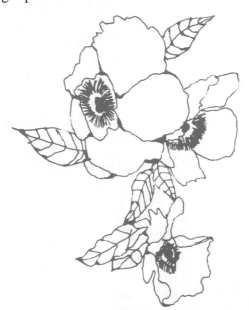

HEAVENLY HASH FUDGE CAKE

A superb, cakelike confection to serve as a dessert for party or buffet supper. A chocolate delight!

  1 (18½-ounce) package commercial butter
     fudge cake mix
½ cup softened butter
¾ cup water
  3 large eggs, room temperature
½ teaspoon vanilla extract
  1 cup toasted sliced pecans or English
     walnuts, divided
34 large or regular-size marshmallows
   Fudge Icing

Combine cake mix, softened butter, water, eggs, and vanilla in a large bowl. Blend with electric beater on low speed until moistened, scrape sides of bowl with spatula. Beat 4 minutes at medium speed. Fold in ½ cup pecans.

Spoon batter into a 13- x 9- x 2-inch pan, well greased, floured, and lined with brown paper. Bake in a preheated 375° oven for 30 to 35 minutes or until cake tests done. Arrange marshmallows on top of cake, spaced close at intervals and return cake to oven. Turn off heat. When marshmallows are melted press down lightly with spatula to make a complete covering and sprinkle with remaining ½ cup nuts. Cool on wire rack. Cover with Fudge Icing. For best cutting results, allow cake to cool for several hours. This cake will make two nice size cakes by cutting it in the middle and lifting out each section with two very broad spatulas. Excellent for bake sales. Yield: 1 (13- x 9- x 2-inch) cake—20 to 22 servings.

Fudge Icing:

2½ cups powdered sugar, sifted
  1 large egg, well beaten
½ cup butter or margarine
  3 (1-ounce) squares unsweetened chocolate
⅓ cup sugar
  3 tablespoons water
¼ teaspoon salt
  1 teaspoon vanilla extract

Combine powdered sugar with well-beaten egg in a large bowl. Melt butter and chocolate over low heat in a saucepan. Bring sugar, water, and salt to a boil over low heat; boil for 1 minute. Pour syrup slowly over egg mixture, then add chocolate mixture and vanilla. Beat until creamy and spread over cake.

TEXAS PECAN CAKE

A great nut cake suitable for any occasion.

 1 cup butter, softened
 3 cups sifted sugar
 5 cups flour, spooned into cup, divided
 7 large egg yolks, beaten
 1 quart chopped pecans
 1 pound candied pineapple, finely chopped
 1 pound candied cherries, finely chopped
 1 teaspoon baking soda
 4 tablespoons red wine
 2 ounces lemon extract
 7 large egg whites, beaten
 ½ cup Jamaican rum (optional)

Cream butter and sugar until light and fluffy using medium speed of electric mixer. Add ¼ cup sifted flour to beaten egg yolks, and sprinkle ¼ cup flour over nuts and candied fruit, each in separate bowls. Add beaten egg yolks to creamed mixture in very large bowl. Dissolve soda in warm wine and add to creamed mixture. Add lemon extract and remaining flour and beat well. Add fruit and nuts. (This makes such a thick batter.) Fold in beaten egg whites with clean hands. Spoon batter into a greased 10-inch tube pan lined with greased brown paper. Bake in a preheated 250° oven for 4 hours. Or you may use three 7-inch round fruit cake tins and one 9-inch fruit cake tin and bake in a preheated 250° oven for 2 to 2½ hours for small cakes, longer for the 9-inch cake. Cakes should test done. Allow cakes to cool 30 minutes before removing from pans. Place on wire rack overnight before wrapping in foil or placing in sealed tins. Dribble 3 tablespoons rum over each cake before wrapping, if desired. This cake will keep well for several weeks. Yield: 6½ to 7 pounds—1 (10-inch) tube cake or 3 (7-inch) and 1 (9-inch) round cakes—20 to 22 servings.

CARROT CAKE

The lowly carrot takes on a lofty air for delicious dessert.

 3 cups coarsely grated raw carrots
1¾ cups sugar
1¼ cups vegetable oil
 4 large eggs, room temperature
 2 cups all-purpose flour
 2 teaspoons baking powder
 2 teaspoons soda
 1 teaspoon salt
 2 teaspoons ground cinnamon
 1 teaspoon lemon extract
 1 teaspoon vanilla extract
 ½ cup chopped pecans or walnuts
    Pineapple Icing

Grate carrots by cutting into 1-inch pieces and placing in blender on "chop". Use coarse grater, if doing by hand. Cream sugar and vegetable oil until light and fluffy, about 2 minutes on medium speed of electric mixer. Add eggs and beat on high speed for 2 minutes. Sift dry ingredients onto a large plate or waxed paper. Add to creamed mixture, 1 heaping tablespoon at a time using medium speed of mixer. Add flavorings to batter mixture and fold in grated carrots and nuts. Divide batter into three 8-inch layer pans, greased, floured, and lined with waxed paper. Bake in a preheated 350° oven for 30 minutes or until cake tests done. Cool on wire rack for 10 minutes and remove from pan. Ice with Pineapple Icing when cake layers are completely cold. Yield: 3 (8-inch) layers—12 servings.

Pineapple Icing:

1 (16-ounce) package powdered sugar
4 tablespoons butter or margarine, softened
1 (8-ounce) package cream cheese, softened
1 teaspoon lemon extract
2 teaspoons vanilla extract
1 (8-ounce) can crushed pineapple, well
    drained

Cream powered sugar, butter, and cream cheese until light and fluffy. Add flavorings and crushed pineapple; spread on cake.

BUTTERSCOTCH CAKE

A delectable cake with an unusual flavor reminiscent of ones your grandmother used to bake. The texture is superb.

1 cup butter, softened
1 cup dark ribbon cane syrup
2 large eggs, room temperature
1 teaspoon vanilla extract
1 (3¼-ounce) package instant butterscotch
    pudding mix
2 cups all-purpose flour, measured after
    sifting
½ teaspoon soda
1 teaspoon baking powder
1 cup commercial sour cream
    Chocolate Icing

Cream butter and syrup in a large mixing bowl with electric beater on medium speed. Beat until mixture is very light, about 8 minutes.

Add eggs one at a time, beating after each addition on high speed. Add vanilla. Sift dry ingredients onto a large plate and add alternately with sour cream to batter with electric mixer on low speed. Add about one-fourth of dry ingredients with each addition. When all ingredients have been added, increase to high speed and beat 1 minute. Spoon batter into two 9-inch layer pans, greased, floured, and lined with waxed paper. Bake in a preheated 350° oven for about 30 minutes or until cake tests done. Cake should be leaving sides of pan. Cool on wire rack 10 minutes, remove from pans. Allow to cool completely before icing. Chocolate Icing melds the flavor of a butterscotch cake to perfection. Yummy! Yield: 2 (9-inch) layers—18 to 20 servings.

Chocolate Icing:

2 (1-ounce) squares unsweetened chocolate
3 egg whites, unbeaten
5 tablespoons cold water
¼ teaspoon cream of tartar
1½ cups sugar
1½ teaspoons light corn syrup
1 teaspoon vanilla extract

Melt chocolate in top of a double boiler over hot water; allow to cool. Cook egg whites, water, cream of tartar, sugar, and corn syrup in a double boiler over rapidly boiling water. Beat with electric or dover beater for 7 minutes or until icing stands in peaks. Remove from stove, add vanilla and fold in cool melted chocolate. Spread icing on cake; approximately a fourth should go between the two layers, a fourth on top, and the rest on the sides.

Candies and Cookies

TOOTIE FAGAN'S SEA FOAM CANDY

Elegant and great for a party or bazaar because the recipe makes a lot. There are three easy steps.

3 egg whites
3 cups sugar
1 cup light corn syrup
⅔ cup water
1 cup sugar
½ cup water
1 cup chopped nuts
1½ teaspoons vanilla extract

In a very large bowl beat egg whites until stiff but not dry. Mixture 1: Combine 3 cups sugar, corn syrup, and ⅔ cup water in a large, flat-bottomed saucepan and cook over low heat, stirring until sugar is dissolved.

Mixture 2: At the same time, combine 1 cup sugar and ½ cup water over low heat, stirring constantly until sugar is dissolved. Turn off heat.

Boil Mixture 1 until it forms hard balls (270° to 290°) when a few drops are tested in cold water. Then turn Mixture 2 on high heat and bring to boiling point without stirring. Pour Mixture 1 slightly over beaten egg whites. Beat mixture as you pour, continuing to beat until mixture is almost stiff. When Mixture 2 has been boiled until it threads (238°), add to bowl mixture. Stir both mixtures together until thickened. Add nuts and vanilla and drop on waxed paper. Speed is essential to avoid hardening before reaching waxed paper. Place bowl in a pan of warm water to slow the hardening process. For best results scoop up ½ teaspoonful candy at a time, scraping candy from bowl of teaspoon with another teaspoon. Two or three agile aids would be helpful. Yield: 10 dozen pieces.

ELIZABETH WINN'S APRICOT BALLS

A tasty delight for a party.

1 pound dried apricots
1 whole thick-skinned orange
   Juice of an additional orange
2 tablespoons lemon juice
2 cups sugar
1 cup powdered sugar
36 pecan halves

Grind apricots and whole orange, skin and all, with a fine blade. Place in a saucepan with fruit juices and sugar; cook over low heat 20 minutes or until juice has cooked out. Cool completely.

Place powdered sugar in a small bowl; drop from teaspoon small amount of apricot mixture and roll in sugar to form a small ball. Place on waxed paper; press one pecan on each ball. Allow to dry. These are best made a day in advance. Yield: about 3 dozen balls.

BOURBON BALLS

3 cups vanilla wafers
1 cup finely chopped pecans
½ cup bourbon or rum
1 cup powdered sugar
½ cup powdered cocoa
3 tablespoons light corn syrup
1 cup powdered sugar, cocoa, or finely grated coconut (optional)

Roll vanilla wafers between two sheets of waxed paper with rolling pin until they are a fine dust. In a large bowl combine vanilla wafer dust and chopped pecans. Place remaining ingredients except optional ingredients in another bowl and mix thoroughly; pour over pecan mixture and mix well. Shape into small balls ½ inch in diameter and roll in powdered sugar, cocoa, or grated coconut, if desired. Yield: about 4 dozen balls.

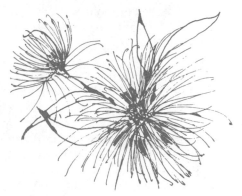

CHOCOLATE COVERED CARAMELS AND PECANS

Scrumptious! A first cousin to Millionaires, this is a very simple recipe to make.

2 (14-ounce) packages commercial caramels
3 tablespoons cold water
2½ cups coarsely chopped pecans
24 ounces commercial milk chocolate bars
1⅓ ounces paraffin (about a fraction more than a fourth of a 4-ounce block)

Use only light caramels; remove the darker colored ones. Melt caramels in water in double boiler over high heat, stirring often. As soon as caramels melt, stir in nuts. Drop by teaspoonfuls on buttered waxed paper. Work as quickly as possible and keep caramel mixture over hot water to keep soft. Place waxed paper on cookie sheet and place in freezer for 30 minutes or in refrigerator for 2 hours.

Melt chocolate and paraffin in double boiler over very hot, but not boiling, water. (If using 8-ounce or 12-ounce chocolate bars, break into small pieces before melting.) With tongs or toothpick, dip and spin each piece of chilled candy in melted chocolate and paraffin mixture and place on waxed paper. Allow candy to stand for at least 1 hour. Yield: 4½ to 5 dozen pieces.

CARAMELS

Simply luscious!

1 cup firmly packed light brown sugar
1 cup white sugar
½ cup butter, sliced
1 (14-ounce) can sweetened condensed milk
1 cup light corn syrup
2 teaspoons vanilla extract
⅛ teaspoon salt
1 cup chopped pecans

Cook sugars, butter, condensed milk, and corn syrup in a large heavy boiler or skillet on low heat until a few drops of mixture dropped in cup of cold water form a hard chewy ball or until candy thermometer reads 250° to 252°. Stir rarely—only to see if mixture is sticking. Remove from heat; add vanilla and salt. Cool 15 minutes and add chopped nuts, stirring only enough to incorporate the nuts. Pour into buttered 13- x 9- x 2-inch baking dish and allow to cool overnight or all day. Cut into squares. Wrap each square in plastic wrap or foil. Yield: 5 to 6 dozen caramels.

BARBARA GLENN'S MERINGUE MINTS

Lovely for a party and may be made ahead of time.

 2 large egg whites, room temperature
 1 teaspoon cream of tartar
¾ cup sifted sugar
   Few drops green food coloring
 1 (6-ounce) package chocolate mint chips

In a narrow deep bowl beat egg whites and cream of tartar to a soft peak, using high speed of electric mixer. Gradually add sugar; beat until stiff. Add food coloring. Fold in mint chips. Drop mints by the teaspoonful onto a cookie sheet lined with brown paper. Place cookies in a preheated 350° oven and turn off heat. Leave in 5 hours or overnight. Yield: 5 dozen mints.

MARGUERITE RUSH'S PEANUT BRITTLE

The best!

1½ cups sugar
 ½ cup light corn syrup
 ⅓ cup water
 2 cups shelled raw peanuts
 3 teaspoons baking soda

Combine sugar, corn syrup, and water in a large boiler (at least 2-quart size) and bring to a boil. When syrup begins to thicken slightly (about 220°), add peanuts and continue to boil until the theremometer reads 300°. If you do not have a candy theremometer, boil until syrup when dropped from a spoon makes a fine, threadlike stream which breaks like a dry, brittle twig. Remove from heat and add soda; blend, do not beat, until soda is absorbed into the syrup. Pour onto a large metal tray or cookie sheet which has been greased with vegetable oil. After about 10 minutes begin lifting around edges until you are able to lift it entirely free of the tray, then turn it over and wipe off surplus oil from back, also wipe off surplus oil from sheet. As it begins to cool, break into desired size pieces. After pieces have cooled, place in 1-pound coffee cans which have a plastic bag as an interlining; twist bag tops tightly and seal can. If kept in an airtight container, this candy will stay fresh for weeks. Yield: fills 2½ (1-pound) cans.

LOUISE STAMM'S CHOCOLATE DELIGHTS

A superb confection—there's nothing like it, and it's so easy a child could make it. This makes a marvelous dessert for a buffet luncheon or supper.

2 cups finely rolled graham cracker crumbs
1 (12-ounce) package chocolate pieces
1 cup coarsely chopped pecans
2 tablespoons light corn syrup
1 (14-ounce) can sweetened condensed milk
1 tablespoon butter
   Topping

In a large bowl combine all ingredients except butter and Topping; mix thoroughly. Butter bottom and sides of a 7- x 11-inch pan. Spread mixture as evenly as possible in pan with spatula. Bake in a preheated 350° oven for 20 minutes. Remove from oven and cover with Topping. Cook 10 minutes longer. While still hot run a knife around sides of pan before cutting into squares. Cool before moving from pan. The squares will keep 10 days to 2 weeks in a tin can provided *you* can leave them alone. Yield: 2½ dozen (1-inch) squares.

Topping:

 1 cup finely chopped pecans
2½ tablespoons light corn syrup

Blend ingredients and use to cover baked mixture.

MARVELOUS FUDGE

This fudge never dries out and is excellent for a party because it makes a large amount.

4½ cups sugar
⅛ teaspoon salt
3 tablespoons butter
1 (13-ounce) can evaporated milk
2 teaspoons vanilla extract
12 ounces semisweet chocolate bits
12 ounces German's sweet chocolate
2 cups commercial marshmallow cream spread
2 cups chopped nuts

Bring first four ingredients to a boil in a large saucepan over medium heat. Boil for 6 minutes. Remove from heat and pour boiling syrup over remaining ingredients. Beat until all chocolate is melted. Pour out onto buttered marble slab or waxed paper. (You need a large area to pour it out.) Allow candy to set for 3 hours before cutting. Yield: about 4 pounds fudge.

CHOCOLATE MERINGUE DELIGHTS

Delicious and easy to make, these are wonderful for any kind of party. Since these vanish so quickly in my home, I cannot tell you how long they will keep.

1 (6-ounce) package chocolate pieces
2 large egg whites, room temperature
½ teaspoon vanilla extract
½ teaspoon vinegar
½ cup sugar, sifted
¾ cup finely sliced pecans or English walnuts
1 teaspoon butter or margarine

Melt chocolate pieces in top of a double boiler over very hot water. Allow to cool. In a small bowl beat egg whites, vanilla, and vinegar at high speed until mixture stands in peaks. Gradually add sugar, one tablespoon at a time. Cut down sides with spatula. Beat until very stiff but not dry. Fold in cool melted chocolate and finely sliced nuts. Cover a large cookie sheet with brown paper and grease with butter. Take well-rounded teaspoon of meringue mixture and ease onto paper with a spatula; arrange about 1 inch apart. Bake in a preheated 350° oven for 10 minutes. Remove from paper with spatula and cool on wire rack. As soon as cool, put into a sealed tin can. Yield: about 2 dozen meringues.

MARGARET NELSON'S DATE NUT LOAF

Luscious!

2½ cups sugar
½ cup evaporated milk
½ cup milk
1 tablespoon light corn syrup
1 cup chopped dates
1 cup chopped pecans
1 tablespoon butter
1 teaspoon vanilla extract

In a large saucepan cook sugar, milks, and corn syrup over medium heat, stirring constantly, until it forms a very soft ball when a few drops are put in cold water. A candy thermometer should read 238°. Add dates and cook 5 minutes longer, stirring frequently to prevent dates from sticking. Add pecans, butter, and vanilla and cool to lukewarm. Beat until thick. Spread on damp cheese cloth and form into a roll with buttered hands. Later transfer to waxed paper and roll in foil. Slice for eating. This will keep refrigerated for months. Yield: 2 pounds.

OPERA CREAMS

A taste delight, this candy improves with age.

 3 cups sugar
½ teaspoon salt
 1 cup half-and-half
 1 tablespoon light corn syrup
 4 tablespoons butter
 2 drops Mapleine
 1 teaspoon vanilla extract
 1 cup sliced pecans

In large heavy saucepan, combine sugar, salt, half-and-half, corn syrup, and butter and cook over low heat, stirring constantly, until sugar is dissolved. Cook to the soft ball stage (238°) or until a few drops of syrup dropped into a cup of cold water can be gathered into a soft ball that will almost hold its shape. Stir occasionally to keep from sticking. When syrup reaches soft ball stage, remove pan from heat and allow to cool. Add flavorings. Pour mixture into a large bowl and beat with electric mixer until creamy. Add pecans. Drop by teaspoonfuls onto buttered waxed paper. Yield: 2½ dozen pieces (1¼ pounds).

Note: The weather is a big factor in candy making. On a hot, humid day it is advisable to cook candy two degrees higher than in cold, dry weather.

DIVINITY

Creamy smooth and delectable!

2½ cups sugar
 ½ cup light corn syrup
 ½ cup water
 2 large egg whites, stiffly beaten
⅛ teaspoon salt
 1 teaspoon vanilla extract
 1 cup chopped nuts

In a large flat-bottomed saucepan stir sugar, corn syrup, and water over low heat until sugar

is dissolved. Once sugar is dissolved, do not stir. Raise heat to medium high and cook until syrup forms long strings when dropped from spoon and makes soft ball when a few drops of syrup are dropped into a cup of cold water. A candy thermometer should read 238°. Pour in thin stream about ½ of syrup into bowl of stiffly beaten egg whites to which you have added salt. Return remaining syrup to stove and cook for 2 to 5 minutes longer until a few drops in cup of cold water make a hard ball. A candy theremometer should register 252°. Remove from heat and pour over beaten egg white mixture. Continue beating until candy sets up—loses its gloss and stands in peaks. Add vanilla and nuts, drop quickly from tip of spoon onto buttered waxed paper or pour into a buttered pan. Yield: about 3 dozen pieces.

ALMOND MACAROONS

Delicious and easy to make, the macaroons will keep fresh in sealed canister for two weeks.

 1 cup almond paste
 1 cup minus 1 tablespoon sugar
 3 large egg whites
½ teaspoon vanilla extract
½ teaspoon almond extract
 3 tablespoons all-purpose flour
⅓ cup powdered sugar
⅛ teaspoon salt

Soften the almond paste into small bits, using either clean hands or a blender. In a large bowl add sugar and blend well; I use a pastry blender for this job, but you can use your hands. Add egg whites and flavorings and work mixture into a paste. Add flour, powdered sugar, and salt, sifting slowly into mixture and working in with a pastry blender.

When thoroughly blended, drop a rounded iced-tea spoonful of batter onto a large cookie sheet fitted with brown paper. Place 1 inch apart; allow to stand uncovered for 2 hours. Using middle shelf of oven, bake in a preheated 300° oven for 25 to 30 minutes or until macaroons test done. Remove from oven and place brown paper lining on a clean towel that has been dipped in water and wrung out. The macaroons will come up easily with a spatula. Cool on wire rack before serving or storing. Yield: about 3½ dozen (2-inch) macaroons.

CHOCOLATE TOP HATS

A conversation piece for a buffet type party, tea, or luncheon. Delicious down to the last crumb. Children love them.

 1 cup all-purpose flour, measured after sifting
½ teaspoon soda
¼ teaspoon salt
½ cup vegetable oil
½ cup sugar
½ cup firmly packed dark brown sugar
 1 large egg, room temperature
½ teaspoon vanilla extract
 1 cup crushed cornflakes
 1 cup quick-cooking rolled oats
½ cup frozen or fresh-shredded coconut
 Chocolate Filling

Sift flour, baking soda, and salt; set aside. Combine vegetable oil, sugars, egg, and vanilla, and beat at medium speed of electric mixer until light and creamy. Add sifted ingredients gradually and beat well. Stir in and blend thoroughly cornflakes, rolled oats, and coconut. This makes a heavy dough. Roll in waxed paper and chill for one hour. Remove one third of dough. Shape remaining two thirds into balls using a level teaspoonful as a mea-

sure. Place on greased cookie sheets. Bake in a preheated 350° oven for 8 to 10 minutes. Cool on wire rack. Shape the reserved dough into balls, using a half teaspoonful as a measure. Bake in a preheated 350° oven for 8 minutes and cool on wire rack.

Spread Chocolate Filling over large cookies and top with small ones. Keep in a cool place until serving. These freeze well. Take out and serve while still cold. Yield: 3⅓ dozen top hats.

Chocolate Filling;

2 cups (12 ounces) semisweet chocolate
   pieces
1 cup powdered sugar
2 tablespoons water
2 (3-ounce) packages cream cheese, softened

Combine chocolate pieces, powdered sugar, and water in top of double boiler over hot, not boiling, water. As soon as chocolate melts, blend in softened cream cheese. Beat until smooth and cool.

SUPER CHOCOLATE COOKIES

Wonderful for a party! These may be made days ahead and stored in a tin can.

 2 (1-ounce) squares of unsweetened
    chocolate
 1 (14-ounce) can sweetened condensed milk
1½ cups well-crumbled vanilla wafers
1½ cups broken pecans
 ½ teaspoon salt
 1 teaspoon vanilla extract

Melt chocolate in the top of a double boiler. Remove from heat and add condensed milk and crushed vanilla wafers. Add pecans, salt, and vanilla. Drop from a teaspoon onto greased cookie sheets. Bake in a preheated 350° oven for 8 to 10 minutes. Watch carefully to keep from burning. Cool on wire rack and store in tin can. Yield: 2½ dozen cookies.

MARIE BARRON'S BLOND TOFFEE BROWNIES

1½ cups all-purpose flour, sifted
2 teaspoons baking powder
½ teaspoon salt
½ cup butter or margarine, softened
1 cup sugar
½ cup firmly packed brown sugar
2 eggs
1 teaspoon vanilla extract
1 cup crushed chocolate covered English toffee bars
Toasted almond slivers (optional)

Sift flour, baking powder, and salt together. Cream butter, add sugars and cream well. Add eggs and vanilla and beat until fluffy. Blend in dry ingredients. Stir in crushed candy, reserving a small amount. Spread batter over bottom of a well-greased 13- x 9- x 2-inch baking pan. Bake in a preheated 350° oven about 30 minutes. Cool and cut into 3- x 1-inch bars. If desired, bars may be frosted with a white or chocolate butter frosting before cutting. Sprinkle reserved candy bits and toasted almond slivers, if desired, over top. Yield: 3 dozen bars.

BROWNIES FOR ANY SIZE CROWD

A marvelous brownie and a quickie delight!

1 cup sugar
2 large eggs, well beaten
½ cup butter
2 (1-ounce) squares unsweetened chocolate
½ cup all-purpose flour (reserve 1 teaspoon for nuts)
½ teaspoon vanilla extract
1 cup chopped pecans or other nuts

In a large bowl add sugar to beaten eggs. Melt butter and chocolate in top of a double boiler over simmering water, not boiling. Add flour and vanilla to beaten egg mixture; add this to chocolate mixture. Sprinkle reserved flour over pecans and fold into batter. Spoon into a greased and floured 9-inch square cakepan and bake in a preheated 325° oven about 30 minutes or until brownies test done. Cool before cutting. Yield: 16 squares.

Note: For a Medium-Size Crowd, double the recipe and use two 9-inch square cakepans or one much larger pan. Yield: 32 squares.

For a Large Crowd, triple the recipe and use as many pans as necessary. Yield: 4 dozen squares.

For a Huge Crowd, quadruple the recipe and use as many pans as necessary. Yield: 6 dozen squares.

THE DELTA'S FINEST BROWNIES

Rich, moist, and luscious, these brownies originated in the Greenville, Mississippi, kitchen of the late Agnes Taylor Lowry, an outstanding cook.

2 cups sugar
6 tablespoons powdered cocoa
⅛ teaspoon salt
4 large eggs, room temperature
½ cup margarine, melted (use cottonseed oil margarine, not corn)
1 teaspoon vanilla extract
1½ cups all-purpose flour, spooned into cup (reserve 1 teaspoon for nuts)
Rounded ½ cup chopped pecans

Sift sugar, cocoa, and salt into a large mixing bowl. Add 1 egg to cooled melted margarine and blend into sugar mixture; do not beat. Add another egg and continue blending. If using an electric mixer, use low speed. Add remaining 2 eggs and blend well. Add vanilla. Sprinkle reserved flour over pecans in another bowl. Gradually sift in flour and blend well. Fold in chopped pecans. Pour batter into a generously greased 9-inch square cakepan. Spread batter evenly with spatula. Bake in a preheated 300° oven for 42 minutes or until brownies test done.

If using an aluminum or glass cakepan, the brownies will be ready in exactly 42 minutes. A stainless steel pan requires a few minutes more cooking. Cool about 20 minutes, cut into squares, and remove from pan. Cool completely on wire rack; then wrap individually in waxed paper. These will keep two weeks or more in a sealed container. These will freeze; remove from waxed paper and allow to thaw on wire rack. Yield: 16 squares.

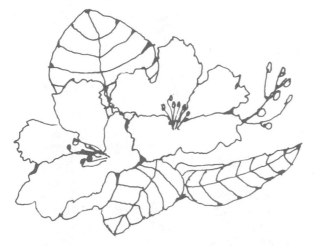

DARK CHOCOLATE CAKELIKE BROWNIES

 3 (1-ounce) squares unsweetened chocolate, melted
½ cup butter or margarine
 3 eggs, room temperature
 1 cup sugar
¾ cup all-purpose flour
½ teaspoon baking powder
½ teaspoon salt
 1 cup chopped pecans or walnuts
 1 teaspoon vanilla extract

Melt chocolate in a double boiler over boiling water and add butter. Stir until dissolved. Beat eggs on high speed, and add sugar slowly. Then add flour sifted together with baking powder and salt. Add nuts, vanilla, and chocolate mixture. Spoon batter into an 11- x 8- x 2-inch pan, well greased and the bottom lined with waxed paper. Bake in a preheated 350° oven for 15 to 20 minutes or until brownies test done. Cool in pan and cut into squares. These keep nicely in a tin container. Yield: 3 dozen (1-inch) squares.

BUTTERSCOTCH BROWNIES

A delicious brownie for those who cannot eat chocolate or eggs. This cake confection is marvelous for serving with coffee at a buffet luncheon, at supper, or to a bridge foursome.

¾ cup butter or margarine (use corn oil margarine if you have cholesterol problems)
 2 cups lightly packed light brown sugar
 1 cup all-purpose flour
 1 teaspoon salt
 2 large eggs, lightly beaten
 2 teaspoons vanilla extract
 1 cup sliced or broken pecans
 1 tablespoon powdered sugar

Melt butter in a heavy skillet over low heat. Then add brown sugar. Allow sugar to run through hands to be sure there are no lumps. Stir into butter until completely blended and smooth in appearance; add flour and salt, and stir until smooth. Remove from heat and allow to cool for 4 or 5 minutes before adding the beaten eggs, vanilla, and nuts. Pour into a greased, 11- x 7- x 3-inch oblong pan. Bake in a preheated 350° oven for 30 minutes or until brownies test done. This may have a slightly sticky feeling because of the richness of the batter. Cool brownies for 20 minutes; then cut into 1-inch squares, but leave in pan for several hours until completely cold. Sprinkle with powdered sugar while still warm. These will keep well in a sealed tin can for a week or more. Yield: 2 dozen (1-inch) squares.

YUMMY BUTTER COOKIES

Rich and crisp, a delightful cookie to serve with tea or coffee.

1 cup butter (or ½ cup butter and ½ cup margarine), softened
1 cup sugar
1 large egg, well beaten
1 teaspoon rum or rum flavoring
2 cups sifted all-purpose flour
⅛ teaspoon salt

Cream butter and sugar until light and fluffy, using an electric mixer on medium speed or by hand. Add beaten egg and rum. Beat well. Combine flour and salt and add to creamed mixture, mixing well. Place mixture in a large bowl, cover and refrigerate overnight. Drop cookies from an iced-tea spoon onto a greased cookie sheet. Bake in a preheated 350° oven 10 to 15 minutes or until golden brown around the edges. Yield: About 5 dozen cookies.

APRICOT DROP COOKIES

If you're in a cookie-making mood, try your talents on these delicious, crunchy, fruity morsels, and enjoy your vitamins the pleasant way.

1⅓ cups all-purpose flour, unsifted
¾ cup wheat germ
1 teaspoon salt
½ teaspoon soda
¼ teaspoon ground nutmeg
1 cup diced dried apricots
1 cup firmly packed light brown sugar
½ cup butter or margarine
2 eggs
1 tablespoon grated orange rind
½ cup coarsely chopped nuts

Sift flour, wheat germ, salt, soda, and nutmeg onto waxed paper; stir well to blend. If dried apricots are very hard, plump before using by placing apricots in colander or sieve over boiling water about 30 minutes. Cream sugar, butter, eggs, and orange rind until light and fluffy. If using electric beater, beat 4 minutes at high speed. Turn to low, and add dry ingredients; mix well. Stir in apricots and nuts. Chill dough about 1 hour. Drop by teaspoonfuls onto greased cookie sheets and bake in a preheated 350° oven for 10 to 12 minutes. Cool on wire racks. (For those who cannot eat nuts, the cookies are almost as delicious without them.) Yield: 4 dozen cookies.

MARGE FRASER'S CHESS COOKIES

This makes a lovely cookie square to serve at a party or buffet supper.

1 cup margarine
1 (16-ounce) package dark brown sugar
1 cup white sugar
4 egg yolks
2 cup all-purpose flour, measured after sifting
1 teaspoon baking powder
¼ teaspoon salt
1 cup chopped nuts
1½ teaspoons vanilla extract
4 eggs whites, stiffly beaten

Melt or cream margarine; add both sugars and egg yolks and beat well. Add flour, baking powder, and salt. Fold in nuts and vanilla; then add stiffly beaten egg whites. Spread in well-greased 13- x 9- x 2-inch pan. Bake in a preheated 350° oven for 30 to 40 minutes or until cookies test done. Allow cookies to cool for 20 minutes; then cut into pieces, but leave in pan for several hours until completely cold. Yield: 2 to 2½ dozen cookies.

MONICA FELDMAN'S BUTTER COOKIES

The best!

½ **cup sweet (unsalted) butter, softened**
¾ **cup sugar**
1 **large egg**
2 **cups all-purpose flour, spooned into cup**
1 **teaspoon baking powder**
1 **teaspoon vanilla extract**
1 **egg yolk**
  Food coloring (optional)

Combine all ingredients in a large bowl except extra egg yolk and food coloring. Knead dough until all ingredients are well mixed; then refrigerate for at least 2 to 3 hours. Using a small amount of dough at a time, roll out on floured board with a lightly floured rolling pin. Cut out cookies with a small glass or cutter about 1½ inches in diameter. Place on a greased baking sheet, and brush with egg yolk which has been blended with food coloring, if desired. Bake in a preheated 350° oven about 10 minutes or until brown around the edges. Yield: 2½ to 3 dozen cookies.

QUICK MIX OATMEAL COOKIES

The best cookie of this kind I have ever eaten and easy to prepare.

2 **cups all-purpose flour, measured after sifting**
1 **teaspoon salt**
1 **teaspoon baking powder**
2 **teaspoons ground cinnamon**
1 **teaspoon soda**
1 **cup firmly packed dark brown sugar**
1 **cup sugar**
2 **large eggs**
2 **tablespoons water**
2 **teaspoons vanilla extract**
1 **cup vegetable shortening**
3 **cups uncooked rolled oats**
1 **cup seedless raisins**

Sift flour, salt, baking powder, cinnamon, baking soda, and sugars into a large bowl. Add eggs, water, vanilla, and shortening. Beat until smooth, about 2 minutes with an electric beater at medium speed. Fold in oats and raisins. Using a rounded teaspoon, shape into small balls and place 2 inches apart on greased cookie sheets. Bake in a preheated 375° oven for 12 to 15 minutes. Remove immediately from pan and finish cooling on wire rack. This is a crisp, crunchy cookie, and they keep well in a sealed tin can. Yield: 4½ to 5 dozen cookies.

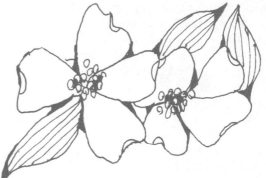

WINNIE'S PRALINE COOKIES

If you are not a candy eater, you may prefer my delicious praline cookie which features pecans too.

½ **cup butter**
½ **cup white sugar**
½ **cup firmly packed dark brown sugar**
1 **large egg, well beaten**
½ **cup all-purpose flour, measured after sifting**
1 **cup chopped pecans**
1 **teaspoon vanilla extract**

Cream together butter and sugars until light and fluffy. Add well-beaten egg; then gradually add flour. Add chopped pecans and vanilla. Drop from teaspoon onto a greased cookie sheet and bake in a preheated 350° oven for 10 minutes. Loosen while warm and cool on wire rack. Yield: 2½ to 3 dozen cookies.

NEW ORLEANS PRALINE COOKIES

Yummy and easy to make. It's a quickie and the recipe is easily cut in half to make 10 cookies.

¼ pound pecan halves or pieces, if halves are not available
20 single honey graham crackers
1 cup butter
2 cups firmly packed brown sugar

Arrange pecan halves in rows on top of graham crackers placed on an ungreased cookie sheet. For a party the halves make the prettier cookies, but pecan pieces are just as tasty. In an iron skillet cook butter and sugar over medium heat until melted together, stirring constantly. Remove from heat, and with a large kitchen spoon, pour mixture slowly over each graham cracker. Bake in a preheated 300° oven for 9 or 10 minutes. Remove from oven and let stand 1 minute. Place on waxed paper with spatula to cool. Yield: 20 cookies.

MAUDE LANE'S LEMON SQUARES

A delicious pastry confection for a morning coffee or afternoon tea.

½ cup butter
1 cup powdered sugar
1 cup all-purpose flour, measured after sifting
Topping

Blend the above ingredients and pat into the bottom of an 8-inch square cakepan. Bake in a preheated 350° oven for 15 minutes. Prepare Topping.

Topping:

2 large eggs
1 cup sugar
2 tablespoons all-purpose flour
⅛ teaspoon salt
½ teaspoon baking powder
5 tablespoons strained lemon juice, divided
Grated rind of 1 lemon
1½ cups powdered sugar

Beat together eggs and sugar. Sift together flour, salt, and baking powder and add to egg mixture. Add 2 tablespoons lemon juice and grated rind; pour over pastry bottom and bake in a preheated 350° oven for 25 minutes. Remove from oven and cool on rack. Mix powdered sugar with remaining 3 tablespoons lemon juice to spreading consistency, and pour over lemon squares. Cut into squares when cool. Yield: 25 squares.

CINNAMON STICKS

Crunchy and wonderful for tea parties or with coffee for a morning brunch.

1 cup butter
1 cup sugar
3 cups all-purpose flour, measured after sifting
4½ teaspoons ground cinnamon
1 large egg, separated
1 teaspoon vanilla extract
1 cup finely chopped pecans
Powdered sugar (optional)

Cream butter and sugar. Combine flour and cinnamon, and gradually add to creamed mixture. Add egg yolk and vanilla. The mixture will be very thick. Spread batter on a buttered cookie sheet and pat down until about ¼ inch thick. Brush top of mixture with unbeaten egg white then press chopped pecans down into dough. Bake in a preheated 350° oven for 30 minutes. Watch carefully as this will burn easily. Cut into oblong pieces or into sticks while hot. Sprinkle with powdered sugar, if desired. Yield: about 3 dozen cookies.

QUICK AND EASY SUGAR COOKIES

Crunchy and yummy, this cookie may be flavored with coconut to make it taste like a macaroon; with vanilla to make a superb sugar cookie.

½ cup margarine
1 cup sugar
1 large egg
1 (5½-ounce) package commercial biscuit mix
1 (2¾-ounce) package instant mashed potatoes
1 teaspoon lemon extract
1 teaspoon coconut extract

In large mixing bowl cream margarine and sugar until light and fluffy on medium speed of electric mixer. Add egg and beat well. Stir in biscuit mix and potato flakes. Add flavorings and blend thoroughly. Drop in 1-inch balls onto greased cookie sheets. Bake in a preheated 350° oven for 10 to 12 minutes or until golden brown around the edges. Yield: about 4 dozen cookies.

Variation; For a plain vanilla cookie substitute 2 teaspoons vanilla extract for the lemon and coconut flavorings.

SUMMIT LEMON SQUARES

A great favorite of Dr. John Nowell of Winston-Salem, North Carolina, the squares are delicious with a morning coffee or as part of a dinner dessert.

1 cup margarine, softened
2 cups all-purpose flour
½ cup powdered sugar
1 tablespoon grated lemon rind
  Topping

Blend ingredients and pat into bottom of a jelly roll pan. Bake in a preheated 325° oven for 15 minutes. Add Topping.

Topping:

4 eggs
2 cups sugar
6 tablespoons strained lemon juice
1 tablespoon grated lemon rind
1 tablespoon all-purpose flour
½ teaspoon baking powder
  Powdered sugar

In mixing bowl beat eggs lightly with a fork. Add remaining ingredients except powdered sugar. Mix well and pour on top of baked pastry. Bake in a preheated 325° oven for 40 minutes. Remove from oven and sprinkle with powdered sugar. Cool and cut into squares. Yield: 4 dozen squares.

MINCEMEAT COOKIES

Unusual and tasty.

1 (9-ounce) package condensed mincemeat
1 cup margarine
1 cup sugar
½ cup firmly packed dark brown sugar
3 large eggs
3½ cups all-purpose flour, spooned into cup
    (reserved ¼ cup for nuts)
1 cup chopped nuts
1 teaspoon soda

Crumble mincemeat onto plate, Cream margarine and sugars in a large bowl on medium speed of electric beater until light and fluffy. Add eggs and beat well. Sprinkle reserved flour on chopped nuts. Gradually sift remaining flour and soda into creamed mixture. Blend in mincemeat and fold in chopped nuts. Drop from spoon onto a greased cookie sheet. Bake in a preheated 350° oven about 10 minutes or until golden brown. Yield: 5 dozen cookies.

OLD-FASHIONED TEACAKES

A delicious crisp cookie relished by young and old. The directions are simple, ingredients inexpensive, but you do need time and patience to roll out the cookies. Go slowly as grandmother did, and you will be completely satisfied with your golden results. For a marvelous treat, serve with ice cold lemonade on a hot day.

4 cups all-purpose flour, measured after
    sifting
2½ cups sugar
⅛ teaspoon soda (large pinch)
1⅓ cups vegetable shortening
4 large eggs
1½ teaspoons vanilla extract

In a large bowl mix together flour, sugar, and soda. Make a well in center of flour mixture and add shortening, unbeaten eggs, and vanilla. Using both hands, scoop up edges of mixture and thoroughly work all ingredients together until well blended. The dough will be soft and sticky like pie pastry. Chill dough for at least 20 minutes.

Roll out a small amount at a time; keep remaining dough chilled until ready to use. Roll out very thin, less than ¼ inch thick, so that you will have to peel dough from the rolling pin and pat down again on a greased cookie sheet. For a large size teacake, 2½ inches in diameter, use a regular glass as a cutter; for smaller size use an orange juice glass. Bake in a preheated 350° oven about 15 to 20 minutes or until light gold or delicately browned. Cool on wire rack. If you wish, place part of dough in refrigerator and bake later. The dough will hold well for a week or ten days. Wrap or cover well with foil or plastic wrap. The teacakes will keep crisp and fresh in a sealed tin can or cookie jar. Yield: 12½ dozen large or 16 dozen smaller teacakes.

Variation: For a spicy flavor use 1 teaspoon vanilla and ¼ teaspoon each ground cinnamon and ground nutmeg.

Homemade pickles and accompaniments add just the right touch of zest to many meat dishes. The recipe for watermelon rind pickle is on page 151, tangy pickled okra pods on page 151, and traditional bread and butter pickles on page 152.

SESAME SEED WAFERS

Different and easy to prepare.

1 (2¼-ounce) jar sesame seeds
6 tablespoons butter or margarine, softened
1 cup firmly packed dark brown sugar
1 large egg, well beaten
½ cup all-purpose flour
¼ teaspoon baking powder
⅛ teaspoon salt
1 teaspoon vanilla extract

Toast sesame seeds in a heavy skillet over low heat about 20 minutes or until golden brown, stirring constantly; cool. Cream butter and sugar until fluffy. Add egg and blend well. Combine flour, baking powder, and salt; add to creamed mixture. Add vanilla and toasted sesame seeds. Using an iced-tea spoon, drop leveled-off amounts onto greased cookie sheets, at least 2 inches apart. Bake in a preheated 350° oven for 8 minutes; cool for 1 minute before removing from cookie sheet. Let wafers finish cooling on a wire rack and place in an airtight container. These keep fresh for several weeks. Yield: about 6 dozen cookies.

PECAN TREASURES

An elegant cookie suitable for any kind of party. It is particularly good for a buffet supper or cocktail party where finger food is part of the menu. It blends as well with a bourbon highball as it does with hot spiced tea.

2½ pounds shelled pecans
1 cup butter, room temperature
1 pound firmly packed dark brown sugar
1 teaspoon soda
½ cup cold water
1 teaspoon freshly ground nutmeg
1 teaspoon freshly ground allspice
2 teaspoons ground cinnamon
3 cups all-purpose flour, spooned into cup (reserve ½ cup for nuts)
3 large eggs, room temperature
1 teaspoon vanilla extract

Break or slice each pecan into 3 pieces. Using electric mixer, cream butter and brown sugar in a large bowl at medium speed until light and fluffy. Dissolve soda in cold water. Place spices in sifter with 2½ cups flour and gradually add to creamed mixture alternating with soda water. Cut down from sides with spatula often and use low speed for blending. Add eggs one at a time and beat well after each addition, changing to a high speed of mixer. Add vanilla and fold in pecans which have been dusted with reserved flour. Mound batter onto an iced-tea spoon and slide onto greased cookie sheets. Bake in a preheated 350° oven for 15 to 20 minutes. Watch carefully because the cookie bottoms can get too brown. Remove to wire rack at once and allow to cool completely; then place in tightly sealed canisters or tin cans. The cookies will keep fresh for a month or longer. If they should lose their crispness, bake at 350° for 1 or 2 minutes. Yield: about 9 dozen cookies.

Freshly baked ham and light, flaky biscuits will bring your family to the dinner table in a hurry. Winifred shares her instructions for cooking a Virginia ham on page 170.

Casseroles

MR. BLUE LAKE'S SOUFFLÉ

The delicate rich flavor of this soufflé is especially good for a hot baked ham dinner. Or enjoy it with cold ham and zippy mustard for lunch. I recommend it for pleasant eating.

1 (16-ounce) can Blue Lake green beans
2 cups diced yellow squash (about 1 pound)
    or 1 (10-ounce) package frozen yellow
    squash
1 teaspoon salt, divided
¼ cup butter or margarine
¼ cup all-purpose flour
⅛ teaspoon dry mustard
⅛ teaspoon ground nutmeg
⅛ teaspoon white pepper
1 cup milk
2 eggs, separated
1 teaspoon lemon juice
½ cup slivered almonds (optional)

Drain bean liquid into a saucepan. Add squash and ¼ teaspoon salt. Cover and cook for 10 minutes. Melt butter in another saucepan; stir in flour, remaining ¾ teaspoon salt, and spices. Gradually add milk and cook until thickened, stirring constantly. Beat egg yolks lightly in a bowl and slowly stir into hot mixture. Add beans, squash, and lemon juice. Beat egg whites until stiff. Add almonds and then fold egg whites into vegetable mixture. Spoon into eight greased 6-ounce custard cups or a 1½-quart casserole. Place in pan with hot water which comes up about halfway on the cups or casserole. Bake in a preheated 350° oven: custard cups for about 30 minutes, casserole for about 50 minutes or until set. Test with a silver knife blade in center. This should come out clean. Serve at once. For a soufflé, this one holds up very well. Yield: 8 servings.

CORN PUDDING SUPREME

Simply yummy!

3 large eggs, room temperature
2½ cups fresh corn or 2 (10-ounce) packages
    frozen whole kernel or creamed corn,
    thawed
½ cup whipping cream
½ cup milk
2 tablespoons all-purpose flour
1 teaspoon salt
2 tablespoons firmly packed dark brown
    sugar
2 tablespoons butter, melted

Beat eggs until light, then add remaining ingredients. Pour into a buttered 1-quart casserole. Bake in a preheated 350° oven for 1 hour. Serve immediately. Yield: 6 servings.

POTATO SOUFFLÉ

A great way to use leftover mashed potatoes. This makes a delightful companion to my meat loaf with a tossed green salad and hot French bread.

2½ cups hot mashed potatoes, fresh or
    leftover
 2 egg yolks
 2 tablespoons all-purpose flour
½ cup whipping cream or undiluted canned
    milk
 1 teaspoon salt
⅛ teaspoon paprika
¼ teaspoon dried green onion
⅛ teaspoon white pepper
¼ teaspoon baking powder
½ cup grated sharp cheddar cheese
 2 egg whites, well beaten

Combine hot potatoes, egg yolks, flour, cream, salt, seasonings, and baking powder; beat well. Fold in grated cheese, then egg whites. Spoon into buttered 1½-quart casserole and bake in a preheated 325° oven about 15 minutes. Serve immediately. Yield: 4 to 6 servings.

ENID'S COTTAGE PIE

1½ pounds Irish potatoes
 4 cups boiling water
 2 teaspoons or more salt, divided
 5 tablespoons butter, divided
1½ pounds ground or English minced beef
 1 cup grated onion
¼ teaspoon pepper
 6 drops Worcestershire sauce
 1 tablespoon all-purpose flour

Peel potatoes. Cook in boiling water with 1 teaspoon salt for 20 to 25 minutes or until potatoes are tender. Drain well and place in a large bowl; add 3 tablespoons butter and remaining 1 teaspoon salt and mash well. Beat with fork until potatoes are fluffy. In skillet, sauté beef in remaining 2 tablespoons butter over medium heat. Add onion, pepper, Worcestershire sauce, and flour, and cook until browned. Pour into a buttered 1½-quart casserole and cover with mashed potatoes. Bake in a preheated 400° oven for 1 hour or until potatoes are crisp and brown. Yield: 6 to 8 servings.

OSCAR OF THE WALDORF'S ESCALLOPED POTATOES

Creamy rich, yet simple to do. This is marvelous with a beef roast or meat loaf.

6 medium-size potatoes, preferably red
1 teaspoon salt
¼ teaspoon freshly ground black pepper
¼ teaspoon paprika
1 tablespoon dried green onion or 1
    medium-size white onion, thinly sliced
    (optional)
  Butter
1 (13-ounce) can evaporated milk, undiluted,
    or 1 pint whipping cream

Wash potatoes, cover with water in a saucepan and boil in their jackets until half done, using high heat. When a fork tine goes in easily they are ready; you do not want squashy potatoes. Drain, cool and peel potatoes, and cut into ¼-inch thick slices. Put in layers in a buttered 1½-quart baking dish. Sprinkle each layer with salt, pepper, paprika, dried green onion or sliced onion, if desired; dot with butter, and cover with undiluted evaporated milk. Bake in a preheated 350° oven for 45 minutes to 1 hour or until the top layer is golden and looks as if it is covered with a thick cheese sauce. Yield: 6 servings.

BAKED CANNED SWEET POTATOES WITH MARSHMALLOWS

Festive, delicious, and easy to prepare.

 1 (30-ounce) can sweet potatoes
½ teaspoon ground cinnamon
¼ teaspoon ground nutmeg
 1 tablespoon orange juice
 4 tablespoons butter
⅛ teaspoon baking powder
 2 large eggs, well beaten
 1 teaspoon vanilla extract
   Sugar (optional)
   Marshmallows

Drain sweet potatoes and reserve liquid. Beat potatoes with an electric mixer or put through a ricer until thoroughly mashed. Add spices, orange juice, butter, ¼ cup reserved liquid, baking powder, beaten eggs, and vanilla. Mix well. Add sugar, if desired, one tablespoon at a time. Butter a 1½-quart casserole and fill half-full with potato mixture. Add a layer of marshmallows, then remaining potato mixture. Bake in a preheated 350° oven for 30 minutes. Remove from oven, add a top layer of marshmallows, and return to oven until marshmallows turn a golden brown. Yield: 6 to 8 servings.

ALMOND RICE WITH PETIT POIS

Superb with crabmeat or veal dishes.

3½ cups water
 1 teaspoon lemon juice
1½ teaspoons salt
1½ tablespoons butter, divided
1½ cups popcorn rice or long grain rice
 ½ cup finely sliced almonds
 1 cup petit pois or tiny English peas, cooked

Combine water, lemon juice, salt, and ½ tablespoon butter in a medium-size saucepan; bring to a boil. Add rice and lower heat; cook uncov-

ered for 20 to 25 minutes until all liquid is absorbed. Stir occasionally to be sure rice does not stick. Taste a few grains; rice should be tender, not hard. Remove from heat and rinse in colander under warm water. Return colander to stove and place over hot water with the heat turned to low. Make a well in center of rice and cover with pan top. The rice will stand in separate grains. Toast almonds in 325° oven with remaining 1 tablespoon butter for 10 to 15 minutes until golden. Just before serving, sprinkle almonds and petit pois in rice; toss with a fork and serve in a mound. This dish may be cooked early in the day and reheated. Yield: 8 servings.

MRS. WHITFIELD HATCH'S RICE CASSEROLE

A very tasty and zesty dish!

1 cup uncooked regular rice
1 cup sliced fresh or canned mushrooms
1 (2-ounce) jar pimientos, finely chopped
2 bell peppers, finely chopped
2 hot peppers, finely chopped
2 medium-size onions, finely chopped
1 teaspoon Worcestershire sauce
1 (10½-ounce) can condensed chicken with
   rice soup
⅛ teaspoon pepper
   Salt to taste
1 (10½-ounce) soup can water
¼ cup butter, melted

In large bowl mix together all ingredients. Pour into 1½-quart oblong baking dish. Bake for 1 hour in a preheated 350° oven. Serve hot. Yield: 6 to 8 servings.

BAKED BEANS

Very tasty and easy to prepare.

 1 (24-ounce) can pork and beans
¾ cup firmly packed light brown sugar
 1 cup catsup
 1 very large onion, diced
 1 teaspoon prepared mustard
 2 or 3 slices bacon (optional)

Combine all ingredients except bacon in a large bowl. Pour into a greased, flat, 2-quart casserole and cover with bacon slices, if desired. Bake in a preheated 350° oven for 1½ to 2 hours. Yield: 12 servings.

ARTICHOKE SUPREME

An artichoke dish pleasing to the palate and easy to make. This gourmet casserole is ideal for a dinner party or buffet supper but it does take time to prepare. You may double the ingredients without difficulty to serve 12 or more. This will freeze and may be made ahead of time.

 4 artichokes, stems cut off
 4 tablespoons salt
 1 lemon, sliced
 1 tablespoon vegetable or olive oil
 2 celery ribs or 1 teaspoon celery seeds
   Sauce
½ cup seasoned or toasted bread crumbs

Soak artichokes in cold water for 30 minutes; drain. Bring enough water to a boil in a large soup kettle or a Dutch oven to cover artichokes; add all ingredients except Sauce and bread crumbs to boiling water. Boil for 45 minutes to 1 hour depending on size of artichokes; drain and cool. Remove leaves and scrape the soft meaty heart from bottom of each leaf onto a plate. Remove the choke, and cut up hearts. Place hearts in a buttered 1½-

or 2-quart casserole. Prepare the Sauce. Pour Sauce over artichoke hearts; top with bread crumbs and bake in a preheated 350° oven for 30 minutes. Yield: 6 to 8 servings.

Sauce:

½ cup chopped onion
½ cup butter
 1 (7¼-ounce) can whole mushrooms, drained
 1 (10¾-ounce) can condensed cream of
   mushroom soup
⅛ teaspoon lemon-pepper marinade
½ teaspoon Worcestershire sauce
½ teaspoon Tabasco
   Artichoke meat from leaves

Sauté onion in butter in a heavy skillet over medium heat about 15 minutes; add remaining ingredients. Blend thoroughly and taste to see if salt is needed. Pour sauce over cut up artichoke hearts.
Variation: For a seafood casserole, add ½ pound cooked or fresh crabmeat or 1 pound cooked shrimp to cut up hearts before pouring sauce over all.

EXOTIC SPINACH

 2 (10-ounce) packages frozen whole spinach
 3 cups commercial sour cream
 1 (1-ounce) package dry onion soup
 2 tablespoons medium-dry sherry
   Bread crumbs (optional)

According to package directions cook spinach in unsalted water. Drain and chop finely. Add sour cream, onion soup, and sherry. Sprinkle bread crumbs over top if desired. Place in a greased 1½-quart casserole and bake in a preheated 325° oven for 15 to 20 minutes. This may be covered with foil and reheated. Yield: 8 to 10 servings.
Note: Fresh spinach may be used, but it takes more time to cook.

SPINACH WITH OYSTERS AND CHEESE

  1 (10-ounce) package frozen chopped spinach
  3 celery ribs, including leaves, chopped
  3 green onions, including tops, chopped
  ½ bunch parsley, chopped
  ½ cup butter or margarine
  1 tablespoon Worcestershire sauce
  ¼ teaspoon Tabasco
  ¾ cup packaged dry corn bread dressing
  ½ pint oysters, chopped
  1 cup shredded cheddar cheese

According to package directions cook spinach until tender; drain. Lightly sauté chopped celery, onions, and parsley in butter. Combine spinach and sautéed vegetables with Worcestershire and Tabasco, corn bread dressing, and chopped oysters. Place in a greased 1½-quart casserole and bake in a preheated 350° oven for 25 minutes. Top with shredded cheese and return to oven for an additional 5 minutes. Yield: 4 to 6 servings.

MOUSSAKA

This casserole, rich with layers of ground beef or lamb, eggplant, and custard sauce is enhanced with interesting spices. A complete meal in itself, it is inexpensive and ideal for informal entertaining. More zesty if prepared the day before, this gourmet dish may be frozen and made even weeks in advance. You cannot make Moussaka in a hurry. Allow yourself at least two hours if you are a fast worker, longer if you are not.

Step 1:

2 (1-pound 4- to 6-ounce) eggplants
1 tablespoon salt
1 cup olive oil (I prefer ½ olive and ½ corn)

Wash and dry eggplants. Slice into ¼-inch rounds and sprinkle with salt. Let stand for at least 30 minutes. Press between paper towels until all excess moisture is removed. Pour 3 tablespoons oil into a large skillet, and turn to high heat. When oil is hot, add eggplant slices and brown on both sides. Adjust heat as you cook and watch closely to prevent burning. Add more oil as needed and repeat until all eggplant has been browned. Drain on paper towels.

Step 2:

1½ pounds ground chuck or lamb (authentic
      Greek recipe uses lamb)
  1 cup finely chopped onion
  1 clove garlic, minced
  1 (8-ounce) can tomato sauce
  2 tomatoes, peeled and chopped, or 2
      (8-ounce) cans tomato sauce
  2 tablespoons chopped fresh, dried, or frozen
      parsley
  2 bay leaves
  ½ teaspoon ground oregano
  ½ teaspoon dried basil leaves
  ½ teaspoon powdered mushrooms
  ½ teaspoon ground cinnamon
  ½ teaspoon salt
  ⅛ teaspoon freshly ground black pepper
  ½ cup Burgundy or dry red wine
  2 large eggs, well beaten
  ¼ cup fine bread crumbs

Use same skillet with oil to brown meat with onion and garlic. Stir constantly over medium-high heat about 10 minutes. Drain off any excess fat. Add tomato sauce and fresh tomatoes, parsley, bay leaves, oregano, basil leaves, powdered mushrooms, cinnamon, salt, pepper, and red wine. Simmer for 20 to 30 minutes until liquid is almost absorbed. Cool slightly and add a little of the hot sauce to the beaten eggs; return eggs to hot mixture and cook over low heat for 2 minutes, stirring constantly. Add bread crumbs and blend well.

Step 3:

Béchamel Sauce:

 4 tablespoons butter
 4 tablespoons all-purpose flour
 ½ teaspoon salt
 4 cups milk, slowly warmed to hot
 4 egg yolks, well beaten
 ⅛ teaspoon ground nutmeg
 ¼ cup fine bread crumbs
 1 cup freshly grated Romano or Parmesan
　　cheese, divided

Melt butter in a heavy saucepan, and stir in flour with a wire whisk. When mixture is smooth, add salt and slowly stir in hot milk. Cook until thickened and smooth. Remove sauce from heat and pour a little of it over beaten egg yolks, then combine the two. Add nutmeg and blend well. Butter two 1½-quart oblong casseroles or one 3-quart casserole. Sprinkle bread crumbs over bottom of casserole. Arrange half of eggplant slices over this, then spoon the meat mixture evenly and cover with ½ cup cheese and remaining eggplant. Pour the Béchamel Sauce over all, and sprinkle with remaining ½ cup cheese. Bake in a preheated 350° oven for 1 hour or until top is golden. It is wise to line the bottom of the oven with foil to catch drippings. Remove Moussaka from oven, and let stand at least 30 to 40 minutes before serving. If frozen, reheat in 300° oven for 45 minutes to 1 hour or until hot. To complete your meal serve hot French bread, a tossed green salad, and a good red wine. Or if you want to go Greek all the way, try retsina—a wine of Greece—and a luscious almond torte for dessert. Yield: 12 servings.

WINIFRED BARRON'S BLUSHED ONIONS

A tasty and colorful casserole to serve with a beef, lamb, or pork roast.

 6 cups sliced medium-size to large onions
　　Water to cover
 1 teaspoon salt
 ⅔ cup catsup
 ½ cup honey
 2 tablespoons butter

Remove outer onion skin before cutting into slices at least ⅛ inch thick. Cover onion slices with water and add salt; cook in boiling water for 5 minutes. Drain and combine with remaining ingredients. Pour into a greased 2-quart casserole and bake, uncovered in a preheated 350° oven for 1 hour. Yield: 4 servings.

ODEL HERBERT'S CARROT CASSEROLE

Even husbands and children will eat carrots served in this tasty way.

 8 whole large carrots
 1 cup finely chopped celery
 1 medium-size onion, finely chopped
 1 tablespoon prepared mustard
 ½ cup mayonnaise
 ½ cup buttered bread crumbs

Scrape carrots, cover with water, and cook in a saucepan until done. (A fork tine should go in easily.) Drain carrots and mash finely. If you do not have a blender, use a rolling pin. In a large bowl combine all ingredients and pour into buttered 1½-quart casserole. Top with buttered bread crumbs. Bake in a preheated 300° oven for 1 hour. Serve hot. Yield: 6 to 8 servings.

ASPARAGUS—ENGLISH PEAS CASSEROLE

2 tablespoons butter or margarine
2 tablespoons all-purpose flour
1 (20-ounce) can asparagus, drained and juice reserved
  Milk
7 ounces (¾ stick) New York State sharp cheddar cheese, grated, divided
1 (⅝-ounce) package cornflakes
1 (8½-ounce) can petit pois
1 (2-ounce) jar pimientos
2 hard-boiled eggs, chopped
1 (3-ounce) can sliced mushrooms

Melt butter in a saucepan over low heat; add flour and blend in with wire whisk. Measure reserved asparagus juice, and add enough milk to measure 1 cup; warm slowly in another saucepan. Add warmed juice mixture to flour mixture, stirring slowly. Cook and stir until sauce is smooth and boiling. Add some grated cheese to sauce. Butter a 1½-quart casserole, sprinkle some of the cornflakes on bottom; reserve rest for top. Add half of asparagus, half of peas, chopped pimientos, cream sauce, chopped eggs, and sliced mushrooms for first layer. Then add a layer of cheese. Repeat process with vegetable combination and cream sauce, then a layer of cheese. If cream sauce has become too thick, thin it with a little milk. Sprinkle remaining cornflakes on top. Bake in a preheated 350° oven for 20 to 25 minutes until bubbly. Yield: 8 to 10 servings.

ASPARAGUS WITH A HUNGARIAN TWIST

In preparing this Hungarian asparagus casserole, I follow the instructions of its cooks and use fresh asparagus, if available, with sour cream and fresh paprika, their favorite condiment. This seasoning accents the sour cream and is a perfect foil for green asparagus. This is delicious served with a beef roast or steak.

1½ pounds fresh asparagus spears or 1 (10-ounce) package frozen or 1 (14½-ounce) can green spears, drained
1 teaspoon sugar
4 pieces thinly sliced white or cheese bread, toasted dry and crumbled
4 tablespoons butter, divided
1½ cups sour cream, divided
1 teaspoon paprika, divided
  Salt to taste

Remove all scales and snap off tough ends of asparagus. Tie in bundles and stand in boiling water sweetened with sugar, leaving tips above water line. Cover and boil until lower ends are tender, about 20 to 25 minutes. Drain in colander. If using frozen asparagus, cook according to package directions, then drain in colander. Brown bread crumbs in 2 tablespoons butter. Place ¾ cup sour cream in a deep, buttered, 12-inch piepan; cover with half the bread crumbs. Follow with a layer of asparagus and cover with remaining ¾ cup sour cream. Sprinkle with half the paprika. Add remaining bread crumbs, paprika, and salt, and dot with butter. Bake in a preheated 375° oven about 25 to 30 minutes until sour cream has bubbled through mixture, and it is browned on top. Yield: 4 to 6 servings.

VIVIENNE WILSON'S ASPARAGUS AND CARROT ESCALLOP

A delightfully seasoned casserole and a quickie.

3 large carrots, cooked and sliced or 1 (16-ounce) can sliced carrots
1 (13-ounce) can cut green asparagus
4 tablespoons butter
1 (10¾-ounce) can condensed cream of celery soup
½ soup can half-and-half or milk
3 or 4 dashes Tabasco
  Coarsely ground cracker crumbs

Layer carrots and asparagus in a buttered 2-quart casserole, making 4 to 6 layers. Dot with butter as you layer; cover with soup blended with cream and Tabasco. Cover with buttered cracker crumbs. This may be prepared early in day, refrigerated, and baked just before serving. Bake in a preheated 350° oven for 20 to 30 minutes until mixture bubbles. Serve hot. This will freeze uncooked, but wait until baking to add buttered cracker crumbs. Yield: 4 to 6 servings.

SPINACH SOUFFLÉ

This has a New Orleans flavor with the use of Creole mustard, horseradish, and a zippy sharp cheese. The dish is quickly prepared and goes well with pork roast or a highly seasoned beef dish like Boeuf Bourguignon.

1 (10-ounce) package frozen whole spinach
1 teaspoon salt
¼ teaspoon lemon bits
3 tablespoons butter or margarine
3 tablespoons all-purpose flour
1½ cups milk
¼ teaspoon salt
⅛ teaspoon paprika
2 egg yolks, well beaten
1 cup shredded sharp, natural white cheddar cheese
1½ teaspoons Creole mustard
1 teaspoon Worcestershire sauce
1 teaspoon prepared horseradish
2 egg whites, stiffly beaten

Cook spinach according to package directions, but use 1 teaspoon salt and ¼ teaspoon lemon bits. Put through food mill or blend in blender;

then drain well. Melt butter over low heat; add flour and blend well. Slowly stir in whole milk and season with ¼ teaspoon salt and paprika. Add beaten egg yolks, shredded cheese, mustard, Worcestershire sauce, horseradish, and drained spinach. Stir constantly until thickened; do not let mixture boil. Cool slightly; then fold in stiffly beaten egg whites. Spoon mixture into an ungreased, 1½-quart casserole dish or 6 individual custard cups. Place in a pan of hot water and bake in a preheated 350° oven for 30 minutes. Serve immediately. Yield: 6 servings.

MUSHROOMS SUPREME

A superb main dish served on Holland rusks or crisp toast. Serve with a fresh fruit salad for a luncheon. It makes an elegant side dish with roast beef or lamb.

6 tablespoons butter, softened
1 tablespoon prepared mustard
¼ teaspoon Tabasco
1 teaspoon salt
1½ tablespoons all-purpose flour
⅛ teaspoon ground nutmeg
1 tablespoon finely chopped fresh, frozen, or dried parsley
1 tablespoon grated onion
1 pound large mushrooms
1 cup whipping cream
½ cup milk

In a small bowl cream butter on medium speed of electric mixer; add prepared mustard and Tabasco. Combine salt, flour, and nutmeg and add to butter mixture. Add parsley and onion. Wash mushrooms in cold water, dry thoroughly on paper towels, and slice lengthwise. Place a layer of mushrooms in the bottom of a buttered 2-quart casserole and dot with butter mixture; repeat layers several more times. Blend cream and milk and pour over mushrooms. Bake in a preheated 375° oven for 55 to 60 minutes. Yield: 6 servings.

SARA HEDERMAN'S BAKED GREEN TOMATOES

A new taste treat!

  8 medium-size to large green tomatoes
¼ teaspoon celery seeds
  1 teaspoon dried green onion
1½ teaspoons salt
  ½ teaspoon white pepper
  2 tablespoons chopped chives
  ⅛ teaspoon curry powder
  **1 teaspoon finely chopped fresh or dried
       basil**
  ¾ cup fresh bread crumbs, toasted
  2 tablespoons butter
  ½ cup grated Parmesan cheese

Wash tomatoes and cut into ¼-inch thick slices; arrange in layers in a greased flat or oblong casserole. Sprinkle each layer with a few celery seeds, dried green onion, salt, pepper, chives, curry powder, basil, bread crumbs and a liberal dotting of butter. Top with Parmesan cheese and bake in a preheated 350° oven for 1 hour. Yield: 6 servings.

ONIONS STUFFED WITH HAM

Tasty and economical. Use leftover ham for the filling.

  **6 medium-size onions (about 2 pounds),
       Texas grown preferred**
**½ cup chopped cooked ham or 1 (4-ounce) can
       deviled ham**
¼ cup chopped green pepper
½ cup softened bread crumbs
  **1 tablespoon butter or margarine, melted
       Salt to taste**
⅛ teaspoon freshly ground black pepper
  1 cup half-and-half or milk
½ cup buttered or seasoned bread crumbs

Peel onions with care to keep shape. Wash and cut a slice from top of each. Pierce each onion through to center with a metal straw or fork tine to keep whole while cooking. Cook onions in small amount of water in a saucepan over medium heat until almost tender. Drain and push out centers. Chop onion centers and mix with ham, green pepper, softened bread crumbs, and melted butter; stir in salt and pepper. Stuff onion cups. Place in a greased oblong baking dish and pour half-and-half around the stuffed onions. Sprinkle tops of onions with buttered or seasoned bread crumbs. Bake in a preheated 375° oven about 30 minutes or until the tops are a golden brown. Yield: 6 servings.

MARY FRANCES BLAKE'S CAJUN EGGPLANT CASSEROLE

A zesty gourmet dish, easy to prepare and inexpensive. If you wish to dress it up for a party or special company, add ½ pound medium or large shrimp, peeled and diced. This dish is delicious with a beef, lamb, or pork roast. It makes a good supper dish on a cold winter night.

  **1 large or 2 small eggplants (2 cups cooked
       eggplant)**
  1 cup water
1½ teaspoons salt, divided
  ¾ cup chopped onion
  4 tablespoons butter, margarine, or corn oil
  ½ cup chopped celery
  ⅔ cup condensed cream of celery soup
  2 tablespoons catsup
  1 tablespoon Worcestershire sauce
  ⅛ teaspoon sweet basil (fresh if available)
  **¾ cup chopped tomato (one medium-size to
       large)**
  ¼ teaspoon freshly ground black pepper
  ¼ teaspoon seasoned salt
  ¾ cup grated sharp cheddar cheese
  **3 tablespoons buttered or seasoned bread
       crumbs**

Peel and dice eggplant, add water and 1 teaspoon salt, and cook in a saucepan over medium heat about 15 to 20 minutes or until just tender. Drain well. Sauté onion in butter over medium heat in a heavy skillet until clear. Add celery and cook until just tender; it should be a little crunchy. Mash 2 cups eggplant and add other ½ teaspoon salt and remaining ingredients except bread crumbs. Pour eggplant mixture into a well-buttered 1½-quart casserole. Top with bread crumbs and bake in a preheated 350° oven for 20 to 30 minutes or until bubbly and bread crumbs are golden brown. Yield: 6 to 8 servings.

MARIAH'S BAKED EGGPLANT WITH SHRIMP

1 large eggplant
2 slices bread
½ cup butter, divided
1 small onion, finely chopped
1 clove garlic, finely chopped
1 celery rib, finely chopped
1 egg, well beaten
¼ teaspoon ground mace
2 teaspoons Worcestershire sauce
  Salt to taste
¼ teaspoon pepper
3 dashes Tabasco
6 to 8 large shrimp
  Cracker crumbs

Steam whole eggplant in boiling salted water for 20 minutes. Cut lengthwise and scoop out center. Soak bread in cold water, then squeeze out water in colander. In a large skillet melt 6 tablespoons butter over medium heat; add onion, garlic, and celery and cook about 12 minutes or until onion is clear. Add bread, egg, eggplant, mace, Worcestershire sauce, salt, pepper, and Tabasco. Cook shrimp separately in boiling water for 3 to 4 minutes. Drain and cut each into three or four pieces. Add shrimp to eggplant mixture and cook for several min-

utes until well blended. Taste and adjust seasonings if needed. Spoon into eggplant shells. Top with cracker crumbs and dot with remaining butter. Place these in pan with enough water to cover bottom of pan. Bake in a preheated 400° oven for 15 to 20 minutes or until brown. Yield: 6 servings.

ZESTY BROCCOLI CASSEROLE

¼ cup chopped onion
6 tablespoons margarine, divided
2 tablespoons all-purpose flour
½ cup water
2 (10-ounce) packages frozen chopped broccoli
1 (6-ounce) jar commercial whipped cheese spread
½ cup grated cheddar cheese
3 eggs, well beaten
½ cup cracker crumbs

Sauté onion in 4 tablespoons margarine in a large heavy skillet over medium heat. Stir in flour and add water. Cook until thickened, stirring constantly. Cook broccoli according to package directions; drain well. Add broccoli and both cheeses to sauce mixture. Add well-beaten eggs. Pour mixture into a flat or oblong baking dish buttered with 1 tablespoon margarine. Use remaining margarine to butter cracker crumbs used for topping. Bake in a preheated 350° oven for 35 to 40 minutes. Yield: 8 servings.

CHICKEN, SOUR CREAM, AND MUSHROOM CASSEROLE

Crunchy and savory. Prepare the chicken and broth a day ahead of time.

  3- to 3½-pound fryer or same amount of chicken breasts
    Water to cover
  3 celery ribs with leaves
  1 teaspoon dried green onion
  2 slices lemon
  1 teaspoon salt
  1 teaspoon Mei-yen powder
  ¼ teaspoon freshly ground black pepper
  ½ cup reserved chicken broth
  ½ cup butter, melted, divided
1½ cups (¼ pound) premium crackers, finely rolled
  ½ (6-ounce) can water chestnuts, finely sliced
  ½ pound fresh mushrooms, sliced lengthwise
  1 (10¾-ounce) can condensed cream of mushroom or chicken soup
  ½ pint commercial sour cream
  ⅛ teaspoon ground nutmeg
  1 tablespoon prepared mustard
  ¼ teaspoon paprika

Combine first eight ingredients in a large saucepan, and bring to a simmering boil. Cover and simmer about 2 hours or until chicken is tender. Test with fork in thick part of thigh. Cool, remove skin and bones from chicken, and cut into bite-size pieces. Strain broth and reserve ½ cup.

To assemble the casserole takes only a few minutes. Be sure to keep the chicken refrigerated until needed. Butter a 2-quart casserole with 2 tablespoons melted butter. Blend remaining 6 tablespoons butter with cracker crumbs. Place chicken on bottom of casserole; add ½ cup reserved broth. Arrange a layer of sliced chestnuts, a layer of mushrooms, and sprinkle generously with buttered cracker crumbs. Combine soup, sour cream, nutmeg,

and mustard, and spread over all. Cover with more cracker crumbs and sprinkle with paprika. Bake in a preheated 350° oven for 25 to 30 minutes or until casserole bubbles and browns on top. It freezes beautifully. Yield: 8 to 10 servings.

MUSHROOMS WINIFRED

A superb casserole to complement a roast or steak, it will also make a delightful main dish for a luncheon. If desired, bake in a ring mold and fill center with petit pois and a few chopped pimientos for color.

 1 pound fresh mushrooms
 5 tablespoons butter, divided
 2 tablespoons finely chopped onion
 ¾ teaspoon salt
 ¼ teaspoon ground nutmeg
 ¼ teaspoon ground ginger
 4 tablespoons all-purpose flour
½ cup milk
3 dashes Tabasco
2 large eggs, well beaten

Buy firm, unspotted mushrooms. Wash gently under cold running water, and dry on paper towels. Do not peel unless skin is brown. Chop mushrooms coarsely.

In a large heavy skillet melt 4 tablespoons butter over medium heat. Add chopped onion and cook about 7 to 10 minutes or until onion is golden, stirring often. Add mushrooms and stir constantly for 5 minutes, long enough for butter to lightly coat mushrooms. Add seasonings and flour; blend. Add milk and Tabasco, and cook until mixture thickens, stirring constantly. You may prepare recipe to this point in the morning or even the day before serving, refrigerate, and bake when ready to serve.

Add well-beaten eggs to mushroom mixture and spoon into a 1-quart soufflé or casserole buttered with remaining 1 tablespoon butter. Bake in a preheated 350° oven for 35 minutes. The top should be a medium brown. Yield: 6 servings.

Variation: If desired, spoon mushroom mixture into an 8-inch ring mold buttered and lined with waxed paper. Complete recipe as follows:

1 (14½- to 16-ounce) can tiny English peas
2 tablespoons butter
  Sprig fresh mint
1 tablespoon chopped pimientos

In a saucepan heat peas with butter and mint; add pimientos. When ring is baked as directed above, go around sides gently with a spatula and turn out on a warm serving tray. Fill center with English pea mixture. The ring will freeze, but be sure to add the pea mixture after the mold has been heated in a 350° oven until hot.

LEBANESE STUFFED SQUASH

12 medium-size yellow, crooked-neck squash
  Cold water to cover
1 tablespoon salt
  Filling
1 (10½-ounce) can tomato puree
2 cups water
1 clove garlic, minced, or ⅛ teaspoon garlic powder
  Pastry

Wash and core squash with a paring knife by first cutting off the small narrow part of the neck. Use a small measuring spoon or melon baller to clean out shell completely. Place squash shells in a saucepan, cover with cold water, and add salt. Prepare Filling; then drain shells and stuff, leaving about a ¾-inch opening unfilled to allow for expansion. Place squash in a large soup kettle or Dutch oven, add tomato puree, water, and minced garlic; cover and cook over low heat for 35 to 40 minutes or until tender. Test to see if a fork tine goes easily into the shell. Drain on wire rack and enclose in Pastry. Bake in a preheated 450° oven for 15 minutes or until a golden brown. Serve hot. (You can do everything but the final enclosing and baking the day before serving.) Yield: 12 servings.

Filling:

  ½ cup pine nuts
  5 tablespoons butter, divided
  1 cup uncooked regular rice, rinsed in cold water
1½ teaspoons salt
1½ pounds ground beef or lamb (lamb makes a more tasty dish)
  ⅛ teaspoon pepper
1½ teaspoons ground cinnamon

Sauté pine nuts in 1 tablespoon butter in a skillet over medium heat for 7 to 10 minutes. Melt remaining 4 tablespoons butter and add to all remaining ingredients in large bowl. Blend together and with clean hands stuff the squash.

Pastry:

1½ cups sifted all-purpose flour
  ½ cup vegetable shortening
  1 teaspoon salt
  5 tablespoons cold water

Blend all ingredients lightly with a pastry blender. Chill. Break off a piece of pastry the size of a medium-size egg; roll out thinly. Place squash on pastry and fold over, enclosing completely.

CAJUN SQUASH

Eudora Welty, one of my best tasters, commented, "This dish has the delicate flavor of squash yet is full of life." The casserole would be perfect served with a beef, lamb, or ham roast. There are two easy steps.

3 pounds yellow squash or 4½ (10-ounce)
**   packages frozen yellow squash**
1 teaspoon salt
1 tablespoon dried green onion
5 tablespoons butter or margarine, divided
¾ cup coarsely chopped onion
¾ cup chopped celery
½ cup chopped bell pepper
1 (10¾-ounce) can condensed cream of celery
**   soup**
2 tablespoons chili sauce or tomato catsup
1 tablespoon Worcestershire sauce
½ (4-inch) hot pepper, seeded and finely
**   chopped or ½ teaspoon Tabasco**
¼ teaspoon freshly ground black pepper
¼ teaspoon seasoned salt
¼ teaspoon baking powder
½ cup grated Parmesan cheese (optional)
**   Seasoned or buttered bread crumbs**

Wash squash and slice thinly, unpeeled. Combine 1 teaspoon salt, dried green onion, and 2 tablespoons butter in a saucepan and cover. Cook over low heat for 15 to 20 minutes or until squash is tender but not mushy. Do not add water; let this cook in its own juice plus the butter. This makes about 3½ cups cooked squash.

In a heavy skillet, sauté onion in 3 tablespoons butter over medium heat until onion is clear. Add chopped celery and bell peppers and cook until barely tender. This mixture should be a little crunchy. Along with cooked squash, add remaining ingredients except Parmesan cheese and bread crumbs. Simmer mixture a minute or two, taste, and add more salt if needed. Divide mixture between two buttered, 1½-quart oblong casseroles; sprinkle tops with Parmesan cheese and bread crumbs. Bake at 350° for 20 to 30 minutes or until casserole is bubbly and bread crumbs are toasted. Casserole can be frozen. Yield: 8 to 10 servings.

CHICKEN-BROCCOLI CASSEROLE

A luscious party dish that may be made ahead of time and put into the oven 30 minutes before serving. There are two easy steps.

Step 1:

5 pounds chicken breasts
3 celery ribs with leaves
1 teaspoon salt
1 teaspoon dried green onion
**   Water to cover**

Place breasts in a large pot or Dutch oven. Add remaining ingredients and cover with water. Bring to a simmering boil over high heat; then lower heat, and cook chicken until tender. Test with a fork; it should go in easily. Pour off liquid broth and save. This makes a good stock for later use, but it must be frozen to keep any length of time. Cool chicken and dice.

Step 2:

3 (10-ounce) packages chopped frozen
**   broccoli**
2 (10¾-ounce) cans condensed cream of
**   celery soup**
1 cup well-seasoned homemade mayonnaise
**   or commercial mayonnaise**
¼ teaspoon curry powder
4 tablespoons freshly strained lemon juice
**   Seasoned or buttered bread crumbs or**
**   commercial bread dressing**

Cook broccoli according to package directions; drain. Combine remaining ingredients including diced chicken from step 1 in a very large bowl and spoon into a buttered 3-quart casserole. Top with bread crumbs and bake in a preheated 350° oven for 25 minutes. This may be reheated, but keep refrigerated until used. Yield: 16 servings.

SQUASH SUPREME

A marvelous casserole, almost a meal in itself. For an economical meal, serve casserole with cold slaw, a chilled peeled tomato, and hot French bread.

**3 pounds fresh yellow or zuchini squash, or
　　2 quarts frozen yellow or zucchini squash**
1 cup chopped onion
1 teaspoon salt
1 carrot, grated
**1 (10¾-ounce) can condensed cream of
　　chicken soup**
1 cup commercial sour cream
½ teaspoon Tabasco
6 tablespoons butter, divided
½ (8-ounce) package herb-seasoned stuffing

Wash squash, cut crosswise into ½-inch thick slices. In a large saucepan cook squash, onion, and salt, covered, over low heat about 20 minutes or until tender. Stir often to prevent sticking since you add no water. Beat with potato masher until mashed to a pulp. Add grated carrot, soup, sour cream, and Tabasco. Use 2 tablespoons butter to grease two flat, 9- x 6-inch casseroles. Divide herb seasoning; sprinkle a fourth over bottom of each casserole. Divide squash mixture and pour a fourth over herb seasoning; sprinkle remaining fourths of herb seasoning over top of each casserole, and dot with butter. Bake uncovered in a preheated 325° oven for 50 to 60 minutes. Serve hot. This casserole freezes beautifully, and freezing seems to enhance the flavor even more. Yield: 12 servings.

GREEN BEAN AND SHRIMP CASSEROLE

A delightful combination.

1 quart water
1 teaspoon salt
1 lemon slice
4 celery tops
¼ teaspoon Tabasco
¼ teaspoon paprika
1 tablespoon Worcestershire sauce
**1 pound fresh or frozen shrimp or 3
　　(4½-ounce) cans shrimp**
**1 (9-ounce) package frozen French-style
　　green beans**
1 tablespoon strained lemon juice
1 teaspoon grated lemon rind
1 teaspoon dried green onion or grated onion
**1 (10¾-ounce) can condensed cream of celery
　　soup**
2 tablespoons chopped fresh or dried parsley
¼ teaspoon ground mace
½ cup grated Parmesan cheese
⅛ teaspoon paprika

For fresh shrimp, bring water, salt, lemon slice, celery tops, Tabasco, paprika, and Worcestershire sauce to a boil in a large saucepan. Boil for 10 minutes. Add shrimp, bring to a rolling boil and boil for 2 minutes. Cook frozen shrimp only half the time stated on the package. Drain shrimp and cut each into 3 pieces. After draining canned shrimp pour ice water over them and let stand 4 or 5 minutes; drain again. In a saucepan cook green beans in unsalted water according to package directions; drain well. Place cooked beans in a well-greased, oblong, 1½-quart casserole; sprinkle shrimp over top. Blend lemon juice and rind, onion, celery soup, parsley, and mace, and pour over shrimp. Cover with cheese and sprinkle with paprika. Bake in a preheated 350° oven for 20 to 25 minutes or until cheese melts and is golden brown. Yield: 6 servings.

TUNA GOALPOST CASSEROLE

A perfect casserole to serve after a football game on a cold winter day. It is also ideal to use for church luncheons. Have each lady prepare a casserole at home and bring to the church kitchen to be baked.

 2 (7-ounce) cans solid light tuna
½ large bell pepper, finely chopped
½ large onion, finely chopped
 1 tablespoon butter
 2 tablespoons all-purpose flour
½ cup milk
 1 (10¾-ounce) can condensed cream of
    mushroom soup
 1 (14½-ounce) can English peas, drained
 2 tablespoons Worcestershire sauce
½ teaspoon Tabasco
    Salt and pepper to taste
 2 cups shredded mild Longhorn cheese
 1 cup cracker crumbs

Run hot water over tuna to remove oil. In a skillet sauté bell pepper and onion in butter over medium heat. Add flour, milk and soup; cook until thickened. Add peas, tuna, Worcestershire, and Tabasco. Taste; you may need to add salt and pepper. Pour mixture into a buttered 1½-quart oblong casserole. Sprinkle cheese over top, then cracker crumbs, and bake in a preheated 350° oven for 20 minutes. Yield: 8 servings.

SCALLOPED OYSTERS

 1 quart oysters, drain and reserve liquid
½ cup oyster liquid
 6 tablespoons butter
 2 cups bread crumbs
½ teaspoon salt
    Cayenne pepper to taste

Wash oysters with ¾ cup cold water in colander and check for shell. Strain and measure liquid. Melt butter; add bread crumbs, salt, and

cayenne pepper. Line bottom of a greased 1½-quart oblong casserole or large shallow baking pan with a fourth of the crumb mixture. Then add half the oysters. Add a fourth of the crumb mixture and the remaining oysters and liquid. Cover with remaining half of the crumb mixture and bake in a preheated 350° oven for 30 minutes. Yield: 6 servings.

MIRLITONS WITH SHRIMP

A zesty casserole! Serve with well-seasoned green beans, whole broiled tomatoes, tossed green salad, and hot French bread for an elegant repast.

 5 mirlitons (enough for 5 cups cooked)
1½ pounds unshelled shrimp
 2 cups cold water
1¼ teaspoons crab boil, divided
 1 small onion, quartered
 1 celery rib
⅔ cup chopped green onion
½ cup minced onion
½ cup chopped celery
¼ cup fresh or dried chopped parsley
 3 tablespoons butter
½ cup chopped ham
 3 slices fresh bread
1½ teaspoons salt
¼ teaspoon Tabasco
 3 tablespoons seasoned bread crumbs

Cover mirlitons with water, and boil for about 1 hour or until tender; test with a fork. Cool, remove center seeds and skin, and cut into cube-size pieces. Cover unshelled shrimp with 2 cups water; add ¼ teaspoon crab boil, quartered onion, and celery rib. Simmer for 10 minutes; drain and reserve liquid. Peel shrimp and cut each into three or four pieces. In a very large skillet cook green onion, minced onion, chopped celery, and parsley in butter over medium heat about 7 minutes or until onion is transparent. Add ham, cut up shrimp, and cubed mirlitons. Take ½ cup shrimp liquid and pour into mirliton mixture. Soak bread in remaining stock and squeeze out in colander. Add salt, remaining 1 teaspoon instant crab boil, and Tabasco, and simmer for 20 minutes. When the liquid from mirlitons has been absorbed, taste and add more salt if needed. Pour into one 2-quart buttered casserole or two 1-quart casseroles, and sprinkle with seasoned bread crumbs. Bake in a preheated 375° oven about 20 minutes or until brown. Serve hot. This dish may be frozen. Mirlitons and shrimp stock may be cooked a day in advance. Refrigerate assembled casserole until ready to bake. Yield: 8 to 10 servings.

Variation: You may substitute zucchini for the mirlitons. Leave zucchini raw; peel and cut into cubes, and follow recipe.

EVELYN WILL'S OYSTER–SPINACH CASSEROLE

A gourmet dish to serve with highly seasoned meats such as beef shish kabobs, lamb, or a beef or pork roast.

2 (10-ounce) packages frozen chopped spinach
½ teaspoon lemon bits
2 teaspoons salt
4 tablespoons margarine, divided
3 green onions including tops, finely chopped
3 celery ribs including leaves, finely chopped
1 tablespoon chopped dried or frozen chopped parsley
1 pint oysters
2 tablespoons Worcestershire sauce
¼ teaspoon Tabasco
1 cup seasoned bread crumbs

According to package directions cook spinach until tender, after adding lemon bits, salt, and 1 tablespoon margarine to cooking water; drain. Melt remaining margarine over medium heat, and lightly sauté chopped onion, celery, and parsley.

Drain oysters and cut in half. Combine sautéed vegetables, spinach, Worcestershire and Tabasco, oysters, and seasoned bread crumbs. Toss mixture lightly with a fork. Spoon mixture into a flat or oblong casserole and bake in a preheated 350° oven for 30 minutes. This casserole reheats well and may be prepared in the morning for serving at night, or it can even be made a day in advance. Freezing is not recommended. Yield: 6 servings.

BAKED SHERRIED FRUIT CASSEROLE

A completely different casserole with the piquant flavor of fresh orange predominating the various canned fruits. Serve with turkey, chicken, ham, or pork. Ideal for a spring luncheon with chicken salad, hot rolls or cheese straws, and a party dessert.

1 (29-ounce) can peach halves
1 (29-ounce) can pear halves
1 (1-pound) can Queen Anne cherries
2 cups boiling water
½ cup white or black seedless raisins
1½ medium-size to large oranges, thinly sliced
1 cup sugar
3 tablespoons all-purpose flour
¼ teaspoon salt
4 tablespoons butter
½ cup medium-dry sherry

Drain and reserve juices from canned fruit. Slice pear and peach halves. Pour boiling water over raisins and sliced oranges, cover and let simmer in a saucepan over medium heat about 20 minutes. Drain and discard water. Sift sugar, flour, and salt into medium-size saucepan and mix with 1½ cups reserved fruit juices and butter; cook over medium heat until thickened; cool and add sherry. Place fruit in a 2-quart buttered oblong baking dish; cover with sauce and refrigerate overnight. Bake in a preheated 350° oven for 1 hour. Yield: 10 to 12 servings.

BAKED APRICOTS

A marvelous casserole to serve with chicken or turkey.

2 (17-ounce) cans unpeeled apricot halves
3 tablespoons firmly packed dark brown sugar
½ teaspoon ground cinnamon
¼ teaspoon ground ginger
3 tablespoons butter
7 round crackers

Drain apricots and reserve ⅓ cup juice; remove seeds from apricots. Combine sugar, cinnamon, and ginger. Butter a round 1½-quart casserole. Arrange a layer of one-half the apricots in bottom of casserole, sprinkle with one-half the spice mixture and dot with butter. Repeat process so that you have two layers or more. Add reserved ⅓ cup apricot juice. (You want just enough to moisten fruit but not make it runny.) Crumble crackers over the top and dot with remaining butter. Bake in a preheated 375° oven for 40 to 45 minutes. Yield: 4 to 5 servings.

BAKED CURRIED FRUIT

An exotic casserole to be served with any meat. This exciting combination of brown sugar, butter, curry powder, and mixed fruit particularly enhances cold sliced turkey, chicken, ham, or pork roast. Ideal for a luncheon or buffet supper.

1 (29-ounce) can pear halves
1 (29-ounce) can peach halves or 8 large ripe peaches, peeled and halved
1 (29-ounce) can pineapple chunks
1 (29-ounce) can unpeeled apricot halves
1 (4-ounce) jar maraschino cherries
½ cup butter
¾ cup firmly packed dark brown sugar
1 teaspoon curry powder

Drain and blot fruit with a paper towel. Butter a 3-quart round or oblong casserole and arrange pear and peach halves in bottom. Add a layer of pineapple chunks and apricots and sprinkle cherries over top.

Melt butter over low heat in a heavy skillet and add brown sugar and curry powder. (If you really like curry, add ½ teaspoon more.) Simmer briefly until blended. Dribble over fruit and bake in a preheated 275° oven for 1 hour. Yield: 10 to 12 servings.

BAKED STUFFED AVOCADO

Rich and tasty, this dish originated in the Arizona kitchen of Mrs. Walker Brock.

3 medium-size to large avocados, fully ripe
  Juice of 1 lime or lemon, strained
2 tablespoons butter
2 tablespoons all-purpose flour
1 cup milk, warmed
½ teaspoon salt
⅛ teaspoon ground mace
4 drops Tabasco
1 teaspoon dried green onion
⅛ teaspoon white pepper
1 cup fresh or frozen crabmeat
1 cup grated mild cheddar cheese (optional)

Cut avocados in half and remove seeds. Sprinkle each half with lemon or lime juice. Melt butter in a saucepan over medium heat. Remove from heat and stir in flour, blending with a wire whisk until smooth. Slowly add warm milk, stirring constantly. Add salt, mace, Tabasco, dried green onion, and white pepper. Cook over low heat until it begins to thicken. Add crabmeat and mix well. Fill avocados with mixture and top with cheese, if desired. Arrange avocados in oblong baking dish with ½ inch water in bottom. Bake in a preheated 350° oven for 20 minutes. Serve hot. Yield: 6 servings.

Crêpes, Quiches, Cheese and Egg Dishes

CHENEY CRÊPES

The technique for making crêpes requires only a deft hand and a bit of practice. Master the art and you open a whole new vista of entrées and dessert dishes to spark your menus.

Prepare crêpe batter two hours ahead of time and allow it to rest, enabling flour to expand and absorb liquid to cook better.

¼ teaspoon salt
1 cup all-purpose flour, spooned into cup
3 large eggs
1 to 1¼ cups whole or skimmed milk, divided
2 tablespoons melted butter or corn oil
3 tablespoons butter or oil for cooking
    crêpes, divided

Sift salt with measured flour into large bowl. Blend eggs and 1 cup milk in another bowl and beat well with wire whisk or wooden spatula. Add to flour mixture; blend well; stir in 2 tablespoons melted butter, and blend until batter is consistency of heavy cream. (You may need to add remaining ¼ cup milk.) Heat a 7- or 8-inch teflon or iron skillet over medium heat. Add 1 tablespoon butter and when it bubbles or sizzles slightly, pour in 3 table-spoons batter (slightly under ¼ cup). With your left hand, tilt pan quickly so that bottom is covered with a thin coating of batter. Keep pan moving. Put it back on heat for 3 or 4 minutes. When edges start to curl and brown, crêpe is ready to turn. Use a flexible metal spatula or catch a curled edge of crêpe between finger and thumb and flip it over for a minute or two on other side. Drain on paper towel.

Repeat this process brushing butter on skillet as needed. For immediate use, place crêpes on a platter in a warm oven. To refrigerate or freeze, first place waxed paper between crêpes. Crêpes freeze well.

Variations: To make dessert crêpes, follow same recipe and flavor batter with 3 table-spoons sugar and 1 tablespoon vanilla or 2 tablespoons cognac or grated lemon rind. Blend well, allow batter to rest, and cook as directed above. Yield: 12 crêpes.

CRÊPES

4 large eggs
2 cups milk
1½ teaspoons melted butter or margarine
1½ cups all-purpose flour, measured after
    sifting
1 teaspoon salt
16 teaspoons shortening, 1 teaspoon for each
    crêpe

In a medium-size bowl beat eggs until light; add milk and melted butter. Sift flour and salt into batter, blending until smooth. Melt 1 tea-spoon shortening in 8- or 9-inch teflon or crêpe skillet over medium heat. Pour in ¼ cup batter; tilt pan quickly so that batter runs and covers bottom. Cook until crêpe edges brown; then turn and cook about a half minute longer or until bottom browns. Flip pan over upside down, turning crêpe onto paper towel. Repeat process with next ¼ cup batter until all crêpes are cooked. Allow crêpes to cool, place waxed paper between them and refrigerate overnight. Yield: 16 crêpes—8 servings.

CRÊPES SPINACH JALAPEÑO

A savory dish, marvelous for a luncheon, yet inexpensive.

¾ cup water
1 (10-ounce) package frozen chopped spinach
1 teaspoon salt
3 tablespoons minced onion
6 tablespoons butter or margarine, divided
¼ cup all-purpose flour
½ cup evaporated milk
¼ cup reserved spinach liquid
¼ teaspoon pepper
¾ teaspoon celery salt
¼ teaspoon garlic salt
1 teaspoon Worcestershire sauce
   Salt to taste
½ (6-ounce) package jalapeño cheese
10 to 14 crêpes
1 (2-ounce) package whole almonds
10 to 14 tablespoons sherry

In a covered saucepan bring water to a rapid boil; add spinach and salt. Cover, bring to boil, lower heat and cook gently for 6 minutes or until tender. Drain in colander and reserve ¼ cup liquid. In a large skillet sauté onion in 3 tablespoons butter over medium heat for about 5 minutes; blend in flour with spoon or wire whisk. Slowly add milk, reserved spinach liquid, and seasonings. Cook until thickened, stirring constantly.

Add spinach and cheese which has been cut into small pieces; stir until melted. Taste and adjust seasonings, if desired. Fill crêpes across the center with a heaping tablespoon of spinach mixture. Fold crêpe over, placing in a large, greased, oblong, 2-quart casserole or a large baking dish.

In a heavy skillet sauté almonds in remaining 3 tablespoons butter. Drain on paper towel and slice thinly. Dribble 1 tablespoon sherry and sprinkle 1 tablespoon finely sliced almonds over each crêpe. Bake in a preheated 350° oven for 20 minutes. Serve hot. These will hold on warm for 30 minutes or more without affecting the texture. Yield: 10 to 14 crêpes.

Variation: For oyster-spinach crêpes, drain well 1 pint oysters on paper towels. Check for shell, chop finely, and add ½ teaspoon Pernod to oysters. Add to spinach mixture after cheese is added, and cook only long enough to blend well. Yield: 14 crêpes (allow 2 crêpes per serving as an entrée).

APRICOT PALATSCHINKEN

A marvelous Hungarian dessert. Spread 1 tablespoon apricot puree on a crêpe and roll up. Serve hot, plain or with a dollop of sour cream or with whipped cream on the side. One cup of puree will fill 12 crêpes. This makes a delicious topping for ice cream or pancakes.

1 cup dried apricots
   Water to cover
1⅓ cups sugar
2 tablespoons dark rum
24 Crêpes (see recipe for Crêpes in this chapter)

Cover apricots with water in saucepan and bring to boil over medium heat. Keep on simmering boil for 35 to 40 minutes. Apricots must be completely tender. Add sugar the last ten minutes of cooking. Puree apricots in blender or put through food mill or ricer; add rum to mixture. Puree will keep under refrigeration for several weeks in sealed pint jar. This freezes also. Yield: 2 cups puree—24 crêpes.

LOUISE C. HAMILTON'S CHICKEN MUSHROOM CRÊPES

The organized hostess prepares her crêpes in advance and refrigerates them. But the hostess with real ingenuity prepares crêpes and filling prior to party time. Here's a winner.

4 large whole chicken breasts, about 3 pounds, skinned
2 tablespoons lemon juice
½ cup butter or margarine, divided
2 tablespoons olive oil
1 pound fresh mushrooms or 2 (7-ounce) cans sliced mushrooms, packed in butter, drained
¼ teaspoon paprika
¼ teaspoon freshly ground black pepper
1 teaspoon salt
1 teaspoon Worcestershire sauce
⅛ teaspoon ground nutmeg
5 tablespoons all-purpose flour
2 envelopes instant chicken broth
2 (13¾-ounce) cans chicken broth
16 crêpes
Parsley

Cut chicken into bite-sized pieces and sprinkle with lemon juice. In heavy skillet heat 6 tablespoons butter and olive oil over medium heat. Add chicken and cook slowly turning often for 8 to 10 minutes; do not brown. Remove with slotted spoon to large mixing bowl. Wash fresh mushrooms and dry on paper towels; slice thinly. Add remaining 2 tablespoons butter to skillet over medium heat and cook mushrooms for 7 to 10 minutes or until tender, stirring often. Stir in all seasonings and cook a minute longer. Using a slotted spoon, remove mushrooms to bowl with chicken. Add flour to liquid in skillet, stirring constantly until smooth. Add instant chicken broth and canned broth and bring sauce to a boil, stirring constantly. At once stir in chicken and mushrooms and boil for 1 minute. Cool in large bowl and refrigerate overnight. About one hour before

serving time, cook filling in double boiler over rapidly boiling water for 30 minutes or until hot. Spoon ⅓ cup filling into center of each crêpe, roll tightly; place seam side down in lightly greased casserole or 13- x 9- x 2-inch baking pan. Bake in a preheated 400° oven for 20 minutes. Garnish with parsley. Yield: 16 crêpes—8 servings.

STRAWBERRY CRÊPES-FITZGERALD

2 (3-ounce) packages cream cheese
6 tablespoons commercial sour cream
2 tablespoons whipping cream
12 dessert crêpes (see recipe for Crêpes in this chapter)
Sauce

In a mixing bowl beat cream cheese, sour cream, and whipping cream until fluffy. Chill; remove from refrigerator 30 minutes before serving. Spoon a heaping tablespoon of mixture into center of crêpe and fold over. Place 2 crêpes per serving on dessert plates and spoon Sauce over each. Yield: 12 crêpes—6 servings.

Sauce:

1 quart ripe strawberries
⅔ cup or more sugar
4 tablespoons butter
½ cup sugar
1 ounce strawberry liqueur
1 ounce kirsch
2 ounces warmed brandy

Wash and slice strawberries into halves; add ⅔ cup sugar to sweeten. In chafing dish or saucepan combine butter, ½ cup sugar, strawberry liqueur, and kirsch. Add sweetened strawberries. Cook until sugar and butter thicken mixture very slightly. Pour warmed brandy mixture over and ignite. Spoon carefully until flame subsides. Ladle over crêpes.

PUDDING CRÊPES

2 eggs
1 (3¼-ounce) package gelatin vanilla pudding
and pie filling
½ cup half-and-half
    Strawberries, halved and sweetened, or fruit
    jam
    Powdered sugar
    Commercial whipped topping (optional)
    Whole strawberries (optional)

Beat eggs until very light and frothy. Add pudding mix and half-and-half, mixing well. Pour ¼ cup batter at a time into hot, well-buttered 10-inch skillet. When golden brown, turn to brown other side. Spoon strawberries into center of each warm crêpe and roll up. Sprinkle powdered sugar over top. Garnish with prepared whipped topping and whole strawberries, if desired. Yield: 5 to 6 crêpes.

SEAFOOD CRÊPES

1 cup white crabmeat or 1 cup raw shrimp,
    peeled and deveined
1½ (10¾-ounce) cans condensed cream of
    shrimp soup
¼ pound fresh mushrooms, sliced
1 tablespoon minced onion
¼ cup minced green pepper
½ cup chicken bouillon
¼ teaspoon ground mace
1 cup shredded sharp cheddar cheese
1 tablespoon lemon juice
1 tablespoon dry white wine or vermouth
    Dash Tabasco
¼ teaspoon white pepper
    Salt to taste
12 to 14 crêpes

Check crabmeat for bits of shell or cut shrimp into small pieces. Combine soup and seafood. Cook mushrooms, onion, and pepper in bouillon over medium heat until tender. Add to soup mixture. Add remaining ingredients except crêpes, and heat slowly just until cheese melts, stirring often. Fill crêpes, roll and place in single layer in a large, ungreased, shallow baking dish or pan with sides. Pour remaining sauce around and over crêpes. Bake in a preheated 300° oven for 1 hour. Yield: 12 to 14 crêpes—6 to 7 servings.

MARIE-ROSE TIZON'S QUICHE LORRAINE

Delicious and easy to make.

1 (10-ounce) package frozen patty shells,
    defrosted, or pastry for one crust pie
1 medium-size onion
2 tablespoons butter
1 cup scalded milk
2 large eggs
¼ teaspoon white pepper
    Dash nutmeg
    Dash cayenne pepper
    Salt to taste
½ cup grated sharp cheddar cheese
4 slices Canadian bacon, cubed

Press patty shells together and roll to fit one 8-inch flan pan or same size circular foil or cakepan with straight sides. Line pan with crust, trim pastry, flute edges, and prick crust. Bake in a preheated 450° oven for 10 minutes. Remove briefly from oven and fill.

Peel and slice onion. Sauté sliced onions in butter over medium heat until soft and golden, but not browned. Place in bottom of pie shell. In a large bowl beat milk, eggs, and seasonings until blended. Add cheese and bacon and cover onions with mixture. Bake at 325° for 30 minutes until custard is firm in center. Test with silver knife. Yield: 1 (8-inch) quiche—6 servings.

QUICHE LORRAINE

For a luncheon or supper serve this delicacy with a crisp green salad, hot French bread, cold white wine, and a light dessert of fruit poached in grenadine.

1 package piecrust mix (single shell) or prepare own recipe
1 egg, lightly beaten
  Custard Filling

Prepare piecrust according to package directions, substituting beaten egg plus enough water to complete the amount of liquid required. Roll out and use pastry to line bottom and sides of an ungreased 9-inch piepan, fluting with a high edge. Prick sides and bottom with a four-tine fork. Chill for half an hour. Bake in a preheated 425° oven for 15 to 20 minutes. When pastry is golden, remove from oven.

Custard Filling:

  1 teaspoon onion puree or 1 tablespoon minced green onion
  1 tablespoon butter
  ¼ pound St. Paulin, Port Salut, Bonbel, or Gruyeré cheese, shredded
  1 (3½-ounce) can Champignons de Paris
  3 egg yolks
  1 whole egg
  ½ teaspoon dry mustard
  1 teaspoon Dijon mustard
  ⅛ teaspoon cayenne pepper or 3 dashes Tabasco
  ½ to 1 teaspoon salt
  1¾ cups half-and-half, scalded

In a skillet, cook onion puree in butter for 3 or 4 minutes. In a bowl, combine shredded cheese and drained mushrooms. Add onion and spread over bottom of pie shell. Beat egg yolks and whole egg; add mustards and seasonings and continue beating until well blended. Beat in scalded half-and-half. Spoon cream over cheese mixture in pie shell. Bake in a preheated 350° oven for 40 to 45 minutes or until knife inserted in center comes out clean. Serve warm or hot. Yield: 1 (9-inch) quiche—6 large servings or countless small servings for hors d'oeurves.

Note: Champignons are cultivated mushrooms with chopped truffles and may be bought at any fine food store. Whole mushrooms broiled in butter and cut in half, either fresh or canned, may be substituted; add half that amount of chopped truffles.

SHRIMP-MUSHROOM QUICHE

⅓ pound raw peeled and deveined shrimp or 1 (5-ounce) can shrimp
1 (3-ounce) can sliced mushrooms, drained or ¼ pound fresh mushrooms, sliced
1 (9-inch) baked pastry shell, cooled
¾ cup shredded pasteurized process American cheese
1 (10¾-ounce) can condensed cream of shrimp soup
¼ cup milk
4 eggs, slightly beaten
  Pinch ground mace
⅛ teaspoon Tabasco

Chop raw shrimp finely. If using canned shrimp, drain, rinse with cold water, and let stand for 5 minutes. Drain again and chop canned shrimp finely. Arrange shrimp and drained mushrooms in baked pastry shell; sprinkle with cheese.

In a small saucepan combine soup and milk, stirring constantly over medium heat. Bring just to boil, stirring constantly. Gradually stir into eggs. Season with mace and Tabasco. Pour soup mixture over cheese. Bake in a preheated 325° oven for 40 to 45 minutes or until knife inserted off-center comes out clean. Let stand 10 minutes before cutting. Yield: 1 (9-inch) quiche—6 servings as entrée for luncheon, or numerous small servings as hors d'ouevres.

EMPRESS HOTEL'S QUICHE LORRAINE

4 thin slices bacon
1 medium-size onion, diced
1 ounce mushroom, chopped
2 teaspoons chopped parsley
1 (9-inch) unbaked pie shell
2 ounces Gruyère cheese, cut into small cubes
3 ounces Old Canadian cheese, cut into small cubes
1 pint half-and-half
4 eggs, beaten
   Dash garlic salt
   Dash white pepper
   Dash ground nutmeg

In large skillet sauté bacon, onion, mushrooms, and parsley over medium heat; drain off any excess fat, and cool. Fill bottom of pie shell with cheeses and sautéed ingredients. Combine cream, beaten eggs, and seasonings and pour into pie shell. Bake in a preheated 400° oven for 10 minutes. Reduce heat to 350° and continue baking for another 30 minutes. Serve warm. Yield: 1 (9-inch) quiche—6 servings.

MACARONI AND CHEESE DELUXE

Very tasty and made without butter or eggs.

3 tablespoons cake flour
3 tablespoons nonfat dry milk powder
1 teaspoon seasoned salt
½ teaspoon monosodium glutamate
⅛ teaspoon white pepper
2 cups warm water
8 ounces elbow macaroni
3 quarts salted water (1 tablespoon salt)
8 ounces sharp cheddar cheese, shredded
1 teaspoon prepared mustard
1 teaspoon Worcestershire sauce
1 tablespoon margarine

Combine first 5 ingredients in a cup. Put warm water in a 1-quart fruit jar, and pour dry ingre-dients on top. Close jar and shake well for a few minutes. Pour into a heavy skillet, and cook over high heat stirring constantly to keep from sticking. The sauce will be thick and smooth.

In a large saucepan boil macaroni in boiling salted water for 8 to 10 minutes or until tender. Drain and run cold water through macaroni; drain again. Grease a 1½-quart casserole with margarine. Line bottom with shredded cheese; then add a layer of macaroni. Continue layer-ing, ending with cheese on top. Add mustard and Worcestershire sauce to hot white sauce and pour over top of cheese. Bake in a pre-heated 350° oven about 30 minutes or until bubbly and lightly browned. This is delicious reheated to serve another day; refrigerate until used. Yield: 8 servings.

ALLAN CHENEY'S LASAGNE

¼ cup olive or salad oil
1 large onion, diced
1 clove garlic, minced
2 tablespoons finely chopped parsley
1 pound ground beef chuck
1 (28-ounce) can Italian tomatoes, undrained
1 (6-ounce) can tomato paste
2 bay leaves
1 teaspoon salt
¼ teaspoon sugar
4 tablespoons butter
1 small onion, diced
3 tablespoons all-purpose flour
2 cups milk
¾ cup freshly grated Parmesan cheese
2 egg yolks, slightly beaten
1 tablespoon salt
½ (1-pound) package lasagne
1 pound ricotta cheese

In a large heavy skillet heat oil over medium heat and sauté large diced onion, garlic, and parsley about 8 minutes or until onion is tender and transparent. Add beef and sauté until well browned, stirring occasionally. Add tomatoes, tomato paste, bay leaves, salt, and sugar and mix well. Bring to simmering boil, reduce heat, cover, and simmer for 1½ hours, stirring occasionally. The sauce should be thick.

In a small saucepan melt butter over medium heat and add small diced onion, and cook about 8 minutes or until onion is tender. Remove onion with slotted spoon, and add flour to melted butter slowly with a wire whisk. When blended add milk and Parmesan cheese, and cook until sauce thickens. Return onions to sauce, add slightly beaten egg yolks, and cook about 10 minutes longer.

In a large soup kettle bring 3 quarts water to boil, add salt and lasagne, 2 or 3 pieces of noodles at a time. Return water to boiling, cook uncovered for 15 to 20 minutes until lasagne is tender when tasted. Drain; rinse under cold water.

To assemble lasagne, grease a 13- x 9- x 2-inch baking dish, place a layer of noodles, a layer of tomato sauce, a layer of cheese sauce, a layer of ricotta cheese. Repeat layers putting ricotta cheese before cheese sauce. (Cheese sauce should be top layer.) Bake at 325° for 20 minutes; then put under broiler until cheese is thoroughly melted. Yield: 6 to 8 servings.

EGGPLANT MANICOTTI

2 medium-size (3- x 6-inch) eggplants
4 tablespoons olive oil, more if needed
1 cup grated Mozzarella cheese
⅓ cup ricotta cheese or dry cottage cheese
½ cup grated Parmesan cheese
1 large egg, well beaten
1 tablespoon minced parsley
1 tablespoon chopped prosciutto or ham
1 teaspoon basil
 Salt and pepper to taste
1 (8-ounce) can tomato sauce

Peel eggplants, cut in half, and slice into thin long slices about ⅛ inch thick. In a heavy skillet sauté each slice in oil over medium heat, turning only once and cooking just long

enough for the eggplant to become limp enough to roll. Cool slices on paper towels.

Combine remaining ingredients except tomato sauce. Spread each eggplant slice with a thin layer of cheese mixture. Roll each slice and place in a large shallow casserole; top with tomato sauce. Bake in a preheated 350° oven for 20 to 25 minutes or until bubbly. Yield: 8 to 10 servings.

EMMA KATHERINE BIRCHETT'S CHEESE SOUFFLÉ

Marvelous, never-fail soufflé, this is best made a day in advance.

1 tablespoon butter
2 cups white bread, crustless and pulled into
    small pieces
2 cups shredded sharp cheddar cheese
2 cups milk
1 teaspoon salt
⅛ teaspoon cayenne pepper
1 teaspoon Worcestershire sauce
1 teaspoon prepared mustard
5 large eggs, well beaten
 Paprika

Butter a 1½-quart casserole, and line with pieces of pulled bread, layer with shredded cheese. Repeat layers until both bread and cheese are used up. Add milk and seasonings, except paprika, to well-beaten eggs. Pour over casserole. Let stand at least 8 hours in the refrigerator. Remove from refrigerator 1 hour before baking. Sprinkle paprika over top. Place casserole in pan of warm water and bake in a preheated 350° oven for 45 minutes to 1 hour. This soufflé will hold without falling. Yield: 6 servings.

111

MARIE-ROSE TIZON'S CHEESE SOUFFLÉ

3 level tablespoons butter
3 level tablespoons all-purpose flour
1 cup milk
1 cup shredded cheese
  Parsley or chives, minced (optional)
  Salt and pepper to taste
3 eggs, separated

In saucepan over low heat blend butter and flour without browning. Add milk gradually and stir until the mixture boils. Add cheese and seasonings and set aside to cool. Beat egg yolks and add to mixture in saucepan. It doesn't have to be entirely cooled. Beat egg whites to a stiff froth and fold into mixture. Turn into deep, well-greased 1-quart baking dish, and bake in a preheated 350° oven about 25 minutes. Serve immediately. Yield: 4 servings.

MICHEL GARRAUD'S MUSHROOM RAREBIT

½ pound fresh small mushrooms
 6 tablespoons butter
 1 small onion, chopped
¼ cup all-purpose flour
   1 cup milk
⅛ teaspoon ground nutmeg
½ teaspoon Worcestershire sauce
   Salt and pepper to taste
1½ cups finely grated Swiss cheese, divided
 8 small slices bread
   Chopped parsley

Rinse, dry, and slice mushrooms. Melt butter in skillet over medium heat, and cook onion for about 7 minutes or until tender. Stir in mushrooms and cook slowly for 3 to 4 minutes, stirring. Sprinkle in flour and remove from heat. Gradually blend in milk; add nutmeg, Worcestershire sauce, and salt and pepper. Return to heat, bring to a boil, then simmer for 2 to 3 minutes, stirring constantly. Remove from heat, stir in ½ cup cheese. Toast one side of bread, top toasted side with mixture. Sprinkle remaining cheese on top. Put under hot grill until golden brown. Garnish with parsley. Yield: 4 servings.

MACARONI LOAF AND PIQUANT SAUCE

Ma cari! Ma caroni! Legend has it that these were the exclamations of joy of an Italian cardinal centuries ago, when he first tasted the delicacy we know today as macaroni. I hope you will want to rejoice over my macaroni loaf for its savory taste, ease of making, and inexpensive cost.

3 quarts cold water
1 tablespoon salt
5 ounces macaroni
1 cup fresh bread crumbs (4 slices bread)
1 cup scalded milk
1 (4-ounce) jar pimientos, finely chopped
¾ cup shredded sharp cheddar cheese
1½ tablespoons finely chopped onion
1 tablespoon finely chopped parsley
½ cup melted butter or margarine
3 eggs, well beaten
1 teaspoon salt, divided
¼ teaspoon cayenne pepper
  Piquant Sauce
  Parsley

In a large kettle bring water to a boil, add 1 tablespoon salt and macaroni. Follow package directions for cooking time, stirring often. The macaroni should be tender but firm to the bite; drain at once. In a large bowl combine macaroni and remaining ingredients in order, except eggs, salt, and cayenne pepper. Add ½ teaspoon salt to the beaten eggs, the remaining ½ teaspoon to the macaroni mixture. Add eggs and cayenne pepper. Pour into a greased 9- x 5- x 3-inch loaf pan. Place in a pan of water and bake in a preheated 300° oven for 1½ hours. Place cooked loaf on a large heated platter and pour Piquant Sauce over it. You may wish to divide loaf and freeze half before you add sauce to it. Add sprigs of parsley for a more festive dish. Yield: 1 (9- x 5- x 3-inch) loaf—8 servings.

Piquant Sauce:

¼ cup butter or margarine
3 tablespoons instant-blending flour
2 cups liquid (mushroom juice and milk)
1 (4-ounce) can mushrooms
2 teaspoons lemon juice
1 teaspoon salt
½ teaspoon monosodium glutamate
⅛ teaspoon white pepper

In a heavy skillet melt butter over low heat. Add flour and blend with wire whisk until smooth. Add warmed, drained mushroom juice with enough milk to make 2 cups liquid, stirring constantly. Add mushrooms and seasonings and coninue stirring until sauce thickens. This makes 2 cups.

SOUFFLÉED CHEESE OMELET

6 eggs, separated
⅓ cup whipping cream
1 teaspoon salt, divided
⅛ teaspoon white pepper
⅛ teaspoon paprika
½ cup grated Gruyère cheese
2 tablespoons butter
Minced parsley or chives

In large bowl beat egg yolks well with wire whisk or electric mixer on high speed. Add cream, ½ teaspoon salt, white pepper, and paprika and beat a few seconds more. In another large bowl beat egg whites with remaining ½ teaspoon salt until they hold stiff peaks. Lightly fold egg yolk mixture along with grated cheese into beaten egg whites. In an ovenproof 9-inch skillet heat butter over

medium high heat and pour in egg mixture, stir for a few seconds and transfer to a preheated 375° oven for 8 minutes until it is puffed and set. Slide omelet, folding it in half, onto heated platter and garnish with minced parsley or chives. Serve with toast and butter. For plain omelet omit cheese. Yield: 4 to 6 servings.

LES OEUFS MIMOSA—EGGS WITH A DASH

From Madame Poulpiquet's kitchen in Paris comes this marvelous and easy way of preparing hard-boiled eggs. A good and inexpensive luncheon dish. Accompanied by a tossed green salad and hot French bread, Les Oeufs Mimosa make a delightful meal.

6 large eggs
1½ teaspoons salt, divided
3 tablespoons butter
3 tablespoons all-purpose flour
1¼ cups hot milk
⅛ teaspoon white pepper
2 tablespoons chopped chives
6 small fresh mushrooms or canned button mushrooms

Place eggs in boiling water with 1 teaspoon salt; reduce heat and keep water just under boiling point. Cook for 30 minutes and plunge into cold water to prevent discoloration of yolks. Peel eggs as soon as they are cooled. Slice eggs in half lengthwise and remove yolks.

Melt butter in teflon or iron skillet over low heat. Blend in flour with wire whisk. Slowly stir in hot milk and continue stirring until mixture is smooth and boiling. Add white pepper, remaining ½ teaspoon salt, and chives. On heated plate arrange the egg whites with a mushroom in the center of each, and cover with cream sauce. Grate egg yolks over top of each egg. Yield: 4 servings.

DEVILED EGGS

12 hard-boiled eggs
¾ cup mayonnaise
 1 teaspoon dry mustard
 1 tablespoon India relish or diced sweet
    pickle
½ teaspoon salt
⅛ teaspoon cayenne pepper
    Parsley sprigs

Halve cooked eggs. Remove yolks, being careful not to break whites. Place yolks in a small bowl and mash with a fork. Add remaining ingredients and mix until smooth. Spoon mixture into egg whites, and decorate with sprigs of parsley. Serve cold. Yield: 24 egg halves.

BOILED CUSTARD

Reynolds' favorite.

 1 quart milk
1½ cups sugar
 ⅛ teaspoon salt
 4 tablespoons all-purpose flour
 6 large eggs, room temperature
 2 teaspoons vanilla extract

Allow milk to warm slowly in top of a large double boiler. Blend sugar, salt, and flour in a small bowl. Beat eggs slightly and add dry ingredients; mix well. Add egg-flour mixture slowly to warmed milk using a wire whisk. Stir constantly with whisk, reaching all over bottom of pan. When mixture thickens and will coat a metal or silver spoon, remove from heat and add vanilla. Cool pan in bowl of ice and stir often. Yield: 1½ quarts.

CREAMED LEFTOVER EASTER EGGS

Serve hot on toast or waffles, in noodle nest, or over cornbread. For brunch serve over sliced tomatoes or cooked asparagus on toast.

¼ cup butter or margarine
 3 tablespoons all-purpose flour
 1 teaspoon salt
⅛ teaspoon pepper
⅛ teaspoon paprika
 1 teaspoon grated onion
 2 cups milk, warmed
 6 hard-boiled eggs, sliced or chopped
 1 tablespoon chopped parsley

Melt butter; add flour and seasonings and blend well. Cook over low heat until bubbly. Add the milk slowly and cook, stirring constantly until thickened. Add eggs and parsley. Heat thoroughly. Add more seasonings if desired. Yield: 2 to 3 servings.

Variation: For a gourmet food, mix with chicken, ham, or tuna, mixed vegetables, broccoli and carrots for a casserole.

CHOCOLATE BAKED CUSTARD

Chocolate at its best.

 3 cups milk
½ cup plus 1 tablespoon semisweet chocolate
    pieces
 4 large whole eggs or 3 egg yolks plus 2 whole
    eggs
½ cup plus 1 tablespoon sugar
 1 teaspoon vanilla extract
⅛ teaspoon salt

Combine milk and chocolate in a saucepan; stir over low heat until chocolate melts. Cool slightly. In a large mixing bowl beat eggs, sugar, vanilla, and salt with a wire whisk just long enough to blend thoroughly. Stir in chocolate mixture and pour into eight 6-ounce cups. Place cups in a pan of hot water 1-inch in depth and bake in a preheated 300° oven for 40 to 45 minutes. Insert silver knife 1 inch from edge of cup; this should come out clean. Cool on wire rack. Serve warm or cold. I prefer to eat mine cold. Keep under refrigeration until used. Yield: 8 (6-ounce) cups.

Variations: For a company dessert serve with whipped cream sweetened with 2 tablespoons sugar, 1 teaspoon brandy or vanilla, and slivered almonds, or serve with a dollop of vanilla ice cream.

If you prefer a more chocolate flavor and not as sweet, use the following ingredients and follow the method given above.

3 cups commercial chocolate milk
⅓ cup semisweet chocolate pieces
4 large eggs
1 teaspoon vanilla extract
⅛ teaspoon salt

EASY-AS-PIE EGG CASSEROLE

5 large hard-boiled eggs
⅓ stick butter, divided
1 (10¾-ounce) can condensed cream of mushroom soup
3 slices bread, toasted and crushed (for a delicate flavor) or 1 cup seasoned commercial bread crumbs (for a highly seasoned flavor)

Put eggs through a sieve. Butter a 1-quart casserole. Place alternate layers of eggs, soup, and bread crumbs in casserole; repeat. Dot top with remaining butter, and place casserole in a pan of hot water. Bake in a preheated 350° oven for 20 minutes. Turn off heat and leave for 10 minutes longer. Serve immediately. Yield: 4 to 6 servings.

DIABETIC'S BAKED CUSTARD

A delightfully smooth custard, easy to make.

7 whole grains saccharine tablets
1 tablespoon hot water
4 large eggs
3 cups milk, whole or high protein
1 teaspoon vanilla extract
Ground nutmeg (optional)

Dissolve saccharine in hot water. Beat together all ingredients except nutmeg in a large bowl until thoroughly blended, using a wire whisk or dover egg beater. Pour mixture into a 1½-quart casserole or into eight 6-ounce pyrex cups; sprinkle nutmeg lightly over top, if desired. Add hot water to pans to at least 1 inch in depth; it should come at least halfway up the sides of the containers. Bake in a preheated 300° oven for 50 minutes to 1 hour. Test with a silver knife blade; if it comes out clean, the custard is done. Serve hot or cold. Cool on wire rack before refrigerating. Yield: 8 servings.

EGG MOUSSE IN INDIVIDUAL POTS

This is a tasty luncheon or supper dish. The mousse may be made in an oblong casserole, cut into squares, and served atop tomato aspic for a very attractive combination.

4 large hard-boiled eggs
1 tablespoon unflavored gelatin
1 cup beef stock or 1 beef bouillon cube dissolved in boiling water
2 teaspoons Worcestershire sauce
1 tablespoon chopped, drained anchovy
1 tablespoon tomato catsup
⅛ teaspoon freshly ground black pepper
1 cup whipping cream
Salt to taste

Put eggs through a sieve. Dissolve gelatin in hot beef stock, add Worcestershire sauce, the anchovy which has been mashed with a fork into a paste, tomato catsup, and black pepper. Set aside ¼ cup liquid mixture for garnish. Add cream to remaining liquid mixture and blend well; add eggs and salt, stirring often until mousse sets. When ready to serve, chop up the reserved ¼ cup liquid which has been allowed to set, and decorate the top of each serving. Yield: 5 servings.

Dazzling Desserts

JANE BROCK'S ALMOND CHOCOLATE JOY

A superb dessert and easy to make. Frozen in 2½-inch foil baking cups, these are extra-rich and a joy to have on hand.

⅔ cup commercial chocolate syrup
⅔ cup sweetened condensed milk
2 cups whipping cream
1 teaspoon vanilla extract
1 teaspoon brandy
1 teaspoon almond extract
⅓ cup slivered almonds
1 tablespoon butter
¾ teaspoon salt

In a large mixing bowl blend chocolate syrup, condensed milk, cream, and flavorings. Refrigerate for 12 hours or overnight. Place slivered almonds on a cookie sheet, avoiding stacking. Cook in a preheated 325° oven for 10 minutes; add butter and stir until almonds are coated. Sprinkle with salt over all and return to oven. Lower heat to 250° and cook for 20 minutes longer. Stir twice during cooking period. The toasted almonds should be a golden brown. Cool on paper towel to remove excess salt. The next day beat syrup-condensed milk mixture until it is light and fluffy and stands in light peaks. Fold in almonds. Place 2½-inch foil baking cups on cookie sheet and, using a ladle, fill each one. Freeze immediately. After they are frozen, place in a plastic bag. For Saint Patrick's Day use green-lined cups and top with a dollop of whipped cream and a green maraschino cherry. Yield: 20 servings.

CHARLOTTE AUX POMMES— APPLE CHARLOTTE

This elegant dessert created for Queen Charlotte of England on the occasion of a state visit to France is unsurpassed for company fare and may be made ahead of time. It is not expensive, but as my Mammy used to say, "It do take time and plenty of elbow grease."

5 pounds (12 large) tart red apples, Rome Beauty, Red Gravestein, Jonathan, or Winesap
2 tablespoons strained lemon juice
4 tablespoons sugar
1 cup apricot preserves
1 cup sugar
3 tablespoons butter
2 tablespoons vanilla extract
¼ cup dark rum

Core, peel, and slice apples; cover with lemon juice and a clean wet dish towel to prevent discoloration while preparing. Place apples and 4 tablespoons sugar in a heavy-bottomed pan and cover; add no water. Cook down into

116

applesauce at medium heat, stirring often. Add apricot preserves and put mixture through sieve. Add 1 cup sugar, butter, and flavorings to mixture and cook about 30 minutes over medium heat. Stir often to prevent sticking. When the puree begins to spit and sputter like a volcano, it is done. Taste to see if more sugar is needed. To complete recipe you need:

1 large loaf thinly sliced sandwich bread
2 cups clarified butter (2 cups plus 2
**   tablespoons butter)**
**   Glaze**

In selecting bread, press the package; you do not want the soft squashy variety. I prefer Pepperidge Farm. To clarify butter, place 2 cups plus 2 tablespoons butter in a heavy iron skillet over low heat; melt slowly. On no condition leave the room when it is cooking or your kitchen could go up in flames. When butter is melted, skim off foam that rises to surface. Set aside a few minutes and then ladle or pour off 2 cups clear butter. Do not allow any of milky sediment to come with it.

Remove crusts from bread. Use a charlotte mold or 1¾-quart cylindrical baking casserole for cooking dessert. To cut bread for bottom of mold turn mold upside down and use for a pattern. Brush one side of bread with clarified butter and place in bottom of mold, butter side down. Cut enough bread into triangles to place around inner edge of mold. After dipping in same butter, lap each piece over the other, pushing bread against sides of mold. Fill mold with a part of apple-apricot puree; cut remaining bread into 1½-inch long strips, dip into butter, and cover apple puree. Continue to alternate additions of bread strips and puree, ending with bread strips on top.

Place a pan of water on rack below mold to prevent bottom from getting too brown. Place on middle rack and bake in a preheated 425° oven for 30 minutes. Slip a knife between bread and sides of mold, if bread is golden brown the charlotte is done. Remove from

oven and cool on a wire rack for 15 minutes. Turn mold over onto a serving tray; lift the mold up a few minutes to see if sides of charlotte will hold. If it appears it might collapse, lower mold over dessert again; it will firm up as it cools. Test every 6 or 7 minutes until mold can be removed. Brush top with Glaze; serve dessert warm or cold with cream, either plain or whipped, or a custard sauce, accompanied by champagne or coffee. Yield: 8 to 10 servings.

Glaze:

½ cup sieved apricot preserves
3 tablespoons dark rum
2 tablespoons sugar

Boil apricot preserves, rum, and sugar in a saucepan over medium heat until thickened. Spread over charlotte.

BANANA MOUSSE

1 egg, well beaten
3 tablespoons sugar
1 tablespoon all purpose flour
1 cup milk
1 cup banana puree (1 large or 3 medium-size
**   bananas)**
**   Pinch salt**
1 teaspoon vanilla extract
1 cup whipping cream, whipped

Combine egg, sugar, flour, and milk in a double boiler over rapidly boiling water; stir until thickened. Allow mixture to cool. Remove white strip from banana and puree.

To cooled mixture, add salt, vanilla, banana puree, and whipped cream. Blend well and freeze. Yield: 4 servings.

APRICOT SOUFFLÉ

The apricot at its best. In making a soufflé, an unlined copper bowl and balloon whip beater do the best job; a portable beater is next best because by moving it around, more air is mixed into the whites. Be sure whites contain no particle of yolk and that bowl and beater are free of any grease. A test for perfect stiffness is to place a whole egg on top of beaten egg whites. If it stays up, you've beaten long enough.

1 cup dried apricots
  Water to cover
1 cup sugar
1 tablespoon dark rum
1 tablespoon strained lemon juice
1 teaspoon grated lemon rind (about half a
  lemon)
1 tablespoon cooked apricot juice
5 large egg whites, room temperature
¼ teaspoon cream of tartar
  Whipped cream (optional)

Cover apricots with water in a saucepan and bring to a boil over medium heat. Cover and keep on simmering boil for 30 to 35 minutes; apricots must be completely tender. Test with fork; the tines should go in easily. Drain and reserve 1 tablespoon juice. Puree apricots in blender or put through food mill or ricer.

To the apricot puree add: sugar, rum, lemon juice and rind, and apricot juice; blend well. Beat whites on low speed of electric mixer until foamy; then add cream of tartar and beat on high speed until whites are stiff and stand in upright peaks. Take a big spoonful and stir into apricot mixture to lighten it. With rubber spatula scoop remaining whites on top. Using spatula, cut down from top center of mixture to bottom of bowl and draw spatula quickly toward you against edge of bowl and up to left and out. Continue this movement at the most for a minute or two or until all whites have been folded into the apricot mixture. Pour mixture gently into a 9-inch soufflé dish. If not pressed for time, cover soufflé dish with a large pot and set aside in a warm place free from drafts for 30 minutes. To bake, set soufflé dish in pan of hot water in a preheated 400° oven. Reduce heat to 375°, and bake for 35 to 40 minutes or until soufflé is browned on top and has risen two to three inches above rim of dish. Serve at once with unsweetened whipped cream or with teacakes or similar type cookies. The soufflé will keep its shape only 5 to 8 minutes in a turned-off oven. Yield: 6 servings.

CAROLYN CLARK'S LEMON ICEBOX DESSERT

A magnificent dessert for beauty and flavor.

  8 egg yolks
1½ cups sugar, divided
  Juice and rind of 2 lemons
1½ tablespoons (1½ envelopes) unflavored
  gelatin
½ cup orange juice
½ cup boiling water
  8 egg whites
1½ dozen lady fingers
½ pint whipping cream, whipped

Beat egg yolks well. Add ½ cup sugar, juice, and rind of lemons. Cook in double boiler until thick. Soak gelatin in orange juice. Add ½ cup boiling water to gelatin and pour in yolks. Let cool.

Beat egg whites and add 1 cup sugar. Fold in yolk mixture. Line bottom and sides of a springform pan with lady fingers. Pour mixture into pan and let stand at least 8 hours. Release mold and serve with whipped cream on top. Yield: 12 servings.

A luscious Beef Tenderloin Wellington adds grace and elegance to any party scene. Special instructions for this delicious pièce de résistance are on page 162.

HALLOWEEN BANANA FROST AND FLAME

For Halloween, light up with this dessert from Barbados.

1 quart coffee ice cream
6 egg whites, room temperature
6 tablespoons powdered sugar
⅛ teaspoon salt
1 teaspoon vanilla extract
3 long ripe bananas, peeled and halved lengthwise
2 tablespoons dark rum

Allow ice cream to soften in a large mixing bowl; do not allow to melt. Refreeze in an empty milk carton or in a 9- x 5- x 3-inch loaf pan. In a mixing bowl beat egg whites at high speed of electric mixer. When eggs begin to stand in peaks, add powdered sugar, 1 tablespoon at a time. Add salt and vanilla, and continue beating at high speed until whites are stiff. Cover a bread board with heavy brown paper, and arrange three banana halves side by side, flat sides up. Place quart block of ice cream on bananas and cover with remaining halves, flat sides down. Gently spoon egg mixture over top bananas so that it completely seals them. Place in a preheated oven for 4 to 5 minutes, keeping a constant eye on the meringue. Remove as soon as it is a light golden color. Heat rum in a metal cup. Slide meringue from the brown paper onto a large metal tray or pyrex platter and pour hot rum over it. Ignite and serve flaming. Yield: 6 servings.

Brunswick stew has always been a popular crowd pleaser. The tempting recipe is on page 228 and is ideal served in big bowls accompanied by hot corn bread muffins.

EMMA CHENEY'S CHARLOTTE RUSSE

Light as a gossamer cloud, its taste is heavenly. Since my beloved mother-in-law never used alcoholic beverages for flavoring, that is the only liberty I took with her recipe. Either way this dessert rates par excellence and is quickly and easily made.

12 almond macaroons
1 envelope (1 tablespoon) unflavored gelatin
½ cup cold milk
1 teaspoon vanilla extract
1 teaspoon brandy or ½ teaspoon almond flavoring
¾ cup sugar, divided
4 large egg whites, room temperature
⅛ teaspoon salt
1 pint whipping cream
1¼ teaspoons brandy or vanilla extract

Line a large cut-glass bowl or a 1½-quart mold with macaroons. Soften gelatin in cold milk in a small saucepan for about 10 minutes; then hold pan over boiling water to dissolve. When dissolved, add 1 teaspoon vanilla, 1 teaspoon brandy or ½ teaspoon almond flavoring, and ½ cup sugar.

Beat egg whites and salt in a small narrow bowl at high speed of electric mixer until soft peaks appear. Gradually add remaining ¼ cup sugar and continue beating until whites are stiff. Whip cream until it stands in soft peaks; add flavoring and continue beating until stiff. Fold beaten egg whites into whipped cream mixture. Fold gelatin mixture into combined egg whites and whipped cream and spoon into bowl or mold. Chill for several hours until set. This will keep beautifully for several days refrigerated and is more delicious when made the day before using. Serve from cut glass bowl or unmold on a large platter. Yield: 10 servings.

Variation: You may substitute ladyfingers for macaroons and Grand Marnier for brandy for a delightful change.

BANANAS FOSTER

A Flaming dessert popular in New Orleans' restaurants.

2 tablespoons butter
3 tablespoons firmly packed dark brown sugar
1 large ripe banana, peeled and halved lengthwise and crosswise
1 tablespoon lemon juice
⅛ teaspoon ground cinnamon
2 ounces white rum
2 tablespoons banana liqueur

In a chafing dish or small skillet melt butter over medium heat; add sugar and cook quartered banana in this mixture until lightly browned. Sprinkle with lemon juice and dust with cinnamon. Add rum and banana liqueur; ignite, basting the banana until the flame dies. Bananas Foster is glorious spooned over crêpes or vanilla ice cream. Yield: 2 servings.

VIENNA GUGELHUPF
(Vienna Coffee Cake)

This traditional coffee cake along with Mocha Choc-A-Bloc are favorites of Roberta Peters, famous opera star. To entertain a host of friends she always serves a choice of at least two confections, one rich and the other mild.

1 cup sweet butter, room temperature
2 cups sugar
6 large eggs, separated
1½ cups sifted all-purpose flour
½ teaspoon salt
2 teaspoons baking powder
6 tablespoons milk
1 teaspoon vanilla extract
Coffee Glaze

Cream butter to consistency of mayonnaise; add sugar gradually and continue to beat until light and fluffy. Add egg yolks one at a time, beating well after each addition. Mix and sift flour, salt, and baking powder. Combine milk and vanilla. To creamed batter add flour mixture and liquids alternately, stirring gently but thoroughly. Spoon into a greased 9-inch (12-cup) Turk's Head mold or a deep 10-inch tube pan. Bake in a preheated 350° oven for 1 hour or until cake tests done. Cool in pan 10 minutes. Gently loosen cake around tube and rim of pan. Invert on cake plate. When cool cover with Coffee Glaze. Yield: 16 to 18 servings.

Variation: You may wish to substitute ½ teaspoon lemon or almond extract or 2 tablespoons grated lemon peel for the vanilla extract.

Coffee Glaze:

Cold strong coffee
2 cups powdered sugar

Mix enough cold strong coffee with powdered sugar until it reaches pouring consistency. Pour evenly over cake, using pastry brush to cover evenly.

"HELLO DOLLY" DELIGHTS

A superb confection and a great finger dessert for any occasion. Serve this smash hit to your family, bridge club, or V.I.P. There's nothing like it. The beauty of "Hello Dolly" is that its exceptional flavor improves with storage. The squares will keep ten days to two weeks in a sealed container.

1 (7¼-ounce) box vanilla wafers
½ cup butter
1 (4-ounce) can sweetened premium coconut shred
1½ cups chocolate pieces
1½ cups finely sliced pecans
1 (14-ounce) can sweetened condensed milk

Roll vanilla wafers between two pieces of waxed paper with rolling pin until very fine crumbs. Butter sides of an 11- x 7-inch pan and place remaining butter in pan to melt slowly in a 300° oven. Sprinkle wafer crumbs evenly over bottom of pan. Spread as evenly as possible in separate layers the coconut, chocolate pieces, and pecans. Dribble condensed milk over layered mixture. Bake in a preheated 350° oven for 35 to 40 minutes. Test with a straw for doneness. Cool in pan for at least 8 hours, preferably overnight. Cut into 1-inch squares and serve with black coffee. Yield: 30 (1-inch) squares.

WINIFRED'S APPLE CHARLOTTE RUSSE

My favorite creation has eye appeal and is light and lovely to taste. Make the apple-apricot puree according to directions in Charlotte aux Pommes. The dessert may be made days in advance.

 1 envelope (1 tablespoon) unflavored gelatin
 1 cup milk, divided
 3 egg yolks
 2 whole eggs
 ⅔ cup sugar
 ⅛ teaspoon salt
 2 cups half-and-half
 2 teaspoons brandy
 1 teaspoon vanilla extract
    Apple-apricot puree
    Frosted Mint Leaves

Dissolve gelatin in ¼ cup cold milk. Beat egg yolks and whole eggs slightly. Add sugar, and salt; place in top of a double boiler and stir in remaining milk and cream. Cook over slowly boiling water about 20 minutes or more until mixture begins to coat spoon, stirring constantly. Add dissolved gelatin in milk and cook about 10 minutes longer. The custard begins to feel thicker when stirred. Remove from heat and add flavorings. Cool pan over ice and stir mixture. Chill to allow custard to set and thicken. Spoon into chilled parfait glasses starting with custard, then puree, and ending with custard. I find a tablespoon does the best job. Chill at least 4 hours before serving. Top with frosted or candied mint leaves. Yield: 14 to 16 parfaits.

Variation: This custard may be combined with fresh ripe strawberries, raspberries, or peaches for a superb dessert.

Frosted Mint Leaves:

 1 egg white
16 mint leaves
    Sugar

Beat egg white until slightly frothy. Spread beaten egg white on washed and dried mint leaves; sprinkle with sugar and allow leaves to dry. (Grapes may be done in the same manner.)

JAKARTA BANANA DELIGHT

This is a delicious hot fruit dish. Use with pork roast, baked ham, chicken, or turkey. As a dessert, serve alone or over a scoop of vanilla ice cream.

 6 fully ripe bananas
 1 tablespoon butter, divided
 1 cup orange juice
 1 cup fimly packed light brown sugar
 ½ cup finely grated fresh, frozen, or canned
       coconut
 ½ cup dry bread or cake crumbs
 ¼ teaspoon ground cinnamon
 ¼ teaspoon ground nutmeg

Peel and remove white threads from bananas; split, and place in a buttered baking dish. Dot with remaining butter. Blend orange juice and brown sugar and pour over bananas. Mix together coconut, dry crumbs, cinnamon and nutmeg, and sprinkle over top of bananas. Bake for 20 minutes in a preheated 350° oven. Serve hot. Yield: 6 servings.

FROZEN ALEXANDER

An ultra special dessert from The Argyle in San Antonio, Texas.

1 quart coffee ice cream
2 ounces brandy
1½ ounces Tia Maria liqueur

Place coffee ice cream in a large mixing bowl and allow to stand 15 to 20 minutes or until softened. Blend in brandy and Tia Maria using electric mixer on low speed for a very few seconds. Return mixture to the quart container and refreeze. Do not allow the ice cream to melt. Yield: 6 servings.

BANANAS WINIFRED

A festive and inexpensive dessert for any occasion—Thanksgiving, Christmas, or Easter. Light and lovely, it can be made ahead of time. At Christmas, decorate each slice with fresh or candied mint leaves and a red cherry. At Easter use mint leaves and candied violets.

1 cup sugar
1 teaspoon vanilla extract
1 teaspoon cider vinegar
1 teaspoon cold water
3 large egg whites, room temperature
⅛ teaspoon salt
½ teaspoon baking powder
Banana Filling

Sift sugar onto a dinner plate. Combine vanilla, vinegar, and water in a glass. In a deep, 6-inch diameter bowl, combine egg whites, salt, baking powder, and vanilla mixture. On high speed of electric mixer beat whites until stiff, then add sifted sugar, 1 tablespoon at a time.

Cover a very large cookie sheet with brown paper and trace around an ice cube tray twice. Lightly butter paper. Divide meringue mixture in half, and shape each half to fit the traced pattern. Bake in a preheated 250° oven for 60

minutes. Remove from oven and cool on wire rack. Prepare Banana Filling while meringue is cooling.

Place one baked meringue form in a freezer tray and cover with Banana Filling. Top with second meringue form and freeze for 3 hours. If you are making dessert days ahead, remove from freezer when you sit down to dinner. It will be exactly the right temperature for eating at dessert time. Yield: 8 servings.

Banana Filling:

1 cup banana pulp (about 3 average-size bananas)
¼ teaspoon salt
1½ tablespoons strained lemon juice
1 cup whipping cream
¼ cup powdered sugar
1 teaspoon brandy (optional)

Remove white threads from banana and whip bananas into a frothy pulp with a fork. Combine pulp, salt, and lemon juice in a bowl; chill in the refrigerator or a bowl of ice.

Chill cream; beat on medium speed of electric mixer in a narrow bowl until cream stands in soft peaks. Fold in powdered sugar and brandy, if desired. Fold whipped cream into banana mixture.

FRESH FIG ICE CREAM

Luscious!

1½ pints ripe Celeste figs, peeled and measured after mashing
1 tablespoon strained lemon juice
2⅔ cups sugar, divided
1 quart milk
4 large eggs
⅛ teaspoon salt
2 tablespoons all-purpose flour
3 teaspoons vanilla extract, divided
1½ pints half-and-half

Crush peeled figs with a fork or wooden spoon in a large bowl; sprinkle with lemon juice and ⅓ cup sugar. Blend well. Heat milk slowly in top of a double boiler.

In another bowl beat eggs lightly with 2 cups sugar, salt, and flour. Add to hot milk slowly, stirring constantly until mixture begins to thicken. Keep water boiling rapidly in bottom of boiler. Remove from heat, add 2 teaspoons vanilla, and allow to cool. Add remaining ⅓ cup sugar to half-and-half with remaining 1 teaspoon vanilla. Combine mixtures and blend thoroughly; freeze in a gallon container. Yield: 1 gallon—about 16 servings.

CUSTARD CHARLOTTE RUSSE

A festive dessert to highlight any occasion. Mother always served this delight at Easter.

  1 egg yolk
  ⅛ teaspoon salt
  1 cup milk
  1 envelope (1 tablespoon) unflavored gelatin
  ¼ cup cold water
  2 tablespoons vanilla extract or brandy or ¼
      cup sherry
  1 pint whipping cream
 12 ladyfingers, halved
      Candied cherries
      Blanched almonds

In a small narrow bowl beat egg yolk until light. Gradually beat in sugar and add salt. Scald milk in top of a double boiler and pour gradually over egg mixture. Return to double boiler and cook over simmering water, stirring constantly until mixture coats spoon. Do not allow water to touch bottom of pan.

Soften gelatin in cold water and add to hot custard as removed from stove; stir until dissolved. Cool. When mixture begins to set, blend in your choice of flavoring. Whip cream and fold into custard.

Line a large cut glass bowl with halved ladyfingers and pour in mixture, or serve with ladyfingers in parfait glasses, or lightly butter a springform pan and line with split ladyfingers. Refrigerate until set. Unmold on a large platter and decorate with candied cherries and blanched almonds. This is best when made one day in advance. Yield: 8 servings.

CATHERINE HAGAMAN'S LEMON DESSERT

  1 (10-ounce) angel food cake (made from a
      packaged mix)
  1 envelope (1 tablespoon) unflavored gelatin
  ½ cup cold water
  ¾ cup lemon juice
  ¾ cup sugar
  6 egg yolks
  2 tablespoons grated lemon rind
  6 egg whites
  ¾ cup sugar
  1 cup whipping cream, whipped

Make angel food cake according to package directions. When cool, break into walnut-size pieces. Sprinkle gelatin over water. Cook over hot water in top of a double boiler, stirring until thickened. Add lemon juice, sugar, egg yolks, and lemon rind. Stir in gelatin mixture and cook until dissolved. Set aside to cool.

Beat egg whites until foamy. Add sugar gradually, beating until stiff. Fold in cooled mixture and cake pieces. Place in a 9-inch springform pan and refrigerate overnight. When ready to serve, unmold and top with whipped cream. Yield: 12 servings.

Note: This dessert can also be made in a shallow 3-quart pan and cut into squares. Yield: 15 servings.

LOVE'S DELIGHT CAKE

This exotic creation comes from a romantic period of old Natchez. Guaranteed to catch a beau.

  ½ (4-ounce) package German's sweet
      chocolate, melted
1½ cups sugar, divided
1¾ cups all-purpose flour, measured after
      sifting
  ¾ teaspoon salt
  ¾ teaspoon soda
  ½ cup vegetable oil, not olive oil
  1 cup buttermilk
  2 large eggs, separated
  ¾ cup crème de cacao
  1 (2-ounce) package ground and toasted
      almonds
      Chocolate Fluff

Bring water to a simmering boil in bottom of double boiler and place chocolate in top boiler. Stir for a few minutes until chocolate begins to melt; remove from heat. Proceed with cake preparation, returning in a few minutes to beat chocolate with wooden spoon. (Smooth chocolate will blend more easily into cake batter.)

Grease and flour two 8-inch cakepans. Sift together 1 cup sugar, flour, salt, and soda into a large bowl. Add oil and gradually pour in buttermilk, beaten egg yolks, and melted chocolate. Beat 1 minute at high speed of electric mixer or with a dover beater, 4 or 5 minutes if beaten by hand. Beat egg whites until frothy with a wire whisk or electric mixer and gradually add ½ cup sugar. Beat until glossy. Fold egg whites carefully into batter. Spoon into two greased and floured 8-inch square cakepans and bake in a preheated 350° oven for 30 to 35 minutes or until cake tests done. Cool on wire rack 10 minutes; remove from pans. When fully cold, split each layer. Dribble crème de cacao over each layer. Divide toasted and ground almonds into four parts. Spread layers with Chocolate Fluff and almonds. Ice all layers and top and sides with Chocolate Fluff. Refrigerate. Allow enough time for cake to lose its chill before serving. It freezes well. Yield: 16 to 18 servings.

Chocolate Fluff:

  2 cups whipping cream
  1 cup powdered sugar
  ⅓ cup powdered cocoa
  ⅛ teaspoon salt
  ¼ teaspoon almond extract

Beat cream until it begins to thicken. Add powdered sugar, cocoa, salt, and almond flavoring. Spread on cake as directed.

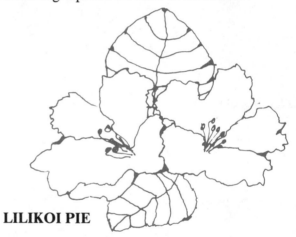

LILIKOI PIE

This special treat comes from May Kodani, outstanding pastry chef at the Coco Palms, Kauai, Hawaii.

  1 envelope (1 tablespoon) unflavored gelatin
  ¼ cup cold water
  4 large eggs, separated, room temperature
  ¾ cup sugar, divided
  ¼ cup passion fruit juice, fresh, frozen, or
      canned; if using canned, add 1 tablespoon
      lemon juice
  1 (9-inch) baked and chilled pie shell

Soften gelatin in cold water for 5 minutes. Beat egg yolks at high speed with electric mixer until light; gradually add ½ cup sugar and continue beating until thick and lemon colored. Add passion fruit juice and mix well. Cook in top of a double boiler over rapidly boiling water about 5 minutes or until mixture thickens, stirring constantly. Remove from heat, add gelatin, and cool. Chill until partly set.

Beat egg whites at high speed with mixer until they stand in soft peaks. Gradually add remaining ¼ cup sugar and continue beating until they stand in firm peaks. Fold into chilled gelatin mixture and spoon into chilled, prepared pie shell. Chill for 3 or 4 hours before serving. Yield: 6 to 8 servings.

Variation: You may substitute cranberry juice for passion fruit juice.

LIME POTS DE CRÈME

A marvelous lime dessert for luncheon or dinner party.

  8 large egg yolks
  1 cup freshly squeezed, strained lime juice
1½ tablespoons grated lime rind
  1 cup sugar
  1 pint whipping cream
  4 large egg whites
  2 tablespoons powdered sugar

Beat egg yolks slightly. Combine egg yolks, lime juice and rind, sugar, and cream in top of a double boiler, and cook over rapidly boiling water using a medium high heat until mixture thickens, stirring constantly. Remove from heat and place pan in a bowl of ice, and stir occasionally until cold.

In a deep narrow bowl beat egg whites until they stand in soft peaks, using a wire whisk or electric mixer on high speed. Add powdered sugar and continue beating until whites are stiff. Fold into the cooked cream mixture. Spoon dessert into demitasse or pots de crème cups and chill. This may be made a day in advance. Yield: 12 servings.

REYNOLDS' CHERRIES JUBILEE

Lovely to behold and to taste!

  1 (17-ounce) can pitted black cherries, drained and juice reserved
  6 tablespoons sugar
1½ ounces brandy
  ½ ounce kirsch
  1 quart premium vanilla ice cream
  6 slices toasted pound cake or 6 meringue cups (optional)

In a saucepan heat reserved cherry juice and sugar until a heavy syrup is formed. Add cherries, pour into brûlot bowl or chafing dish, and add liqueurs. As soon as mixture becomes hot, ignite with a long-handled match to avoid burning fingers. As it flames, spoon liquid over cherries with a long-handled spoon or ladle. Ladle cherries and juice over ice cream. If you wish to make it even fancier, place the ice cream in meringue cups or on toasted pound cake. Yield: 6 servings.

CATHERINE HAGAMAN'S CRÈME DE MENTHE DELIGHT

  1 teaspoon (⅓ envelope) unflavored gelatin
  1 tablespoon cold water
25 regular-size marshmallows
  ¾ cup milk
  ⅓ cup crème de menthe
  1 pint whipping cream, whipped
  1 (5½-ounce) can commercial chocolate syrup

Sprinkle gelatin over water. Dissolve marshmallows in milk in a double boiler over boiling water. Add gelatin to marshmallows and stir until dissolved; cool. Add crème de menthe and fold in whipped cream. Pour into a bundt pan or mold and chill overnight. When ready to serve, unmold, cut into slices, and spoon 1 or 2 teaspoons chocolate syrup over each serving. Yield: 12 servings.

BLUEBERRY BUCKLE

Fresh-picked blueberries are best for this lus-cious English dessert. It's simple to make and a joy to eat.

1¼ cups sugar
 ½ cup butter or margarine, softened
 2 large eggs
 2 cups sifted all-purpose flour, divided
 2 cups fresh blueberries
 2 teaspoons baking powder
 ½ teaspoon salt
 ½ teaspoon ground cinnamon
 ½ cup milk
 1 teaspoon lemon extract
   Crumb Topping

Cream sugar and butter for 3 or 4 minutes or until light and fluffy using medium speed of electric mixer. Add eggs and beat at high speed for 2 minutes. Sprinkle ¼ cup flour over blue-berries that have been washed and dried on a paper towel. Gently mix with your hands until the berries are lightly coated. Sift together remaining 1¾ cups flour, baking powder, salt, and cinnamon. Add flour mixture alternately with milk to creamed mixture, beating well after each addition. Add lemon extract. Fold in berries carefully so you do not crush them. Lightly grease and flour a 9-inch square baking pan. Spread batter evenly in pan and make Crumb Topping.

Sprinkle Crumb Topping over batter as evenly as possible; it will spread as it bakes. Bake in a preheated 375° oven for 45 to 50 minutes or until a toothpick inserted into the center comes out clean. Cut into squares and serve warm. This will keep well in the pan two or three days if you can leave it alone. Yield: 9 (3-inch) squares.

Crumb Topping:

½ cup sugar
¾ cup sifted all-purpose flour
 6 tablespoons softened butter or margarine
¾ teaspoon ground cinnamon

In a medium-size bowl combine all ingredients with a pastry blender or two knives used scis-sor-fashion until mixture resembles coarse crumbs.

HEAVENLY MERINGUES

Beautiful and always a sure-fire success as a dessert. Inexpensive and very low in choles-terol, it provides an ideal confection for cho-lesterol watchers. The recipe makes a 10-inch meringue shell for a pie, serving 8, or 12 meringues. Be sure the eggs are fresh.

 3 large egg whites, room temperature
⅛ teaspoon salt
½ teaspoon baking powder
 1 teaspoon vanilla extract
 1 teaspoon cold water
 1 teaspoon vinegar
 1 cup sifted sugar

In a narrow deep mixing bowl place egg whites, salt, baking powder and vanilla, cold water, and vinegar which have been combined in a cup. Set mixer on high speed and beat until egg whites stand in soft peaks. Gradually add sifted sugar 1 tablespoon at a time. Cut from sides with spatula and continue beating until whites are very stiff, but not dry.

For individual meringues cut brown paper to fit a large cookie sheet. Round egg white mixture on soup spoon and ease onto paper with a knife; lightly press in sides around top to form a slight well. Place at least 2 inches apart. For the pie shell, lightly butter brown paper cut to fit pie shell and heap the egg white mixture gently on top. Shape meringue with a spatula or knife giving it a heavy edge like a tart or pie. Bake meringues in a preheated 250° oven for 1 hour. Cool on wire rack about 20 minutes. Place in a sealed tin can for later. They keep for a week or more. Freeze the pie shell in its pan in a plastic bag to prevent breakage. Allow the frozen shell to reach room temperature before serving. Yield: 12 individual meringues or 1 (10-inch) pie shell.

GRASSHOPPER PIE

A light and luscious pie combining two of my favorite liqueurs, crème de menthe and crème de cacao. Use this colorful and elegant dessert for cherished company. It is an excellent peace offering to soothe over wounded feelings in case of domestic difficulties.

Crust:

22 chocolate wafers, finely rolled
4 tablespoons butter, melted

Mix rolled chocolate wafers with melted butter and pat into a 9-inch greased pie plate. Bake crust in a preheated 350° oven for 8 minutes and set aside to cool.

Filling:

22 regular-size marshmallows
¾ cup milk
1 tablespoon green crème de menthe
3 tablespoons white crème de cacao
½ pint whipping cream, whipped
Grated German's sweet chocolate

Melt marshmallows with milk in top of a double boiler over rapidly boiling water; cool. Add crème de menthe and crème de cacao. Let mixture stand until syrupy and thickened. Fold in whipped cream and pour into pie shell. Chill in refrigerator for several hours or overnight. At serving time sprinkle grated German's sweet chocolate lightly over top of pie. Yield: 6 to 8 servings.

PINK VALENTINE PIE

Cupid's best!

½ teaspoon finely grated orange peel
1 tablespoon plus 1 teaspoon
Triple Sec
22 chocolate wafers, finely rolled
4 tablespoons melted butter
22 regular-size marshmallows
¾ cup milk
3 tablespoons crème de cacao
1 drop red food coloring
½ pint whipping cream, whipped

Marinate orange peel in Triple Sec overnight.

Combine rolled chocolate wafers with melted butter and pat into a 9-inch greased pie plate. Bake in a preheated 350° oven for 8 minutes; set aside to cool.

Melt marshmallows with milk in top of a double boiler over rapidly boiling water; cool. Add Triple Sec with orange peel and crème de cacao. Let stand until syrupy and thickened. Add red coloring, fold in whipped cream, and pour into pie shell. Yield: 6 to 8 servings.

CREAMY BAKED CUSTARD

This is very nourishing and ideal to take to a sick friend. It makes a delightful dessert at the end of a rich meal, and the recipe is easy and foolproof.

> **8 rounded teaspoons firmly packed dark brown sugar**
> **3 large egg yolks and 1 whole egg or 4 large eggs**
> **½ cup sugar**
> **3 cups whole or skimmed milk**
> **3 tablespoons nonfat dry milk powder**
> **⅛ teaspoon salt**
> **1½ teaspoons vanilla extract**
> **Ground nutmeg**

Place 1 rounded teaspoon dark brown sugar in each custard cup. Break eggs into a large bowl; add remaining ingredients except nutmeg. Beat mixture lightly with a wire whisk or fork until thoroughly blended. Ladle into custard cups and sprinkle with nutmeg. Place cups in enough hot water to come halfway up the outside of each cup and bake in a preheated 300° oven for 40 to 45 minutes or until a silver knife inserted 1 inch from edge of cup comes out clean. Serve hot or cold. Yield: 8 (6-ounce) custard cups.

Variations: For a richer custard, use whole milk instead of nonfat dry milk powder. For a very fancy custard, omit nutmeg and top with a teaspoon of orange marmalade or your favorite preserves and cover with Meringue.

Meringue:

> **2 egg whites, room temperature**
> **⅛ teaspoon salt**
> **¼ teaspoon cream of tartar**
> **¼ cup sugar**

Beat egg whites, salt, and cream of tartar in a narrow deep bowl at high speed of electric mixer until whites stand in soft peaks. Add sugar gradually; continue beating until whites are stiff but not dry. Spread lightly over each custard cup. In spreading meringue do not bring it to edge of cup. Bake in a preheated 325° oven for 10 minutes. Allow custards to cool on wire rack; then chill in refrigerator.

BLUEBERRY FLUFF

A luscious dessert in three easy steps.

Pastry:

> **½ cup butter, softened**
> **1 cup all-purpose flour**
> **2 egg yolks, beaten**
> **1 tablespoon cold water**

In a large bowl cut softened butter into flour with a pastry blender. Add egg yolks beaten until thick and lemony. Add water and stir well. With fingers press flour and egg mixture into a 9-inch square cakepan or a 9-inch deep dish pie plate. Prepare Filling.

Filling:

> **4 cups washed blueberries**
> **¾ cup sugar**
> **1 tablespoon strained lemon juice**
> **2 tablespoons all-purpose flour**
> **¼ teaspoon ground nutmeg**
> **Grated rind of 1 lemon**

Drain berries in colander. Gently blend all ingredients in a large bowl and sprinkle evenly over pastry bottom. Bake in a preheated 375° oven for 10 minutes; lower heat to 350° and cook 25 minutes longer. You may use frozen berries straight from the freezer. The dessert may be made to this point in advance. About half an hour before serving prepare the Topping.

Topping:

 2 egg yolks, beaten
½ cup sugar
 1 cup commercial sour cream
 3 egg whites

Blend egg yolks, sugar, and sour cream. Beat egg whites until stiff but not dry. Fold into yolk and sour cream mixture. Spoon over top of blueberries. Bake in a preheated 350° oven for 20 minutes; cool 10 minutes before serving. Serve hot for perfection, but it is good cold. Yield: 1 (9-inch) square pie—8 to 10 servings.

COFFEE CLOUD FILLING

Add this airy and unbeatable flavor delight to my meringue recipe and have twelve individual coffee angel pies. Delicious on sliced pound or sponge cake. Served alone this makes 4 servings, each with 120 calories.

 3 teaspoons instant coffee
 1 cup water
 1 (3½-ounce) package vanilla Whip and Chill
½ cup skimmed milk, very cold
 1 teaspoon vanilla extract
¼ teaspoon pure mocha extract
 1 large egg white
 1 tablespoon sugar

Boil coffee with water in a saucepan over high heat until it cooks down to ½ cup liquid; chill. In a small deep narrow bowl thoroughly blend Whip and Chill and cold milk at low speed of electric mixer. Beat at high speed for 1 minute. Add flavorings to chilled coffee and slowly blend at low speed into Whip and Chill. Beat for 2 minutes. Chill for 10 to 15 minutes or until mixture begins to set.

Beat egg whites until stiff and add sugar; fold into coffee mixture. If using meringues, place several large scoops of coffee cloud atop each one. Refrigerate overnight for best results. These will hold up for several days. I place toothpicks on the top and cover with plastic wrap to prevent drying. Yield: filling for 12 meringues.

ORANGE ICEBOX CAKE

A beautiful and delicious creation.

 1 cup sugar
2¾ cups water, divided
 2 envelopes (2 tablespoons) gelatin
 1 cup orange pulp
 1 cup orange juice
 2 tablespoons lemon juice
 4 packages plain ladyfingers
 1 cup chopped pecans, divided
 1 pint whipping cream
32 regular-size marshmallows, quartered

Boil sugar and 2 cups water slowly for 20 minutes. Soak gelatin in remaining ¾ cup cold water and add to boiled sugar water. Put orange pulp in blender for 1 minute. Add orange pulp and orange and lemon juices to gelatin mixture. Chill in refrigerator until thickened. Line a springform cakepan (with sides at least 4 inches high) with waxed paper. Snip off bottoms of ladyfingers so that they will stand level and arrange around sides of pan. Crumble remaining ladyfingers and place some on bottom of pan. Sprinkle ½ cup chopped pecans over bottom of pan. Whip cream and add quartered marshmallows. When gelatin mixture has thickened, put in bowl and whip with electric mixer until light. Add slowly to whipped cream mixture. Spoon half of the mixture into pan; sprinkle with remaining ladyfinger crumbs and ½ cup pecans. Top with remaining mixture. Chill for several hours in refrigerator or overnight. Yield: 10 to 12 servings.

LEMON ICE

1½ teaspoons unflavored gelatin
  1 cup milk
  ½ cup sugar
  ⅓ cup lemon juice
  2 tablespoons grated lemon rind
  1 large egg white, room temperature
  ⅛ teaspoon salt
  2 tablespoons sugar

In a saucepan heat gelatin, milk, and sugar until gelatin and sugar are dissolved. Add lemon juice and lemon rind. Beat egg white with salt until soft peaks form; then add sugar gradually. Beat until stiff. Stir lemon mixture into beaten egg white and freeze in an ice-cube tray. Yield: 4 servings.

PEACHY RASPBERRY AMBROSIA

Delectable! Delectable!

5 large fully ripe peaches, a tart variety such
    as Red Haven, Dixie Belle, or Georgia
    Belle
  2 tablespoons lemon juice
  1 tablespoon lime juice (if not available use
    1 additional tablespoon lemon juice)
¼ cup plus 1 tablespoon sugar
    Raspberry Puree

Peel peaches and cut into large slices. Place in a flat 9-inch square casserole or serving dish. Arrange slices close together all going the same way. Pour combined lemon and lime juices over fruit and sprinkle with sugar. Taste. If you prefer a sweeter dessert, add 2 more tablespoons sugar. Spoon Raspberry Puree over peaches and chill until serving time. Serve with rose geranium sauce (see Sauces).

Raspberry Puree:

  2 pints fresh raspberries
1½ cups superfine sugar or 1¼ cups sugar
    Or
  2 (10-ounce) packages frozen raspberries,
    thawed
  1 cup superfine sugar or ⅔ cup sugar

The puree may be made with either fresh or frozen berries. Use the ingredients given first for fresh berries and those given last for frozen ones. Mash berries through a sieve. Reserve juice from one package of thawed berries to add to puree. Place mashed berries in a blender with sugar and blend 3 minutes, or place berries and sugar in a deep narrow bowl and beat on high speed of electric mixer for 8 to 10 minutes. Chill. Spoon over chilled peach mixture. Yield: 6 servings.

ORANGE BEIGNETS

Orange Beignets or fritters, with fewer calories than pie or cake, are a delightful combination of the Old World cuisine and the new. They are delicious served as a light dessert or as a side dish and are particularly good for a brunch.

  2 large navel oranges
  5 tablespoons sugar
  2 eggs, separated
  1 cup unsifted all-purpose flour
  1 tablespoon butter, melted
  2 tablespoons brandy
¼ teaspoon salt
    About ½ cup cold water
    Vegetable oil
    Powdered sugar

Peel oranges and remove all the white inner skin. Section evenly and remove seeds. Sprinkle with sugar and set aside in a glass bowl for 1 hour. At that time drain off the formed juice and reserve for later use.

Beat egg yolks until thickened in a large mixing bowl. Slowly add flour and reserved orange juice; beat until light. Pour in melted butter and brandy. Add salt and thin with water to the consistency of very thick starch; you may not need the entire ½ cup water suggested. Beat egg whites until very stiff, but not dry, and add to batter.

Using a large cooking spoon, dip sliced fruit into batter mixture. Batter must be thick enough to coat fruit but not so thick as to be tough. Drop each slice of coated orange into deep hot vegetable oil (250°). It takes only a few minutes for fritters to become crisp and golden. Drain on brown paper or paper towel. Serve hot, sprinkled generously with powdered sugar. If promptly refrigerated, batter may be prepared three or four hours ahead of time. Yield: 12 to 14 fritters—4 to 6 servings.

Variation: Many Creole cooks substitute white wine, sherry, or lemon juice for the brandy.

ORANGE CAKE

A true orange flavor.

1 cup butter or margarine, softened
2 cups sifted sugar
1 teaspoon vanilla extract
2 tablespoons grated orange rind
5 large eggs, room temperature
3 cups all-purpose flour, measured after sifting
1 tablespoon baking powder
⅛ teaspoon salt
½ cup orange juice
¼ cup milk
  Grand Marnier Glaze

In a large mixing bowl cream butter and sugar about 5 minutes on medium speed of electric mixer until light and fluffy. Cut down batter from sides with spatula. Add vanilla and orange rind. Add eggs one at a time, beating well after each addition. Sift together twice the flour, baking powder, and salt. Add dry ingredients to creamed mixture a small amount at a time, alternating with orange juice and milk. Begin and end with dry ingredients. Beat well. Spoon batter into a greased and floured 10-inch tube pan. Bake on lowest rack of a preheated 350° oven for 1 hour or until cake tests done. Cool on wire rack 10 minutes. Make a Grand Marnier Glaze. Yield: 1 (10-inch) tube cake.

Grand Marnier Glaze:

¼ cup butter
⅔ cup sugar
⅓ cup Grand Marnier

Combine all ingredients and cook over low heat until sugar is dissolved. With a fine straw or slender toothpick punch holes in top of cake and dribble glaze over it.

MOCHA CHOC-A-BLOC

Roberta Peters' rich confection.

2 (4-ounce) packages German's sweet chocolate
½ cup strong coffee
2 egg yolks, slightly beaten
½ teaspoon vanilla extract
12 lady fingers

Melt chocolate in top of a double boiler over hot water. Add coffee and stir until smooth. Pour a little chocolate on egg yolks and blend; return yolk mixture to remaining chocolate mixture. Cook over hot water, stirring constantly until slightly thickened. Add vanilla and cool to room temperature. Split lady fingers; place 3 halves close together and spread with chocolate mixture. Repeat, crossing layers until lady fingers are all used. Spread remaining chocolate mixture on sides. Chill. Cut into 4 to 6 slices. Yield: 4 to 6 servings.

FREDERICK MERRILL'S PEACHES FLAMBÉ

  Juice of 1 orange
  Juice of 1 lemon
 2 tablespoons granulated sugar
 ½ teaspoon grated orange rind
 ½ teaspoon grated lemon rind
 3 teaspoons butter
 ½ cup fresh peach slices or drained canned
     peach slices
 1 ounce peach brandy
 1 ounce brandy
 4 slices pound cake
 1 quart top-quality vanilla ice cream

In a small skillet combine fruit juices, granulated sugar, and grated orange and lemon rinds. Over high heat cook mixture until it is reduced to one-half of its volume. Stir as it boils so that you include the portions that caramelize (almost burn) around the sides of skillet. Remove from heat. Stir butter into mixture. Add peaches and 1 ounce peach brandy and simmer over low heat. When you are ready to serve, simmer remaining 1 ounce brandy in a saucepan, ignite, pour over peaches, and spoon the flaming peaches over sliced pound cake topped with two scoops of ice cream. Serve immediately. Yield: 4 servings.

POIRES MONT BLANC

You may never see the beauty of Mont Blanc in the French Alps but you may taste a sample of its namesake, Poires Mont Blanc. An exquisite dessert and low-calory.

6 pears with stems, ripe but firm, Bartlett or
     Anjou
1 (3-inch) lemon rind about ½ inch wide
1 cup sirop de grenadine (French preferred) or
     12 ounces American grenadine
1 large egg white, stiffly beaten

Peel pears with potato peeler, leaving stems intact. If pears are very large, cut in half and remove cores. (I prefer them whole and poached longer.) Add lemon rind to grenadine, and bring to a boil in a saucepan over medium heat. Simmer 10 minutes; add pears to boiling syrup and poach. If pears are fully ripe, simmer in sauce 10 minutes, if more on the green side, simmer 20 to 30 minutes. Rotate pears, testing with a straw or toothpick for tenderness. Remove each pear as it is done and place in a baking dish. When all are done, spoon remaining syrup over pears. Mound stiffly beaten egg white on stem of each pear and place in a preheated 450° oven for 3 to 5 minutes or until egg white is golden. Serve either hot or cold. I prefer the chilled pear for a more exotic taste. Yield: 6 servings.

MARILLEN SCHAUMTORTE
(Apricot Meringue Torte)

My apricot meringue torte is *am allerschönsten.* According to the Viennese this is a super superlative denoting the "most beautiful of them all." Mine is for beauty of taste.

 1 cup butter, softened
 ½ cup sifted sugar
 5 large egg yolks, divided
 2 tablespoons milk
 1 teaspoon vanilla extract
 ½ teaspoon salt
 ½ teaspoon baking powder
 2 cups cake flour, spooned into cup
 1 (12-ounce) jar apricot preserves
   Meringue
 1 pint commercial sour cream

In a large mixing bowl beat butter, sugar, and 2 egg yolks on high speed of electric mixer about 5 minutes or until light and fluffy. Add remaining 3 yolks and continue beating. Reduce to low speed and blend in milk, vanilla, salt, and baking powder. Beat well. Sift flour and add gradually until thoroughly blended. Spread batter evenly in three 9-inch round layer pans greased on the bottom only. Spread ⅓ apricot preserves on each layer. Prepare Meringue.

Divide meringue into thirds and spread lightly over preserves. Bake in a preheated 350° oven for 35 to 40 minutes until light golden brown or until cake tests done. Allow cake to cool in pans 15 minutes. Turn layers with meringue side up on wire racks to cool completely. Stack layers with meringue side up and spread sour cream between layers. Leave meringue top plain. Chill several hours or overnight. Yield: 16 servings.

Meringue:

1⅓ cups finely grated coconut, fresh, canned, or frozen
5 large egg whites, room temperature
¼ teaspoon salt
1 cup sifted sugar
1 teaspoon vanilla extract

Allow frozen coconut to thaw completely. In a small narrow bowl beat egg whites and salt at high speed of mixer until soft peaks appear. Gradually add sugar and continue beating until glossy, stiff peaks form. Fold in coconut and vanilla.

FLAMING BAKED PINEAPPLE

The fruit on Barbados is so luscious that pineapple and bananas are featured in many marvelous desserts.

1 medium-size whole pineapple, golden ripe
4 tablespoons sugar
4 tablespoons dark rum, divided
1 teaspoon ground cinnamon

Cut pineapple head off evenly and reserve. Scoop out pineapple meat with a curved or grapefruit knife, being careful not to pierce the shell. Discard the hard white pith, and dice fruit over a bowl to catch any juice. Roll dried fruit in sugar and return to shell. Pour any juice and 2 tablespoons rum over fruit in shell and sprinkle with cinnamon. Using skewers or cocktail sticks, attach the pineapple head to the shell. Bake in a preheated 375° oven for 30 minutes or until tender. Remove skewers, heat 2 remaining tablespoons rum and pour over entire pineapple. Light with a match and serve flaming. Yield: 4 to 6 servings.

HAWAIIAN ORANGE CHIFFON PIE

A frothy mile-high fresh orange pie from the famous pie chef, May Kodaini, at the beautiful Coco Plams Hotel on the Island of Kauai.

1 envelope (1 tablespoon) unflavored gelatin
¼ cup cold water
4 large eggs, separated
1 cup sugar, divided
½ cup orange juice
1 tablespoon lemon juice
½ teaspoon salt
1 tablespoon grated orange rind
1 (9-inch) baked pie shell
1 cup whipping cream
2 tablespoons powdered sugar
2 teaspoons Grand Marnier

Soften gelatin in cold water for 5 minutes. Beat egg yolks; add ½ cup sugar, orange and lemon juices, and salt; mix well. Cook in top of a double boiler over boiling water, stirring constantly until custard is slightly thickened, about 5 minutes. Add dissolved gelatin and orange rind, and stir well. Chill bowl over ice until mixture mounds slightly when dropped from a spoon. Beat egg whites at high speed of electric mixer until stiff but not dry. Gradually add remaining ½ cup sugar and beat until very stiff. Fold egg whites into custard mixture and spoon into prepared pie shell. Chill until firm. Whip cream and sweeten with powdered sugar and Grand Marnier; spread over pie. Yield: 6 to 8 servings.

ICE CREAM ANGEL CAKE

Easy to make and pretty as a picture. This frozen dessert keeps well for a long time in the freezer.

½ gallon top-quality vanilla ice cream
1 large angel food cake, broken into small
  pieces
1 (10-ounce) package frozen strawberries,
  thawed
1 (8¼-ounce) can crushed pineapple, drained
½ pint whipping cream, whipped

Place ice cream in a large mixing bowl and allow to soften. Add small pieces of angel food cake, thawed strawberries, and crushed pineapple. Beat on low speed of electric mixer until smooth. Fold in whipped cream and pour into angel food cake pan and freeze. Remove from freezer and slice when ready to serve. Top with a dollop of whipped cream, a large ripe strawberry, and a sprig of mint, if available. Yield: 18 to 20 servings.

PEACHES CARDINAL

Peaches and raspberries have an affinity for each other and make an exquisite summer and early fall dessert when they are usually available. Frozen raspberries may be used but its puree is not as thick.

8 large, firm ripe peaches
6 cups water
2 cups sugar
2 slices lemon
2 tablespoons vanilla extract
  Raspberry Puree

Drop peaches into boiling water in a large kettle for 2 or 3 minutes. Drain and put into cold water. The skins will usually slip off without using a knife. Combine water, sugar, lemon slices, and vanilla in a large saucepan and bring to a boil; add peaches. When syrup returns to a simmering boil, test with a toothpick or straw to see if it goes into the peach easily. Remove from heat and cool in syrup. Drain peaches on wire rack; place peaches in a casserole and chill. Reserve syrup; it may be used for poaching other fruit. Prepare Raspberry Puree.

When peaches and puree are thoroughly cold, arrange peaches in an oblong casserole and pour puree over all. Chill, and serve in crystal sherbet glasses and decorate with fresh mint leaves. Yield: 8 servings.

Raspberry Puree:

2 pints fresh raspberries
1½ cups superfine sugar or 1¼ cups sugar
  Or
2 (10-ounce) packages frozen raspberries,
  thawed
1 cup superfine sugar or ⅔ cup sugar
  Mint leaves

The puree may be made with either fresh or frozen berries. Use ingredients given first for fresh berries and those given last for frozen ones. Mash berries through a sieve. Reserve juice from one package of thawed berries to add to its puree. Place mashed berries in blender with sugar and blend 3 minutes or in a deep narrow bowl and turn on high speed of electric mixer for 8 to 10 minutes. Chill.

PRUNE WHIP OR SOUFFLÉ

After fifty years I remember how great this dessert tasted the first time I ate it while visiting in a cousin's home. I could not believe it was made with prunes, my pet aversion. As our patriotic duty during World War I my father had insisted we eat stewed prunes three times a day. Every morning he collected the prune seeds and took them to a special pick-up spot to be used in the making of gas masks. Only a superb concoction like this could redeem the prune from its former ignominy. It is an ideal dessert for people who have cholesterol problems.

11 pitted prunes
   Water to cover
 1 teaspoon lemon extract
½ tablespoon softened margarine
¾ cup sifted sugar
 5 large egg whites, room temperature
⅛ teaspoon salt
½ cup broken nuts (optional)
   Whipped cream (optional)

Cover prunes with water in a small saucepan and bring to a boil. Lower heat and simmer until tender, following directions on prune box. Place 2 tablespoons prune liquid and prunes in a blender and puree; add lemon flavoring. Grease a 1½-quart casserole or 6 individual casseroles with margarine. Sprinkle sugar in casserole; turn upside down to let excess sugar fall out.

Beat egg whites and salt in a large bowl until soft peaks are formed, using a wire whisk or electric beater on a high speed. Add remaining sugar gradually, 2 tablespoons at a time, until whites are stiff. Fold in prune puree and nuts and spoon into prepared molds. Place several layers of brown paper in bottom of a large pan and fill halfway with boiling water; set casseroles in this and bake on lowest oven shelf in a preheated 350° oven for 30 to 40 minutes. The soufflé is done when there is a faint line of shrinkage from the sides of pan. Cool on wire rack; then chill for 3 or 4 hours before serving. Unsweetened whipped cream makes it even more delicious. Yield: 6 servings.

MERINGUE MOUSSE AU CHOCOLAT

Simply luscious, rich and fluffy with the flavor of mocha and Grand Marnier. For a Parisian touch, dot whipped cream topper with crystallized violets. Serve with black coffee or salted nuts for a wonderful contrast of flavors.

7 (1-ounce) squares semisweet chocolate
2 teaspoons instant coffee
¼ cup boiling water
7 extra large eggs, separated, room
   temperature
⅔ cup sugar, sifted
2 teaspoons vanilla extract, divided
4 tablespoons Grand Marnier, divided
⅛ teaspoon salt
1 tablespoon butter
¼ cup fine dry bread crumbs
1 cup whipping cream
3 tablespoons superfine sugar or ¼ cup
   powdered sugar

Melt chocolate in top of a double boiler over hot, not boiling, water. Dissolve coffee in ¼ cup boiling water and add to chocolate. Cover and let stand over very low heat, stirring occasionally with a wire whisk. When chocolate is almost melted, beat smooth with wire whisk.

In a large mixing bowl beat egg yolks until thick and lemon colored with electric mixer on high speed. Gradually add sugar to yolks. Gradually add chocolate into egg mixture and continue beating. Add 1 teaspoon vanilla and 3 tablespoons Grand Marnier. Beat egg whites and salt in another large bowl until stiff, but not dry. Stir a fourth of the beaten whites into chocolate mixture. Gently fold in remaining whites until blended. Dust a well-buttered 9-inch pie plate with dry bread crumbs. Spoon mousse mixture into pie plate so that it comes just level with the edge. Bake in a preheated 350° oven for 25 minutes, then turn off heat, and bake for 5 minutes longer. Remove and cool for 2 hours on wire rack. Do not be alarmed when the cooked mousse sinks in the middle to form a pie shell. This part of recipe may be prepared the day before.

Three hours before serving, whip cream until stiff, and add remaining 1 teaspoon vanilla, 1 tablespoon Grand Marnier, and superfine sugar. Gently spread over pie. Chill. This will keep several days under refrigeration. Yield: 8 to 10 servings.

OLD-FASHIONED PLUM PUDDING

The tastiest! Easy to prepare, the recipe requires a morning's work. The result is worth it. Cook in foil containers for bazaars or Christmas gifts. The flaming pudding makes an exciting holiday dessert.

    2 cups (½ pound) finely chopped beef suet
    1 (16-ounce) box plus 3 tablespoons firmly
        packed dark brown sugar
    1 cup milk
    4 eggs, well beaten
    2½ cups sifted all-purpose flour, divided
    1 (11-ounce) box dried currants
    2 pounds chopped mixed candied fruits,
        citron, orange and lemon peel, cherries
    2 cups sliced blanched almonds
    2 teaspoons soda
    2 teaspoons salt
    1 teaspoon freshly grated nutmeg
    2 teaspoons ground cinnamon
    ½ teaspoon ground mace
    2 cups soft bread crumbs
    ½ cup brandy
        Hard Sauce

Ask butcher for white, fresh beef suet. After removing any thin veins of skin, chop suet finely and measure. In a large mixing bowl combine suet, brown sugar, milk, and well-beaten eggs. In another large bowl blend ½ cup flour with currants, chopped candied fruit, and almonds. Sift remaining 2 cups flour with soda, salt, and spices into suet mixture; mix well. Add fruit and bread crumbs, and stir until thoroughly blended. Turn into two well-greased 2-quart covered pudding molds. Steam for 3 hours by placing mold in a large kettle in the oven; pour boiling water to ½ depth of mold. If a pudding mold is not available, spoon batter into well-greased brown paper lined fruitcake pans or ungreased foil containers.

Invert mold onto a hot platter. Heat brandy in a small saucepan. Pour over pudding, ignite, and bring flaming pudding to the table. Serve with Hard Sauce. The recipe may be divided or multiplied successfully. Yield: 6 pounds—3 (4½-inch) and 1 (6½-inch) pudding molds or 6 (16-ounce) foil molds.

Note: The pudding freezes well. Reheat frozen or refrigerated puddings in top of a double boiler until hot to the touch.

Hard Sauce:

    ½ cup butter, softened
     2 cups sifted powdered sugar
    ⅛ teaspoon salt
     1 teaspoon vanilla extract
     2 teaspoons brandy

Beat softened butter until light; add sugar gradually, and continue beating until well blended. Add salt, vanilla, and brandy. When sauce is very smooth, chill thoroughly before serving.

MACAROON PUDDING

Light and luscious and easy to make.

    2 cups milk
    3 large eggs, separated
    ¾ cup sugar
    1 envelope (1 tablespoon) unflavored gelatin
    ¼ cup cold water
    1 teaspoon vanilla extract
    3 teaspoons dark rum, divided
    12 almond or coconut macaroons
    ½ pint whipping cream, whipped
    2 tablespoons powdered sugar
        Cherries or pecans (optional)

Heat milk in top of a double boiler. Beat egg yolks until very light, add sugar, and continue beating. Add fully warm milk to egg mixture and cook in double boiler until thickened, stirring constantly. Dissolve gelatin in cold water and add to hot custard mixture. On high speed of electric mixer beat egg whites until very light but not stiff. Pour cooked custard over beaten whites. Add vanilla and 2 teaspoons dark rum. Set aside to cool.

Break macaroons into small pieces. Spoon half the cooled mixture into a glass bowl or 1-quart mold. Sprinkle with half the macaroon pieces and place in refrigerator for 30 minutes. Cover with remaining custard mixture and remaining macaroon pieces. Chill. When pudding is firm, cover with whipped cream sweetened with powdered sugar and remaining 1 teaspoon dark rum. For a festive touch dot with cherries or pecans. Yield: 6 to 8 servings.

LINDA LACEFIELD'S PERSIMMON PUDDING

A delightfully different dessert using native ripe persimmons. The large California variety are not suitable.

   Ripe persimmons (2 cups pulp)
  2 large eggs
1¼ cups sugar
  ½ teaspoon baking powder
  ½ teaspoon soda
  ¼ teaspoon ground cinnamon
  ¼ teaspoon ground cloves
  ¼ teaspoon ground nutmeg
1¼ cups all-purpose flour
1½ cups milk
  2 tablespoons butter
  Whipped cream (optional)

Wash ripe persimmons and run through a colander or sieve. Place pulp in a large bowl with eggs and sugar; mix thoroughly. Sift dry ingredients including spices onto a piece of waxed paper or a large flat platter. Using an electric mixer on low speed add flour mixture alternating with milk to the persimmon mixture; blend well. Melt 1 tablespoon butter in each of two 8- or 9-inch cake pans. Divide batter into pans. Bake in a preheated 325° oven for 40 to 50 minutes. The pudding will puff up and pull away from sides of pan and begin to crack across the top when done. Do not overcook. The pudding falls as it cools. Serve in square or wedge shapes. Top with whipped cream, if desired. Yield: 16 to 20 servings.

ALZINA PIERCE'S BREAD PUDDING

Original recipe from the famous Bon Ton Restaurant in New Orleans, Louisiana.

1 loaf French bread
1 quart milk
3 eggs
2 cups sugar
2 tablespoons vanilla extract
1 cup seedless raisins
3 tablespoons margarine, melted
  Whiskey Sauce

Soak bread in milk; crush with hands until well mixed. Add eggs, sugar, vanilla, and raisins and stir well. Pour margarine in bottom of a thick, oblong baking pan, add bread mixture, and bake until very firm. Let cool; then cube pudding and put into individual pyrex dessert dishes. When ready to serve, add Whiskey Sauce and heat under broiler. Yield: 8 to 10 servings.

Whiskey Sauce:

½ cup butter or margarine
 1 cup sugar
 1 egg, well beaten
  Whiskey to taste

Cream butter and sugar and cook in top of a double boiler until very hot and thoroughly dissolved. Then add beaten egg and whip rapidly so egg does not curdle. Let cool and add whiskey.

137

LOUISIANA PLANTATION BREAD PUDDING

A tasty bread pudding with a custardlike texture and not too much bread, delicately flavored with ribbon cane syrup.

  3 slices stale cinnamon bread or white bread
  2 tablespoons butter or margarine, softened
  ½ cup seedless raisins
  2 cups milk, 1 cup whole and 1 cup
      evaporated, undiluted, or 2 cups
      half-and-half
  3 large eggs, separated
  ½ cup ribbon cane syrup or light molasses
  ⅛ teaspoon salt
  1 teaspoon vanilla extract
    Meringue

Toast bread lightly if fresh. Butter both sides of stale or toasted bread and break into small pieces. Arrange on bottom of shallow baking pan and sprinkle with raisins. Beat together milk, eggs, syrup, salt, and vanilla in a mixing bowl with a wire whisk until thoroughly blended. Pour mixture into a baking dish and place in a pan of hot water. Bake in a preheated 350° oven for 35 to 40 minutes. An inserted knife should come out clean. Cool 10 minutes on wire rack and cover with Meringue. Bake in a preheated 300° oven for 15 to 20 minutes. Allow to cool slowly. Yield: 8 servings.

Meringue:

  3 egg whites
  ¼ teaspoon cream of tartar
  1 tablespoon water
  6 tablespoons sugar
  1 teaspoon vanilla extract
  ⅛ teaspoon salt

Combine egg whites, cream of tartar, and water in a small deep narrow bowl and beat at high speed for 3 minutes. Add sugar gradually, 1 tablespoon at a time. Add vanilla and salt. Beat at high speed approximately 4 or 5 minutes or until mixture stands in peaks.

OLD-TIME RICE PUDDING

Creamy and lovely!

1½ cups water
  ⅓ cup regular rice, uncooked, or 1 cup
      leftover cooked rice
  3 egg yolks
  1 cup sugar
  1 teaspoon vanilla extract
  1 (13-ounce) can evaporated milk or 2 cups
      whole milk
  ¼ teaspoon salt
  2 tablespoons butter, softened
  ½ cup dark or white seedless raisins
  ½ teaspoon ground nutmeg
  2 teaspoons plum or blackberry jelly
    Meringue

Bring water to boil in a saucepan over high heat. Stir in ⅓ cup uncooked rice and cover tightly. Reduce heat to low and cook until all water is absorbed, about 25 minutes or until rice is tender. In a large bowl beat egg yolks; blend in sugar, vanilla, milk, salt, softened butter, raisins, and cooked or leftover rice. Pour into a buttered oblong 1½-quart casserole and sprinkle top with nutmeg. Bake in a preheated 325° oven about 45 to 50 minutes or until firm. A silver knife inserted near center should come out clean. Cool on wire rack. Spread lightly with dabs of jelly and cover with the Meringue.

Pile Meringue lightly on top of pudding and spread lightly, covering entire top. Bake in a preheated 300° oven for 15 to 20 minutes. Cool slowly. Serve hot or cold. Refrigerate after it has become fully cold. Yield: 6 to 8 servings.

Meringue:

 3 egg whites
 ¼ teaspoon cream of tartar
 6 tablespoons sugar
 1 teaspoon vanilla extract

In a narrow deep bowl beat egg whites and cream of tartar at high speed of electric mixer until stiff. Beat in sugar ½ teaspoon at a time until meringue holds its shape well. Add vanilla.

MARMADUKE PUDDING

A superb dessert for V.I.P. company. Great for bazaars or holiday giving. Quick and easy.

 1 cup (¼ pound) finely chopped beef suet
 ½ cup firmly packed dark brown sugar
 ⅓ cup orange juice
 2 eggs, well beaten
 1¼ cups unsifted all-purpose flour (reserve ¼ cup for nuts)
 1 teaspoon soda
 1 teaspoon salt
 1 teaspoon ground cinnamon
 2 tablespoons grated orange rind
 1 cup soft bread crumbs
 1 cup finely sliced almonds
 ¾ cup orange marmalade
   Hard Sauce

Combine suet, brown sugar, orange juice, and well-beaten eggs. Sift flour, soda, salt, and cinnamon into mixture. Add orange rind and bread crumbs to suet mixture. Mix well. Sprinkle reserved ¼ cup flour over almonds; add marmalade last with almonds. Put waxed paper in bottom of a well-greased 8-inch tubular fruitcake pan. turn dough into pan, cover top with aluminum foil, and tuck under tightly. Steam 1½ hours. Put into steamer or improvise by using a large soup kettle with a small pan upside down over cakepan in larger kettle.

You may cut pudding in half and freeze, or you may divide batter into orange juice cans filling ⅔ full to bake and give as presents. Remove pan from oven and test with straw for doneness. Put in a preheated 275° oven for 20 minutes. Turn onto a hot platter and serve hot with Hard Sauce. Serve with coffee; the two complement each other. Yield: 12 servings.

Variation: If you wish, heat ½ cup brandy in a small saucepan, light brandy, and bring pudding to table flaming.

Hard Sauce:

 2 cups sifted powdered sugar
 ½ cup softened butter
   Dash salt
 1 teaspoon vanilla extract or brandy

Beat sugar into softened butter until light and fluffy; add salt and vanilla or brandy.

VALENTINE STRAWBERRY PIE

 1 pint ripe strawberries
 1 cup sugar
 2½ level tablespoons cornstarch
 1 (10-ounce) bottle lemon-lime carbonated beverage
   Few drops red food coloring
 1 (9-inch) baked pie shell
 ½ pint whipping cream, sweetened and whipped

Wash strawberries and cut into halves. Combine sugar, cornstarch, and lemon-lime carbonated beverage in a saucepan and cook until mixture is clear and thickened. Cool. Add a few drops red food coloring. Pour mixture into pie shell and top with whipped cream. Yield: 6 servings.

ZOLLIE KIMBROUGH'S LEMON SAUCE FOR MERINGUES

A rich lemony sauce to fill a dozen meringues

- 1 cup sugar
- 1¼ cups water
- 1 tablespoon butter (no substitute)
- ¼ cup cornstarch (not quite level)
- 3 tablespoons cold water
- 6 tablespoons freshly squeezed, strained lemon juice
- 1 teaspoon grated lemon rind
- 3 egg yolks, well beaten
- 2 tablespoons milk

Combine sugar, 1¼ cups water, and butter in a saucepan over medium heat. When sugar dissolves add cornstarch and 3 tablespoons cold water. Stir constantly and cook slowly until mixture is clear. This will begin to thicken. Add lemon juice and rind, and cook for 2 minutes. Slowly add egg yolks beaten with milk, and bring to a boil. Remove from stove and cool. Chill and spoon over meringues just before serving. Yield: filling for 12 meringues.

TIPSY CAKE

A "Tipsy Cake" is one of the great desserts of any time. It is served at festive occasions whenever the family gathers together. For over 140 years this has been a traditional dish in my clan. My grandmother would announce after Grace, "Be sure to save a place for the pièce de résistance." With that the younger children would whoop and say, "We're going to have tipsy cake today, aren't we, Grandmother?"

Grandmother would then remind us of when Tipsy Cake first came to Kentucky: Her great-grandmother cherished this recipe enough to carry it in her walnut *escritoire papeterie* from eastern Maryland to the land of the Dark and Bloody Ground later known as Kentucky. She traveled by Concord coach to the Cumberland Gap and from there by pack mule over the Wilderness Road to a spot where Elizabethtown now stands. Upon her arrival the caravan was attacked under cover of darkness. Several persons were killed including her husband and her aunt. When a snowstorm arose during the night, she escaped with her sons and some other women to the woods nearby where she gave birth to a daughter. Later the Indians were driven off and order was restored. The new settlement named the town Elizabeth after its first born citizen.

This delicious dessert must be prepared two or even three days ahead for the best results. The cake has a large sherry content and wisdom dictates not eating it on an empty stomach. Take your best sponge cake recipe or use my simple one.

Sponge Cake:

- 6 large eggs, separated, room temperature
- 1½ cups sugar, divided
- ½ teaspoon salt
- 1½ cups all-purpose flour, measured after sifting
- 4½ tablespoons cold water
- 1 teaspoon vanilla extract
- 1½ teaspoons baking powder
- 2 cups sherry

Beat egg yolks until light. Sift and gradually add ¾ cup sugar. Beat at high speed until mixture is thick and a creamy yellow. In another bowl beat egg whites at high speed until light. Sift and gradually add remaining ¾ cup sugar. Fold egg white mixture into yolk mixture. Add salt to measured flour in sifter. Fold in flour and water alternately to the egg mixture; start and end with flour mixture. Add vanilla and baking powder. Pour cake batter slowly into an ungreased 10-inch tube pan. Bake on lowest rack in a preheated 350° oven for 25 to 30 minutes. When cake begins to reach a golden brown and starts leaving sides of pan, test with straw in center for doneness. Remove from oven and invert on cake rack until entirely cold.

Slice through middle of sponge cake, making two layers. Place each layer on a large platter. Dribble 1 cup sherry over each and set aside. The next day make a thick boiled custard.

Custard:

1½ cups sugar
⅛ teaspoon salt
2 tablespoons all-purpose flour
6 large eggs
1 quart milk
2 teaspoons vanilla extract

Combine sugar, salt, and flour. Beat eggs slightly and add dry ingredients; blend well. Heat milk in top of a double boiler until warm. Test a drop on wrist. Pour 1 cup warm milk into sugar mixture; then pour entire mixture into remaining warm milk, stirring constantly. Cook until mixture coats spoon and becomes thickened. Remove from heat and add vanilla. For cooling quickly, place top of double boiler over ice and stir until cool. There should not be any lumps; if there are, strain through sieve.

Icing:

1 pint whipping cream, whipped
3 tablespoons sugar
2 teaspoons vanilla extract
1 (8-ounce) glass apple jelly
1 (8-ounce) can blanched almonds

When ready to serve cake, whip cream and add sugar when it begins to thicken. Add vanilla.

To finish cake spread one-half the apple jelly over bottom layer, sprinkle with one-third of the almonds and cover with one-half the custard. Place top layer of cake over this and repeat the same process. Cover cake with plastic wrap or waxed paper and refrigerate until next day.

Ice with whipped cream and place remaining one-third of the almonds on top. I reserve some of the custard and whipped cream to add to each slice. This dessert will keep a week provided you return to refrigerator after each serving. Serve with coffee. Yield: 20 servings.

RASPBERRY PEACH ALASKA

Glamorous and easy to make.

1 quart raspberry sherbet
1 (9-inch) pastry shell, baked and frozen
1 (10-ounce) package frozen sliced peaches in syrup or 1½ cups fresh peaches, peeled and sliced
⅓ cup sugar, for fresh peaches only
1 tablespoon lemon juice, for fresh peaches only
3 large egg whites, room temperature
½ teaspoon vanilla extract
⅛ teaspoon salt
3 tablespoons powdered sugar

Spoon raspberry sherbet into baked, frozen pastry shell, spread evenly, and freeze overnight or until firm. Thaw frozen peaches but keep chilled until ready to serve dessert. If using fresh peaches, sprinkle with sugar and add lemon juice; cover and chill.

At serving time, make meringue. In a small narrow bowl beat whites, vanilla, and salt at high speed of electric mixer until soft peaks appear. Gradually add powdered sugar and continue beating until stiff peaks form. Working quickly, drain chilled peaches and spread over surface of frozen sherbet. Spread meringue over fruit, and seal meringue well to edge of pastry. Place pie plate on a cutting board. Bake in a preheated 450° oven for 3 or 4 minutes until meringue is golden brown. Cut into slices and serve at once. Dipping a sharp knife into water facilitates cutting. Yield: 8 servings.

PINK LADY WHIPPED CREAM CAKE

Lovely! Serve on silver or crystal cake platter with your prettiest china and an arrangement of pink roses.

1½ cups cake flour, measured after sifting
¼ teaspoon salt
1½ teaspoons baking powder
1 cup whipping cream
2 extra-large eggs, room temperature
1 cup sugar
1 teaspoon vanilla extract
Pink Peppermint Icing

To measured flour, add salt, and baking powder and sift three times. Whip cream until stiff in a large mixing bowl. Drop in eggs one at a time and continue to beat; add sugar using high speed of electric mixer. Sift in flour mixture and add vanilla, using medium speed. Spoon into two well-greased and floured 8-inch cakepans lined with waxed paper. Bake in a preheated 375° oven for 20 to 25 minutes or until cake tests done. Cool on wire rack 10 minutes; remove from pan and finish cooling on rack. A double recipe will make a big stem loaf pan or 3 (9-inch) layers. Frost with Pink Peppermint Icing. Yield: 2 (8-inch) layers.

Pink Peppermint Icing:

3 large egg whites, room temperature
1½ cups sugar
1½ teaspoons light corn syrup
¼ teaspoon fresh cream of tartar
5 tablespoons cold water
1 drop oil of peppermint
1 drop red food coloring
¼ cup (4 sticks) finely crushed peppermint
**   stick candy**
1 teaspoon vanilla extract

Combine egg whites, sugar, corn syrup, cream of tartar, and water in top of a double boiler over rapidly boiling water and beat until thoroughly blended. Continue to beat with electric mixer, rotary beater, or wire whisk for 7 minutes or until icing begins to stand in peaks. Remove from heat, add peppermint oil, red food coloring, crushed candy, and vanilla. Spread on cake.

RASPBERRY WINE TORTE

A superb dessert created for Dr. E. L. Posey, Jr., this wine torte features the delicate flavor and color of the luscious red berry. The recipe has four easy parts and uses individually frozen berries. To achieve its perfection, the cake must be made at least three days in advance so that the torte may ripen fully.

Raspberry Cake:

6 large eggs, separated, room temperature
1½ cups sifted sugar, divided
½ teaspoon salt
1½ cups all-purpose flour
4½ tablespoons cold water
1½ teaspoons baking powder
1 teaspoon vanilla extract
2 cups Raspberry Bandon Wine

Beat egg yolks until light, and gradually add ¾ cup sifted sugar. Continue beating with electric mixer on high speed until yolks are thick and creamy yellow. At the same speed beat egg whites in another bowl until light and standing in soft peaks. Gradually add remaining ¾ cup sifted sugar, beating until whites are stiff but not dry. Fold egg white mixture into yolk mixture. Add salt to measured flour in sifter. Fold flour and water alternately into egg mixture. Begin and end with flour mixture. Add baking powder and vanilla.

Pour cake batter into an ungreased 10-inch tube pan. Bake on lowest rack in a preheated

350° oven for 25 to 30 minutes until cake turns a golden brown and starts leaving sides of pan and until cake tests done. Remove from oven and invert on rack until cold. Run spatula gently around cake. If cake clings to bottom of pan, return to oven just long enough to heat the pan fully warm, and the cake will come out with ease. Slice crosswise through middle of cake, making two layers. Place layers on a large platter and dribble 1 cup raspberry wine over each. Set aside. The next day make Custard Filling.

Custard Filling:

  1 quart milk
1½ cups sugar
 ⅛ teaspoon salt
  4 tablespoons all-purpose flour
  6 large eggs, room temperature
  2 teaspoons vanilla extract

Warm milk slowly in top of a large double boiler. Blend sugar, salt, and flour in a small bowl. Beat eggs slightly and add dry ingredients; mix well. Add egg-flour mixture slowly into warmed milk using a wire whisk. Stir constantly with wire whisk, reaching all over bottom of pan. When mixture thickens and will coat a metal or silver spoon, remove and add vanilla. Cool pan in bowl of ice and stir often.

Other Ingredients Needed:

  1 (8-ounce) glass raspberry jelly
  1 (8-ounce) can blanched almonds, sliced
  1 (3½-ounce) package vanilla Whip and Chill
 ½ cup milk
  1 (10-ounce) package individually frozen
      raspberries
  2 tablespoons lemon juice
  2 tablespoons brandy, preferably almond
  1 drop red food coloring (optional)

Crabapple or another tart jelly may be used in place of raspberry. Spread a thin layer of jelly evenly over one layer of cake. Sprinkle with sliced almonds and ice with chilled custard. Add second cake layer and repeat icing process. Refrigerate until next day or until you plan to serve dessert. Place Whip and Chill in a small deep narrow bowl and mix at low speed of electric beater with milk. Whip at high speed 1 minute.

Allow raspberries to thaw completely. Drain juice into a separate bowl. Place berries on paper towels to dry. Measure out ½ cup berry juice; add lemon juice and brandy. Add juice mixture to milk and beat at low speed; then whip at high speed for 2 minutes. For a deeper pink add 1 drop red coloring. Chill 10 minutes and ice entire cake with mixture.

Whipped Cream:

½ pint whipping cream, very cold
  2 tablespoons sugar
  2 tablespoons Triple Sec or brandy

Whip cream; add sugar and Triple Sec. Immediately before serving decorate torte with raspberries and rosettes of whipped cream. Serve torte on a large silver or crystal cake platter. This is ideal for a Valentine party with coffee or punch and salted nuts. When serving, top each slice with a dollop of whipped cream. If you prefer a dessert with less calories and less cholesterol, omit whipped cream. Yield: 20 to 22 servings.

CLAUDIA WHITNEY'S PEACH ICE CREAM

4 to 6 peaches (1½ cups puree)
1 tablespoon lemon juice
1 cup whipping cream
1 cup powdered sugar

Peel peaches and remove pits. Put peaches and lemon juice into blender. Cover, blend, and puree until smooth. Whip cream until it holds a soft peak. Add powdered sugar and continue to beat until stiff. Fold in 1½ cups peach puree. Pour into refrigerator tray and freeze for 2 to 4 hours or until firm. Yield: 4 to 6 servings.

WATERMELON CHARLOTTE RUSSE

Serve this exquisite dessert laced with lady fingers in a large cut glass bowl. Its flavor is indescribably lovely.

2⅔ cups strained watermelon juice, divided
  2 envelopes (2 tablespoons) unflavored
    gelatin
  ⅔ cup sugar, divided
  ⅛ teaspoon salt
  2 tablespoons strained lemon juice
  2 large egg whites, room temperature
  ½ pint whipping cream, chilled
  1 tablespoon powdered sugar
  2 teaspoons crème d' almond brandy, divided
  8 ladyfingers, split in half
    Mint sprigs

One fourth of a large fully ripe watermelon will yield about 3 cups juice. Cut melon into cubes and remove seeds. Liquify in blender or mash through strainer. Sprinkle gelatin over 1 cup juice in a medium-size saucepan. Cook over low heat about 5 minutes until gelatin is dissolved, stirring constantly. Add ⅓ cup sugar and salt, and stir until dissolved. Pour into a large mixing bowl and add remaining watermelon juice and lemon juice. Chill, stirring occasionally, until mixture mounds slightly when dropped from a tablespoon. In a small narrow bowl beat egg whites on high speed of electric mixer until they stand in soft, stiff peaks. Gradually add remaining ⅓ cup sugar and beat until very stiff. Fold beaten egg whites into watermelon mixture.

Whip cream until stiff, adding powdered sugar as soon as cream begins to stand in peaks. Add crème d' almond. Fold whipped cream into watermelon mixture. Stand split lady fingers around edge of bowl and gently pour in Charlotte Russe. Chill about 2 hours or until set. Garnish with mint sprigs. You may use the Charlotte Russe in a baked 10-inch graham cracker crust or pastry shell. Yield: 8 to 10 servings.

ZOLLIE KIMBROUGH'S SCHAUMTORTE

A superb dessert, festive enough for any special occasion. Easily made, it must be prepared two or three days ahead for proper aging.

2 cups sugar, superfine preferred
6 large egg whites, room temperature
1 teaspoon vanilla extract
1 tablespoon vinegar
1 pint whipping cream
  Frosted green mint leaves, frosted violets, or
    fresh strawberries

Sift sugar for lumps. Using vegetable oil on a paper towel, lightly grease two 8- or 9-inch cakepans, preferably type with a center lever for easy removal. The 8-inch pan makes a higher, more spectacular torte.

In a large bowl beat egg whites at high speed until fairly stiff. Add sugar slowly, 1 tablespoon at a time. Add vanilla and vinegar; beat well. Taste; if there is any feel of sugar grain, continue to beat. Take spatula and see if you can make a wide swath through center of beaten eggs. If the sides hold back, divide meringue evenly into two pans. Bake in a preheated 250° oven for 1 hour. Test with straw in center for doneness; if straw comes out sticky bake 10 minutes longer. Remove immediately. Cool for 1 hour.

Chill a bowl and electric beaters. Beat cream until very stiff. Spread whipped cream between the two layers and on the outside and top of the torte. Refrigerate for at least one or two days. I place my torte on a china or crystal cake plate and decorate top with frosted green mint leaves and frosted violets. You may like to decorate top with a circular or heartshaped design with large, washed and dried strawberries. Arrange just before serving. Yield: 10 to 12 servings.

SPECTACULAR RASPBERRY CLOUD

The luscious raspberry at its best. Take your favorite angel food cake recipe or use a commercial angel food mix and prepare a 10-inch tube pan lined on bottom with waxed paper. Bake according to package directions; cool completely. With a sharp knife loosen cake from sides of pan and gently remove. Cut crosswise 1 inch from top and remove top layer. Being careful not to damage remaining cake's outer shell, scoop out insides and tear into pieces about the size of a pingpong ball. Make this filling which is low in calories and cholesterol.

½ **cup sliced almonds, divided**
2 **tablespoons margarine**
1 **(10-ounce) package frozen red raspberries, partially thawed**
2 **large egg whites, room temperature**
1 **cup sifted sugar**
1 **tablespoon strained lemon juice**
2 **teaspoons crème d'almond brandy**
1 **tablespoon raspberry brandy**
½ **(9-ounce) container commercial whipped topping, frozen, divided**

Toast sliced almonds in margarine and divide in half. Place berries, egg whites, sugar, lemon juice, and brandies in a large mixing bowl and beat at high speed 15 minutes. Cut down from sides with spatula during process. Divide mixture in half and place other half in another large bowl. Add whipped topping to first bowl; fold in pieces of cake and ¼ cup toasted almonds.

Fill cake with this mixture, replace top layer, and ice with remaining bowl of raspberry filling. Sprinkle remaining ¼ cup toasted almonds on top. Freeze at once. At serving time remove from freezer and slice. If you plan to keep the cake longer than 1 day, cover with foil after it has frozen. For best results use within 2 weeks of making. Serve with black coffee and salted pecans. Yield: 18 servings.

Jellies, Pickles, and Accompaniments

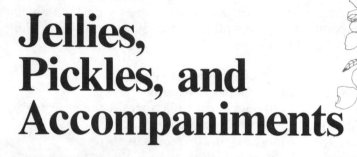

ROSE GERANIUM JELLY

Crab apples make a tart jelly with the geranium flavor while regular apples produce a sweeter jelly with the same flavor.

> **5 pounds whole crab apples or 12 medium-size apples, Jonathan, Rome Beauty, Winesap, or Stayman**
> **24 to 26 geranium leaves**
> **5 cups water**
> **2 (4-ounce) blocks paraffin**
> **1 (1¾-ounce) package powdered fruit pectin**
> **8 cups sugar**

Wash apples and remove blossom ends. Leave crab apples whole, but cut regular apples into small pieces. *Do not peel or core.* Wash geranium leaves lightly and shake off moisture. Add water to apples; cover and simmer for 15 minutes. Crush with masher and simmer 5 minutes longer. Place in jelly bag and allow to drip overnight for clearest jelly. (I find a man's cotton handkerchief clipped with clothes pins to a strainer or colander makes a very handy jelly bag.) If you are in a hurry, you may squeeze out juice. There should be about 7 cups of juice. If there is a slight shortage of juice add water.

Sterilize jars and lids; scald and drain. Melt paraffin in a heavy glass jar in boiling water.

Measure strained juice. Mix fruit pectin with juice in a 6- to 8-quart saucepan over high heat. Bring to a hard boil, stirring occasionally. Add sugar at once. Bring to a hard rolling boil that cannot be stirred down, stirring constantly. Boil 1 minute, remove from heat, and skim off foam with a metal spoon. Place one geranium leaf in each glass and pour jelly over it. Remove first leaf as it shrivels and replace with a fresh leaf to be left in. Leave ½ inch space at top and cover with melted paraffin. Jelly will keep in refrigerator for two months without paraffin but sealed with lid. Allow jelly to sit for 24 hours before moving to store. Yield: 12 to 13 (8-ounce) glasses.

Note: For softer jellies, use ¼ cup more juice; for stiffer jellies, ¼ cup less juice.

MUSCADINE JELLY

> **2 quarts muscadines**
> **1½ (4-ounce) blocks paraffin**
> **1 (1¾-ounce) package powdered fruit pectin**
> **7 cups sugar**

Wash and drain muscadines. Place in a 6- to 8-quart saucepan and cover with cold water. Bring to a boil and simmer 15 minutes with kettle covered. Crush muscadines with masher and simmer five minutes longer. Place in jelly bag and squeeze out juice. There should be 6 cups. If there is a slight shortage of juice, add water. Sterilize, scald, and drain jars and lids. Melt paraffin in a heavy glass jar in boiling water. Measure strained juice. Mix fruit pectin with juice in saucepan over high heat. Bring to a hard rolling boil that cannot be stirred down, stirring constantly. Add sugar slowly and boil for 1 minute. Remove from heat, skim off foam with metal spoon. Pour at once into glasses, leaving ½-inch space at top, and cover with ⅛ inch melted paraffin. Jelly will keep in refrigerator for 2 months without paraffin but sealed with a lid. Allow jelly to sit for 24 hours before moving to store. Yield: 11 to 12 (8-ounce) glasses.

Note: For softer jellies, use ¼ cup more juice. For stiffer jellies use ¼ cup less juice.

POMEGRANATE JELLY

A beautiful and piquant jelly. Spread over baked or sliced ham, pork chops, or baked Canadian bacon for an exotic dish. Good with any meat or fowl.

6 very large and fully ripe pomegranates or 8 medium-size pomegranates
6 cups cold water
2 tablespoons strained lemon juice
1 (¾-ounce) box fruit pectin
6 cups sugar
Paraffin

Cut pomegranates in half and scrape out ripe seeds with a spoon or ream on a juice squeezer. Combine seeds and water, bring to a simmering boil, and boil 10 minutes. Place juice in jelly cloth or bag and squeeze out juice. This should make 5 cups. Place measured juice, lemon juice, and pectin in a large saucepan and bring to a boil over high heat, stirring constantly. Stir in sugar at once. Bring to a full rolling boil and boil 1 minute.

Test for jelly since this fruit has no pectin. Dip spoon into boiling syrup; two large drops will form, one on either side, along the spoon's

edge. When these two drops come together and fall as one drop, the "sheeting stage" has been reached (220° to 222°). This makes a firm jelly. Remove pan from heat, skim off foam with metal spoon, and pour quickly into sterilized jelly glasses. Cover with hot melted paraffin. Be sure to melt paraffin over a very low flame or over hot water. I have a metal teapot which I use for this purpose only. Yield: 8 (8-ounce) glasses.

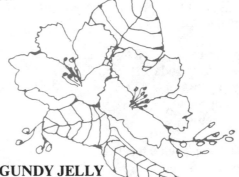

BURGUNDY JELLY

Clear as crystal and delectable to eat! Try it with any meat. You can make this in twenty minutes. Put up in attractive and inexpensive juice glasses, the jelly makes ideal gifts for holiday giving or for bazaars. Seal with paraffin and cover with foil muffin cups turned upside down and taped.

2 cups Burgundy
3 cups sugar
1 (6-ounce) bottle liquid fruit pectin
1 (4-ounce) block paraffin

Combine wine and sugar in top of a double boiler over rapidly boiling water. Stir constantly 2 to 10 minutes, depending on temperature of wine, until sugar is dissolved. Do not allow wine-sugar mixture to boil; heat only to dissolve sugar. When dissolved, stir in fruit pectin at once, pour into sterilized jelly glasses, and seal with melted paraffin. You may use other wines to suit your taste: sauterne, muscatel, tokay, claret, or champagne. Yield: 5 (8-ounce) glasses.

FIG PRESERVES

A simple and easy way to make beautiful fig preserves. Proportions are for both peeled and unpeeled figs. I would not recommend working with more than 1½ gallons of figs at one time; with the syrup, this amount fills a dishpan within an inch of the top of the pan. Allow yourself two hours to prepare, cook and pack the preserves into jars. One and a half gallons of figs makes approximately 6 pints with the jars packed tightly.

For 1 cup unpeeled figs use:
    Baking soda
1⅓ cups water
  1 cup sugar
    Lemon slices

For 1 cup peeled figs use:
1⅓ cups water
  ¾ cup sugar
    Lemon slices

Pick through figs and remove those which are overly ripe, split, or broken. Fill a dishpan nearly full of water and bring to a boil; add figs gently. If you are using unpeeled figs, immediately pour in 4 heaping tablespoons baking soda for every 5 quarts of water. This will foam. (Stand back so that you will not be burned should it run over the sides.) Allow figs to stay in soda water only a minute or two. Stir figs gently with wooden spoon and drain off liquid by pouring figs into a large colander. Rinse thoroughly with at least two changes of water.

Measure ingredients for number of cups of figs you are using. Boil water, sugar, and lemon slices over medium heat, stirring contantly until sugar is dissolved. For every 10 or more cups of figs, use 2 washed lemons, sliced as thinly as possible. Allow mixture to boil gently for 15 to 20 minutes; then add figs a few at a time. After all figs have been added, raise heat until the mixture begins to boil briskly.

Lower heat to a simmering boil. Stir often with a plastic or wooden spoon. Remove any thick heavy foam that may rise to the top.

Sterilize jars and keep in boiling water until ready to use. When the figs become clear and a toothpick goes in easily, pack the figs into the jars and arrange with an iced-tea spoon. Cover with boiling syrup and seal immediately. Yield: 1½ gallons of figs makes 6 pints fig preserves.

JAMAICAN BANANA JAM

Savor the exotic flavor of the West Indies in the easiest and quickest jam you will ever make.

5½ pounds (about 12 large) ripe bananas
  ½ lime
  1 cup cold water
  2 pounds sugar
  4 teaspoons lime juice
  2 (4-ounce) blocks paraffin

Peel and scrape off banana's outer fuzz and slice bananas very thickly. Wash lime, slice thinly and cut into tiny pieces. (Lemon may be substituted if fresh lime is unavailable.) In a large 4- to 6-quart kettle combine water, sugar, and tiny pieces of lime; bring to a boil and allow to simmer 15 minutes with kettle covered. Add lime juice and bananas, and cook for 25 to 30 minutes, until mixture thickens. Stir often. Ladle jam into sterilized jars leaving ½ inch space at top; cover at once with paraffin that has been melted in a saucepan over low heat. Place lids on jars, screw bands on tightly, and invert. To seal without paraffin, use two-piece metal lids leaving ⅛ inch space at top of jar when filling with jam. Screw bands on tightly and invert; when all are sealed, stand upright and cool. Yield: 4 pints.

AUNT SARAH'S STRAWBERRY PRESERVES

The best and easy to make. These berries are luscious.

2 pints firm ripe strawberries
4 cups sugar
¾ tablespoon red cider vinegar

Wash and cap berries. Combine sugar and berries in a large covered kettle and cook over low heat. When the sugar has melted, raise heat to medium and allow mixture to come to a boil. Boil exactly 3 minutes. Add vinegar and boil hard for an additional 8 minutes. Remove from heat and lightly skim foam from top. Cover and stir occasionally until completely cold. Cover and let stand overnight. Bottle cold in sterilized jars. This recipe works best in small quantities. You may cook several batches at the same time, but make each one separately. Yield: 4 (8-ounce) jars.

GINGER JELLY

5 pounds whole crab apples or 12
    medium-size Jonathan, Rome Beauty,
    Winesap, or Stayman apples
5 cups water
8 cups sugar
1 (1¾-ounce) box fruit pectin
24 to 26 Jamaica gingerroots
2 (4-ounce) blocks paraffin

Wash apples and remove blossom ends. Leave crab apples whole, but cut the others into small pieces. *Do not peel or core.* Add water to apples, cover and simmer 15 minutes. Crush with potato masher and simmer 5 minutes longer. Place in jelly bag and allow to drip overnight for clearest jelly. (I find a man's cotton handkerchief clipped to a strainer or colander with clothes pins makes a very handy jelly bag.

There should be about 7 cups of juice. If there is a slight shortage of juice, add water.

Sterilize jars and lids; scald and drain. Melt paraffin in a heavy glass jar in boiling water. Measure strained juice. Mix juice and fruit pectin in a 6 to 8 quart saucepan over high heat. Bring to a hard boil, stirring occasionally. Add sugar at once. Bring to a hard rolling boil that cannot be stirred down, stirring constantly. Remove from heat and skim off foam with a metal spoon. Place two ginger roots in each glass and pour jelly over them. Leave ½ inch space at top of glass and cover with melted paraffin. Jelly will keep in refrigerator for two months without paraffin but sealed with a lid. Allow jelly to sit for 24 hours before moving to store. Yield: 12 to 13 (8-ounce) glasses.

Note: For softer jellies, use ¼ cup more juice; for stiffer jellies, use ¼ cup less juice.

SCOTCH MARMALADE

This is hard to beat for taste or cost.

1 grapefruit, white or pink
1 large or 2 small smooth-skinned oranges
1 large lemon
3 quarts cold water, divided
5 pounds white sugar

Wash fruit and cut into small pieces, removing seeds. Combine 1½ cups fruit and ½ cup water in blender and chop. Repeat until all fruit is chopped finely. Put in stainless steel or enamel pan, and add remaining water. Measure depth of mixture with kitchen spoon handle before turning on heat. Bring to a hard boil over high heat and cook down until reduced to one half its original volume. Add sugar and bring to boil again; lower heat, and boil slowly, but at more than a simmer. Remove any thick white foam from marmalade while cooking. Stir occasionally. When two drops of syrup hang together on spoon, marmalade is done. Put up in hot sterilized jars; seal. Yield: 5 pints.

SOUR PICKLES INTO SWEET

Easy to do and makes inexpensive friendship gifts and bazaar donations.

1 gallon sour pickles, drained
1 (1½-ounce) box black peppercorns
1 (1½-ounce) box whole mixed pickling spices
2 tablespoons vegetable oil
4 cloves garlic, chopped
5 pounds sugar, minus 2 cups

Slice pickles into ¼-inch rounds. Combine all ingredients in a large enamel, glass, or stainless steel bowl. Stir until thoroughly mixed, then cover bowl with plastic. Stir twice a day for 5 days. Pack into sterilized jars, adding enough juice to cover pickles and seal. Be sure and distribute chopped garlic cloves evenly among jars. Yield: 8 pints.

SWEET PICKLED FIGS

A rare treat! Easy to do but requires a good memory.

4 quarts water
½ cup soda
3½ pounds (1 gallon plus 1 pint) ripe firm figs, unpeeled
2½ pounds sugar
½ cup water
1 cup red cider vinegar
3 tablespoons whole cloves
3 sticks cinnamon
2 tablespoons whole allspice

Boil 4 quarts water in large saucepan or dishpan. Add soda and drop in figs. Stir 1 to 2 minutes and pour off water. Rinse figs carefully with two changes of water and allow to drain in a colander. In a large enamel or stainless steel kettle, add sugar, ½ cup water, vinegar, and spices; bring to a full boil. Drop figs into boiling syrup and bring to a rolling boil.

At this point turn off heat and cover kettle immediately. Set aside and let stand overnight. Repeat cooking process the next morning and again that same afternoon or evening. Repeat cooking process the second morning for the final time. Remove figs with a slotted spoon and arrange in hot, sterilized jars; cover with boiling syrup. Divide cloves, allspice, and broken cinnamon sticks, placing a little in each jar. Seal. Yield: 4 pints.

SALLIE JORGENSEN'S PICKLED GARDEN RELISH

Colorful and tasty. Serve on a meat platter as a salad or a vegetable.

½ small head cauliflower
2 carrots, pared
1 green pepper
2 to 3 celery ribs
1 (4-ounce) jar pimiento, drained
1 (3-ounce) jar pitted green olives, drained
¾ cup wine vinegar
½ cup olive or salad oil
2 tablespoons sugar
1 teaspoon salt
½ teaspoon dried basil or oregano leaves
¼ teaspoon pepper
¼ cup water

Cut cauliflower into flowerets and slice. Cut carrots and green pepper into 2-inch strips. Cut celery into 1-inch strips and measure out 1 cup; cut pimientos into strips.

In a large skillet, combine all ingredients. Bring to boil, stirring occasionally. Reduce heat, cover, and simmer 5 minutes. Cool; then refrigerate at least 24 hours. Drain well. Yield: 6½ to 7 cups or 6 servings.

Tender pork chops attractively garnished with orange sections and fresh parsley can turn any meal into a special occasion. Winifred's delicious Pork Chops in Ginger Ale recipe may be found on page 172.

PICKLED OKRA PODS

Serve as zesty hors d'oeuvres with alcoholic beverages or sliced in a green salad.

½ pound (about 22 to 25) small tender okra
    pods
3 small hot peppers, red or green
1 tablespoon dill seeds
½ tablespoon mustard seeds
3 cloves garlic
⅔ cup cider vinegar
2 tablespoons salt
⅓ cup water

Wash okra and clip stem, but do not remove cap. Pack pods stem-end up into a hot 1-pint sterilized jar. Add hot peppers, dill and mustard seed, and garlic. Bring vinegar, salt, and water to a hard boil and pour over okra. Seal and allow to stand several weeks before using. Yield: 1 pint.

LOUISE CARLISLE'S WATERMELON RIND PICKLE

7 pounds watermelon rind (1 large
    watermelon)
1 small bottle Lilley lime (available at most
    drugstores)
½ tablespoon salt
6 pounds sugar
  About 2 quarts vinegar
1 tablespoon whole allspice
1 tablespoon whole cloves
4 sticks cinnamon

Cut green rind and red meat from watermelon. Cut rind into small pieces or strips. Soak rind

Trout with Véronique sauce adds an extra elegance to the dinner table. Serve with a chilled white wine for those special guests. Winifred's Trout Véronique is on page 194.

in lime overnight. Wash 3 times in clear water. Cover rind with water, add salt, and boil 25 minutes. Wash 3 times again; drain. Cook in sugar, vinegar, and spices until clear. Leave overnight; then boil 10 minutes. Pack pickles in hot, sterilized jars, and pour syrup over them. Yield: 10 pints.

ICEBERG GREEN TOMATO PICKLE

Take those small green tomatoes left on the vine or find some at a farmers' market and make a luscious party pickle.

7½ pounds small green tomatoes
1 bottle Lilley's lime (made into solution
    according to label directions)—available
    at most drugstores, or 3 cups lime
    dissolved in 3 gallons of water
12 pounds sugar
8 pints cider vinegar
2 teaspoons whole cloves
2 teaspoons whole allspice
4 sticks cinnamon
  Green food coloring

Wash tomatoes, remove blossom end, slice thinly, and soak 24 hours in lime water solution. Drain and soak in fresh water for 4 hours, changing every hour; drain. In a large enamel or stainless steel dishpan, place sugar, vinegar, and spices. Bring to a boil over medium heat. Stir mixture until all sugar is dissolved. When mixture reaches a boil add tomatoes and let stand overnight. The next morning allow mixture to boil for 1 hour or until tender, stirring often. Add a few drops of food coloring and seal in sterilized glass jars. If larger tomatoes are used you will need wide-mouthed canning jars. Yield: 6 pints.

AUNT SALLY'S PICKLED PEACHES

This recipe takes about two hours if you work fast. The results are rewarding—the tastiest golden peaches.

  8 pounds firm, ripe clingstone peaches
3½ pounds sugar
  2 cups cider vinegar
  3 cinnamon sticks, broken into pieces
  1 tablespoon or more whole cloves, or
      enough to put 3 cloves in each peach

Pour boiling water over peaches in large dishpan and let stand two or three minutes. Drain and cover peaches with cold water. Peel peaches; place in plastic bag to keep from turning brown. When you are halfway through peeling, combine sugar, vinegar, and cinnamon in a saucepan over medium heat. Stir until sugar is dissolved; then bring to boiling point and boil 15 minutes. Place 3 cloves in each peach; remove clove head first to keep syrup from darkening. Add peaches to boiling syrup and cook until a straw can be inserted into the peaches with ease. Place peaches in hot, sterilized, wide-mouthed jars; cover to keep hot. Cook syrup about 10 minutes longer and pour it boiling hot over peaches. Place a piece of cinnamon stick in each jar. Seal jars at once. This recipe doubles easily. Yield: about 5 pints.

BREAD AND BUTTER PICKLES

A tasty and easily prepared pickle that does not have to be sealed airtight. These may be placed in a plastic or glass gallon jar with a clean screw-on top. Keep a pint in the refrigerator—crisp and cool for use with hamburgers.

  8 medium-size white onions
  1 gallon (6 pounds) small sliced cucumbers
  2 large bell peppers
½ cup salt
  5 cups sugar
  5 cups white vinegar
  2 tablespoons mustard seeds
  1 tablespoon celery seeds
½ teaspoon whole cloves
1½ teaspoons ground tumeric

Wash onions, cucumbers (outer skin removed), and bell peppers; slice into ⅛-inch thick slices. (If onions affect you, use an underwater mask to cover eyes.) Place in a large enamel or stainless steel dishpan and cover with salt. Mix thoroughly with clean hands. Cover with 10 pounds of chopped ice. Let stand for 3 hours, then drain off liquid. Place prepared vegetables and remaining ingredients in dishpan and bring to a boil over medium heat, stirring often. Allow the mixture to boil for 15 minutes or longer until the onion and cucumbers become transparent. Put up in thoroughly scalded jars with clean lids. Yield: 10 pints.

SHERRIED PEPPERS

This is a gourmet seasoning which adds a magic flavor to soups and stews. It creates savory sauces and makes a Bloody Mary stand on its head and a dry Martini par excellence. The sauce makes an attractive gift in a decanter for the gourmet cook who has everything.

  1 quart jar or whiskey decanter
¾ to 1 pound red hot peppers, plus a few
      green peppers for color
  Boiling water to cover
12 whole cloves
  1 teaspoon lemon bits
12 black peppercorns
  1 teaspoon Beau Monde seasoning
  3 cups (or enough to cover peppers) dry or
      cocktail sherry

Sterilize jar or decanter. Pour boiling water over peppers and allow to sit for 2 or 3 minutes; drain. Arrange some peppers in the jar, stem end up; use iced-tea spoon to help in arranging. Drop in a few cloves, lemon bits, and peppercorns. Add more peppers halfway along with Beau Monde seasoning. When all peppers are placed in jar, add remaining spices. Cover with sherry and screw lid on tightly. As peppers absorb sherry, add enough to keep them covered. (Once is usually sufficient.) Allow sauce to sit at least four weeks before using. This will keep indefinitely. Yield: 1 quart.

Note: For Bloody Marys and Martinis, add only a few drops of sauce.

GREEN TOMATO RELISH

An excellent relish to serve with meats or for making slaw. Easy to make but requires time; the recipe is a large one.

  1 quart chopped cabbage
  1 quart chopped onion
  1 gallon thinly sliced green tomatoes
 10 red and green bell peppers (red for color only)
     Salt
  1 quart chopped celery
1½ quarts red cider vinegar
  4 pounds sugar
  1 cup all-purpose flour
  1 tablespoon mustard seeds
  1 tablespoon celery seeds
  1 teaspoon ground turmeric
  1 quart diced sweet pickle
 ½ teaspoon alum

In a large enamel or stainless steel dishpan place cabbage, onion, tomatoes, and peppers and sprinkle with a good-size handful of salt; let stand overnight. The next morning, drain off liquid and put dishpan on stove with vegetables. Add chopped celery and enough fresh water to cover. Bring to a boil over medium high heat; drain. Add vinegar, sugar, flour, mustard and celery seeds, and turmeric. Cook 15 minutes or until tender; taste. Add diced pickles and alum to mixture just long enough before canning to heat them thoroughly. Pour into sterilized pint jars and seal immediately. Yield: 39 pints.

OKRA COO-COO

An unusual cooked okra side dish that comes from Barbados. It is served mainly with fried or steamed flying fish for which the island is noted. The Bajans use a coo-coo stick to remove the lumps from the cornmeal, but my wooden kitchen spoon proved very satisfactory. Coo-coo can be made with breadfruit or with canned tomatoes.

  6 tender okra pods
1½ cups water
  1 teaspoon salt
 ½ cup white cornmeal
  2 tablespoons butter
 ½ teaspoon hot sauce or Tabasco (optional)

Wash and slice okra. Bring water to a boil; add salt and sliced okra. Cook about 15 minutes or until tender; a fork should go in easily. Drain okra in colander and reserve liquid. Return okra to saucepan with 4 tablespoons reserved liquid. Stir in cornmeal with coo-coo stick or wooden spoon, pressing against sides of saucepan to remove all lumps. Gradually add remaining liquid, butter, and hot sauce, if desired, cooking until mixture is thick and smooth. Yield: 4 servings.

BRANDIED STRAWBERRIES

The real thing! Tastes like fresh strawberries, yet has the fragrant bouquet of good brandy. Put up as much as you like. Give a jar to that special friend for a joyous occasion.

1 pint fresh ripe firm strawberries
1 cup sugar
½ cup good brandy

Remove hulls, wash, and drain strawberries in a colander. Sterilize or wash thoroughly a ½-gallon jar or crock. Place some berries in jar, cover with some of the sugar and part of the brandy. Continue until all the ingredients are used. Cover, but do not put lid on tightly; the mixture needs a little air. Gently stir mixture daily until all sugar is dissolved, then stir occasionally for a month or more. In the early fall put up in attractive jars and seal the lids. Yield: 2 (8-ounce) jars.

Variations: Use 1 cup seedless grapes with 3 cups strawberries, 2 cups sugar, and 1 cup brandy for Christmas giving. This makes a delicious and colorful combination. The brandy solution will not hold its flavor longer than 12 months. Make a fresh batch every year for best results.

WILD SPRING PLUM CONSERVE

Tart and tasty! This is great with chicken, turkey, ham, or pork roast.

5 cups plum pulp
1½ to 2 cups sugar (depending on tartness of fruit)
1 (1¾-ounce) package powdered fruit pectin
1 teaspoon almond extract
1 (4-ounce) block paraffin

To prepare pulp, strain juice for jelly and remove seeds by putting through a fine colander or ricer. In a very large saucepan combine pulp, sugar, and fruit pectin and bring to a simmering boil. Cook 5 minutes, stirring constantly. Remove from heat; skim off any foam with a metal spoon. Add almond extract and stir well. Pour at once into glasses, leaving ½ inch space at top. Cover with melted paraffin. Yield: 6 (8-ounce) glasses.

SHERRIED SOUR CHERRIES

An unusual relish to serve with roast pork or ham.

1 (16-ounce) can pitted sour cherries
Cider vinegar to cover
Sugar
Dry sherry
1 tablespoon whole cloves
Red food coloring (optional)

Cover cherries with cider vinegar in a glass, enamel, or stainless steel bowl and let stand overnight; drain. Measure equal amounts of sugar and of cherries. Add 1 ounce dry sherry for each cup of cherries; mix. Add 1 tablespoon whole cloves. Cover and place in refrigerator, stirring once a day for one week. Add a few drops of red coloring, if desired. Divide into small jars to give as gifts. This must be kept refrigerated. Yield: 3½ to 4 (8-ounce) glasses.

HORSERADISH MOLD

A relish mold delicious with hot or cold beef, lamb, ham, and pork roasts.

1 (3-ounce) package lemon-flavored gelatin
1 cup boiling water
1 tablespoon apple cider vinegar
¾ teaspoon salt
¾ cup drained prepared horseradish
½ cup commercial mayonnaise
1 cup whipping cream, whipped

Dissolve gelatin in boiling water. Add vinegar and salt. When partially set or thickened, fold in horseradish, mayonnaise, and whipped cream. Put into mold. This keeps nicely in refrigerator for over a month. Yield: 2½ cups.

MANGO CHUTNEY

This unusually flavored chutney adds zest to any cold meat and is a fitting companion to any kind of curry.

4 firm ripe mangoes
2⅔ cups firmly packed light brown sugar
1⅓ tablespoons salt
⅔ cup preserved or fresh green ginger
1⅓ cups rice or white wine vinegar
2 cups white seedless raisins
1⅓ cups lime juice (juice from about 8 large limes)
2 medium-size garlic cloves, minced
1⅓ cups chopped onion
1 hot pepper, finely chopped
4 whole cloves
½ teaspoon Tabasco
2 (3½- to 4-inch) sticks cinnamon, broken
2⅔ tablespoons mustard seeds

Peel and seed mangoes; measure out 4 cups mango pieces. Combine all ingredients in a large, flat-bottomed kettle and bring to a simmering boil over medium heat. Stir until sugar is dissolved. Cover and allow mixture to stand overnight, stirring occasionally. The following morning bring mixture to a slow boil over medium heat. Do not cover. Stir occasionally. This process should take 15 to 20 minutes. Allow chutney to cool, stirring often while cooling. Spoon into sterilized jars and seal. Remove cloves and broken pieces of cinnamon before spooning into jars. If you prefer, you may tie these spices into a small piece of cheesecloth or an old white handkerchief before cooking. Yield: 6½ pints.

FIG CHUTNEY

A rare flavor in a chutney to accompany beef, lamb, pork, or wild fowl.

1 medium-size lemon
1 medium-size lime
4 cups ripe figs, measured after peeling and quartering
1 (8¼-ounce) can crushed pineapple, drained
2 tablespoons molasses
4 cups sugar
½ teaspoon salt
1½ cups seedless white raisins
3 red hot peppers
1½ teaspoons Tabasco
1 teaspoon whole cloves
1 (16-ounce) can whole-berry cranberry sauce
1 cup finely sliced pecans

Wash and finely slice lemon and lime. Put into blender and chop. Combine fruit slices and remaining ingredients except pecans in a large heavy kettle and cook over medium heat 45 to 60 minutes or until thick. Stir often to prevent sticking. Add sliced pecans about 5 minutes before removing from heat. Remove hot peppers. If you like a hot chutney, chop the peppers and leave in. Pour mixture into sterilized jars. Seal immediately with paraffin or tight fitting lids. Yield: 4 (8-ounce) glasses.

ELTA POSEY'S ORANGE CHUTNEY

This is a delightful and zesty relish to serve with chicken, turkey, ham, pork, or lamb. Easy to prepare and inexpensive.

11 medium-size to large thin-skinned oranges
1½ quarts water
** 3 cups sugar**
** 3 cups water**
** 1 cup vinegar**
1½ (16-ounce) cans whole-berry cranberry
**   sauce**
** 3 brimming tablespoons molasses**
** 1 cup seedless raisins**
** 1 tablespoon salt**
1½ teaspoons Tabasco
** 5 (3-inch) pieces stick cinnamon**
** 5 pieces whole gingerroot**
** 1 teaspoon whole cloves**
** ½ cup orange juice**
** 1 tablespoon curry powder**

Put whole washed oranges in a large saucepan and add 1½ quarts water. Bring to a boil and boil 20 minutes or until tender. Drain and cut oranges into eighths and then into sixteenths. Then cut into thirty-seconds. Combine sugar, 3 cups water, and vinegar and place over low heat, stirring until sugar is dissolved. Add remaining ingredients; bring to a boil and simmer about 20 minutes. Ladle into hot sterilized jars and seal with paraffin or cover and store in refrigerator. Yield: 13 cups.

BRANDIED PINEAPPLE

Easily made, this is wonderful used with a fresh fruit compote or served over ice cream, sherbet, or sliced pound cake. Makes a lovely gift or a good bazaar item.

1 very large fully ripe pineapple that smells
**   luscious—about 4 to 5 cups**
Sugar
Brandy

Slice pineapple, peel, and remove core and eyes; cut into 1-inch strips or chunks. Add sugar and brandy. Use 1 cup fruit to 1 cup sugar to 2 ounces brandy. For 4 cups fruit use 4 cups sugar and 8 ounces brandy; for 5 cups fruit use 4 cups sugar and 10 ounces brandy. A 2-ounce jigger is useful for measuring brandy. Use a good domestic or an imported brandy; I prefer cognac.

Pour mixture into a half-gallon, wide-mouthed jar that has been washed thoroughly and sterilized. (A honey or fruit juice jar does a good job.) Use a long-handled spoon to stir the pineapple mixture every day until sugar is completely dissolved. This usually takes about three to four weeks. Put up in sterilized jars and seal. Yield: 1½ quarts.

PEAR RELISH

Excellent with meats and for use on hamburgers and in coleslaw.

4 quarts ground sand or hard pears, peeled
2 quarts (about 10 pounds) peeled ground
**   onion**
8 red peppers, seeds removed, ground
4 green bell peppers, seeds removed, ground
2 (4-ounce) jar pimientos, ground
2 (8-ounce) jars sweet pickles, ground
2 quarts red vinegar
4 cups sugar
4 tablespoons salt
3 tablespoons turmeric
3 tablespoons dry mustard
3 tablespoons mustard seeds
8 tablespoons all-purpose flour

Use medium grinder or food chopper on pears, vegetables, and pickles. In grinding vegetables, put colander in an oblong baking dish to separate juice from vegetables. Discard juice. Reserve juice from grinding pears and use enough to make vegetables completely moist but not runny. Add vinegar to ground ingredients in large dishpan. Combine dry ingredients and seasonings and add to mixture. Bring to a boil over medium heat and boil 30 to 40 minutes or until relish is tender and transparent. Stir constantly to prevent sticking. Seal in hot sterilized jars. Yield: 18 to 20 pints.

MY BEST COOKED APPLES

Simple to do and the tastiest.

8 medium-size to large tart apples, Jonathan, Winesap, or Rome Beauty
1 cup water
2 cups sugar
2 tablespoons freshly squeezed lemon juice
1 teaspoon ground cinnamon
⅛ teaspoon ground nutmeg
8 teaspoons butter (optional)

Wash and core apples, and peel ½ way down from stem end. Combine water, sugar, lemon juice, cinnamon, and nutmeg in a large saucepan or skillet and bring to a boil. Place apples in skillet and cook over medium heat, basting constantly, until a straw goes in easily. Place apples in an ungreased 2-quart oblong casserole and cover with syrup. Add 1 teaspoon butter to the center of each apple, if desired. Cover and bake at 350° about 30 minutes. Serve hot or cold. Yield: 8 servings.

Variation: For festive cinnamon apples follow the cooking directions given above and add ¼ cup cinnamon drops omitting ground cinnamon, nutmeg, and butter. If desired, fill the apple tops with blanched almonds or nutmeats and raisins.

FRESH MINT JELLY

A refreshing and fragrant jelly, a fitting companion for a crown roast of lamb or pork.

1½ cups firmly packed mint leaves and stems
Water to cover

Wash mint leaves and crush each leaf separately with a masher or bottom of water glass. Place in a large kettle and cover with water. Bring quickly to a boil. Remove from heat and cover. Let stand 10 minutes and then strain through cheese cloth. Yield: about 1⅔ cups mint infusion.

1⅔ cups mint infusion
2 tablespoons strained lemon juice
Few drops green food coloring
3½ cups sugar
½ (6-ounce) bottle liquid fruit pectin

Place mint infusion in a large saucepan; add lemon juice, food coloring, and sugar. Bring mixture to a quick boil, stirring constantly. Add liquid pectin at once. Bring to a rolling boil and boil hard 1 minute, stirring constantly. Remove from heat, skim off thick foam, and pour into hot sterilized glasses. Seal with paraffin. Yield: 5 (6-ounce) glasses.

Note: If you have 2 cups or more of the infusion add ¼ cup more sugar to the mixture.

EXOTIC PEACH HALVES

A tasty accompaniment for chicken, lamb, or pork.

¼ teaspoon ground ginger
¼ teaspoon lemon bits
 1 tablespoon firmly packed dark brown sugar
 4 canned peach halves, well drained

Combine ginger, lemon bits, and brown sugar. Place peach halves in a 1-quart baking dish and sprinkle dry ingredients over the top. Place baking dish on middle rack in oven and broil for 5 minutes. Watch closely; some broilers work more quickly than others. Serve hot. Yield: 2 servings.

HOT PEPPER JELLY

Hot pepper jelly has a tangy bite and should be eaten with caution. This condiment is delicious with lamb, pork, or beef roast. It is a tasty and colorful tidbit on seasoned cream cheese as an hors d'oeuvre.

1½ cups cider vinegar, divided
 1 cup (about 2 large peppers) finely chopped
    bell pepper
 ⅓ cup finely cut hot peppers
6½ cups sugar
    Green or red food coloring
 1 (6-ounce) bottle liquid fruit pectin
    Melted paraffin

Put ½ cup vinegar into a blender and add peppers. Reduce to a fine puree. Pass through a sieve if no blender is available. Be sure to wear rubber gloves if using a sieve. Strain pepper mixture through a fine cheese cloth, squeezing hard. Pour juice into a large, flat-bottomed kettle and add remaining 1 cup vinegar, sugar, and a few drops food coloring. Bring mixture to a full rolling boil that cannot be stirred down, stirring constantly. Remove from heat and cool 5 minutes. Skim off thick foam that rises to top. Add liquid pectin and stir well. Pour into hot sterilized glasses. Cover jelly with melted paraffin, ⅛ inch thick. Yield: 7 (8-ounce) glasses.

Note: If you wish to use large-size baby food jars, the recipe will fill 9.

Meats

CRANBERRY POT ROAST

For Thanksgiving with a difference try my cranberry pot roast recipe. The berries give a delicious tangy flavor to the roast with a gravy that will delight you.

2 cups cranberries
½ cup water
½ cup all-purpose flour
2 teaspoons salt
½ teaspoon monosodium glutamate
½ teaspoon lemon-pepper marinade
1 (3½- to 4-pound) chuck roast
2 tablespoons shortening
16 whole cloves
¾ cup water
2 to 3 tablespoons all-purpose flour
1 tablespoon sugar

Wash cranberries and place in a saucepan with ½ cup water. Cook about 5 minutes or until the skins pop. Remove from heat to use later. In a large bowl mix the flour, salt, monosodium glutamate, and lemon-pepper marinade. Coat the beef evenly with this mixture.

In a preheated broiler, melt shortening in a roasting pan placed on the lowest shelf. Place meat in the pan and broil about 10 minutes or until brown on top and sides. Watch carefully to keep from burning it. Pour cooked cranberries over roast and arrange cloves evenly on top. Add ¾ cup water and seal tightly with roaster cover or aluminum foil. Bake in a preheated 325° oven for three hours. Check once during cooking period to see whether more water is needed. Test meat with fork for tenderness. Strain drippings and add enough water to have 1½ cups of liquid.

To make gravy, use a wire whisk and thicken with 2 to 3 tablespoons flour depending on consistency desired. Taste. If gravy is too tart, add 1 tablespoon sugar. Serve with saffron rice, tossed green salad and hot French bread. Yield: 6 to 8 servings.

NORMA WATKINS' PARTY BRISKET ROAST

Delectable. Thinly sliced, this makes a great hors d'oeuvre or sandwich served on melba rounds or thin-sliced rye bread spread with mayonnaise.

2 (0.7-ounce) packages commercial Italian dressing mix
¼ cup vinegar
2 tablespoons water
⅔ cup vegetable oil
1 (14- to 14½-pound) boneless brisket roast
1 (20-ounce) bottle catsup
1 teaspoon liquid smoke
12 drops Tabasco
1 tablespoon Worcestershire sauce

Blend Italian salad mix, vinegar, water, and oil according to salad package directions. Add to remaining ingredients and place in a large bowl; mix well. Baste roast in marinade mixture for 30 minutes, turning often; then place in a large plastic bag and pour in mixture. Refrigerate in a large pan for at least 24 hours, preferably 48. Bake in a preheated 250° oven for 4 to 5 hours. Test with fork for tenderness. Yield: 60 servings.

BEEF RIB-EYE STEAKS AU POIVRE VERT

Add new dimension to your cooking with green peppercorn. Steamed fresh green asparagus with lemon-butter sauce, tossed green salad, and hot French bread or rolls along with these delicious steaks will give you a memorable meal.

4 (1-inch thick) rib-eye steaks from heavy beef
1 (6-ounce) can sliced mushrooms or ½ pound fresh mushrooms, sliced
¼ cup butter
4 teaspoons green peppercorns
1 teaspoon salt
Juice of 1 lime, strained
1½ tablespoons butter and 1½ tablespoons oil or beef fat for each skillet
1 cup whipping cream or undiluted evaporated milk
½ teaspoon Creole or Dijon mustard
¼ cup brandy

Cut off a piece of fat from steak and render it in a heavy skillet. Trim off excess fat and dry steaks thoroughly on paper towels. Sauté fresh mushrooms in butter for 5 to 7 minutes. Drain peppercorns and rinse in colander.

Thirty minutes before cooking mash peppercorns and spread over both sides of the beef. At serving time, sprinkle salt and lime juice on both sides of steaks. Use two heavy skillets just large enough to hold the meat. Put butter and oil or beef fat in each skillet and turn the heat to medium high. When the foaming butter begins to subside or the beef fat is almost smoking, sauté the steaks for 3 minutes on both sides. Watch the heat and turn down to keep meat from burning, but you do want a hot fire. The steak is rare when you see a little of the red juice oozing out on top of the steak. To be sure, take a sharp knife and cut a small incision in the meat and touch with finger. If it is hot in the middle, it's ready. For medium rare steaks cook the meat a minute or two longer. Place the steaks on a hot platter or hot plates. Remove any excess fat from skillets and scrape the juices into one skillet with a wooden spoon. Stirring constantly, add cream, mustard, brandy, and mushrooms. When the sauce simmers, pour over the steaks and serve. Yield: 4 servings.

BEEF RIB-EYE ROAST

Serve for a special occasion, such as honoring a new son-in-law or having the president of the company to dine. Heaven comes only once; enjoy it.

1 (6-pound) rib-eye roast, choice or prime beef
2 tablespoons Worcestershire sauce
3 tablespoons lime or lemon juice
2 teaspoons green peppercorns
1 teaspoon seasoned salt
1 pound thick-sliced bacon

The morning of the day you plan to serve the roast, remove from refrigerator and rub Worcestershire sauce, and lime or lemon juice into the meat. Wash, drain and mash green peppercorns; pat mashed peppercorns on both sides of meat and let stand at room temperature until time to cook. Sprinkle roast with seasoned salt and wrap in bacon, securing with toothpicks.

Place roast in an open roasting pan or one with a 1- or 2-inch side. Insert meat thermometer to half the depth of meat. Bake in a preheated 325° oven 15 to 18 minutes per pound for very rare meat, 140° on meat thermometer. Remove from oven when thermometer reaches this for the meat will continue to cook from the contained heat. For a medium roast allow 22 to 25 minutes to the pound, 160°; for a well-done roast allow 27 to 30 minutes to the pound, 170°. For a small roast, allow the longer period of cooking; for a large roast a shorter period. Other cuts of beef may be used in this manner if tender enough to be served rare. With this savory roast serve broiled fresh mushrooms and stuffed baked tomatoes. Yield: 12 to 14 servings.

ROAST BEEF WITH BLUE CHEESE MARINADE

Blue cheese marinade gives this roast a marvelous flavor which makes it ideal for cold sliced sandwiches. The meat provides its own gravy.

 1 (4-ounce) package blue cheese, crumbled
½ cup lemon juice (about 3 lemons)
 3 tablespoons all-purpose flour
½ tablespoon salt
 1 tablespoon dry mustard
 1 teaspoon coarsely ground black pepper
½ teaspoon Worcestershire sauce
 4 dashes Tabasco
 3 cloves garlic, finely chopped
 1 cup water
 1 teaspoon dried green onion
 1 (4- to 6-pound) beef roast, any cut of oven
     roast. I prefer a boneless Boston roll.

Mix all ingredients except water and green onion into a paste and smear on meat. Let stand in refrigerator for 2 days. Sprinkle onion over roast, place in a roasting pan along with 1 cup water. Bake in a preheated 300° oven for 3 hours. Strain the gravy and serve with saffron rice. Yield: 6 to 8 servings.

Note: Any leftover roast I cut into small pieces and combine with a can of beef bouillon, ¼ teaspoon dried green onion, and remaining rice and cook in baking dish at 350° until moisture is absorbed, about 30 minutes.

STIFATO—GREEK BEEF STEW

The Greeks serve this aromatic beef stew during the winter as one of their few beef dishes. They use a cheap cut of beef chuck and cook it with wine and herbs. Cows are scarce in Greece and the people treasure their herds.

 2 pounds beef, boneless chuck or roast
½ cup olive oil
 2 pounds small onions
 2 cloves garlic
 2 tablespoons wine vinegar
 1 cup dry red wine
 2 bay leaves
¼ teaspoon freshly ground black pepper
1¼ teaspoons salt
 3 tablespoons tomato paste
½ cup hot water

Have meat at room temperature several hours before cooking. Remove fat and cut meat into walnut-size pieces. Pour olive oil into a very large skillet over high heat. Drop a small piece of bread into hot oil, if color changes gradually add meat; do not cool oil by adding meat all at once. Turn meat and cook until it has a nice brown crust; remove and place in a heavy pot or Dutch oven. Wash onions and remove outer skin, but do not cut off navel end. Add to skillet and keep turning onions as they cook. When they turn a rosy color, put aside in a bowl. Brown whole garlic quickly in oil, and add to meat in heavy pot. Add wine vinegar, red wine, bay leaves, pepper, salt, and tomato paste dissolved in ½ cup hot water. Stir well and cover pot as soon as mixture comes to a simmer over low heat. Do not stir again or peep. Shake pan if you must. After cooking 30 minutes add onions and bring to boil again; cover and simmer for 1 hour or longer until onions are tender. If there is too much liquid, remove meat and onions and boil quickly. Serve with hot, crusty French bread. The gravy is so delicious you may serve with cooked rice or potatoes. Yield: 6 to 8 servings.

TASTY BEEF STEW

Use leftover roast or steak in this low caloried way. If cholesterol is a problem, omit leftover gravy and use a can of beef bouillon or dissolve 2 beef cubes or 2 packages of instant beef bouillon in 2 cups boiling water.

2 cups meat
2 cups beef stock or leftover gravy
½ cup chopped onion, fresh or frozen
½ cup chopped celery plus a few tops or 1 teaspoon celery seeds
¼ cup chopped bell pepper, fresh or frozen (optional)
½ teaspoon seasoned salt
½ teaspoon lemon-pepper marinade
3 tablespoons port, sherry, or white wine

Trim off fat from meat and cut into bite-size pieces. Put this into a saucepan with remaining ingredients except wine and bring to a simmering boil over medium heat. Cover pan and allow to simmer for 1 hour. After 30 minutes of cooking, add wine and taste to see if more salt is needed. Serve with cooked rice or noodles. Yield: 4 servings.

Variations: You may wish to add 1 can whole boiled onions and 1 can of small whole potatoes to saucepan. Cook until vegetables are thoroughly heated.

ALLAN CHENEY'S BEEF STROGANOFF

1½ pounds lean beef chuck cubes
2 tablespoons all-purpose flour
½ teaspoon salt
¼ teaspoon pepper
2 tablespoons shortening
1 (10½-ounce) can beef consommé
3 tablespoons Worcestershire sauce
3 tablespoons catsup
2 tablespoons dry mustard
1 (4-ounce) can mushrooms
½ pint commercial sour cream

Dredge beef cubes in flour seasoned with salt and pepper. In a skillet brown beef cubes in shortening over medium high heat. Add consommé, Worcestershire sauce, catsup, and dry mustard, Cook over low heat in a covered skillet or Dutch oven about 2 hours. The last 15 minutes of cooking time add mushrooms. Just before serving add sour cream. Serve over cooked rice. Yield: 6 servings.

BEEF TENDERLOIN WELLINGTON

Cincinnatti's Maisonette offers the superb creation of Chef Pierre André. Follow the easy directions closely and serve the masterpiece at home. Bordelaise or Perigourdine sauce is a fine accompaniment. A *bouquetière* of fresh vegetables would be delicious with the meat.

Salt and freshly ground black pepper
1 (3- to 4-pound) prime tenderloin, fully trimmed
¼ cup salad oil
2 tablespoons butter
1 small onion, finely chopped
½ pound fresh mushrooms
2 ounces cognac
½ teaspoon powdered rosemary
2 (5-ounce) cans imported pâté de foie gras with truffles
1½ pounds puff paste or 2 (10-ounce) packages puff pastry shells, defrosted
1 egg
1 tablespoon milk

Salt and pepper the tenderloin on all sides. Preheat oil in a baking pan and roast in a preheated 450° oven for 10 to 15 minutes making sure it stays very rare. Remove from oven and cool. Pour off oil from the tenderloin and using the same pan, add butter. Sauté onions and mushrooms until tender over a medium heat. Add cognac, remove from heat and cool. When cool, chop mushrooms very finely, add rosemary and foie gras with a fork and make a very fine liver paste. When tenderloin is cooled, spread its entire surface with liver mushroom paste.

Roll out puff pastry to ¼ inch thickness. If you use pastry shells, work them together so as to make one ball of dough. Roll this out also to ¼ inch thickness and wrap the coated tenderloin. Trim edges of pastry, moistening edges with water and sealing by pressing together. Brush crust with egg beaten with milk. Make two holes on top of tenderloin to allow steam to escape. Decorate with pieces of dough making grapes, flowers, leaves, etc., according to your artistic ability. Bake in a preheated 425° oven for 20 to 25 minutes. Yield: 8 to 10 servings.

SIRLOIN DE ROQUEFORT

Food lovers beware! This is indeed an epicurean treat. Ask your butcher for a first cut sirloin steak of choice heavy beef, a full 1½ inches thick—large enough to serve the number of guests invited. Have him cut a deep pocket in the meaty side.

    Sirloin steak
 1 clove garlic, crushed or ⅛ teaspoon garlic
      powder
½ teaspoon monosodium glutamate
 1 teaspoon salt
½ teaspoon dry mustard
¼ teaspoon finely ground Java black pepper
 1 (4-ounce) can sliced mushrooms or ½ pound
      fresh mushrooms, sliced
 1 (3-ounce) package Roquefort cheese,
      crumbled

Rub inside of steak pocket with garlic. Mix remaining seasonings in a bowl. Put half seasoning mixture into the pocket along with half the sliced mushrooms, and most of the crumbled cheese. Preheat the oven to 500° and place broiler pan in oven to become sizzling hot. Sprinkle remaining ingredients on sides of steak. Turn oven control to broil and cook meat 20 to 25 minutes for rare and 30 minutes for medium. For well-done, cut off heat and let meat stay in 5 minutes longer. Turn meat once during cooking process. The steak may be cooked on an outside grill. A first cut sirloin of heavy beef (2½ to 3 pounds) will serve 5 to 6, depending on appetites of your family or guests. Yield: 5 to 6 servings.

TALLARENE

 1 pound ground beef
 2 tablespoons shortening
 1 medium-size onion, diced
 1 clove garlic, chopped
 1 (16-ounce) package medium-size egg
      noodles
 1 (8-ounce) can tomato sauce
 1 (4-ounce) can mushrooms, stems and
      pieces
    Salt to taste
1½ cups water
 1 cup whole kernel corn
 1 (2-ounce) can stuffed green olives, cut into
      pieces
1½ cups shredded cheddar cheese

Cook meat in a large skillet in a small amount of shortening, stirring constantly until it is no longer red. Add onions, garlic, noodles, tomato sauce, mushrooms, salt, and water. Cook noodles length of time indicated on package. Remove from heat and gently stir in the corn and olives; mix gently. Alternate layers of mixture in casserole with shredded cheese. Bake in a preheated 350° oven for 45 minutes. Turn off heat and let casserole stay in oven 15 minutes longer. Yield: 10 to 12 servings.

STASSI'S MEATBALLS

An outstanding recipe from Laurel, Mississippi.

2 pounds chuck, ground twice
2 cups dry bread crumbs
3 large eggs
4 green onions including tops, finely chopped
1 clove garlic, crushed
½ cup grated Parmesan cheese
1 cup freshly snipped parsley or 2 tablespoons dried parsley
1 tablespoon salt
1 teaspoon freshly ground black pepper
¼ cup water
⅓ cup olive or corn oil
  Spaghetti Sauce

In a large bowl combine all ingredients except oil and Spaghetti Sauce and shape into 33 meatballs. In a large skillet cook balls in oil over medium heat until all are browned. Add to Spaghetti Sauce after it has reached the proper consistency.

Spaghetti Sauce:

1 large onion, finely chopped
2 tablespoons olive oil
3 cloves garlic, crushed
1 (28-ounce) can Italian-style tomatoes with basil
2 (8-ounce) cans Spanish-style tomato sauce
  5 (8-ounce) cans water
1 tablespoon sugar
1 bay leaf
½ teaspoon oregano
½ teaspoon sweet basil or 1 teaspoon Italian seasoning
2 (12-ounce) packages spaghetti

In a large soup kettle or Dutch oven sauté onion in oil over medium heat until golden brown. Add remaining ingredients, cover, and cook at a simmering boil over low heat for 1½ to 2 hours. Add browned meatballs and simmer 1½ hours longer. Serve over spaghetti cooked according to package directions. Yield: 33 large meatballs with sauce and spaghetti —about 24 servings.

Note: If you plan to use for hors d'oeuvres, make about 48 balls. Simmer in sauce about 1 hour or until sauce is thick.

CLAUDIA WHITNEY'S MEAT SPAGHETTI

Excellent and easy to prepare. Serve with a tossed green salad and hot French bread.

1 pound lean ground chuck
2 tablespoons corn or olive oil
1 large onion, finely chopped
1 large green pepper, finely chopped
1 clove garlic, finely chopped
3 (8-ounce) cans tomato sauce
1 teaspoon chili powder
⅛ teaspoon cayenne pepper
1 tablespoon paprika
  Salt to taste
1 (7-ounce) can mushroom bits and pieces
5 quarts boiling water
2 tablespoons salt
12 ounces Italian thin spaghetti
  Ripe olives
1 cup grated Parmesan cheese

Break ground chuck into very small pieces. Place oil in a large heavy skillet over medium heat and cook onion, green pepper, and garlic, until onion is transparent, stirring constantly to prevent onion's scorching. Add beef and brown lightly, stirring constantly. Add tomato sauce and seasonings and bring to a simmering boil. Lower heat and simmer for 1 hour. Add mushrooms the last 15 minutes of cooking.

In a large saucepan bring water to boil, add salt, and spaghetti. Boil 10 to 15 minutes, stirring occasionally. Do not over cook; the spaghetti should be tender to the bite. Drain water from spaghetti in colander and pour cold water over it. Mix with sauce in a large bowl and serve on heated platter, garnished with ripe olives. Sprinkle each serving generously with Parmesan cheese. Yield: 12 servings.

BEEFBURGER AU POIVRE VERT

These patties are ideal for campers, skiers, or boaters who like to take along a man-size meat dish.

     1 teaspoon green peppercorns
1½ pounds ground beef
     1 teaspoon seasoned salt
     ½ teaspoon salt
     1 egg, slightly beaten
     ½ cup whipping cream or undiluted
         evaporated milk
     3 tablespoons butter, divided
     2 tablespoons chopped fresh or dried green
         parsley
     2 small green onions, finely chopped
     1 cup dry red wine of good vintage
     1 (6-ounce) can sliced mushrooms

Thirty minutes before serving time drain peppercorns and rinse well. Mash finely and add to beef in a large bowl. Add seasoned salt, salt, beaten egg and cream. Work mixture with clean hands or a two-pronged fork. Form into four equal-size patties. Place 2 tablespoons butter in a heavy 9-inch skillet and sauté patties over medium high heat. Turn about three times during cooking process, pressing meat down lightly. A nice crust will form on top. Keep heat high enough to evaporate juices as

they form. These patties are fairly thick and it will take about 10 to 12 minutes for very rare, 13 to 15 minutes for medium rare, and 18 to 20 minutes for well done.

Place cooked patties on heated plates or hot toasted sliced buns. Add remaining 1 tablespoon butter to skillet, using a high heat. When it foams, add parsley and onions. Stir for a few moments, add wine and mushrooms. Be sure to scrape loose all meat particles in pan and stir well. When the wine bubbles and turns brown, simmer for a minute. Taste to see if salt is needed. Pour sauce over patties and serve at once with cooked rice or baked potatoes. Freeze in individual aluminum foil containers or baking ware you can transfer immediately to stove. To thaw, bake in a preheated 375° oven for 45 minutes to 1 hour. Yield: 4 servings.

SUCCULENT MEAT LOAF

A tasty meat loaf with lots of energy-giving power.

1½ pounds "English minced" or ground beef
         chuck
     ⅔ cup wheat germ
     1 (4-ounce) can sliced mushrooms, drained
     1 tablespoon dried green onion or chives or
         1 tablespoon chopped white onion,
         cooked with a little water for 10 minutes
     ⅔ cup chili sauce
     1 large egg, beaten
1¼ teaspoons salt
     ⅛ teaspoon pepper
     1 tablespoon prepared horseradish (optional)

Combine all ingredients in a large mixing bowl and blend thoroughly with clean hands. Shape firmly into a loaf and place in a shallow baking pan. Cover with foil and bake in a preheated 350° oven for 45 minutes to 1 hour. Serve hot, but this is also delicious sliced cold for sandwiches. Yield: 6 to 8 servings.

LE BOEUF BOURGUIGNON

This is not a difficult dish to make. For a festive occasion use giant mushrooms in place of small buttons. Serve this culinary masterpiece with cooked white or saffron rice or as a true *Français* would with boiled *pommes de terre* (Irish potatoes.)

2 pounds lean beef, round, rump, chuck or heavy aged beef or leftover rare roast, rump or sirloin tip
1½ cups red wine
¼ teaspoon ground thyme
1 bay leaf
1 medium-size onion, thinly sliced
4 sprigs parsley, finely chopped
6 shallots or green onions, finely chopped
1 carrot, scraped and thinly sliced
2 tablespoons butter
1 tablespoon all-purpose flour
1 teaspoon salt
½ teaspoon coarsely ground black pepper
⅛ teaspoon oregano
1½ cups beef or chicken stock or 1½ cups water with dissolved beef bouillon cubes or with a veal knuckle
1 (4-ounce) can button mushrooms
2 tablespoons brandy

Cut beef into 1-inch pieces and place in a glass bowl. Add wine, thyme, bay leaf, onion, parsley, shallots, and carrot. Marinate for at least 3 hours or overnight if possible. (This is not mandatory but it ensures more flavor and tenderizes the meat.) Remove beef from marinade and strain remaining ingredients from wine.

Melt butter in a large iron skillet or Dutch oven. When it bubbles, brown beef quickly and remove from fire to a large bowl. Brown sliced onion and shallots and add to meat. You may need an additional tablespoon butter to keep onions from sticking. Blend flour with salt, pepper, and oregano; sprinkle into a skillet and brown. Slowly add warm stock, stirring constantly. Add wine marinade and return beef

and onions to the sauce. Cover skillet tightly and simmer for 3 hours, stirring occasionally. The last 15 minutes of cooking add mushrooms and brandy. Yield: 8 servings.

POTPOURRI OF LEFTOVER MEAT

Only a cup of meat finds its way into this savory casserole. When I created it I had half a cup of lamb roast and half a cup of steak pieces.

1 tablespoon butter or margarine
½ cup chopped onion, fresh or frozen
½ cup chopped celery and green tops
½ cup chopped bell pepper, fresh or frozen
1 package instant beef bouillon or 1 chicken or beef bouillon cube
½ cup boiling water
1 (10¾-ounce) can condensed cream of mushroom soup
1 cup leftover meat
1 teaspoon Beau Monde seasoning
⅛ teaspoon lemon-pepper marinade
½ teaspoon salt
3 to 4 drops Tabasco
1 can Chinese noodles or 1 can shoestring potatoes

Melt butter in an iron skillet over medium heat and cook onion, celery, and bell pepper for 10 to 15 minutes or until onion is clear and transparent. Dissolve the instant beef bouillon or bouillon cube in boiling water and add to mushroom soup, meat, Beau Monde seasoning, lemon-pepper marinade, salt, and Tabasco; add to onion mixture. Cook for 3 to 4 minutes, stirring constantly. Taste to see if more salt is needed.

Lightly butter a 1-quart casserole. Cover and bake potpourri in a preheated 350° oven for

30 minutes. Pour meat mixture over uncooked noodles and cook for 10 minutes more. For a truly thrifty meal use the canned shoestring potatoes in the same manner as the noodles. For a heartier meal serve over cooked elbow or shell macaroni. Yield: 4 servings.

MARGE FRASER'S SWEET AND SOUR BEEF BALLS

A very delightful and unusual combination.

1 pound ground beef, chuck or round
1 large egg
1 tablespoon cornstarch
1 teaspoon salt
2 tablespoons finely chopped onion
⅛ teaspoon freshly ground black pepper
¼ cup vegetable oil, not olive
   Sauce
4 slices pineapple
2 large bell peppers, cut into lengthwise strips

Mix first 6 ingredients together and form into 18 or more small balls. Brown in oil quickly in a large skillet over medium heat. Drain on paper towel. Prepare Sauce.

Add cooked meatballs to Sauce. Place in an 8-inch square casserole or a 1½-quart oblong casserole and top with pineapple slices and bell pepper strips. Bake in a preheated 350° oven for 20 minutes. This is good with rice or noodles. Yield: 6 to 8 servings.

Sauce:

1 tablespoon vegetable oil
1 cup pineapple juice
3 tablespoons cornstarch
1 tablespoon soy sauce
3 tablespoons vinegar
6 tablespoons water
½ cup sugar

Over low heat cook oil and pineapple juice. Add mixture of cornstarch, soy sauce, vinegar, water, and sugar and cook until juice thickens, stirring constantly. This part of the recipe may be made in advance.

SPICED ROUND

Try this delectable beef tidbit from old Virginia for your next party or holiday gathering. Begin the process at Thanksgiving for the meat requires three weeks to age properly.

1 (10-pound) top round beef
2 cups salt
1 (2-ounce) bottle saltpeter
4 tablespoons ground nutmeg
4 tablespoons ground cinnamon
1 (2-ounce) can ground allspice
1 teaspoon ground mace
1 cup firmly packed light brown sugar
1 cup firmly packed dark brown sugar
1 cup water

Have your butcher remove any excess fat from roast and tie it into shape. Mix the salt and saltpeter and rub thoroughly into meat. Blend nutmeg, cinnamon, allspice, mace, and sugars and rub mixture over entire meat surface. Place beef in a large bowl, crock, or enameled dishpan; cover and place in a cool room. Turn roast daily and baste with its forming juice. At the end of three weeks rinse meat several times with warm water. Weigh beef before cooking because several pounds will have been lost in shrinkage. Add 1 cup of water to beef in roasting pan, cover, and bake in a preheated 325° oven for 20 minutes per pound. Spiced Round will keep refrigerated for months. Yield: if sliced very thinly, 150 servings.

Note: There are many ways to use this delightful treat. Slice thinly when cold and serve on assorted crackers or hot buttered or beaten biscuits. Shred a little over a tossed green salad for a special fillip or cut into small portions and wrap attractively for an unusual gift to a cherished friend. This delicacy is delicious served with highballs or eggnog.

NATCHITOCHES MEAT PIES

Natchitoches, Louisiana, is famous for its meat pies. This fine recipe originated in Mr. Tom Whitehead's kitchen.

2 pounds ground lean beef
1 pound ground pork
2 teaspoons shortening
5 green onions, finely chopped
3 medium-size onions, ground with juice
2 bell peppers, finely chopped
2 tablespoons finely chopped parsley
1 clove garlic, minced
   Cayenne pepper, black pepper, and salt to
     taste
¼ teaspoon paprika
2 tablespoons all-purpose flour
2 tablespoons water, if needed
   Pastry

In a heavy skillet cook meat in shortening over medium heat, stirring often until it is mealy in appearance and crumbles. Add onions, bell pepper, parsley, garlic, and seasonings and cook 10 minutes more. Remove from heat and stir in flour and water; blend ingredients together. Cool; then freeze for 30 minutes. Prepare Pastry.

Put 1 tablespoon meat mixture in the center of each pastry round. Fold over in half and press with fork. Fry in deep fat at 350° until golden brown. Yield: 24 pies.

Pastry:

4 cups all-purpose flour
1 teaspoon salt
4 teaspoons baking powder
2 eggs
1 cup milk
½ cup shortening

Sift dry ingredients into a large bowl. Work shortening in with pastry blender. Beat eggs and add to milk. Add to dry ingredients gradually and knead until consistency to roll out. Roll as thin as possible. Cut into rounds using a tea saucer as a guide.

STUFFED HERB MEATBALLS

Zesty! An excellent meat dish for children. They love it and it's amazing to see how far a pound of beef will go. You may make up three pounds at one time and freeze what you do not need.

1 pound ground chuck, chilled
⅓ cup evaporated milk
1 teaspoon salt
⅛ teaspoon lemon-pepper marinade
3 tablespoons butter or margarine
1 cup hot water
1 cup commercial seasoned stuffing
   Sauce

Mix ground chuck, evaporated milk, salt, and lemon-pepper marinade in a large bowl. Divide into 6 parts and roll between two sheets of waxed paper until flattened into a wide circle. Melt butter in hot water in a saucepan and add stuffing. Toss lightly to blend. Place a rounded tablespoonful of herb mixture in center of flattened meat circles and seal together with hands, completely enclosing the herb mixture and forming the meatballs. Prepare Sauce.

Pour sauce over meatballs and bake in a preheated 350° oven for 40 to 50 minutes; serve hot. Frozen meatballs will take longer to cook. These are delicious served with rice, baked potatoes, or cooked noodles. Yield: 6 servings.

Sauce:

1 (10½-ounce) can condensed cream of celery or mushroom soup
2 teaspoons Worcestershire sauce
1 tablespoon chili sauce or catsup
¼ teaspoon Tabasco

Combine all the ingredients and cook over medium heat until very hot, stirring constantly.

VEAL MEDAILLONS PIERRE

From the Maisonette, Cincinnati, Ohio.

12 (2- to 3-ounce) medaillons of veal (veal escallopine)
2 ripe avocados, peeled
Salt to taste
¼ teaspoon white pepper
All-purpose flour for dredging
2 tablespoons butter
3 shallots, chopped, or ½ onion, chopped
1 cup chablis
1½ cups whipping cream
1 tablespoon chopped fresh or dry tarragon
6 (3 to 4-ounce) wedges imported Swiss cheese

Select veal from loin or tenderloin and have butcher cut and flatten medaillons very thin. Dice avocados. Salt and pepper veal and dredge in flour. Place butter in a preheated heavy skillet or saucepan. Sauté medaillons on both sides until golden brown. Remove to a serving platter and keep hot.

Remove excess fat from skillet. In the same skillet add chopped shallots or onions, and cook for 10 minutes. Add chablis and cook until wine is ¼ of its original volume. Use a very high heat for reducing. Add whipping cream and cook until reduced to ½ of its original volume or until sauce coats spoon. Taste for seasoning. Add chopped tarragon and diced avocados, cook 2 more minutes; the sauce should not be too thick or too thin. The quality of the cream is very important. (If sauce is too thin, thicken with 1 teaspoon cornstarch diluted with wine.) Pour sauce over medaillons and arrange Swiss cheese on top of veal covering all the meat. Place platter under a preheated 550° broiler and let cheese melt about 2 minutes or until it becomes very soft. Serve at once with boiled potatoes or noodles. I like a tossed green salad, hot rolls, French pastry, and coffee to complete my meal. Yield: 4 to 6 servings.

MRS. SAM HOUSTON'S VEAL LOAF

1 pound veal round
2 celery ribs
3 hard-boiled eggs
½ teaspoon onion salt
⅛ teaspoon cayenne pepper
½ teaspoon Worcestershire sauce
3 tablespoons homemade mayonnaise
1 package (1 tablespoon) unflavored gelatin

In a saucepan cover veal with water; add celery ribs, cover, and boil until tender. Test with a fork tine. Remove meat from broth and cut into small pieces. Return meat to broth and boil about 25 minutes more. Put meat and eggs through a meat grinder.

Place ground meat in a large bowl; add onion salt, cayenne pepper, Worcestershire sauce and mayonnaise. Dissolve gelatin in 1½ cups hot veal broth, cool and combine with meat mixture. Mold in an oiled 9- x 5- x 3-inch pan. Keep refrigerated until served. Yield: 5 to 6 servings.

MAXINE RANDOLPH'S CALF LIVER LOAF

Tastes like pâté foie gras. Serve thinly sliced on melba rounds for a cocktail party.

1 pound liver
1 small onion
1 clove garlic
4 slices bacon
⅛ teaspoon powdered sage
⅛ teaspoon black pepper
1 egg, beaten
¾ cup dry bread crumbs
1 teaspoon salt
⅛ teaspoon powdered thyme
½ cup milk

Force liver, onion, garlic, and bacon through a meat chopper (medium blade). In a large bowl add remaining ingredients reserving ¼ cup milk. Form into loaf in a greased or oiled 7- x 3- x 2-inch bread pan and pour reserved milk over top. Set in a pan of water to bake. Bake in a preheated 350° oven for 45 minutes. Unmold on a hot oval platter and serve hot. With or without tomato sauce it makes a delicious luncheon entrée. Yield: 4 to 6 servings.

MISSISSIPPI STUFFED HAM AND DRESSING

Bake ham half-done. Skin, remove excess fat (½ inch). Turn over and insert small vegetable knife at the hock and split, following the bone carefully. Cut bone out of the meat, leaving as little meat on it as possible. When bone is removed, fill cavity with the highly seasoned dressing, pressing it well into all cut places. Pour in a little melted butter and sew up the ham with a cord. Make enough dressing to cover the entire ham ½ inch thick. Moisten covering with ham juice and wrap in cheese cloth. Bake in a preheated 275° oven for 25 to 30 minutes per pound. Keep cheese cloth on until ham is cold; allow to cool naturally. A 12-pound ham sliced for a cocktail party will serve 100.

Dressing:

1 pound bread crumbs
3 cups crumbled corn bread
1 teaspoon ground cloves
1 teaspoon ground allspice
1 teaspoon ground ginger
1 teaspoon ground mace
1 teaspoon onion salt
1 teaspoon garlic salt
1 teaspoon pepper
½ cup molasses
2 tablespoons mustard
3 eggs, well beaten

Combine crumbs, corn bread, and all spices; mix well. Add molasses, mustard, and eggs. Moisten with juice of ham and fill cavity.

VIRGINIA HAM

Place ham in a boiler skin side down and cover with water. Simmer for 20 minutes per pound keeping ham covered by adding hot water as needed. Allow ham to cool in cooking water. Remove skin carefully to avoid tearing fat. Cover with a layer of brown sugar and bake long enough to get a rich brown color.

To fry ham, cut ¼-inch thick slices from ham as is. Trim off rind (but not fat) and smoke-blackened edges. Stand against side of skillet, fat edge down. Cook over moderate heat until fat has rendered out and turned golden brown. Lay slice down to fry slightly on both sides. Do not overcook.

Note: Ham should be soaked overnight for a milder flavor; discard soaking water and cook in fresh water.

SANCTIFIED HAM BALLS

A marvelous solution for using leftover ham. Serve these delicately seasoned ham balls with their subtle sour cream sauce to your family and friends, and they will add their blessing to mine for the day I found my way up the Old Natchez Trace to the old mission church of Saint Matthew's in Kosciusko, Mississippi.

In a conversation about recipes with Mrs. William Davis, a parishioner, this particular one caught my fancy. I tried it out in my own kitchen and gave it a title worthy of its origin.

1 small onion, finely chopped
2 tablespoons vegetable oil
2 pounds cooked ham, ground
¼ teaspoon freshly ground black pepper
2 tablespoons prepared horseradish
1 large egg
1 cup cornflakes
  Sauce

Sauté onion in oil in a heavy skillet over medium heat. In a large bowl combine onion with remaining ingredients except Sauce, and shape into egg-size balls. Place in an uncovered well-greased casserole. Bake in a preheated 350° oven for 30 minutes. Pour Sauce over ham balls and bake an additional 10 minutes. Yield: 10 to 12 ham balls—6 to 7 servings.

Note: This is delectable with candied sweet potatoes, broccoli served with drawn butter, and a fresh grapefruit and hearts of artichoke salad with Roquefort dressing. If you wish,

make balls and sauce early in the morning, refrigerate, and bake the last 10 minutes before serving.

Sauce:

2 tablespoons butter or margarine
2 tablespoons all-purpose flour
1 pint commercial sour cream
⅛ teaspoon ground marjoram
⅛ teaspoon Tabasco
½ teaspoon salt
½ teaspoon dill seeds

Melt butter in a saucepan over low heat; blend in flour. Add sour cream and seasonings. Cook over low heat for 10 minutes. *Do not boil.*

SAUSAGE WITH RAVISHING RICE

A zesty meal in itself for a cold winter night when the wind is howling—inexpensive too.

1 pound hot sausage
5 cups boiling water
2 envelopes chicken noodle soup mix
½ cup uncooked regular rice
1 cup chopped onion
1 large bell pepper, chopped
1 cup finely chopped celery
¼ cup slivered almonds
⅛ teaspoon paprika
6 sprigs parsley, fresh or frozen

Cook sausage in a heavy skillet over low heat. Crumble with kitchen spoon or potato masher and continue cooking until done. Drain thoroughly on paper towel. Bring water to a boil and add soup mix and rice; boil for 7 to 10 minutes. Add onion, bell pepper, celery, and sausage. Pour mixture into a 2-quart buttered casserole or several smaller ones. Top with almonds and sprinkle with paprika. Bake in a preheated 350° oven for 45 to 50 minutes or until liquid is absorbed. Garnish with parsley before serving. Yield: 10 to 12 servings.

PORK CHOPS IN GINGER ALE

 2 large onions, sliced
¼ cup butter, divided
 5 (¾- to 1-inch thick) pork chops
 2 tablespoons firmly packed brown sugar
 1 tablespoon tomato puree or chili sauce
 1 tablespoon all-purpose flour
 1 cup ginger ale
    Salt and black pepper to taste

In a skillet sauté onions in ⅛ cup butter over medium heat until golden brown. Remove onions and place in a 2-quart oblong baking dish. In the same skillet brown chops in remaining ⅛ cup butter over medium heat. Remove and place on top of onions. Sprinkle with brown sugar. Blend tomato puree and flour together in a small bowl; add ginger ale and pour over chops. Sprinkle generously with salt and pepper and cook in a preheated 350° oven for 1 hour or until chops are tender. Test with a fork tine. Yield: 5 servings.

STUFFED PORK CHOPS WITH SHAKER APPLE DRESSING

This unusual recipe comes from the historic Golden Lamb in Lebanon, Ohio. Baked honey acorn squash, braised red cabbage, or buttered rutabaga are a fine complement to this dish.

 6 (10-ounce) pork chops
 1 teaspoon salt
¼ teaspoon pepper
 2 tablespoons butter or bacon drippings
    Shaker Apple Dressing
 2 cups beef stock or bouillon or 2 cups boiling
      water with 2 beef cubes
 1 medium-size onion, finely chopped
 1 carrot, finely chopped
 2 celery ribs, finely chopped
 6 peppercorns
 1 bay leaf

Ask your butcher to cut pork chops 1½ inches thick and make deep pockets in the side. Trim excess fat and wipe chops with a damp cloth. Salt and pepper meat and brown in butter in skillet over high heat. Remove chops and stuff pockets with Shaker Apple Dressing.

Place chops on a rack in a covered roasting pan with stuffing side up. Pour 2 cups beef stock or boiling water with dissolved beef cubes into bottom of pan and around chops. Add finely chopped vegetables, peppercorns, and bay leaf. Bake in a preheated 350° oven for 1 hour. Remove cover last 10 minutes to brown chops. Thicken gravy if desired. Yield: 6 servings.

Shaker Apple Dressing:

 3 tablespoons butter, divided
 1 medium-size onion, minced
1½ cups dried bread crumbs
½ tablespoon ground sage
½ teaspoon fresh thyme
½ teaspoon finely chopped basil
¼ cup chopped celery leaves
½ teaspoon pepper
½ teaspoon salt
¼ cup water
1½ cups sliced peeled apples
 3 eggs

Melt 1½ tablespoons butter in a skillet over medium heat; sauté minced onion but do not brown. Add to bread crumbs in a large bowl; stir in all herbs, celery leaves, pepper, and salt. Heat ¼ cup water in a saucepan and add remaining butter; mix well into dressing mixture. Add sliced apples and eggs; blend thoroughly.

ROAST CHINESE SPARERIBS

Pork at its best!

2 pounds pork spareribs
1 cup chicken stock or 1 package instant chicken bouillon broth or 1 cube chicken bouillon
2 tablespoons soy sauce
2 cloves minced garlic or 1 teaspoon garlic powder
2 teaspoons salt
¼ cup honey
¼ cup catsup
2 teaspoons cornstarch

Place spareribs in a large baking dish or stainless steel roaster. If using instant or cube chicken bouillon dissolve in 1 cup boiling water. Combine all ingredients except cornstarch and pour over ribs. Marinate for 4 hours or overnight. Turn ribs two or three times.

Bake ribs in a preheated 450° oven for 10 minutes. Lower heat to 325° and cook for 1 hour, basting often with marinade. Test with fork for tenderness. Before serving, separate ribs with a sharp knife. The Chinese always cut and eat their meat in bite-size pieces. For a delicious gravy add enough water to baking pan to make a cup of liquid, thicken with cornstarch dissolved in a little cold water and cook until thickened. Any leftover cold meat makes excellent sandwiches. Yield: 3 to 4 servings.

SLICED LAMB NECK

A unique dish and an economical, complete meal with a salad and bread.

1½ pounds (1-inch thick) lamb neck
¼ cup cider vinegar
1 teaspoon salt
½ teaspoon ground ginger
½ teaspoon lemon-pepper marinade
2 tablespoons bacon drippings
¼ cup all-purpose flour
½ tablespoon dried or fresh parsley
1 teaspoon dried green onion
1½ cups strong coffee

Trim excess fat and wipe off outside surface of lamb with vinegar. Combine salt, ginger, and lemon-pepper marinade and rub into meat. Brown quickly in a skillet over high heat in bacon drippings, turning on both sides. Sprinkle with flour; add parsley, dried green onion, and coffee. Cover skillet with a tight-fitting lid and simmer for 2 hours on low heat. Turn meat occasionally and stir to prevent sticking. At the end of 1 hour, add the vegetables of your choice. I add:

4 carrots, scraped and cut lengthwise
4 medium-size potatoes
1 (16-ounce) can Blue Lake string beans, drained (optional)

You may prefer to omit potatoes and serve with saffron rice or cooked noodles. Yield: 3 servings.

LAMB STEAK WITH CHILI SOUR CREAM

Yummy!

½ pint commercial sour cream
1 canned green chili, seeded and finely
    chopped
½ cup shredded sharp cheddar cheese
    Salt
6 (¾- to 1-inch thick) lamb shoulder steaks
½ teaspoon lemon-pepper marinade
1 tablespoon Worcestershire sauce

Combine sour cream, chopped chili, shredded cheese, and a dash salt. Cover and let stand at room temperature for 2 to 3 hours. Preheat broiler. Sprinkle salt generously on each side of the lamb steaks along with lemon-pepper marinade, and Worcestershire sauce. Place steaks 3 to 4 inches from heat and broil for 6 to 8 minutes on each side. Serve with chili sour cream spread over top. Yield: 6 servings.

CREOLE LEG OF LAMB

Colorful and delightfully different.

1 (6- to 6½-pound) leg of lamb
2 cloves garlic or ½ teaspoon garlic powder
½ cup vinegar
2 tablespoons Worcestershire sauce
2 teaspoons salt
¼ teaspoon lemon-pepper marinade
½ teaspoon freshly ground black pepper
1 (16-ounce) can stewed tomatoes
¼ cup catsup
½ cup coarsely chopped onions, fresh or
    frozen
½ cup chopped bell pepper, fresh of frozen
1 tablespoon sugar
    Gravy

Have your butcher remove strong gland from lamb; wipe with a damp cloth. Insert one garlic clove in gash made by butcher; make another cut on the underside and insert remaining clove. Rub vinegar into lamb and douse with Worcestershire sauce. Sprinkle with 2 teaspoons salt, lemon-pepper marinade, and pepper.

In a saucepan blend tomatoes which have been pureed in blender, catsup, chopped onions, bell pepper, and sugar. Cook for 5 minutes over medium heat. Spoon as much sauce as will adhere to the surface over lamb in a roasting pan. Bake in a preheated 300° oven for 35 minutes per pound or until a meat thermometer reaches 170°. Baste every 30 minutes, using up remaining sauce. Add water to keep juices from drying out. Prepare Gravy. Serve with rice, a tossed green salad, and broiled canned peach halves filled after cooking with my orange chutney. Yield: 8 to 10 servings.

Gravy:

2 cups hot water
3 tablespoons all-purpose flour
1 teaspoon salt
¼ teaspoon black pepper

For a tasty gravy, remove lamb to a hot platter, pour off all but 4 tablespoons fat in a pan. Add 2 cups hot water, scraping bottom and sides of pan to dissolve the meat essence. Thicken with flour that has been blended with a little cold water. Bring mixture to a boil slowly; add salt, pepper, and remaining tomato sauce that was in the pan.

STUFFED LEG OF LAMB

"Delicious!" was Eudora's comment on my new lamb discovery. Everyone at the table cleaned their plates down to the last bite so that I felt repaid for rising at dawn to shake a lamb's leg.

1 (7- to 8-pound) leg of lamb
1 pint fresh mushrooms or 1 (6-ounce) can
    sliced mushrooms
1 (4½-ounce) jar stuffed green olives
1 cup chopped onion
2 tablespoons butter or margarine
4 slices white bread, pulled to pieces
1½ cups seasoned bread crumbs
1½ teaspoons freshly ground black pepper
¼ cup chopped parsley, fresh, frozen, or dried
2 tablespoons celery seeds
1 teaspoon powdered mushrooms
1 egg, slightly beaten
4 tablespoons whipping cream
6 slices bacon
1¼ cup white wine vinegar, divided
2 teaspoons salt, divided
2 tablespoons Worcestershire sauce, divided
½ teaspoon lemon-pepper marinade, divided
1 cup water, divided

Have your butcher remove the bone from leg of lamb, then tie the meat securely to prevent drying out.

Wash and dry fresh mushrooms. Cut fresh mushrooms and olives into thin slices. Cook chopped onion in butter in a skillet over medium heat about 15 minutes or until clear.

In a large bowl combine all ingredients except bacon slices and one half of vinegar, salt, Worcestershire sauce, lemon-pepper marinade, and water. Add just enough of the remaining vinegar to moisten well; it may take an entire cup. Untie the meat and stuff with dressing mixture. Remember, stuffing expands during cooking, so pack lightly. Fasten all loose ends of meat to roast with skewers or toothpicks.

Wipe off surface of lamb with remaining ¼ cup vinegar. Sprinkle with remaining salt, Worcestershire sauce, and lemon-pepper marinade. Cover with 5 or 6 slices bacon secured with toothpicks. Place roast on a rack with stuffed side up in a shallow baking pan. Bake in a preheated 325° oven for 40 minutes per pound. Pour remaining ½ cup water in bottom of pan and add an additional ½ cup if necessary. Baste three or four times during cooking process. This is delectable hot or cold. Yield: 10 to 12 servings.

MICHEL GARRAUD'S LAMB GEISHA

Exotic lamb dish.

1 pound lamb (boned best end of neck or
    other cut)
4 tablespoons olive oil
1 medium-size onion, thinly sliced
¼ cup all-purpose flour
1 teaspoon salt
¼ teaspoon black pepper
1 (8-ounce) can pineapple chunks, drained
    and liquid reserved
½ pound button mushrooms, fresh or canned
1 tablespoon cider vinegar
2 tablespoons soy sauce
1 cup water
1 chicken bouillon cube
2 tomatoes, peeled and quartered
    Chopped parsley

Cut lamb into 1-inch cubes, and trim off any excess fat. In a heavy skillet or Dutch oven heat oil over medium heat, add sliced onion and cook until slightly brown; remove from pan. Blend flour, salt, and pepper. Roll meat in mixture and fry until browned in skillet. Mix in any remaining flour with cooked onion, reserved pineapple liquid, mushrooms, vinegar, soy sauce, water, and bouillon cube. Bring to boil; adjust seasoning and cover with foil. Place in a preheated 300° oven and cook for 2 hours. Before serving, add pineapple chunks, quartered tomatoes, and garnish with parsley. Yield: 2 to 3 servings.

LAMBBRATEN

A gourmet specialty of Old Salem Tavern, Winston-Salem, North Carolina. The lamb may be broiled inside or grilled outside on the patio.

1 (3½- to 4-pound) leg of lamb
1 clove garlic, minced or ⅛ teaspoon garlic powder
1½ cups dry vermouth
2½ tablespoons butter
3 tablespoons all-purpose flour
1 egg yolk
½ cup whipping cream
1½ tablespoons small capers
⅛ teaspoon white pepper
1¼ teaspoons salt, divided
⅛ teaspoon freshly ground black pepper

Have your butcher slice lamb into ¼-inch thick slices; place in an oblong glass casserole; add minced garlic and cover with vermouth. Marinate overnight in refrigerator. Strain marinade and place in a small saucepan over low heat. In a heavy-bottomed saucepan or skillet, melt butter over low heat; blend in flour, stirring constantly with a wooden spatula or spoon. Cook for 2 minutes and remove from heat. As soon as the butter-flour mixture stops bubbling, pour in hot vermouth marinade and beat well with a wire whisk to blend thoroughly.

Over a moderately high heat stir until sauce comes to a boil; boil 1 minute and continue to stir. Beat together egg yolk and whipping cream with a wire whisk until well blended. Adding a few drops at a time, beat in ½ cup hot sauce. Slowly beat in remaining sauce and return mixture to saucepan. Cook over moderately high heat, stirring constantly until sauce comes to a boil. Boil 1 minute; add capers, ⅛ teaspoon white pepper, and ¼ teaspoon salt. Reduce heat and simmer; check seasoning. Keep sauce warm in top of a double boiler until ready to serve over grilled lamb.

Sprinkle lamb with remaining 1 teaspoon salt and black pepper. Broil 3 to 4 minutes on one side; turn and broil the other side. Place 2 to 3 slices on each warmed plate and spoon sauce over top. Yield: 8 to 10 servings.

LAMB WITH DATE VÉRONIQUE SAUCE

White grapes, white wine, and diced pureed dates make a festive roast for a holiday table.

1 (6- to 7-pound) leg of lamb
¼ cup white wine
2 teaspoons garlic powder
2 teaspoons onion powder or dried green onion
2½ teaspoons salt
1 teaspoon lemon-pepper marinade
    Basting Mixture and Véronique Sauce

Wipe meat with wine. Sprinkle with seasonings. Place lamb fat side up on a roasting rack in an uncovered pan. Bake in a preheated 325° oven for 30 minutes per pound or until meat thermometer registers 170°.

Basting Mixture and Véronique Sauce:

4 tablespoons butter
½ cup firmly packed dark brown sugar
1 (8-ounce) package diced dates, divided, or whole dates, finely chopped
2½ cups white wine, divided
1 cup peeled seedless white grapes

Melt butter in a saucepan over low heat, add brown sugar and ½ package diced dates; blend together thoroughly. Add 1 cup wine to mixture and stir constantly. Bring to a boil and remove from heat. Puree mixture in blender or put through a ricer. Place peeled grapes and remaining dates in another bowl, cover with 1 cup wine. Set aside. When the lamb has been roasting about 1½ hours or when meat thermometer registers 155°, brush pureed date sauce over roast. Continue to baste often until meat is done and thermometer registers 170°. Place lamb on a warm serving platter.

To complete the sauce, blend remaining ½ cup wine with drippings in roasting pan, stirring well with a spoon. Add any remaining basting mixture and cook over medium heat, stirring constantly. Add grape, wine, and date mixture and cook until sauce begins to boil, then remove from heat. Slice lamb and top with a generous serving of sauce. Garnish with spiced fruit and bunches of white grapes. Yield: 10 servings.

COFFEE ROASTED LAMB

Basting with coffee gives the lamb a subtle and delicious flavor.

  1 teaspoon salt
  ½ teaspoon lemon-pepper marinade
  ¼ cup all-purpose flour, divided
  ½ teaspoon ground ginger
  1 (5-pound) leg of lamb
  2 cups strong coffee
  1¼ cups water
    Salt and pepper to taste

Combine salt, lemon-pepper marinade, ⅛ cup flour, and ginger. Mix well and rub over entire surface of lamb. Place on rack in a shallow roasting pan and pour coffee over lamb. Bake in a preheated 325° oven for 30 to 35 minutes per pound or until meat thermometer registers 170° for medium doneness. Baste often.

When the roast is done, remove to a heated platter and keep warm in oven until serving.

For gravy, pour drippings into a measuring cup. Skim off and discard all but ¼ cup fat; pour drippings into skillet. Blend remaining ⅛ cup flour with a little of the water; stir into drippings with remaining water. Stir constantly over medium heat about 2 minutes or until gravy boils. Add salt and pepper. Yield: 6 to 8 servings.

Note: I usually buy a full leg of lamb and have my butcher cut two or three sirloin steaks, leaving ¾ of a leg. This makes a nice size roast and you have the benefit of the expensive steaks for another meal by wrapping in foil and freezing.

LIB HOLLERS' LAMB SHANKS

This economical and tasty recipe gives a new dimension to lamb.

  2 lamb shanks
  2 tablespoons cider vinegar
  ¼ teaspoon salt
  ⅛ teaspoon lemon-pepper marinade
  2 tablespoons bacon drippings or corn oil
  1 tablespoon all-purpose flour
  ½ cup port or 4 tablespoons cider vinegar
  1 tablespoon Worcestershire sauce
  ⅛ teaspoon ground thyme
  ½ teaspoon dried parsley
  ½ teaspoon dried green onion or chives
  1 tablespoon soy sauce (optional)
  1 cup beef or chicken bouillon

Trim lamb of excess fat and wipe with 2 tablespoons vinegar. Sprinkle with salt and lemon-pepper marinade and brown quickly in bacon drippings in a hot skillet over a medium high heat. Turn on all sides; sprinkle with flour and pour wine over meat. Add remaining ingredients. Cover skillet with a tight-fitting lid and simmer slowly for 2 hours. Baste occasionally. The meat juices form a delicious gravy. Add a small amount of hot water if needed to stretch gravy. Serve with saffron rice or boiled potatoes. For a delicious complete meal with only one skillet to wash, the last hour of cooking add 2 peeled potatoes, 4 scraped carrots left whole, and 3 medium-size white onions with skin removed. Yield: 2 servings.

Neptune's Harvest

CRABMEAT AND SHRIMP CASSEROLE QUICKIE

A marvelous seafood quickie using canned crabmeat and shrimp.

  1 (6½-ounce) can crabmeat
  4 tablespoons butter
  4 tablespoons all-purpose flour
1½ cups milk, warmed
  2 teaspoons Worcestershire sauce
  2 (4½-ounce) cans shrimp, drained
  4 teaspoons grated onion
  4 teaspoons finely chopped bell pepper
  3 teaspoons prepared mustard
  2 large eggs, slightly beaten
⅛ teaspoon freshly ground white pepper
    Salt to taste
  1 cup fine bread crumbs
  3 tablespoons grated Parmesan cheese

Carefully pick through crabmeat for shell; then place in colander and pour ice water over to freshen. Melt butter in saucepan over low heat, add flour and blend in well. Slowly stir in warmed milk. Add Worcestershire sauce and cook until smooth, stirring constantly with a wire whisk. When mixture is thick, set aside to cool.

In a large bowl combine crabmeat, shrimp, grated onion, bell pepper, mustard, beaten egg,

and white pepper. Taste to see if salt is needed. Stir cooked sauce into this mixture and pour into a buttered, 1½-quart casserole. Butter, then toast bread crumbs and roll fine; mix with grated Parmesan cheese and sprinkle over top of casserole. Bake in a preheated 350° oven for 20 minutes. Serve with saffron rice, hot French bread, and a tossed green or grapefruit salad. Yield: 6 servings.

Variation: You may substitute an additional 7½-ounce can crabmeat for the canned shrimp.

EXOTIC SHE-CRAB QUICKIE

The easiest gourmet dish you will ever want to prepare. In less than 20 minutes you are ready to serve a creation fit for a king.

½ cup fresh mushrooms
      or ½ cup large button mushrooms in
      butter sauce
¼ cup butter
  1 (10½-ounce) can She-Crab soup
⅓ cup milk
⅛ teaspoon ground mace
¼ teaspoon dried green onion
½ cup cooked and deveined shrimp
  1 tablespoon dry sherry

Sauté fresh mushrooms in butter over medium heat for 5 to 7 minutes. Dilute soup with milk in top of double boiler over slowly boiling water. Add mace, and dried green onion and stir until blended. Add mushrooms and shrimp and continue cooking for 5 to 7 minutes. Remove from heat and add sherry. Serve in ramekins with tossed green salad and toasted French bread. A dry white wine makes a fitting companion. Yield: 3 servings.

MARIAH'S CRAB BISQUE

Superb! Crisply browned crabmeat patties in a marvelous bisque. This is a very filling dish and may be served as a first course or as an entrée.

 3 tablespoons butter, divided
⅓ cup minced onion
 2 cloves garlic, minced
 2 celery ribs, finely chopped
 1 pound fresh, frozen, or canned crabmeat
 3 slices white bread
 1 teaspoon salt
¼ teaspoon freshly ground black pepper
¼ teaspoon ground mace
 1 large egg, beaten
¼ cup olive or vegetable oil
    Bisque

Melt 1 tablespoon butter in a skillet over medium heat. Cook onion, garlic, and celery

about 15 minutes or until tender, not brown. Carefully pick through crabmeat with clean hands for bits of shell. Thaw frozen crabmeat completely and dry on paper towels. Place canned crabmeat in colander and pour ice water over it to freshen flavor; drain well. Remove cooked onion and garlic mixture to a large bowl. Soak bread in colander with cold water; squeeze out and crumble it in bowl containing onion-garlic mixture. Add salt, pepper, mace, and beaten egg and shape into nice size patties.

Place remaining butter and oil in same skillet over moderately high heat. When you see that the butter foam has almost subsided, arrange 4 or 5 crabmeat patties in skillet. Do not crowd. Fry on one side for 4 or 5 minutes, regulating heat so that fat is very hot but is not burning. Turn and fry patties on other side for same length of time. Each pattie should be crisply browned. Continue with remaining patties, in the same manner adding more butter and oil as needed. Keep warm in heated bowls or plates while preparing Bisque. Pour Bisque over crabmeat patties and serve. Have plenty of hot French bread available to enjoy with it. Yield: 8 servings.

Bisque:

 1 tablespoon butter
 1 tablespoon all-purpose flour
 1 celery rib, finely chopped
 1 clove garlic, finely chopped
¼ cup finely chopped onion
 1 (16-ounce) can stewed tomatoes
 1 tablespoon Worcestershire sauce
    Salt and pepper to taste

Use skillet in which you browned crabmeat patties; do not wash. Melt butter over medium heat; add flour and stir constantly. Tan flour, but do not brown. Add celery, garlic, onion, and tomatoes; mix well and allow to simmer for 15 minutes. Add seasonings and cook a few minutes longer.

STUFFED CRAB

Great for a luncheon or supper dish and easy to make.

½ pound crabmeat, fresh, frozen, or canned
1 clove garlic, minced
1 small onion, finely chopped
1 celery rib, finely chopped
⅓ cup finely chopped bell pepper
3 tablespoons butter or margarine, divided
1 slice fresh white bread
½ cup milk
1 egg, well beaten
⅛ teaspoon ground mace
⅛ teaspoon baking powder
    Salt to taste
½ cup bread crumbs

Carefully pick through crabmeat for particles of shell. Allow frozen crabmeat to thaw completely and dry on paper towel. Place canned crabmeat in a fine strainer and pour ice water over it to freshen. In a heavy skillet sauté garlic, onion, celery, and bell pepper in 2 tablespoons butter over a medium heat about 12 minutes or until onion is transparent. Soak slice of bread in cold water and squeeze out in colander. Add to garlic mixture with milk and blend well, breaking up the bread into fine pieces with cooking spoon or potato masher. Add well-beaten egg, mace, baking powder, and crabmeat. Taste to see if salt is needed. Arrange mixture in crab shells, pyrex cups, or a 1-quart casserole. Sprinkle with bread crumbs and dot with remaining butter. Bake in a preheated 400° oven until brown. Yield: 5 servings.

CHAMPIGNONS DU ROI

François la Varenne, the renowned Gallic chef, introduced his superb *Champignons Farcis* for Louis XIV's pleasure. In making king crowned mushrooms, use fresh ones if available. If not, try Sexton's colossal button variety. This recipe may be served as an hors d'oeuvre, an entrée at a luncheon, or a first course at a formal dinner. Preparation takes less than 10 minutes.

1 pound large fresh mushrooms or 1
    (16-ounce) can colossal button
    mushrooms, drained
4½ tablespoons butter
    Stuffing

Remove stems of mushrooms by twisting gently; reserve for use in other dishes. Wipe caps of fresh mushrooms with a soft damp cloth or wash under a slow stream of cold water. Never soak mushrooms, but dry immediately on paper towels. Melt 4 tablespoons butter in a heavy skillet over medium heat; sauté mushrooms in butter (avoid piling). When edges are golden, after about 10 minutes, turn with a spatula. This may be done the night or morning before being used. Drain on a paper towel.

Sauté canned mushrooms about 5 minutes.

Stuffing:

½ pound canned, frozen, or fresh crabmeat
1½ tablespoons butter, divided
1 slice white bread
1 teaspoon onion puree, fresh or canned
½ teaspoon dried green onion
⅛ teaspoon ground mace
¼ teaspoon salt
⅛ teaspoon baking powder
1 egg, beaten
2 tablespoons seasoned or toasted bread
    crumbs

Carefully pick through crabmeat for small pieces of shell and tissue. Frozen crabmeat must be thawed completely and drained on a paper towel. Melt 1 tablespoon butter in a skillet over medium heat. Add bread which has been soaked in cold water in colander and squeezed out. Add crabmeat, seasonings, baking powder, and beaten egg; mix well using a potato masher. Spoon stuffing into mushroom caps, sprinkle with bread crumbs and dot with remaining butter. Bake in a preheated 400° oven for 10 minutes or until lightly golden. Serve hot. Good cold too. Allow two or three mushrooms as an entrée. Yield: 14 to 16 mushrooms.

CRABMEAT REMICK

A superb dish that may be served either as an appetizer or as an entrée. I make a very highly seasoned mayonnaise as a base for the sauce. You may use a commercial brand if pressed for time.

  2 egg yolks, cold
  ⅓ cup lemon juice, strained and chilled, divided
  2 cups corn or other vegetable oil, chilled
  1 teaspoon salt
1½ teaspoons Tabasco
1¾ teaspoons dry mustard
1¼ teaspoons paprika
  1 teaspoon tarragon vinegar
  ½ cup chili sauce
  5 strips lean bacon
  1 pound lump crabmeat

Chill a deep narrow bowl before making mayonnaise. Place egg yolks and 1 teaspoon lemon juice in a bowl and beat at high speed of electric mixer until mixture becomes thicker, then slowly add some oil and continue beating. When mayonnaise begins to thicken, add salt, Tabasco, mustard, and paprika. Add a small amount of lemon juice. Gradually add remaining oil. Use lemon juice often to keep mixture from becoming too thick. To every 1½ cups mayonnaise add given amounts of vinegar and chili sauce; blend well. Cook bacon over medium heat in a skillet until crisp; drain on a paper towel. Carefully pick through crabmeat to remove any tiny pieces of shell. Divide crabmeat into seven piles. Place crabmeat into individual ramekins and top with sauce and bacon strips. Bake in a preheated 400° oven for 10 minutes, change heat to broiler for 1 minute until sauce is bubbling hot. This is delicious with parslied new potatoes or stuffed baked potatoes. Yield: 7 servings.

Note: If you use a commercial mayonnaise, prepare sauce as follows:

1½ cups commercial mayonnaise
  1 teaspoon tarragon vinegar
  ½ cup chili sauce
  1 teaspoon dry mustard
  2 tablespoons strained lemon juice
  1 teaspoon paprika
  1 teaspoon Tabasco

Blend all ingredients in a bowl and pour over crabmeat. Top with bacon and bake as directed above.

PERKINS FLIPPIN'S STUFFED CRABS

A delightfully different recipe from Old Virginia.

  2 cups crabmeat
  2 hard-boiled eggs
  1 cup mayonnaise
  1 teaspoon grated onion
  1 teaspoon chopped parsley
  2 tablespoons lemon juice
  ½ teaspoon Worcestershire sauce
  ½ teaspoon prepared mustard
  3 tablespoons sherry
  1 cup buttered bread crumbs, divided

Combine all ingredients except ¼ cup bread crumbs for garnish, and place in a buttered 1½-quart casserole or individual crab shells. Sprinkle reserved bread crumbs on top and bake in a preheated 400° oven for 15 to 20 minutes. Yield: 6 to 8 servings.

SARAH B. MORRIS' CRABMEAT CASSEROLE

Superb! Serve for an announcement party or your new son-in-law's first meal in your home. Serve with fluffy, cooked white or saffron rice, a grapefruit and avocado salad for a gourmet meal.

2 cups half-and-half
½ cup butter
4 tablespoons all-purpose flour
⅛ teaspoon freshly ground white pepper
¼ teaspoon salt
¼ teaspoon Tabasco
⅛ teaspoon ground mace
2 tablespoons good dry sauterne
3 (14-ounce) cans artichoke hearts, cut in halves
1 (8-ounce) can buttered chopped mushrooms
1 pound lump crabmeat

Warm half-and-half slowly in a saucepan. Make cream sauce in double boiler or teflon skillet. If using a skillet, melt butter over low heat. Add flour and blend with a wire whisk. Slowly stir in hot cream, add white pepper, salt, Tabasco, and mace, and cook until smooth and boiling; continue stirring. Adjust seasoning; salt may be needed. Add sauterne.

In another saucepan heat the artichoke hearts and mushrooms over low heat. Arrange these in a large, well-buttered, flat-bottomed casserole. Add lump crabmeat and cover with sauce. Cover with foil and bake in a preheated 325° oven for 25 to 30 minutes or until sauce bubbles. Do not overcook for that destroys the marvelous flavor of the fresh crabmeat. Just heat thoroughly. Yield: 10 servings.

ZESTY CREOLE OYSTER PIE

The marvelous flavor of this oyster pie makes it an excellent dish to serve on a cold winter night. You need only a tossed green salad and toasted French bread to complete the meal.

2 cups all-purpose flour, divided
2¼ teaspoons salt, divided
⅓ cup vegetable shortening
1 tablespoon cold water
1 quart oysters, drained
¼ teaspoon freshly ground black pepper
⅛ teaspoon ground mace
¼ teaspoon paprika
2 slices bacon, diced
1 small onion, minced
1 tablespoon minced green pepper, divided
8 to 10 drops Tabasco
2 tablespoons lemon juice
1 tablespoon minced parsley, fresh, frozen, or dried
2 tablespoons butter

In a large bowl blend 1 cup flour, ¼ teaspoon salt, shortening, and water. Roll to ¼ inch thickness on a lightly floured board. Using a regular-size glass as a cutter, cut dough into six rounds, 2¾ inches in diameter. Remove the center of each round with a 1-inch biscuit cutter. Set pastry rounds aside while preparing rest of pie.

Dry drained oysters on paper towels. Roll in mixture of remaining 1 cup flour, 1 teaspoon salt, pepper, mace, and paprika. Sauté bacon and onion until crisp and brown. Place a layer of oysters close together in a buttered 10- x 6- x 2-inch baking dish. Sprinkle half of bacon-onion mixture over oysters. Combine minced green pepper, Tabasco, remaining 1 teaspoon salt, lemon juice, and parsley. Sprinkle half of this mixture over oysters. Repeat layers. Dot with butter and place all pastry rounds on top. Bake in a preheated 450° oven for 25 minutes or until pastry rounds are golden. Serve at once. Yield: 6 servings.

Highly seasoned tomato sauce enhances the shrimp flavor to make Shrimp Creole a special favorite. Winifred's zesty recipe for this Cajun favorite is on page 184.

QUICK OYSTER RAREBIT

A hearty rarebit suitable for dinner on a cold winter's night takes less than 30 minutes to prepare.

 1 pint oysters
 2 tablespoons butter
¼ pound mild cheddar cheese, shredded
¼ teaspoon salt
⅛ teaspoon pepper
 8 drops Tabasco
   Reserved oyster liquor
 2 large eggs, well beaten
 2 teaspoons sherry (optional)
 1 teaspoon Worcestershire sauce
   Parsley
   Paprika

Drain oysters and reserve liquor. Melt butter in top of a double boiler over medium high heat; add shredded cheese and seasonings, stirring until cheese melts. Add reserved oyster liquor with well-beaten eggs and cook until mixture thickens. Add sherry, if desired, and Worcestershire sauce. Remove from heat and add oysters. Serve at once on toast, crackers, or Holland rusks. For an attractive plate, garnish with parsley and sprinkle lightly with paprika. This keeps well in a chafing dish for late guests. Sliced sour pickles add dash to this rarebit. Yield: 4 servings.

SCRUMPTIOUS SESAME SHRIMP

The taste is so delicate and marvelous you do not need to serve any sauce. Beer or dry white wine make an ideal accompaniment.

Southerners always find innumerable ways to prepare their favorite seafoods. The Neptune's Harvest chapter includes favorites from Mobile, Virginia's Tidewater region, and Louisiana.

1 pound medium-size to large raw shrimp, unpeeled
3 tablespoons butter, margarine, or salad oil
3 tablespoons sesame seeds
3 tablespoons freshly squeezed lime juice

Snip shrimp down center back with kitchen shears and remove vein; don't peel. Melt butter in skillet over medium heat; add sesame seeds, lime juice, and shrimp. Cook over medium heat about 15 to 20 minutes or until shrimp are a bright orange-pink and seeds are golden brown. Turn shrimp frequently while cooking. Drain on absorbent paper. Serve hot with French fried potatoes or hush puppies. Allow each person to shell his own shrimp. Yield: 3 servings.

BILOXI BARBECUED SHRIMP

Good dipped in red sauce with cocktails or served as an entrée. This recipe has been served at the Biloxi Shrimp Festival banquet for many years.

5 pounds headless raw shrimp, peeled
1 pound melted butter or margarine
5 cloves garlic, minced
   Paprika
   Salt and pepper to taste
5 tablespoons Worcestershire sauce
2 teaspoons Tabasco
   Juice of 1 or 2 lemons, to taste

Combine all ingredients, seasoning as desired. Sauté over low heat for 1½ to 2 hours in a heavy skillet or bake in a preheated 350° oven for 45 minutes in a covered roasting pan. Yield: 20 servings.

OUT-OF-THIS-WORLD SHRIMP

A VIP casserole, ideal for a party of any kind particularly a bride's luncheon or for a visiting dignitary. The recipe is increased easily; a 5-pound box of shrimp will serve 36. This amount requires five batches of sauce. Serve with saffron rice and a whole tomato filled with my Secret Salad Dressing.

1½ quarts water
 ¼ teaspoon dried green onion
 1 slice lemon
 1 tablespoon plus 1 teaspoon salt
 1 tablespoon Worcestershire sauce
 ½ cup celery tops
 ¼ teaspoon instant crab or shrimp boil
   or ¼ teaspoon Tabasco and ¼ teaspoon
   paprika
1½ pounds shrimp, fresh or frozen, peeled and
   deveined.

Bring water and seasonings to a boil and add shrimp. Return to a boil for 1 minute, then allow to cool in water 2 to 3 minutes after removing from heat. Drain at once.

Sauce:

 2 tablespoons butter
 2 tablespoons all-purpose flour
1¼ cups milk, warm to hot
 ½ teaspoon salt
 ⅛ teaspoon freshly ground white pepper
 3 tablespoons sherry
 1 (14-ounce) can artichoke hearts, washed
   and drained
 1 (16-ounce) can colossal mushrooms
   or 1 pound fresh mushrooms
 ⅛ teaspoon paprika
 4 tablespoons grated Parmesan cheese

Melt butter in top of a double boiler over rapidly boiling water or in a teflon skillet over low heat. Add flour and blend with a wire whisk. Slowly stir in heated milk. Add salt and white pepper. Cook and stir until sauce is smooth and boiling. Remove from heat and add sherry. Place artichoke hearts in a large buttered square or oblong casserole. Scatter the shrimp and mushrooms over hearts. If using fresh mushrooms, wipe off with a damp cloth and sauté in ½ cup butter over medium heat for 6 to 8 minutes.

Cover mushrooms with white sauce and sprinkle generously with paprika and Parmesan cheese. Bake in a preheated 350° oven for 30 minutes or until the sauce is bubbling up. Yummy! This dish may be made the day before using and kept refrigerated. Yield: 6 servings.

Variation: For a richer sauce, substitute half-and-half for the milk. For 8 servings use the preceding recipe and increase shrimp to 2 pounds in the first part. For the sauce, use 3 tablespoons butter, 3 tablespoons flour, and 2 cups warm milk or half-and-half, 1 teaspoon salt, ¼ teaspoon white pepper; everything else stays the same.

CREOLE SHRIMP

A superb dish and easy to prepare.

 1 medium-size onion, chopped
 1 celery rib, chopped
 ½ bell pepper, chopped
 1 clove garlic, chopped
 2 tablespoons bacon drippings
 3 tablespoons all-purpose flour
 1 (16-ounce) can tomatoes
 2 peeled tomatoes, chopped
 1 tablespoon Worcestershire sauce
 ½ teaspoon ground mace
 ½ teaspoon lemon-pepper marinade
 1 beef bouillon cube
 1 cup boiling water
1½ pounds shelled and deveined shrimp
 2 tablespoons catsup (optional)
   Salt to taste

Cook onion, celery, bell pepper, and garlic in a skillet with bacon drippings over medium heat about 15 minutes or until onion is clear and transparent. Add flour, canned and chopped fresh tomatoes, Worcestershire sauce, mace, and lemon-pepper marinade; blend well. Use a potato masher to break up tomatoes into small pieces. Dissolve beef bouillon cube in boiling water and add with shrimp to sauce. Bring to a simmering boil, lower heat, and cook for 45 minutes to 1 hour, stirring often. If tomato pulp is not very acid, add catsup for a better flavor. Add salt. Add additional water if necessary to prevent sticking. Pour shrimp mixture into a lightly buttered, 1½-quart casserole, and brown in a preheated 400° oven about 20 minutes. Serve with cooked rice and toasted French bread and tossed green salad for a complete meal. Yield: 6 servings.

PLANTATION SHRIMP PILAU

1 pound fresh or frozen shrimp or 3 (5-ounce) cans shrimp
4 slices bacon
1 cup uncooked rice
2 tablespoons butter
½ cup finely chopped celery
½ cup finely chopped bell pepper
½ cup finely chopped onion
1 teaspoon Worcestershire sauce
1 tablespoon strained lemon juice
1 tablespoon all-purpose flour
¼ teaspoon ground mace
⅛ teaspoon cayenne pepper
  Salt to taste

Shell and devein fresh and frozen shrimp; if shrimp are large cut each into three pieces. Drain canned shrimp, pour ice water oven them, and let stand 4 or 5 minutes; drain again. In skillet over medium heat fry bacon until crisp, turning often; drain on paper towel. Add bacon drippings to water in which rice will be cooked, follow package directions for cooking

rice. When rice is tender, drain in colander. Using same skillet melt butter over medium heat and add celery, bell pepper, and onion and cook about 12 to 15 minutes or until onion is clear. Sprinkle shrimp with Worcestershire sauce and lemon juice. Dredge in flour and add to vegetable mixture. Add mace. Stir and allow mixture to simmer until flour is cooked. Add cayenne pepper, cooked rice, and salt. If mixture seems too dry add another tablespoon or more of butter. Stir in crumbled bacon and serve on a heated platter. Yield: 4 to 6 servings.

BARBECUED SHRIMP

A zesty seafood treat that may be served with cocktails, dipped in a tomato sauce, or as an entrée.

2½ pounds (about 36) jumbo headless raw shrimp
2 tablespoons lemon juice
½ pound melted butter or margarine
¾ cup olive oil
2 teaspoons paprika
1½ teaspoons salt
¼ teaspoon freshly ground black pepper
3 cloves garlic, minced
1 teaspoon Tabasco
¼ cup parsley, fresh, frozen, dried, or minced

Peel and devein shrimp, leaving tails on. Add shrimp to remaining ingredients which have been thoroughly mixed in a large glass or stainless steel bowl. Marinate for several hours in refrigerator before cooking. Preheat broiler and place shrimp in a heavy shallow pan and broil for 4 minutes on each side, or sauté in a large heavy skillet on a grill for 1½ to 2 hours over low heat. Two skillets may be needed. Turn shrimp often if they are stacked in layers. To serve as an entrée, place in a soup bowl with lots of butter sauce and accompany with hot French bread. Yield: 8 to 10 servings.

SHRIMP BUTTER

Two pounds of heads and shells is equivalent to 1 pound of shells, always use equal amount of butter to quantity of shells.

1 pound butter
6 peeled and deveined shrimp
2 pounds heads and shells of Boiled Shrimp
1 teaspoon French vermouth

Melt butter in skillet and keep hot. Pour boiling water into blender, remove water and quickly put in shrimp, shells, and hot melted butter. Turn indicator to chop; when the shells are completely blended, put mixture through a sieve with a wooden spoon. Add French vermouth. Refrigerate for immediate use or freeze. Marvelous on melba rounds or combined with whipped cream cheese in equal quantities as an hors d'oeuvre with drinks. Yield: 1 pint.

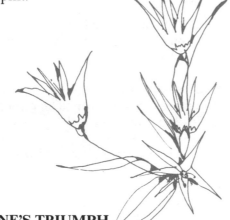

NEPTUNE'S TRIUMPH

When I served this easily prepared casserole for the first time to a group of my husband's friends, all men-folk, they said, "You should call it a Zippy Zee dish." Being a former Latin teacher, I would rather give credit to the old God of the Sea for his delicious wares.

The casserole must be made at least four hours ahead of baking — preferably the night before you plan to serve it.

Shrimp:

1 quart water
1 teaspoon salt
1 lemon slice
4 celery tops
¼ teaspoon Tabasco
¼ teaspoon paprika
1 tablespoon Worcestershire sauce
1 pound fresh or frozen shrimp
**   or 2 (6½- to 7¼-ounce) cans crabmeat,**
**   Alaskan or Japanese**

Combine all ingredients except shrimp in a large kettle. Bring to a boil and continue boiling for 10 minutes. Add fresh shrimp and return to a rolling boil; boil for 2 minutes. Cook frozen shrimp only half the time stated on package. Drain shrimp, reserving ½ cup liquid. Cut shrimp into small pieces.

1 pound fresh or frozen white crabmeat
**   or 2 (6½- to 7¼-ounce) cans**
**   crabmeat, Alaskan or Japanese**
Shrimp
1 cup cooked lobster or its equivalent
**   canned (optional)**
1½ cups yellow rice, cooked
1 hot green pepper, minced
2 tablespoons capers
½ cup finely chopped onion
½ cup finely chopped parlsey
½ (8-ounce) can water chestnuts, thinly
**   sliced**
3 tablespoons lemon juice
2 tablespoons finely chopped pimientos
½ cup reserved shrimp liquid
2 teaspoons soy sauce (optional)
1½ cups commercial mayonnaise

Carefully pick through crabmeat for bits of shell. In a large bowl combine cut shrimp, crabmeat that has been separated, and lobster, if desired. Toss with yellow rice, adding remaining ingredients except mayonnaise. Stir in mayonnaise and place mixture in a buttered

8- x 13- x 2-inch casserole. Cover with foil and let stand in refrigerator for several hours. Bake in a preheated 325° oven for 30 minutes. This is delicious with grapefruit and avocado salad and fresh green asparagus. The casserole will freeze. Yield: 8 to 10 servings.

MARIAH MITCHELL'S CREOLE SHRIMP

The best—easy to prepare. Fresh shrimp are preferable and give tastier results, but frozen ones may be used if the sauce is cooked for 45 minutes before adding shrimp. Cook the shrimp only long enough to get done, 7 to 8 minutes at most. Overcooking makes shrimp tough.

2 pounds medium-size to large raw shrimp
1 large white onion, chopped (about 1 cup)
2 celery ribs, chopped
1 clove garlic, chopped, or ⅛ teaspoon garlic powder
½ cup bell pepper, chopped
2 tablespoons bacon drippings or butter
3 tablespoons all-purpose flour
2 (16-ounce) cans peeled tomatoes
1 teaspoon dried green parsley
½ teaspoon ground mace
1 tablespoon Worcestershire sauce
⅛ teaspoon sugar
⅛ teaspoon soda
2 beef bouillon cubes dissolved in 1 cup boiling water
¼ teaspoon Tabasco
Salt to taste

Peel and devein shrimp by cutting up the back and removing the black vein of sand. In a large skillet brown onion, celery, garlic, and bell pepper in bacon drippings over a medium heat, stirring constantly. Add flour and blend well; then add tomatoes, parsley, mace, Worcestershire sauce, sugar, soda, and shrimp. Continue stirring and add beef broth and Tabasco. Later, if necessary, add additional water to prevent sticking while cooking. Let sauce simmer over low heat for 45 minutes with the top only partially covered. You do not want steam to reduce the strength of sauce. Pour shrimp into a 2-quart oblong casserole and brown in a preheated 425° oven about 10 minutes. Serve hot with fluffy cooked rice and hot French bread. Yield: 6 to 8 servings.

CREOLE JAMBALAYA

A savory, one-dish meal. May be served with French bread and a green salad.

4 tablespoons vegetable oil
4 tablespoons all-purpose flour
1 cup finely chopped onion
1 cup finely chopped celery
1 clove garlic, minced
1 bell pepper, finely chopped
1 pound cooked ham, cubed
2 cups tomatoes, fresh or canned
1½ teaspoons seasoned salt
1 teaspoon Tabasco
2 tablespoons paprika
Pinch sugar
2 pounds shrimp, peeled and deveined
3 cups regular or quick-cooking rice
1 bay leaf
2 tablespoons butter

In a heavy skillet heat oil over medium heat. Add flour and stir until golden brown. Add onion, celery, garlic, and bell pepper and sauté until onion is transparent. Add ham, tomatoes, seasoned salt, Tabasco, paprika, and sugar. Cook 5 minutes over medium heat; set aside. Cook shrimp in boiling water 3 or 4 minutes until pink; drain and reserve liquid. Cook rice in reserved shrimp liquid with bay leaf until tender. Melt butter in another skillet, add shrimp just to heat through. Add shrimp mixture to rice. Combine with cooked onion mixture and heat through. Taste to see if more salt is needed. Serve hot. Yield: 8 servings.

BOILED SHRIMP

Delicious for a patio supper with cold beer or Sangría (see Beverages).

2 pounds shrimp in shells, fresh or frozen
2 quarts water
1 tablespoon salt
1 teaspoon ground thyme
1 teaspoon celery seeds
1 tablespoon dried green parsley
1 lemon, juice and rind
1 teaspoon garlic powder or 1 clove garlic, peeled
1 teaspoon dried green onion or 1 onion studded with cloves
8 cloves to be used with dried green onion
¼ teaspoon instant crab boil

Wash fresh shrimp and cut down the back with kitchen scissors. Remove sand vein and rinse well but do not remove shells. Bring water with remaining ingredients to a boil in a deep kettle. Add shrimp; return to a boil and reduce heat. Simmer 2 to 5 minutes, depending on size. Remove from heat and allow to cool in the kettle in the juices. Cook frozen shrimp according to package directions. Remove from heat and cool in liquid for 20 minutes. Leave shrimp in shells and serve hot with lemon butter or chill and serve with cocktail sauce. Yield: 4 to 6 servings.

FRAMPTON SHRIMP-CRAB CASSEROLE

Colorful and luscious, this casserole originated in the Orangeburg, South Carolina, kitchen of Frances Frampton, a marvelous cook. For a luncheon I serve string beans cooked with diced ham, a grapefruit-avocado salad served on Boston lettuce with poppy-seed dressing, hot biscuits, and my orange pie.

2 cups cooked rice
½ cup finely chopped onion
½ cup finely chopped bell pepper
1 cup finely chopped celery
1 cup tomato juice
½ cup milk
1 egg, well beaten
1 (3-ounce) can sliced mushrooms
2 teaspoons Worcestershire sauce
1 teaspoon salt
½ teaspoon mace
1½ cups (1-pound) raw shrimp, shelled and deveined
1 pound claw or lump crabmeat
1 cup homemade or commercial mayonnaise made with lemon juice
1 tablespoon butter
Buttered bread crumbs
¼ cup slivered almonds

Cook rice according to package directions; drain well. In a large bowl place onion, bell pepper, celery, and tomato juice. In a small bowl add milk to beaten egg and pour into vegetable mixture; blend well. Add mushrooms and seasoning along with shrimp, rice, crabmeat, and mayonnaise; stir well. Pour mixture into a buttered 13- x 9- x 2-inch casserole or a 2-quart baking dish. Sprinkle top with buttered bread crumbs, cover, and bake in a preheated 325° oven for 40 minutes or until shrimp are done; taste one to be sure. Remove cover and sprinkle with slivered almonds. Raise heat to 375° and cook about 5 minutes or until almonds are lightly browned. This freezes well. Yield: 8 to 10 servings.

SHRIMP ARNAUD

This gourmet appetizer or salad is completely different from any other shrimp dish you have ever eaten. It is easy to prepare but requires time. Arnaud's is a famous French restaurant in the Vieux Carré in New Orleans, Louisiana.

Count Arnaud, its founder, was a close

friend of my brother, Marcellus Green, who gave me the recipe. How he learned to make the unique creation I do not know except he had a marvelous sense of taste and was a great cook. You need a good zippy French dressing for a base. I find mine does a better job than a commercial dressing.

2 pounds medium-size cooked, peeled and deveined shrimp
2 cups French Dressing
1 cup finely chopped mild onions
1 cup finely chopped parsley, fresh or frozen
5¾ ounces Creole mustard
1 teaspoon paprika
½ teaspoon salt

If you use small shrimp, increase the French and Arnaud dressings by half, as these absorb so much of the sauce. The small shrimp do not need deveining.

Combine ingredients in a large glass or stainless steel bowl; mix well. Serve over a bed of shredded lettuce with hot French bread. A dry white wine is an excellent companion. Yield: 10 to 12 servings.

French Dressing:

¾ cup powdered sugar
¾ tablespoon paprika
¾ tablespoon salt
½ tablespoon dry mustard
2 cups vegetable, olive, or corn oil
¼ cup fresh lemon juice (about 2 lemons)
¾ cup fresh orange juice (about 1½ oranges)
½ cup cider or wine vinegar
½ tablespoon Worcestershire sauce
⅛ teaspoon garlic powder
**   or 1 clove garlic, whole**

Blend dry ingredients in a small mixing bowl. Add oil, fruit juices, vinegar, and Worcestershire sauce. Beat vigorously with a dover or electric beater until thoroughly blended. Pour into a quart jar, add garlic and refrigerate.

ZOLLIE KIMBROUGH'S SHRIMP CASSEROLE

Exotic!

2½ pounds peeled and deveined raw shrimp
1 tablespoon fresh, frozen, or canned lemon juice
3 tablespoons olive oil
¾ cup raw regular or 1 cup quick-cooking rice
¼ cup minced green pepper
¼ cup minced onion
2 tablespoons butter or margarine
1 teaspoon salt
⅛ teaspoon black pepper
⅛ teaspoon ground mace
**   Dash cayenne pepper**
1 (10¾-ounce) can tomato soup, undiluted
1 cup whipping cream
½ cup sherry
¾ cup slivered almonds, divided

One day before using, cook shrimp in boiling salted water for 4 minutes; drain. Place in a 2-quart casserole and sprinkle with lemon juice and olive oil. Cook rice according to package directions; drain. Refrigerate everything.

About 1 hour and 10 minutes before serving preheat oven to 350°. Reserve 6 or 8 shrimp for garnish. In a skillet sauté green pepper and onion in butter over medium heat for 5 minutes. Add rice, salt, pepper, mace, cayenne pepper, soup, cream, sherry, and ½ cup almonds to shrimp in casserole. Toss well. Bake, uncovered, in a preheated 350° oven for 35 minutes. Top with reserved shrimp and remaining ¼ cup almonds and bake at 350° for 20 minutes more or until mixture is bubbling and shrimp are slightly browned. Yield: 6 to 8 servings.

CREAMED SHRIMP

Perfect for a party. Serve in patty shells or on toasted English muffins.

  4 tablespoons butter
  4 tablespoons all-purpose flour
  1 teaspoon salt
  2 cups milk, warmed
1½ pounds raw shrimp, shelled and deveined
  2 hard-boiled eggs, chopped
  1 teaspoon Worcestershire sauce
  2 teaspoons onion juice
  8 patty shells or toasted English muffins
  ¼ teaspoon paprika

Melt butter in a skillet over low heat; add flour and salt and stir constantly until mixture is smooth. Add warmed milk and continue stirring until sauce thickens. Add shrimp, chopped hard-boiled eggs, Worcestershire sauce, and onion juice and cook a few minutes until shrimp turn pink. Taste to see if more salt is needed. Spoon into warmed patty shells and sprinkle with paprika. Yield: 8 servings.

GALATOIRE'S TROUT MARGUERY

Trout sublime! My sweetheart's favorite. He has never ordered anything else the many times we have eaten at this wonderful old restaurant.

 1 (2½-pound) trout
½ teaspoon salt
½ teaspoon white pepper
 1 tablespoon olive oil
 1 cup water
   Hollandaise Sauce

Clean, skin, and bone trout. Sprinkle fillets with salt and white pepper. Fold fillets and place in a shallow baking pan; cover with oil and water. Bake in a preheated 425° oven for 15 minutes or longer. Test with a fork to see

Hollandaise Sauce:

  1 cup butter, divided
  2 egg yolks, slightly beaten
  3 tablespoons strained lemon juice, warmed
    Salt to taste
⅛ teaspoon cayenne pepper
12 lake shrimp, peeled and deveined
 ½ (4-ounce) can sliced mushrooms, finely cut
  2 truffles, cut julienne style

Place ½ cup butter in a small saucepan with slightly beaten egg yolks. Hold saucepan over hot water; do not allow water to boil. Stir constantly with a wire whisk until butter melts. Add remaining butter and warmed lemon juice. Stir until mixture thickens. Test to see if salt is needed. Add cayenne pepper, shrimp which have been boiled for 2 or 3 minutes, mushrooms, and cut truffles. Pour over fish and serve.

Variation: For a more highly seasoned dish, rub saucepan with a garlic clove. In addition to salt and pepper, add ½ teaspoon Worcestershire sauce and 1 tablespoon diced pimiento to Hollandise Sauce.

CRÈME DE SAUMON

This delectable recipe for salmon was brought to Barbados from England many years ago by my hostess's mother. It is very old and I had to use a magnifying glass to decipher the faded ink script.

½ pound canned or cold boiled salmon
 2 tablespoons melted butter, cooled
 1 tablespoon fine bread crumbs
2 eggs, well beaten
 1 tablespoon minced parsley
   Salt and pepper to taste
   Sauce

Drain liquid from salmon and reserve ¼ cup.

Chop fish finely and place in a large bowl; add melted butter and blend into a smooth paste. Beat bread crumbs into the beaten eggs. Season with parsley, and salt and pepper. Work mixture together and put into a buttered ring mold. Steam or boil for ½ hour. As you serve the salmon pour the sauce over it. Potato or avocado salad may be used in center of ring mold. Yield: 6 servings.

Sauce:

1 cup milk
1 tablespoon cornstarch
1 heaping tablespoon butter
1 teaspoon anchovy paste
⅛ teaspoon ground mace
⅛ teaspoon cayenne pepper
¼ cup reserved salmon liquid
1 egg

Bring milk to a slow boil and thicken with cornstarch. Add butter, anchovy paste, mace, and cayenne pepper. When mixture begins to thicken, add reserved salmon liquid and stir constantly. Add egg and boil for 1 minute very gently.

POACHED FISH WITH COURT BOUILLON

Trout, red snapper, red fish, sheepshead—any good eating fish makes a superb meal.

1 (3- or 4-pound) dressed fish, fresh or frozen
   Court Bouillon
   Paprika
   Fish Sauce

Thaw frozen fish. Clean and scale fresh fish. Place fish in poacher or roasting pan and cover with strained Court Bouillon. Bring to boiling point, reduce heat, and simmer for 25 to 30 minutes or until fish flakes easily when tested with a fork. The smaller fish will take less time.

Remove fish from poacher or pan; drain well. Place on a hot platter, garnish with paprika, and serve hot with Fish Sauce or your favorite sauce. To serve cold, allow Court Bouillon to jell to thick consistency. Yield: 6 servings.

Court Bouillon:

1 large carrot, diced
2 medium-size onions, chopped
2 celery ribs and leaves, diced
2 tablespoons vegetable oil or butter
   Fish trimmings (heads, bones, tails, and fins) or 2 beef bouillon cubes
1 cup dry white wine
1 lemon, quartered, squeezed, including rind
4 cloves
2 bay leaves
½ cup fresh, chopped parsley or 2 tablespoons dried parsley
1 teaspoon thyme
2 cloves garlic (optional)
2 tablespoons salt
4 peppercorns, bruised
1 hot pepper
3 quarts cold water

In a 4-quart saucepan cook carrot, onions, and celery in oil over medium heat about 20 minutes or until vegetables are tender. Tie fish trimmings in a cheesecloth bag. Add remaining ingredients and bring to a simmering boil. Cover and simmer 30 minutes. Cool; remove fish trimmings and strain. Yield: about 3 quarts Court Bouillon.

Fish Sauce:

1½ cups mayonnaise
1 tablespoon dry mustard
3 tablespoons lemon juice, strained
6 drops Tabasco

Blend all ingredients together with a wire whisk. Any leftover sauce will keep refrigerated for at least two weeks.

POACHED FLOUNDER FILLETS

This is a delicious and easily prepared dish using frozen fillets, if fresh ones are not available.

   1 pound flounder fillets, fresh or frozen
1½ tablespoons butter
   2 teaspoons dried green onions, divided
   ½ teaspoon salt
   ⅛ teaspoon white pepper
   ¼ teaspoon paprika
   1 teaspoon ground mace
   ½ cup dry white sauterne
   ¾ cup white vermouth
   ½ cup water
   ¼ teaspoon lemon-pepper marinade
   1 tablespoon lemon juice

Thaw frozen fillets completely; dry excessive moisture on paper towel. Butter an oblong baking dish and sprinkle 1 teaspoon green onions in bottom of dish. Combine salt, white pepper, paprika, and mace and sprinkle lightly over both sides of fillets. Place fillets in a baking dish, cover with remaining teaspoon of onions, and dot with butter. Mix sauterne, vermouth, water, lemon-pepper marinade, and lemon juice in a small bowl and pour over fish; place pan over medium heat and bring to a boil; cover pan with buttered waxed paper or brown paper and transfer to oven. Bake in a preheated 350° oven for 10 to 12 minutes, depending on size of fillets. Test with fork for doneness; when the tines pierce the flesh easily, remove from heat and drain off liquid. The fish may be kept warm by putting the covered pan over slowly boiling water. Yield: 4 servings.

LAURA S. STURDIVANT'S CRAWFISH ÉTOUFÉE

Buy about 10 pounds live crawfish in order to have enough peeled crawfish tails for this delicious *étoufée*.

10 pounds live crawfish (2 pounds crawfish tails)
   1 tablespoon salt
   2 dried red peppers
   ½ cup chopped celery tops
   ½ lemon
      Salt and pepper to taste
   ½ cup butter or margarine
   ¾ cup chopped onions
   ½ cup chopped celery
   ½ cup chopped bell peppers
      Crawfish fat
   2 cups chicken stock, divided
      Salt, black pepper, Worcestershire sauce, and Tabasco to taste
   2 teaspoons cornstarch
   ¼ cup mixed chopped green onion tops and parsley
   2 tablespoons sherry (optional)

Fill kitchen sink with cold water, and salt heavily. Pour in live crawfish (use a wooden spoon to keep them from crawling out). This soaking will rid them of sand and extraneous mud. Meanwhile, fill a large iron pot with enough water to cover crawfish, at least 4 inches. Add 1 tablespoon salt, dried red peppers (chilipiquins are best), celery tops, and lemon. Bring to a boil, put in crawfish, turn off heat immediately, cover, and leave them in for 5 minutes.

Remove crawfish for peeling. Separate heads from tails. Be sure to save all the fat (the yellow deposit usually just inside the head portion). The fat is the ingredient that gives the unique crawfish flavor to the dish. Peel crawfish tails and reserve the fat. Season crawfish tails with salt and pepper.

Melt butter in a deep, heavy iron skillet. Add onions, chopped celery, and bell pepper and cook until onions are clear, stirring constantly. Add crawfish fat, 1½ cups chicken stock, crawfish tails, and seasonings. Simmer over slow heat for about ½ hour, stirring occasionally. Dissolve cornstarch in ½ cup chicken stock, stir until lumps disappear, then add to mixture.

Add green onion tops and parsley mixture and cook about 10 minutes. Turn off heat and let set for a few minutes. Serve over boiled rice with a good tossed green salad. Add sherry about 5 minutes before heat is turned off, if desired. Yield: 4 to 6 servings.

FLOUNDER FILLETS DU ROI LOUIS XIV

When I was a student in France in 1929, I ran across a delicious yet simple way of preparing flounder using finely chopped shrimp and white wine as a sauce. The recipe is attributed to the court of Louis XIV who raised French cuisine to a very high level with the aid of François Pierre de la Varenne, his famous chef. De la Varenne's cookbook altered cookery standards in France and throughout Europe.

My only addition to this historic recipe is the small amount of mace which an expert Creole cook told me always enhances the flavor of any seafood. This recipe is a quickie; in less than 30 minutes you are ready to bring to the table a culinary masterpiece actually created for a king and truly fit for one.

4 large flounder fillets, fresh or frozen
½ teaspoon salt
¼ teaspoon ground mace
2 tablespoons butter (not margarine)
½ cup dry white wine
¼ cup finely chopped boiled or canned shrimp

If you use fresh fish, remove all skin from fillets and wash thoroughly; dry on paper towels. Thaw frozen fillets completely and dry. Combine salt and mace and sprinkle both sides of fillets. Place in a greased baking dish and dot with butter. Broil in a preheated 550° oven for 8 to 10 minutes or until crisp on top. Remove from stove and pour on wine and sprinkle with chopped shrimp. Lower oven heat to 350° and bake for 10 minutes or until fillets are tender; a fork tine should go in easily.

My Creole oyster soup makes a splendid first course for the flounder. These two delicacies will give you an epicurean meal when served with a tossed green salad and hot French bread. Yield: 4 servings.

SALMON OR TUNA SOUFFLÉ

Delicately seasoned and easy to make.

1 slice fresh white bread
1 pound can inexpensive salmon or tuna packed in water, drained
¼ cup butter or margarine
¼ cup all-purpose flour
1 cup milk, warmed
1 teaspoon Mei-yen powder
1 teaspoon finely chopped parsley, dried or fresh
¼ teaspoon salt
⅛ teaspoon white pepper
1 teaspoon dried green onion
2 large egg yolks, well beaten
½ teaspoon baking powder
2 large egg whites, well beaten
½ cup finely shredded mild cheddar cheese (optional)
3 crisp crackers, finely crumbled

Moisten bread with cold water in a colander, and press out gently. In a large bowl crumble up bread and salmon (bones and all). In a skillet melt butter over low heat, blend in flour with wire whisk, and slowly add warmed milk, stirring constantly. Add Mei-yen powder, parsley, salt, white pepper, and dried green onion; cook until sauce is smooth and boiling. Remove from heat and beat in egg yolks. Taste to see if seasoning is correct. In a large mixing bowl add baking powder to salmon-bread mixture along with hot sauce. Blend on medium speed of electric mixer. Fold in beaten egg whites and grated cheese. Pour into a buttered, 1½-quart casserole. Sprinkle top with cracker crumbs. Bake in a preheated 375° oven for 25 to 30 minutes. Yield: 4 to 6 servings.

BAKED FLOUNDER FILLETS

Crunchy and tasty, flounder fillets rolled in wheat germ and baked.

  1 pound flounder fillets, fresh or frozen
  2 tablespoons strained lemon juice
  ½ teaspoon salt
  ¼ teaspoon paprika
  ⅛ teaspoon ground mace
  ¼ teaspoon lemon-pepper marinade
  1½ tablespoons mayonnaise
  7 tablespoons wheat germ

Thaw frozen flounder fillets completely and dry on paper towels. Sprinkle strained lemon juice over dry fillets. Blend salt, paprika, mace, and lemon-pepper marinade in a saucer and sprinkle over both sides of fillets. Spread each side lightly with mayonnaise. Sprinkle wheat germ on a large plate and roll each fillet in it. Place fillets on a greased cookie sheet and bake in a preheated 375° oven for 20 to 25 minutes. These will puff up and turn a beautiful golden brown. Serve hot with tartar sauce or highly seasoned mayonnaise. Yield: 4 servings.

FISH FILLETS IN LOW-CALORY SAUCE

This sauce enhances the true flavor of fish, asparagus, or baked potatoes, and is easily prepared.

  2 beef bouillon cubes
  2 cups boiling water
  ¼ cup fresh lemon juice
  1 teaspoon dried green onion, divided
  ¼ teaspoon lemon-pepper marinade
  ½ teaspoon salt
  ⅛ teaspoon ground mace
  ¼ teaspoon paprika
  1 to 1½ pounds (3 medium-size) fish fillets: trout, red snapper, flounder
  1 tablespoon margarine (optional)

Dissolve beef bouillon cubes in boiling water and add lemon juice. Sprinkle half of the dried green onion in an oblong baking dish. In a separate saucer blend lemon-pepper marinade, salt, mace, and paprika. Score both sides of fish fillet with a knife. Sprinkle both sides with seasonings and place fillets in baking dish. Pour bouillon mixture over fish, reserving some for basting. Sprinkle remaining green onions over top of fillets and dot with margarine. Bake in a preheated 450° oven for 5 minutes and then baste; repeat this twice more. At the end of 20 minutes, your fish will be done. Test with fork to be sure it is tender. If not serving immediately, cover with foil and keep in warm oven. Yield: 3 to 4 servings.

Variations: To use the sauce for vegetables, blend all seasonings together and add to beef bouillon cubes dissolved in boiling water. Add lemon juice and margarine. Cook asparagus in this mixture in place of water until tender. Serve hot.

TROUT VÉRONIQUE

My version of the New Orleans' Ponchartrain Hotel's famous dish is a twin sister and equally as delicious. There are three steps, all very easy.

First make the never fail Hollandaise Sauce. It may be prepared a long time ahead. Set aside and chill. When needed, place sauce over hot water in a small saucepan to reheat. Stir constantly with a wire whisk until it is hot.

  4 trout fillets
  ½ teaspoon salt
  ¼ teaspoon freshly ground white pepper
  ¼ teaspoon ground mace
  ¼ teaspoon paprika
  2 cups white wine (preferably Pinot Chardonnay)
  2 small bunches halved white seedless grapes (about 16 to 20 grapes)

Ask your butcher to cut the fillets from 2 trout weighing between 1¼ to 1½ pounds each. Dry excessive moisture from fillets with paper towels. Sprinkle fillets lightly on both sides with salt, white pepper, mace, and paprika. Place in a 12- x 7- x 2-inch baking dish and cover with wine. Place pan over medium heat and bring to a slow boil. Poach for 7 minutes. Test with fork to see if trout is tender. The meat should be very white. Drain and place fish on an ovenproof plate. Boil wine down briskly until it measures about 4 kitchen tablespoons. Add warmed Hollandaise sauce and stir rapidly. Place sliced grape halves on trout, cover with sauce, and place about 2 inches below broiler until it attains a golden brown glaze. Yield: 4 servings.

Hollandaise Sauce:

½ cup butter or margarine, divided
2 egg yolks, slightly beaten
1 tablespoon strained lemon juice, warmed
⅛ teaspoon salt
⅛ teaspoon cayenne pepper
⅛ teaspoon dry mustard

Put ¼ cup butter into a small saucepan with slightly beaten egg yolks. Hold the saucepan over hot water; do not allow water to boil. Stir constantly with wire whisk until butter melts. Add remaining butter and warmed lemon juice. Add salt, cayenne pepper, and dry mustard; stir until mixture thickens. Serve at once or remove from heat until needed. Should the sauce separate, beat in 1 tablespoon cream or undiluted canned milk. If this reoccurs, add cream and heat again. A double boiler may be used, but hold the top pan over the steam never permit it to touch the boiling water.

TRUITE DU LAC OLIVA

My version of LeRuth's superb trout is very easily prepared and the result satisfying and delicious.

1¼ teaspoons salt
¼ teaspoon freshly ground white pepper
⅛ teaspoon ground mace
6 (8-ounce) fillets of trout (king mackerel may be used)
3 egg whites, well beaten
½ cup all-purpose flour
¾ cup buttery vegetable oil
1 cup butter
½ cup lemon juice, strained
1 (7½-ounce) can Alaskan or Japanese crabmeat or 1 cup backfin lump fresh crabmeat
1 cup cooked and deveined shrimp
1 (14-ounce) can artichoke hearts, small size or cut the large in two
Parsley sprigs
Lemon slices

Blend salt, white pepper, and mace in a saucer and sprinkle on both sides of fillets. Dip fillets in beaten egg whites and coat well with flour. I spread the flour evenly on a large piece of waxed paper and hold each fillet with tongs. Heat oil in a large iron skillet over a medium heat and sauté fillets about 7 minutes or until golden on both sides. Set aside on an oblong casserole or platter and keep warm in oven until ready to serve.

Remove any excess oil from skillet and brown butter over medium heat. It should be the color of chestnuts. Remove skillet from heat and slowly add lemon juice using a wire whisk for stirring. Add crabmeat, cooked shrimp, and artichoke hearts; reheat. Place fillets on very hot serving plates and spoon sauce over them. Garnish with sprigs of parsley and lemon slices. Do not hold the fillets over 30 minutes in a warm oven for the heat tends to make the crust tough. Serve with a tossed green salad and hot French bread. Yield: 6 servings.

NEW ENGLAND CLAM-STUFFED EGGPLANT

The clam stuffing gives eggplant a piquant flavor and gives you an economical meal in itself; serve with a tossed green salad or a combination of avocado and grapefruit with French dressing and hot French bread.

  1 large eggplant (2½ cups cooked)
½ cup water
  1 teaspoon salt
  2 tablespoons minced parsley
  1 leaf fresh basil, minced or ¼ teaspoon dried basil
¼ teaspoon sugar
  1 cup finely chopped onion
  3 tablespoons butter or margarine (reserve ½ tablespoon for topping)
  5 dashes Tabasco
  2 teaspoons Worcestershire sauce
  2 thin slices white bread
¼ teaspoon ground mace
¼ teaspoon baking powder
  1 (8-ounce) can minced clams, drained and rinsed
  2 tablespoons seasoned cracker crumbs
  Butter

Wash eggplant, cut off top, slice in half lengthwise, and scoop out pulp, leaving shell intact. Place pulp in a saucepan with water, salt, minced parsley, basil, and sugar. Cover and steam over medium heat about 25 minutes or until tender.

In a large iron skillet sauté onion in butter over medium heat about 7 to 10 minutes or until clear. Mash cooked eggplant to remove any stringy pulp. Add mashed eggplant to onion in skillet. Add Tabasco, Worcestershire sauce, bread which has been soaked in cold water and squeezed out in a colander, mace, baking powder, and clams. Taste and adjust seasoning. Cook for 3 or 4 minutes to allow seasonings to permeate the mixture. Fill eggplant shells, sprinkle with cracker crumbs and dot with butter. Bake in a preheated 350° oven for 30 minutes or until golden brown. Yield: 4 servings.

PARGO BONNE FEMME
(Red Snapper Fillets)

  6 red snapper fillets
  1 teaspoon salt
¼ teaspoon freshly ground white pepper
¼ teaspoon ground mace
½ cup white wine
  3 tablespoons butter
  4 tablespoons all-purpose flour
1¼ cups reserved fish liquor
1¼ cups milk, warmed
  1 (4-ounce) can sliced mushrooms, drained

Dry fillets on a paper towel and sprinkle with salt, white pepper, and mace. Roll fillets, secure with wooden cocktail sticks, and place in an oblong baking dish. Cover with white wine and bake in a preheated 350° oven for 15 minutes. Pour off fish liquor and reserve 1¼ cups. Cover fish with foil to keep warm.

In a heavy skillet cook butter and flour slowly together about 2 minutes until they foam and froth. Remove from heat and beat in hot fish liquor, then the milk; bring to a boil slowly and boil for 1 minute. The sauce should be thickened and smooth; continue cooking slowly if it is not. Add sliced mushrooms and adjust seasonings if necessary. Cover fillets with sauce and serve with rice or potatoes. Yield: 6 servings.

Pies and Pastry

larger portion as thinly as possible for the bottom crust. Roll the dough in one direction only. Cut it 1 inch larger than the 9-inch piepan. To lift pastry from the board, fold it in half, lay the fold across the center of the pan, then unfold pastry. Press down edges with a fork and prick pastry with a fork in several places.

Roll out smaller portion and cut into narrow strips about ½ inch wide.

Fill piepan with cooked Filling.

Don't use this crust

DAISY WALKER'S APPLE PIE *recipe wrong ratio of shortening!*

The best apple pie you will ever eat and made with canned apples. The pastry defies description.

Pastry:

1½ cups all-purpose flour, measured after
    sifting
 ¼ teaspoon salt
  1 cup vegetable shortening, divided
  5 teaspoons ice water

Sift flour and salt into a large bowl. Divide the shortening into two parts. Cut ½ cup shortening into flour mixture with a pastry blender or two knives until mixture resembles coarse meal. Cut in the remaining ½ cup shortening until mixture is the size of large peas. Sprinkle ice water over mixture and blend in lightly. Remove dough from bowl and work with hands. When the dough holds together so that it may be gathered up in a ball, chill it for 30 minutes. If possible, chill overnight.

Divide dough into two parts, one slightly larger than the other. Reserve smaller part for top strips. On a lightly floured surface roll out

Filling:

1 (16-ounce) can Comstock sliced apples
1 cup sugar
1 teaspoon ground cinnamon
2 tablespoons lemon juice
4 tablespoons butter, divided

Place apples, sugar, cinnamon, lemon juice, and 3 tablespoons butter in a saucepan, and cook over high heat until mixture begins to simmer. Turn down heat. Cook mixture until nearly all liquid is absorbed. Spoon into pie crust; dot with remaining butter. Place narrow pastry strips in lattice fashion across top. Bake on center rack in a preheated 375° oven for 20 to 25 minutes or until bottom and top crusts brown. Serve hot with a sharp cheese or a dollop of vanilla ice cream. Yield: 1 (9-inch) pie—6 servings.

Note: Use the same pastry recipe for banana cream pie by reducing the shortening to ¾ cup.

APPLE DUMPLINGS

An apple lover's delight in two easy steps.

Step 1—Pastry:

 2 cups all-purpose flour, measured after
     sifting
 3 teaspoons baking powder
½ teaspoon salt
 4 tablespoons vegetable shortening
½ cup milk

Sift dry ingredients into a large bowl. Add shortening and cut into dry ingredients with a pastry blender or two knives until mixture is the consistency of coarse meal. Make a hole in center of mixture and pour milk slowly into it. Stir well until dough is free from sides; this takes only a minute. Knead gently on a lightly floured board and roll out to ⅛-inch thickness. Cut into 4- x 7-inch pieces.

Step 2—Apple Filling:

 6 medium-size to large apples, tart juicy
     variety: Winesap, York, Rome Beauty, or
     Jonathan
 2 cups sugar, divided
 1 teaspoon ground cinnamon
 5 tablespoons butter
 6 tablespoons lemon juice, divided
½ cup firmly packed dark brown sugar
 1 cup water

Peel and core apples. Combine ½ cup sugar and cinnamon. Fill center of each apple with 1 tablespoon cinnamon sugar and 1 teaspoon butter. Fold pieces of dough up around apples and pour ½ tablespoon lemon juice over each one. In a large skillet combine remaining 1½ cups white sugar and brown sugar, remaining butter, and water, and cook into a syrup over medium heat.

Place apples in a skillet or a 9- x 5- x 3-inch baking dish, and bake in a preheated 350° oven for 45 minutes to 1 hour or until crust is a light golden brown. About 10 minutes before baking time is up, dip a small amount of syrup and dribble over pastry. Pour remaining syrup over apples and serve at once while still hot. To prepare in the morning for dinner that evening, reheat oven to 375° and cook apples 10 minutes. Coffee makes an ideal accompaniment. Yield: 6 servings.

Note: For a festive occasion, add 1 teaspoon either mincemeat or seedless raisins to center of apples and serve with lightly sweetened whipped cream.

APPLES IN A BASKET

Festive apples and inexpensive. For Christmas add several drops of food coloring to apples and place candied green cherries in center of each. Mincemeat or golden raisins may also be used in center of apples for a party.

 6 medium-size baking apples (Rome Beauty,
     Winesap, York, Jonathan)
 1 cup sugar
½ cup water
 1 teaspoon ground cinnamon
 2 teaspoons powdered fruit pectin
 2 teaspoons strained lemon juice
 6 teaspoons butter
 1 (12-ounce) tube refrigerated caramel
     Danish rolls with nuts
   Sweetened whipped cream or vanilla ice
     cream

Core and peel apples. Use an 11-inch iron or similar skillet. Combine sugar, water, cinnamon, pectin, and lemon juice and cook over medium heat, stirring until dissolved. When syrup comes to a boil, add apples placing 1 teaspoon butter in center of each one. Baste constantly and cook about 25 minutes or until tender. A straw should pierce the apples with ease. Remove apples and place in a 13- x 9- x 2-inch baking pan to cool. Cook syrup until thickened and pour over apples.

To make the basket, unwind caramel rolls into strips of dough. Wrap each apple from bottom up using one or more strips. Crumble nut topping provided in package over each apple before using a strip of dough for basket handle. Bake in a preheated 400° oven for 12 to 14 minutes. *Watch carefully.* Remove when pastry is golden, even though time may not be up. Serve hot or cold with a dollop of sweetened whipped cream or vanilla ice cream. Yield: 6 servings.

GREEN APPLE PIE

 8 medium-size or 10 small apples
½ cup sugar
½ cup firmly packed dark brown sugar
½ teaspoon ground cinnamon
    Pinch ground nutmeg
 1 tablespoon lemon juice
 1 tablespoon cornstarch
¼ cup water
 1 (9-inch) pie shell
 2 tablespoons butter
 1 cup shredded cheddar cheese (optional)

Peel, core, and cut apples into very thin slices. Place slices in a saucepan with white and brown sugars, cinnamon, nutmeg, lemon juice, and cornstarch. Simmer mixture gently for 10 to 15 minutes. Add water if apples are very dry.

Line a 9-inch piepan with your favorite pastry recipe or use a frozen pastry shell. Place apple mixture in pricked crust and dot with butter. Cover with thin strips of pastry in lattice design or with a pricked upper crust. Bake in a preheated 400° oven for 10 minutes; reduce heat to 350° and bake for 25 to 30 minutes or until pastry is golden. If desired, you may bake pie without upper crust at 400° for 20 minutes and then sprinkle 1 cup shredded cheddar cheese over top and melt under broiler. Yield: 1 (9-inch) pie—6 servings.

REAL BUTTERSCOTCH PIE

A rare treat from Barbados.

 3 tablespoons butter, divided
 4 tablespoons all-purpose flour
 2 cups milk
 1 cup sugar
 2 egg yolks, well beaten
 1 teaspoon vanilla extract
 1 (9-inch) pie shell, baked
½ pint whipping cream
 2 tablespoons powdered sugar
 2 teaspoons brandy

Melt 1 tablespoon butter in a heavy saucepan or skillet over medium heat; stir in flour. When butter is absorbed, thin with milk and continue cooking until sauce is smooth and comes to a boil, stirring constantly. In another heavy skillet melt remaining 2 tablespoons butter; add sugar, stirring constantly until sugar turns a light brown and becomes syrupy. Stir into hot sauce over low heat. The caramel will harden but continue stirring, and it will dissolve shortly and give you a rich butterscotch mixture.

Remove from heat and stir in well-beaten egg yolks and vanilla. Put through a strainer in case there should be any tiny lumps. Allow mixture to cool, and pour into a baked 9-inch pie shell. Whip cream in a narrow bowl. When it stands in peaks, add powdered sugar and then brandy. Cover pie with whipped cream and chill until ready to serve. This may be made a day in advance. Serve with black coffee and salted nuts. Yield: 1 (9-inch) pie—6 to 7 servings.

BANANA CREAM PIE

A lovely creation with a true banana flavor.

Single 9-Inch Pie Crust:

1⅓ cups all-purpose flour
½ teaspoon salt
½ cup vegetable shortening
3 tablespoons ice water

Sift flour before measuring; spoon lightly into cup and level without shaking and packing down. In a mixing bowl combine flour and salt, and cut in shortening with a pastry blender or two knives until mixture resembles coarse meal. Sprinkle with water, 1 tablespoon at a time, then toss with a fork and work dough into a firm ball with your hand. Press dough into a flat circle with smooth edges. On a lightly floured surface, roll dough into a circle about 1½ inches larger than an inverted pie plate. Ease dough into plate without stretching. Trim ½ inch beyond edge of plate and fold under to make a double thickness of dough around rim; flute with fingers or fork. Prick bottom and sides thoroughly with fork. Bake in a preheated 425° oven for 10 to 15 minutes until golden brown. Cool on wire rack.

Custard Filling:

1 cup sugar
2 tablespoons all-purpose flour
⅛ teaspoon salt
4 eggs, slightly beaten
2 cups milk
3 large ripe bananas, peeled
2 teaspoons vanilla extract, divided
2 tablespoons powdered sugar
½ pint whipping cream, whipped

In a mixing bowl blend sugar, flour, and salt; add slightly beaten eggs. In top of a double boiler over rapidly boiling water, heat milk until hot to the touch; add egg mixture and stir constantly until it begins to thicken. The custard should coat a silver or metal spoon. Strain through a sieve if you have any lumps. Cool.

Scrape white threads from bananas and slice fruit about ½ inch thick into custard; add 1 teaspoon vanilla. Pour cooled custard into cooled pie crust. Add powdered sugar to whipped cream and add remaining 1 teaspoon vanilla. Using a spatula, cover top of custard filling with whipped cream. Serve at once or refrigerate and serve chilled. This may be made the day before using. Yield: 1 (9-inch) pie—7 servings.

MY BLACK BOTTOM PIE

A luscious pie that takes its name from the rich bottom lands that dot the Mississippi Delta. This recipe is easy to make if you follow the directions carefully.

Crust:

14 ginger snaps
¼ cup softened butter or margarine

Roll ginger snaps into fine crumbs; mix well with softened butter. Line an ungreased 9-inch piepan, pressing crumbs against the bottom and sides. Bake in a preheated 300° oven for 10 minutes. Remove and cool.

Plain Custard Filling:

1¾ cups milk
4 egg yolks, well beaten
1 tablespoon plus 1 teaspoon cornstarch
⅛ teaspoon salt
½ cup sugar
1 envelope (1 tablespoon) unflavored gelatin
¼ cup cold water

Scald milk; then pour slowly into beaten egg yolks in top of a double boiler over rapidly boiling water. Blend cornstarch, salt, and sugar and stir into egg mixture, stirring constantly. Cook about 20 minutes or until mixture coats spoon. Soak gelatin in cold water and dissolve in a metal cup over hot water and add to 1 cup hot custard; set aside to cool.

Chocolate Custard Filling:

1 cup hot custard (without gelatin)
2 (1-ounce) squares unsweetened chocolate, melted
1 teaspoon vanilla extract

Blend melted chocolate into hot custard, beating well. As custard cools add vanilla. Pour into pie crust and chill.

Rum Filling:

4 egg whites, room temperature
⅛ teaspoon cream of tartar
½ cup sugar
2 tablespoons rum or rum flavoring
1 cup reserved cooled custard-gelatin
1 cup whipping cream
2 tablespoons sugar
4 drops almond extract
½ square semisweet chocolate, shaved

Beat egg whites until foamy, sprinkle in cream of tartar, and beat until stiff but not dry using high speed of electric mixer. Gradually add ½ cup sugar. Add rum. Fold egg white mixture into 1 cup reserved, cooled custard-gelatin mixture until well blended. Do not beat; handle gently. Pour over chocolate custard filling and chill until set. Whip cream and add 2 tablespoons sugar and almond extract. Spread over chocolate custard layer in pie crust and sprinkle with shaved chocolate. Serve at once. Yield: 1 (9-inch) pie—6 servings.

LIME PIE

A spring and summer favorite to be made when the limes are fresh and plentiful.

3 egg yolks
1 (14-ounce) can sweetened condensed milk
⅔ cup fresh lime juice (about 6 limes)
1 teaspoon grated lime peel
½ teaspoon vanilla extract
Several drops green food coloring
1 (9-inch) baked pastry shell or graham cracker crust, chilled
Meringue

Beat egg yolks until light and fluffy; add remaining ingredients and pour into crust. Top with Meringue. Bake in a preheated 300° oven for 15 to 20 minutes. Cool on a wire rack and refrigerate until served. Yield: 1 (9-inch) pie—7 to 8 servings.

Meringue:

3 egg whites
⅛ teaspoon salt
¼ teaspoon cream of tartar
6 tablespoons sugar
1 teaspoon vanilla extract

In a small mixing bowl beat egg whites, salt, and cream of tartar at high speed of electric beater until soft peaks form. Add sugar gradually; then add vanilla, beating constantly until stiff peaks form. Spread over pie crust; be sure egg whites go all the way to edge.

201

FRENCH SILK CHOCOLATE PIE

Smooth and lovely! No cooking required except melting the chocolate and baking the pie shell.

½ cup butter, softened
¾ cup sugar
1 (1-ounce) square unsweetened chocolate, melted
2 large eggs, room temperature
1 teaspoon vanilla extract
1 (9-inch) pie shell, baked
½ pint whipping cream
1 tablespoon powdered sugar
¼ teaspoon almond extract

Cream butter until very light and fluffy using a wooden spoon or electric mixer on medium speed. Add sugar gradually. Place chocolate in a metal cup that has been greased with vegetable oil. Place cup in a pan of very hot water to melt chocolate. Beat melted chocolate into creamed butter mixture. Add 1 egg and beat 3 minutes with electric mixer or 5 minutes by hand. Add remaining egg and repeat beating process. Add vanilla. Place bowl in refrigerator until mixture sets. Stir again and spoon into baked pie shell, chill for several hours or overnight. Whip cream sweetened with powdered sugar; add almond flavoring and serve on top of pie. Yield: 1 (9-inch) pie—7 to 8 servings.

BLACK BOTTOM PIE

This recipe comes from Weidman's Restaurant in Meridian, Mississippi, and has been a favorite of its clientele for almost a hundred years.

Crust:

14 gingersnaps
5 tablespoons melted butter

Roll gingersnaps into fine crumbs. Add melted butter to crumbs and pat evenly into an ungreased 9-inch piepan. Bake in a preheated 300° oven for 10 minutes. Cool.

Plain Custard Filling:

4 egg yolks, well beaten
2 cups scalded milk
½ cup sugar
1¼ tablespoons cornstarch

Add eggs slowly to hot milk. Combine sugar and cornstarch; blend into milk and egg mixture. Cook in top of a double boiler for 20 minutes, stirring constantly until mixture coats spoon. Remove from heat and reserve 1 cup hot custard.

Chocolate Custard Filling:

1½ (1-ounce) squares unsweetened chocolate, melted over hot water
1 teaspoon vanilla extract

Add melted chocolate to 1 cup reserved custard and beat well. When custard cools, add vanilla and pour into pie crust; chill.

Bourbon Filling:

1 envelope (1 tablespoon) unflavored gelatin
4 tablespoons cold water
4 egg whites, room temperature
¼ teaspoon cream of tartar
½ cup sugar
2 tablespoons bourbon
1 cup whipping cream, whipped
½ square German's sweet chocolate, shaved

Thoroughly blend gelatin and cold water; add to remaining 1 cup hot custard. Let cool but do not allow to thicken. Beat egg whites until frothy and add cream of tartar. Gradually add sugar until mixture stands in peaks, using a wire whisk or electric beater on high speed.

Fold into plain custard-gelatin mixture. Add bourbon. When chocolate custard sets and becomes firm, add bourbon filling to pie. Chill again until set. Cover with whipped cream and shaved chocolate. Keep pie chilled. Yield: 1 (9-inch) pie—6 servings.

MY BEST CHOCOLATE PIE WITH CRUST

You will never eat a more delicious pie. It is easy to make in the old-time way, the filling cooked in an unbaked shell.

Pastry:

1½ cups all-purpose flour, measured after
    sifting
 1 teaspoon baking powder
 1 teaspoon salt
½ cup plus 1 level tablespoon vegetable
    shortening
½ cup ice water, divided
¼ cup all-purpose flour

Combine 1½ cups flour, baking powder, salt, and shortening in a large mixing bowl. Use a spoon, two knives, or a pastry blender to cut shortening thoroughly into dry ingredients until the mixture resembles coarse meal. Use hands to finish task. Sprinkle ¼ cup ice water over the mixture and blend in lightly. If the dough will hold together so that it may be gathered up in a ball, stop handling. If not, use remaining ¼ cup water and work with hands, keeping moisture out and air in.

Dust pastry board with ¼ cup flour. Roll out dough 1 inch larger than piepan, always rolling in the same direction. To lift the pastry from the board, fold it in half, lay the fold across the center of the pan, and unfold it. You may roll it around the rolling pin and unroll it onto the pan. Use fork tines to press pastry around sides of the pan. Prick with fork in several places. Chill for at least 30 minutes; if possible, chill for 12 hours.

Chocolate Filling:

1½ cups sugar, measured after sifting
 3 level tablespoons powdered cocoa
 2 tablespoons all-purpose flour
 3 large eggs, separated
 1 whole egg
1½ cups half-and-half or 1 (13-ounce) can
    evaporated milk
 1 teaspoon vanilla extract
 1 (9-inch) unbaked pie shell
 6 tablespoons sugar
 ½ teaspoon vanilla extract

Blend 1½ cups sugar, cocoa, and flour together in a large bowl until all lumps are out. Beat egg yolks and whole egg until light and lemon-colored; add a small amount of the half-and-half to eggs. Add eggs and remaining cream to sugar mixture; mix well. Add 1 teaspoon vanilla. Pour into an unbaked pie shell and cook in a preheated 425° oven for 10 minutes. Lower heat to 375° and bake for 25 to 30 minutes longer or until a straw or a silver knife blade inserted in the center comes out clean.

Beat egg whites until they stand in soft peaks. Gradually add 6 tablespoons sugar and continue beating until whites are stiff. Add ½ teaspoon vanilla. Spoon meringue onto top of filling; pile lightly with a spatula. Be sure egg whites cover the filling completely. Lower heat to 325° and cook meringue about 10 minutes or until golden brown. Cool on a wire rack and serve hot or cold. This pie does not slice firmly, but the taste makes up for it. Yield: 1 (9-inch) pie—8 servings.

CHOCOLATE ANGEL PIE

For best results, prepare at least 12 hours or one day in advance.

Meringue:

1 cup sifted sugar
3 large egg whites, room
    temperature
⅛ teaspoon salt
½ teaspoon baking powder
1 teaspoon water
1 teaspoon vanilla extract
1 teaspoon vinegar

Sift sugar into large plate. Combine remaining ingredients in a glass and then place in a deep 6-inch bowl. Beat mixture on high speed of electric mixer until egg whites are stiff. Add 1 tablespoon sugar at a time. Beat 1 or 2 minutes on high speed after all sugar has been added. Cut down from sides of bowl with spatula. Line the bottom of a 10-inch pie plate with brown or waxed paper; lightly butter. Spoon meringue into pie plate and gently shape as you would a tart. Bake in a preheated 250° oven for 60 minutes. Test with straw to see if sticky; if so, cut off heat and allow to cool in oven. If straw is clean, remove and cool on a wire rack. Fill with Chocolate Filling.

Chocolate Filling:

1 cup whipped cream
3 teaspoons Swel or powdered cocoa
2 tablespoons sugar
½ teaspoon vanilla extract
1 teaspoon brandy
1 ounce German's sweet chocolate, finely
    grated

Whip cream and add Swel, sugar, vanilla, and brandy. Fill meringue shell with filling. Sprinkle grated chocolate over pie just before serving. Yield: 1 (10-inch) pie—8 servings.

MRS. PAINE LENOIR'S CHOCOLATE FUDGE PIE

½ cup margarine
2 (1-ounce) squares unsweetened chocolate
4 large eggs, well beaten
2 cups sugar
1 cup broken pecans
⅛ teaspoon salt
2 tablespoons powdered cocoa
1 teaspoon strained lemon juice
2 (9-inch) unbaked pie shells

Melt margarine and chocolate in top of a double boiler over hot, not boiling, water. Beat eggs until light; add sugar. Blend in melted margarine and chocolate; add pecans, salt, cocoa, and lemon juice. Divide batter between pie shells and bake in a preheated 375° oven for 10 minutes. Lower heat to 350° and bake for 20 minutes longer. Yield: 2 (9-inch) pies—12 to 14 servings.

CHOCOLATE FUDGE PIE

2 (1-ounce) squares semisweet chocolate
½ cup butter or ¼ cup butter and ¼ cup
    margarine
2 eggs, well beaten
1 cup sugar
¼ cup all-purpose flour
⅛ teaspoon salt
1 teaspoon vanilla extract
¾ cup broken nuts
    Whipped cream or ice cream (optional)

Melt chocolate and butter in top of a double boiler over hot, not boiling, water. Add well-beaten eggs to chocolate mixture. Stir in sugar, flour, salt, vanilla, and nuts. Pour mixture into a buttered 9-inch pie plate and bake in a preheated 325° oven for 30 minutes. Test with straw in center; there may be a slight trace of chocolate but it should not be sticky. For a super dessert serve with whipped cream or ice cream. Yield: 1 (9-inch) pie—6 to 8 servings.

CHOCOLATE GIRDLE-BUSTER PIE

Guaranteed to please!

1 quart coffee ice cream
1 (9-inch) baked graham cracker crust
1 (14-ounce) can sweetened condensed milk
2 (1-ounce) squares unsweetened chocolate
¼ cup sugar
½ cup water
½ teaspoon vanilla extract
⅓ can chopped nuts (optional)

Allow ice cream to soften enough to pack in a chilled crust. Spoon ice cream into crust and refreeze until hard. In top of a double boiler over rapidly boiling water, heat condensed milk, chocolate, sugar, and water and stir until chocolate melts and mixture thickens. Add vanilla and allow to cool slightly. Spread on top of frozen ice cream and refreeze. Remove from freezer about 30 minutes before serving; cut into wedges. For a complete bust, sprinkle chopped nuts on top. Yield: 1 (9-inch) pie—6 to 8 servings.

CREAM PUFFS AND ÉCLAIRS

Delectable!

1 cup water
½ cup butter
¼ teaspoon salt
1 cup all-purpose flour, measured after sifting
3 large or 4 small eggs
  Custard Filling

Combine water, butter, and salt in a saucepan and heat gradually over low heat. As soon as butter melts, raise heat and bring quickly to a boil; add flour all at once. Stir briskly and constantly until batter forms a smooth ball and leaves sides of saucepan clean. Remove at once and stir until smooth and velvety (stirring makes puffs lighter). Cool until lukewarm. Add eggs, one at a time, beating until well blended after each addition. Drop spoonfuls of batter in 2-inch rounds on a greased pan or cookie sheet. Allow 2 inches between puffs. Shape batter with a spoon for éclairs 5 inches long; heap batter high in center. Bake in a preheated 400° oven for 30 minutes. Reduce heat to 350° and bake 5 minutes longer. Test puffs by removing one from oven; if it does not fall, it is done. Slit hot puffs with a sharp knife to allow steam to escape. Cool and fill with custard, sweetened whipped cream, chocolate, or fruit filling. Yield: 12 large cream puffs or éclairs or 70 (1-inch) puffs.

Custard Filling:

2 cups milk
2 eggs
¾ cup sugar
¼ cup all-purpose flour
1 tablespoon butter
¼ teaspoon salt
1 teaspoon vanilla extract
1 cup whipping cream (optional)

Scald milk in top of a double boiler. Beat eggs in a bowl and add sugar, flour, butter, and salt and continue beating until blended. Gradually add to scalded milk, stir, and cook until custard coats the spoon and is thickened. Cool and add vanilla. For a superb filling fold in whipped cream when custard is cold. Fill cream puffs or éclairs.

Variation: For chocolate éclairs fill with Chocolate Fluff (see Dazzling Desserts), and top with Quickie Fudge Icing (see Cakes and Icings).

CHERRY SQUARES

  1 cup butter
1½ cups sugar
  4 eggs, well beaten
  2 cups sifted all-purpose flour
  1 teaspoon vanilla extract
  1 teaspoon lemon or orange extract
  1 (20-ounce) can cherry pie filling
    Powdered sugar

In a large mixing bowl cream butter and sugar until light and fluffy. Add eggs, flour, and flavorings; blend well. Spread batter into a greased 13- x 9- x 2-inch pan. Cut surface of batter into squares. Spoon several cherries and some filling onto center of each square. During baking, batter puffs up around pie filling. Bake in a preheated 350° oven for 45 to 50 minutes or until golden brown. Cut again into squares. Sprinkle top with powered sugar. Cool, and remove squares from pan. Yield: 20 to 24 squares.

NANCY GRAVES' CREAM CHEESE TARTS

A wonderful companion for luscious strawberries, cherries, or blueberries, or bing cherries that have been soaked in brandy or bourbon.

  2 (8-ounce) packages cream cheese, softened
¾ cup sugar
  3 eggs, separated
⅓ stick butter, melted
  1 cup finely rolled graham crackers
    Filling

In a large bowl beat softened cream cheese and sugar on medium speed of electric mixer. Add 3 egg yolks and blend well. In a small narrow bowl beat egg whites stiff but not dry. Fold egg whites into creamed mixture. Grease miniature muffin pans with melted butter. (⅓ stick butter will do all 48 muffin cups.)

Sprinkle generously or dust all pans with graham cracker crumbs. Turn upside down for a moment to remove excess crumbs. Put about 1 teaspoon creamed cheese mixture in each tin. Bake in a preheated 325° oven for 15 minutes. Cool pans on wire rack until mixture sinks in middle. Fill hollows with filling.

Filling:

1 pint commercial sour cream
5 tablespoons sugar
2 teaspoons vanilla extract

Blend all ingredients and fill each hollow. Bake filled tarts in a preheated 350° oven for 5 minutes; cool slightly. Remove from muffin pans carefully and cool on wire racks. These freeze well in plastic egg cartons lined with plastic wrap, 24 to a carton. Yield: 48 tarts.

FRENCH COCONUT PIE

Smooth and rich.

  1 egg white, lightly beaten
  1 (9-inch) unbaked pie shell
1½ cups sugar
  ½ cup butter, melted
  3 large eggs, slightly beaten
    Pinch salt
  1 tablespoon champagne vinegar
  1 teaspoon vanilla extract
  1 teaspoon coconut extract
  1 cup grated fresh or frozen coconut

Brush a little egg white on unbaked pie shell and bake in a preheated 400° oven for 1 minute. Remove pie shell and lower heat to 300°. Mix sugar and melted butter; add slightly beaten eggs. Add remaining ingredients and pour into pie shell. Bake at 300° for 55 minutes to 1 hour or until straw or silver knife inserted in center comes out clean. Yield: 1 (9-inch) pie—6 to 8 servings.

APRICOT ICEBOX PIE

Tart and creamy!

1 (29-ounce) can peeled whole apricots
1 (14-ounce) can sweetened condensed milk
  Juice from 3 large lemons (about 6
    tablespoons)
1 (9-inch) pie shell or enough vanilla wafers
    to line a 9-inch pie plate

Drain apricots and puree either by pressing through a sieve or in a blender. Add condensed milk and beat well. Add lemon juice. Pour into your own cooked pie shell or vanilla wafers arranged on bottom and sides of a 9-inch pie plate. Chill at least 1 hour before serving. Yield: 1 (9-inch) pie—6 to 7 servings.

OLD-FASHIONED LEMON PIE

1⅓ cups water
  1 cup sugar
  2 tablespoons all-purpose flour
  ⅓ cup softened butter
  3 egg yolks
  1 tablespoon lemon rind
  ¼ cup strained lemon juice
  1 (9-inch) pie shell, baked
    Meringue

Put water on to boil. Mix sugar and flour in a saucepan and cream with softened butter. Add egg yolks and beat well. Gradually add boiling water and blend until smooth. Cook over low heat about 10 minutes or until mixture thickens, stirring constantly. Add lemon rind and juice just before removing from heat. Cool. Pour into baked pie shell and top with Meringue. Be sure filling is completely covered. Bake in a preheated 300° oven for 15 to 20 minutes or until lightly golden. Cool on a wire rack. Delicious warm or cold. Refrigerate only if you keep pie overnight. Yield: 1 (9-inch) pie—6 to 8 servings.

Meringue:

  3 large egg whites
  1 tablespoon water
¼ teaspoon cream of tartar
  6 tablespoons sugar
⅛ teaspoon salt
  1 teaspoon vanilla extract

Beat egg whites, water, and cream of tartar at high speed of electric mixer for 3 minutes until whites stand in soft peaks. Add sugar gradually, 1 tablespoon at a time. Add salt and vanilla and continue beating until egg whites are stiff. Pile lightly on top of filling.

FIDELIA CAMPBELL'S LEMON CHESS PIE

Piquant and delightful!

  2 cups sugar
  1 tablespoon all-purpose flour
¼ teaspoon salt
  1 tablespoon cornmeal
¼ cup strained lemon juice
    Grated rind of 2 lemons
¼ cup milk
¼ cup melted margarine
  4 large eggs, room temperature
  1 (9-inch) unbaked pie shell

In a large bowl mix dry ingredients. Add lemon juice and rind, milk, and melted margarine. Add eggs one at a time and beat well. Spoon into pie shell, and bake in a preheated 350° oven for 50 minutes. Serve hot or cold. Yield: 1 (9-inch) pie—6 to 7 servings.

PINK LEMONADE CIRCUS PIE

A colorful and delicious pink lemonade dessert. A real quickie, its flavor is unbelievable.

½ gallon premium vanilla ice cream
1 (6-ounce) can frozen pink lemonade
    concentrate, thawed
1 (9-inch) graham cracker crust, baked and
    chilled
2 tablespoons nonpareil decors

Blend ice cream in a large bowl until mushy, using medium speed of electric mixer. Add thawed lemonade concentrate and pour into chilled cracker crust. Sprinkle top of pie with nonpareil decors. This will keep for several weeks in the freezer when placed in a plastic bag after being frozen. Yield: 1 (9-inch) pie—6 to 8 servings.

KEY LIME PIE

A delightful taste treat!

Butter Crunch Crust:

½ cup butter, softened
¼ cup firmly packed brown sugar
1 cup sifted all-purpose flour
½ cup chopped pecans or walnuts

In a large bowl combine all ingredients and mix well with clean hands. Spread mixture in an oblong, 13- x 9- x 2-inch baking pan. Bake in a preheated 400° oven for 12 to 15 minutes or until golden. Remove from oven and stir at once with a spoon. Quickly press crumbs against bottom and sides of a 9-inch pan; cool. Reserve some crumbs to sprinkle on top of pie.

Filling:

1 envelope (1 tablespoon) unflavored gelatin
1 cup sugar, divided
¼ teaspoon salt
4 eggs, separated
½ cup key lime juice
¼ cup water
1 teaspoon grated lime rind
    Few drops green food coloring
1 cup whipping cream, whipped

Blend gelatin, ½ cup sugar, and salt in a saucepan. Beat 4 egg yolks, lime juice, and water; stir into gelatin mixture. Cook over medium heat, stirring constantly until mixture comes to a boil. Remove from heat, stir in grated rind and a few drops green food coloring. Chill, stirring occasionally until mixture mounds slightly when dropped from a spoon. Beat egg whites on high speed of electric mixer until they stand in soft peaks, gradually add ½ cup sugar and continue beating until whites stand in stiff peaks. Fold gelatin mixture into egg whites and then fold in whipped cream. Pile into shell and chill. Yield: 1 (9-inch) pie—7 to 8 servings.

COVENTRY GODCAKES WITH MINCEMEAT

These are baked and sold around Coventry in Warwickshire, England, to celebrate New Year's Day.

1 cup all-purpose flour
    Pinch salt
    Water
1 cup butter or margarine, softened
2 cups mincemeat
1 egg white
    Powdered sugar

Combine flour, salt, and enough water to make dough pliable, not sticky or dry. Place on a floured board or marble and knead lightly until smooth. Roll out into an oblong shape. Press out the butter until it is almost half the size of the pastry. Place butter on top of dough and fold dough in half. Press the edges tightly together; then roll out dough to the same thickness as before, and fold in thirds. Do this twice more, but the last time roll it to an ⅛-inch thickness. Cut out triangular shaped pieces of pastry. Place mincemeat in the center of each triangle, and place another piece of pastry on top, moistening to make them stick. Press pastry firmly together and slash one or two cuts on top; then bake in preheated 425° oven about 15 minutes on greased cookie sheet. When done, remove and glaze the top with the stiffly beaten egg white and dust with powdered sugar. Return to oven and bake 3 minutes longer. Cool on a rack. Yield: 6 servings.

QUICKIE MINCEMEAT

   3 (9-ounce) packages condensed mincemeat
4½ cups warm water
   1 medium-size apple, finely chopped
   2 tablespoons sugar
½ cup seedless raisins
   1 (16-ounce) jar commercial orange
      marmalade
   3 tablespoons brandy or 4 tablespoons
      sherry

Mix mincemeat according to package directions, adding warm water, chopped apple, sugar, and raisins. Cook until thickened, stirring constantly. Add marmalade and brandy and remove from stove. For a single pie use 2 cups filling in your own uncooked pastry and dot with butter before adding top crust. Keep the remainder in the refrigerator in a glass jar. Yield: 3 (10-inch) pies—22 to 24 servings.

Variation: If you prefer a nonalcoholic pie, substitute 3 tablespoons orange juice for the brandy or sherry.

GLADY HALES' CHESS PIE

One of the best!

½ cup butter
1 cup sugar
2 tablespoons yellow cornmeal
2 large eggs
1 teaspoon vanilla or lemon extract
1 (9-inch) unbaked pie shell

Cream butter, sugar, and cornmeal in a large bowl. Add eggs one at a time, beating well after each addition. Add vanilla. Spoon filling into pie shell and bake in a preheated 375° oven for 15 minutes. Lower heat to 350° and bake for 20 minutes longer or until crust is golden brown. Serve hot or cold. Yield: 1 (9-inch) pie—6 to 7 servings.

AUNT ELISE'S PECAN ICEBOX PIE

Deliciously different! Rich and yummy!

   3 large egg whites, room temperature
   1 cup sifted sugar
   1 teaspoon baking powder
½ cup chopped pecans or walnuts
24 round rich crackers, rolled into fine crumbs
   1 teaspoon vanilla extract
½ pint whipping cream, whipped
½ (4-ounce) can extra moist shredded
      coconut

Beat egg whites in a small narrow bowl at high speed of electric mixer until they stand in soft peaks. Gradually add sugar, 1 tablespoon at a time. Add baking powder and fold in nuts, fine cracker crumbs, and vanilla. Spoon mixture into a (9-inch) greased piepan and bake in a preheated 350° oven for 20 to 25 minutes. Cool on a wire rack. Top with whipped cream and sprinkle with coconut. Place in refrigerator for at least 2 hours before serving, or make one day in advance and chill. Serve with black coffee. Yield: 1 (9-inch) pie—7 to 8 servings.

SUGAR PLANTATION MOLASSES PIE

The distinctive flavor of this pie brings to mind the luscious sugar cane that grows along the Bayou Lafourche and runs through the heart of Georgia Plantation. You will never taste a better one.

2 cups Louisiana cane syrup
1 cup butter
½ cup whipped cream or undiluted evaporated
   milk
4 large eggs, room temperature
⅛ teaspoon salt
2 teaspoons vanilla extract
1 (10-inch) unbaked pie shell

Bring syrup to boil in a medium-size saucepan. Set aside to cool for 10 minutes, then add butter. When butter is completely melted and mixture is cool enough to feel barely warm when tested on inside of wrist, add cream and whip for several minutes. Add eggs, salt, and vanilla; beat well for 2 minutes. Pour mixture into pie shell and bake in a preheated 400° oven for 10 minutes. Lower heat to 275° and continue to bake for 50 minutes longer. Test with straw in center for doneness. Cool on wire rack. Serve warm or cold. The pie becomes much firmer and easier to cut when cold. Coffee and salted pecans make an ideal accompaniment. This is very rich. Yield: 1 (10-inch) pie—8 servings.

TARTE TATIN

In the nineteenth century a waitress tripped while serving a simple apple pie. Extraordinary? Yes, for her misfortune brought fame to the "Auberge des Soeurs Tatin" near the Pont Neuf. When the girl hastened back to the kitchen with the broken pieces of pie, her mistresses carefully examined what was left and noted how the caramel had hardened into a crust on top. The next day they prepared the pie in the same way and served it turned upside down to achieve this caramelized effect. The unusual flavor of the dish captured the fancy of their patrons, and this became a specialty of the house. Later other fine French chefs copied the idea with their own variations.

I would like for you to try my version of Tarte Tatin which I picked up in Paris many years ago and worked out to my satisfaction. Tarte Tatin requires a special French pastry that is a delight to eat. I find it a great time-saver to make this a day or even weeks ahead. The recipe makes enough for two tarts or pies and will keep frozen for a year. If making both the same day, prepare apples first and allow them to sit while preparing the pastry.

Apples:

6 medium-size to large apples, Golden
   Delicious, Rome Beauty, York Imperial,
   or Winesap
½ cup firmly packed dark brown sugar
¼ cup lemon juice
1 teaspoon lemon peel

Peel and slice apples lengthwise, ⅛ inch thick, and place in a large bowl. Sprinkle with sugar, lemon juice and peel. Cover and allow to sit while preparing pastry.

French Pastry:

6 tablespoons hard cold butter, sliced into
   small pieces
2 tablespoons vegetable shortening
1 tablespoon sugar
1 cup unsifted all-purpose flour
⅛ teaspoon salt
⅓ cup ice water

Place butter, shortening, sugar, flour, and salt into a small deep bowl. Blend for 1 minute with electric mixer on medium speed. Add ice water and beat 1 or 2 minutes or until mixture holds together in a mass. Form this into a ball and wrap in plastic. Chill in refrigerator for at least 2 hours. Remove and divide dough in half. Keep one half refrigerated or frozen. On a lightly floured board, roll remaining half into a top crust ⅛ inch thick and just larger than the baking utensil you plan to use. I place my tart in a 7- or 8½-inch round iron skillet or a shallow baking dish approximately the same size. You will need a deep, 9-inch round pyrex dish when you reverse the tart. The glass bottom allows you to see when the tart is done.

Filling:

½ cup butter, softened, divided
1 cup sugar, divided
   Apples
1 teaspoon ground cinnamon, divided
¼ cup firmly packed dark brown sugar
2 tablespoons powdered sugar

Spread one-third of butter generously on bottom and sides of skillet. Sprinkle ⅔ cup sugar on top of butter and spread evenly. Arrange slices of apples closely together, making a large outside ring and working toward the center. On the next layer, scatter apples about and dot with some of the butter, sugar, and ½ teaspoon of cinnamon. Fill with remaining apples and sprinkle with remaining ½ teaspoon cinnamon, remaining butter, and brown sugar. Cover with top crust, allowing its edges to fall against the inside edge of the skillet. Cut 5 or 6 holes or gashes in the pastry to allow steam to escape. Bake in a preheated 425° oven for 10 minutes, then remove and go around pastry with sharp knife. Turn upside down into a deep, 9-inch baking dish. Lower temperature to 375°. Sprinkle with powdered sugar and continue baking for 35 to 40 minutes longer until the caramelized base hardens to form a stiff icing. Watch carefully and do not allow to burn. The French serve this hot or cold with whipped cream or with Crème Fraîche. If you want perfection, try the latter. Yield: 6 to 8 servings.

Crème Fraîche:

½ pint commercial sour cream
1 pint whipping cream

Beat sour cream with fresh cream in a bowl with a wire whisk until thoroughly blended. Heat mixture in a saucepan over low heat just long enough to remove the chill. Allow to sit overnight without refrigeration. As soon as mixture thickens, refrigerate. This will keep 10 days. Crème Fraîche is delicious over fresh fruit and fruit pies and mincemeat.

OLD-TIME MOLASSES PIE

3 large eggs, room temperature
1 cup unsulphured molasses (Louisiana cane, if possible)
2 cups sugar
1 cup all-purpose flour
1 cup milk
⅛ teaspoon salt
1 teaspoon vanilla extract
1 (9-inch) unbaked pie shell

Beat eggs lightly with a wire whisk; add molasses and blend well. Add sugar, flour, milk, salt, and vanilla; mix well. Pour into unbaked pie shell and bake in a preheated 400° oven for 10 minutes. Lower temperature to 325° and continue baking for 35 minutes. Serve hot or cold. I prefer it hot. Yield: 1 (9-inch) pie—6 to 8 servings.

COURTNEY'S PECAN TARTS

Pastry:

1 (3-ounce) package cream cheese
½ cup butter, softened
1 cup unsifted all-purpose flour

Blend cream cheese, butter, and flour together. Lightly flour 10 muffin cups and pat mixture into tins, leaving a hollow in the center of each tart.

Filling:

3 tablespoons butter, melted
1 egg, slightly beaten
¾ cup firmly packed dark brown sugar
1 cup chopped pecans

Combine all ingredients and put into hollows. Bake in a preheated 350° oven for 25 minutes. Yield: 10 tarts.

PLANTATION PECAN PIE

Superb hot or cold, the recipe is easy to prepare.

¼ cup butter, not margarine
1 cup firmly packed dark brown sugar
1 cup light corn syrup
1 tablespoon evaporated milk or whipping cream
¼ teaspoon salt
3 large eggs, room temperature
2 tablespoons vanilla extract
1½ cups broken pecans
1 (9-inch) unbaked pie shell

Cream butter, add sugar gradually, then add syrup and evaporated milk. In another bowl add salt to eggs and beat until light. Stir well into first mixture; add vanilla and pecans. Use 1 cup nuts for halves or 1½ cups if broken into pieces. The halves make a prettier pie, but I like the pieces. Pour mixture into a 9-inch unbaked pie shell. Bake pie in a preheated 400° oven for 10 minutes. Lower heat to 350° and bake for 35 to 40 minutes longer or until a silver knife inserted in filling comes out clean. Yield: 1 (9-inch) pie—6 to 8 servings.

SOUR CREAM RAISIN PIE

Unusual!

1 cup sugar
1 large egg, room temperature
1 cup halved seedless raisins
1 cup commercial sour cream
½ teaspoon ground nutmeg
¼ teaspoon salt
½ teaspoon ground cinnamon
  Dash of ground cloves
1 (9-inch) unbaked pie shell, chilled

Combine all ingredients in a large bowl and blend well; do not beat egg separately. Pour mixture into chilled pie shell. Bake in a preheated 400° oven for 15 minutes. Reduce heat to 350° and cook for 30 minutes more. Serve hot or cold. I prefer it hot. Yield: 1 (9-inch) pie—6 to 8 servings.

MILDRED REYNOLD'S FRENCH NUT PIE

Rich and spicy, this pie is marvelous to serve at a dessert-bridge party.

½ cup butter or margarine
2 cups sugar
4 large eggs, well beaten
1 cup white or dark seedless raisins
1 cup finely chopped nuts
2 tablespoons all-purpose flour
1 teaspoon ground cloves
1 teaspoon ground cinnamon
2 teaspoons vinegar
2 (9-inch) unbaked pie shells

In a large bowl cream butter and sugar until light and fluffy. Add well-beaten eggs and continue beating. Dredge raisins and nuts in flour; add to creamed mixture with spices and vinegar. Spoon into unbaked pie shells. Bake in a preheated 325° oven about 45 minutes. A silver knife inserted in center should come out clean. Cool on a wire rack and serve cold. This pie freezes well. Yield: 2 (9-inch) pies—14 to 16 servings.

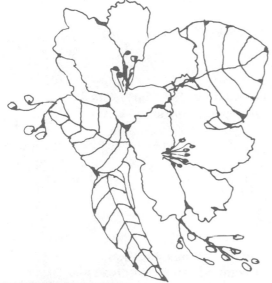

TOFFEE DELIGHT

A frozen taste delight in which you may use either chocolate or coffee ice cream as the base.

12 (1⅛-ounce) commercial toffee bars, frozen
  1 quart chocolate or coffee ice cream, softened
  4 teaspoons Tia Maria or Kahlua, divided
  2 (9-inch) graham cracker crusts, baked and frozen
  1 pint whipping cream

Grate frozen toffee bars in blender or by hand. Blend softened ice cream in a large mixing bowl with 2 teaspoons coffee liqueur. Divide ice cream and place in frozen pie crusts; refreeze.

When mixture is frozen, whip cream and remaining 2 teaspoons coffee liqueur. Fold in finely ground toffee bars. Divide whipped cream mixture with a light hand and cover frozen ice cream. Refreeze pies. I cover with a plastic bag to preserve their airy quality. To serve, remove pies from freezer at beginning of your meal. Yield: 2 (9-inch) pies—12 to 14 servings.

PINEAPPLE MERINGUE PIE

Exotic and lovely!

2 cups firmly packed, undrained, crushed pineapple
1 cup sugar
2 large egg yolks, well beaten
1 tablespoon all-purpose flour
1 teaspoon lemon juice
⅛ teaspoon salt
1 tablespoon butter
1 (9-inch) baked pie shell
3 large egg whites
¼ teaspoon cream of tartar
1 tablespoon water
6 tablespoons powdered or granulated sugar
¾ teaspoon vanilla extract

In top of a double boiler blend crushed pineapple with juice, 1 cup sugar, well-beaten egg yolks, flour, lemon juice, and salt. Cook over rapidly boiling water until thickened, stirring constantly. Remove from heat, add butter, and pour into baked pie shell. Beat egg whites, cream of tartar, and water in a small mixing bowl at high speed of electric mixer. Add 6 tablespoons sugar, 1 tablespoon at a time. Add vanilla. Continue beating at high speed for 4 to 5 minutes until whites stand in peaks. Pile mixture lightly on filled pie shell with a spatula. Bake in a preheated 300° oven for 15 to 20 minutes or until lightly golden. Allow pie to cool slowly. Serve hot or cold. Yield: 1 (9-inch) pie—6 servings.

ORANGE CREAM PIE

A superb pie with the delicate taste of the pure orange. Delicious served warm or cold. Use your favorite pastry recipe or a frozen pastry for a single 9-inch pie crust or shell.

  1 large or 2 medium-size oranges
2½ cups milk or undiluted evaporated milk
  2 large eggs
1½ cups sugar
  1 tablespoon all-purpose flour
  ⅛ teaspoon salt
  1 tablespoon finely grated orange rind
  1 to 2 teaspoons unflavored gelatin
      (optional)
  1 (9-inch) pie shell, baked
      Meringue (optional)

Squeeze oranges for ⅓ cup juice. Place milk in top of a double boiler over boiling water. When it becomes hot, add slightly beaten eggs, sugar, flour, and salt. Add grated orange rind. Stir constantly until mixture thickens. Remove from heat and add orange juice. Pour into pie shell. For a firm pie, dissolve gelatin in mixture and slice only when fully cold. You may make a meringue or cover with ½ pint whipped cream sweetened with 1 tablespoon sugar and 1 teaspoon vanilla.

Meringue:

 3 large egg whites, room temperature
 1 tablespoon water
 ¼ teaspoon cream of tartar
 6 tablespoons sugar
 ¾ teaspoon vanilla extract
   Pinch salt

Beat egg whites, water, and cream of tartar in a small narrow bowl at high speed until whites stand in soft peaks. Gradually add sugar 1 tablespoon at a time, then add vanilla and salt. Continue beating at high speed about 2 or 3 minutes or until egg whites stand in stiff peaks.

Pile lightly on the completely cooled filling and spread over top. If you use the gelatin, allow pie to cool completely before putting on meringue. Bake in a preheated 300° oven for 15 to 20 minutes or until lightly golden. Allow pie to cool slowly. Serve warm or after it is cold; chill in refrigerator. Yield: 1 (9-inch) pie—6 or 7 servings.

BOURBON PIE

A Kentucky favorite.

Crust:

22 chocolate wafers, finely rolled
 4 tablespoons butter, melted

Combine chocolate wafer crumbs with melted butter and pat into a 9-inch greased pie plate. Bake in a preheated 350° oven for 8 minutes. Set aside to cool.

Filling:

24 regular-size marshmallows
 1 (13-ounce) can evaporated milk
 ¼ cup bourbon
 ½ pint whipping cream, whipped, divided
 ½ ounce unsweetened chocolate, shaved

In a saucepan melt marshmallows in evaporated milk over medium heat; do not boil. Cool; add bourbon and one half of the whipped cream. Pour into chocolate crumb crust; chill. When ready to serve, top with remaining whipped cream and sprinkle with shaved chocolate. Yield: 1 (9-inch) pie—6 to 8 servings.

Pecan pie has long been a traditional Southern favorite, particularly during the Thanksgiving and Christmas holiday seasons. The secret for Plantation Pecan Pie is located on page 212.

STELLA STEPHEN'S PEACH SUPREME

A taste thrill.

Pastry:

4 tablespoons cold water
4 teaspoons melted butter
1 (11-ounce) package butterflake pie crust
mix

Combine water and butter in a large bowl; pour over pie crust mix, and stir with fork until dough holds together. Form into two balls and chill for 30 minutes. Make filling while pastry is chilling.

Filling:

2 (16-ounce) cans peach halves, drained and
1 cup juice reserved
1 cup sugar, divided
2 teaspoons powdered fruit pectin
¼ teaspoon ground nutmeg
½ teaspoon almond extract
3 tablespoons butter, divided

Slice peach halves; peach slices do not work as well. Combine sliced peaches, reserved 1 cup juice, ½ cup sugar, fruit pectin, and nutmeg; cook over medium heat in a large saucepan about 20 to 25 minutes or until juice thickens. Add almond extract. Cut two pieces waxed paper 12 inches long. Place one ball of dough between sheets and roll into a 9-inch square. Repeat with remaining ball of dough. Place half of cooked peaches with syrup in an 8½-inch square baking dish. Dot with 2 tablespoons butter and cover with one pastry square, gash with knife and brown in a pre-

---

Fresh fruit salad with a spicy dressing, flavorful tomato aspic, or a colorful tossed salad—all of which are included in the Salads and Salad Dressings chapter—make a delicious accompaniment to a rich entrée.

heated 475° oven about 12 minutes or until golden brown. Remove from heat, add remaining peaches, cover with remaining dough, gash with knife, and bake again for 5 minutes. Remove from oven and spread with mixture of remaining 1 tablespoon butter and ½ cup sugar. Run under broiler to glaze; watch carefully to prevent burning. Serve hot; this may be reheated. It is good cold. I do not recommend freezing. Yield: 10 to 12 servings.

NUT'S FOLLY

My dear friend Eudora Welty bestowed this title on my latest creation at Sunday dinner. The nuts used in the delectable dessert are almonds sliced wafer thin and buried deep in a creamy lemon filling and covered with almond flavored and encrusted whipped cream.

1 (9-inch) graham cracker crust, baked
2 large egg yolks
1 (14-ounce) can condensed milk
⅓ cup strained lemon juice
2 teaspoons vanilla extract, divided
2 teaspoons crème d'almond flavoring,
divided
⅓ cup blanched, wafer-thin almonds
½ pint whipping cream
½ tablespoon sugar
1 teaspoon brandy

Chill baked crust. Beat egg yolks with condensed milk until very light. Add lemon juice and mix well. Add 1 teaspoon vanilla and 1 teaspoon crème d'almond. Add most of the almonds; reserve some for garnish. Spoon filling into crust and chill for several hours or overnight.

An hour or two before serving, whip cream until thick, add sugar, remaining teaspoons vanilla and crème d'almond, and brandy. Spread cream over pie, sprinkle remaining almonds over top, and serve with black coffee. Yield: 1 (9-inch) pie—6 servings.

FRESH PEACH CHIFFON PIE

A peachy quickie when the luscious fruit is in season.

  ¾ cup sugar
2½ tablespoons cornstarch
  ¾ cup water
  3 tablespoons peach flavored gelatin
     Few drops almond extract
  4 cups sliced ripe fresh peaches
  1 tablespoon lemon juice
  2 (7-inch) baked pie shells
  ½ pint whipping cream, whipped

Combine sugar, cornstarch, and water in a saucepan and cook over medium heat until thickened. Add gelatin and almond extract and cool. Slice peaches and sprinkle with lemon juice. Fold peaches into the cooled gelatin mixture. Divide and pour into the pie shells. Cover with whipped cream and chill. Serve cold: Yield: 2 (7-inch) pies—12 servings.

CANTALOUPE COBBLER

A marvelous dessert; easily and quickly made.

  3 cups ripe cantaloupe pieces
  2 cups ripe peach pieces
  4 tablespoons lemon juice
  ¼ teaspoon almond extract
1¼ cups sugar
  3 tablespoons butter or margarine
  1 (16-ounce) tube refrigerated sugar cookies
  1 teaspoon cinnamon sugar

Peel fruit and cut into 1-inch pieces. Butter the bottom of an 11- x 7- x 2-inch casserole or pan. Place fruit, lemon juice, almond extract, and sugar in a large bowl and mix well. Spread mixture evenly in casserole and dot with butter. Slice cookie roll ¼ inch thick and cover fruit mixture completely. You may have to cut the cookies to fill in small empty places.

Sprinkle top of cobbler with cinnamon sugar. Bake in a preheated 375° oven for 25 minutes; lower heat to 300° and continue baking for 25 minutes or until the top of cobbler is a golden brown. This is best when served at once; good used the same day. This will not freeze. Yield: 8 servings.

MARY FRANCES BLAKE'S SODA CRACKER PIE

Luscious.

  1 cup crushed soda crackers
  1 cup sugar
12 dates, chopped
  ¼ cup chopped nuts
  1 teaspoon baking powder
  4 egg whites, stiffly beaten
  1 teaspoon vanilla extract
     Whipped cream

Combine all dry ingredients and then add to beaten egg whites; add vanilla. Fold together and put into a well-greased 9-inch pie plate. Bake in a preheated 350° oven for 30 minutes. Top with whipped cream. Yield: 1 (9-inch) pie—6 servings.

PEACH FILLING FOR SHORTBREADS

  8 ripe peaches, peeled and sliced
    Water to cover
⅛ teaspoon salt
2½ tablespoons strained lemon juice
¼ cup butter or margarine
  2 teaspoons cornstarch
⅔ cup sugar
    Shortbread
    Whipped cream

In a saucepan cover peaches with water and add salt, lemon juice, and butter. Cook over medium heat and bring to a simmering boil. Add cornstarch and sugar and cook until thickened. Arrange single shortbread on dessert place and cover with some of peaches with syrup and top with whipped cream. Yield: 8 servings.

OLD-FASHIONED SHORTCAKE ROUNDS

Serve these with crushed, freshly washed strawberries, sweetened to taste and topped with sweetened whipped cream.

½ cup butter or margarine
 1 tablespoon sugar
 1 egg yolk, beaten
½ cup milk
 2 cups sifted all-purpose flour
 1 scant tablespoon baking powder
½ teaspoon salt
   Melted butter

Cream butter and sugar. Add yolk and blend well. Pour milk into creamed mixture. Smooth out large lumps with a spoon. Sift together flour, baking powder, and salt. Add milk mixture to the dry ingredients all at once. Mix gently to combine all ingredients, but do not knead. Warning: do not mix too thoroughly.

The milk and the butter combine separately with the flour and produce an uneven-colored dough, but this is as it should be. Chill dough in refrigerator for 1 hour (not absolutely necessary, but it helps if you have the time).

Pat or roll out on a floured board to a little over ¼ inch thick; prick dough with fork. Cut out dough with a large biscuit cutter or rim of a large glass. Place on greased baking sheets, leaving space betweeen each biscuit to permit thorough baking. Brush with melted butter. Bake in a preheated 450° oven about 15 minutes. Yield: about 2 to 2½ dozen rounds.

Note: If you like a sweet shortcake, you can safely increase the sugar to 2 tablespoons.

WILD SPRING PLUM PIE

Take the leftover plum pulp after straining the juice for jelly and remove seeds.

2½ cups plum pulp
¾ cups sugar
 2 tablespoons cornstarch
 2 tablespoons butter, divided
½ teaspoon almond extract
   Pastry for (8-inch) unbaked, double pie
     crust
 1 teaspoon cinnamon sugar

Place plum pulp, sugar, cornstarch, and 1 tablespoon butter in a medium-size saucepan, and cook over low heat until mixture comes to a boil and begins to thicken. Add flavoring and pour into bottom pie crust. Dot with remaining 1 tablespoon butter and top with pastry rolled to ⅛-inch thickness. Cut 2 or 3 gashes in top of crust to allow steam to escape or top with pastry cut into ½-inch wide strips arranged lattice fashion. Sprinkle crust lightly with cinnamon sugar. Bake in a preheated 400° oven for 30 minutes or until crust is golden brown. Delicious hot or cold. Yield: (8-inch) pie—6 to 8 servings.

SOUR CREAM LEMON PIE

3 large egg yolks
1 cup sugar
2 tablespoons all-purpose flour
¼ cup butter, melted
¼ cup strained lemon juice
1 tablespoon finely grated lemon rind
1 cup milk
1 cup commercial sour cream
1 (9-inch) pie crust, baked
  Meringue

Beat egg yolks slightly with a wire whisk or dover egg beater in top of a double boiler. Add sugar, flour, melted butter, and lemon juice and rind; mix well. Blend in milk and cook about 15 minutes over rapidly boiling water, stirring constantly until mixture thickens. Allow filling to cool; then fold in sour cream and pour into pie crust. Prepare Meringue.

Meringue:

3 large egg whites
¼ teaspoon cream of tartar
1 tablespoon water
6 tablespoons sugar
⅛ teaspoon salt
1 teaspoon vanilla extract

Beat egg whites, cream of tartar, and water in a small bowl on high speed of electric mixer for 3 minutes or until whites begin to stand in peaks. Add sugar, 1 tablespoon at a time. Add salt and vanilla. Continue beating at high speed until whites are stiff. Pile lightly on filled pie crust; be sure meringue completely covers the filling. Bake in a preheated 300° oven for 15 to 20 minutes or until meringue is golden brown. If you serve this pie warm, the filling will be slightly runny. When cold, it cuts well. My taste buds prefer it warm. Yield: 1 (9-inch) pie—6 servings.

ZOLLIE KIMBROUGH'S SHORTBREADS

These are great with sliced fresh peaches or for making strawberry shortcake.

2 cups all-purpose flour
½ teaspoon salt
⅔ cup vegetable shortening
1 teaspoon lemon juice
1 large egg, well beaten

Sift flour and salt into large bowl; cut in shortening with two knives or pastry blender. Add lemon juice and egg to flour mixture, and work together with clean hands. Turn out onto a marble or working area and knead until well blended. Shape into a roll about 2½ to 3 inches in diameter. Place in double waxed paper, roll tightly and twist at both ends. Chill overnight. Slice ¼ inch thick and place on an ungreased cookie sheet. Bake in a preheated 350° oven about 15 minutes. Remove from pan at once and cool on a wire rack. Yield: 16 shortbreads.

Poultry and Game

CHICKEN BREASTS CHERRIES JUBILEE

I discovered this recipe by chance—the chance that my Scotch blood might freeze at the thought of throwing away anything. The morning after a gala dinner party ending in the festive aura of Cherries Jubilee, I was faced with a leftover cup of Bing cherry juice and ½ cup brandy. Up for grabs were also six chicken breasts which demanded immediate attention because they had been inadvertently thawed during the freezer's breakdown. This chicken has a delightful and unusual flavor and is the color of cherries. The sauce would be delicious over cooked rice or noodles. Serve with fresh string beans, hot French bread, and a mélange of fresh fruit: peaches, nectarines, green grapes, cherries, and watermelon balls doused with several tablespoons Cointreau.

¼ teaspoon Mei-yen powder
   About ½ teaspoon salt
⅛ teaspoon freshly ground white pepper
 6 large chicken breasts, skinned
 1 cup Bing cherry juice
½ cup brandy
⅓ stick butter or margarine

Sprinkle Mei-yen powder, salt, and pepper over chicken breasts and arrange meaty side down in a flat-bottomed casserole. Then pour cherry juice followed by the brandy over these and dot with butter. Cover with foil and bake in a preheated 350° oven for 45 minutes. Turn breasts, baste, and cook 15 minutes longer or until tender. Test with fork; this should go in easily. Yield: 6 servings.

DICK BARNES' ITALIAN-STYLE CHICKEN

Highly seasoned and a quickie!

 6 large chicken breasts or 1 whole
    fryer
¾ teaspoon salt
¼ teaspoon freshly ground black pepper
¼ cup butter or margarine
 1 bottle commercial Italian dressing

Cut fryer into serving-size pieces. Wash and dry breasts or pieces using paper towels. Sprinkle chicken with salt and pepper. Melt butter in a heavy skillet over medium heat and brown chicken. Place chicken skin side down in an oblong casserole and douse with Italian dressing. Cover with foil and bake in a preheated 350° oven for 45 minutes to 1 hour or until a fork tine pierces the meat easily. These will freeze. Preheat covered. Yield: 6 servings.

CHICKEN DELLA ROBBIA

A colorful and unusually flavored chicken dish, this is as pretty as a picture painted by the Italian artist, Della Robbia. Serve for a dinner party with fluffy rice, tiny English peas, a tossed green salad, and chocolate angel pie. For my family I use one 3- to 3½-pound frying chicken; for company or a party, 8 chicken breasts or 5 breasts and 3 whole legs.

    1 (3- to 3½-pound) frying chicken, skinned
        and cut into serving pieces
    6 tablespoons corn oil margarine
    1 large onion, sliced in rings
    ½ pound sliced fresh mushrooms or 1
        (8-ounce) can sliced mushrooms
    ¼ cup lemon juice
    1¼ cups water
    4 teaspoons salt
    2 teaspoons monosodium glutamate
    ½ teaspoon ground ginger
    ½ teaspoon freshly ground allspice
    ½ teaspoon ground cloves
    ¼ teaspoon lemon-pepper marinade
    ½ cup dark seedless raisins
    ½ cup white seedless raisins
    1 cup almonds, pecans, or walnuts
    3 tablespoons all-purpose flour blended with
        ½ cup cold water
    1 pound (2 cups) seedless grapes, washed
        and drained
    4 medium-size oranges, peeled and cut into
        sections
    1 (11-ounce) can mandarin orange sections,
        drained and rinsed
    1 (4-ounce) bottle maraschino cherries

In a large iron skillet or Dutch oven sauté chicken in margarine over medium heat until golden. Add onions and fresh mushrooms, and cook for 4 to 5 minutes. Add lemon juice, water, salt, monosodium glutamate, ginger, allspice, cloves, lemon-pepper marinade, and raisins. Simmer covered for 40 to 45 minutes or until tender; the tines of a fork should go into the chicken easily. Turn the pieces every 15 minutes. Add nuts. Remove chicken to a hot platter. Stir blended flour water into the chicken broth until smooth and thickened; return chicken to skillet and add grapes, orange sections, and cherries that have been washed and drained. Heat for 2 or 3 minutes. Serve at once. Yield: 8 servings.

PARTY CHICKEN LOAF OR RING

An ideal dish for a wedding luncheon or supper, this is tasty, colorful, and easy to prepare but takes time. Make a day ahead and reheat. (For a bridal luncheon, scoop out half a watermelon and fill with cantaloupe, watermelon, honeydew balls and other seasonal fruit topped with poppy-seed dressing.) Serve with cheese straws, hot rolls, wedding cake and coffee. Champagne always adds a festive touch.

Step 1:

    1 (5-pound) hen or 2 fryers equivalent in
        weight or 1 (4- to 6-pound) frozen turkey
        breast, thawed
    3 celery ribs with leaves
    1 teaspoon dried green onion
    1 teaspoon Mei-yen powder
    1 teaspoon salt

Place chicken in a large heavy pot. Cover with water and add remaining ingredients. Bring to a boil over medium heat and cook until done, about two hours for the hen, less time for fryers and much less time for the turkey. Test with fork in thick part of thigh for tenderness. Cool, skin, and bone; dice chicken into a large bowl.

Step 2:

1½ cups cooked commercial saffron rice
  3 slices cheese or white bread, crusts
     removed
  ½ cup chicken broth
  ½ cup half-and-half
  ¼ cup sliced water chestnuts
  ¼ cup chopped pimientos
  1 teaspoon dried green onion
  1 teaspoon onion puree or 2 teaspoons liquid
     onion
  ⅛ teaspoon cayenne pepper
1½ tablespoons finely chopped parsley
  ¼ cup chopped buttery sliced mushrooms
  ½ teaspoon Tabasco
  1 tablespoon Worcestershire sauce
  1 teaspoon salt
  ⅛ teaspoon white pepper
  ¼ cup sherry (optional)
  4 eggs, well beaten

Follow package directions to cook saffron rice. Soak bread, with crusts removed, in blended chicken broth and half-and-half; then add to bowl of diced chicken. Slice water chestnuts thinly and cut into pieces. Blend remaining ingredients with diced chicken, adding well-beaten eggs last. Pour mixture into two 9- x 5- x 3-inch loaf pans or one 10-inch flat pan greased with olive or vegetable oil and bottom lined with waxed paper. Set pans in hot water and bake, uncovered, in a preheated 325° oven for 35 to 40 minutes. Test with straw for doneness. Remove from oven and let stand 15 minutes to firm up. Serve sliced with sauce.

Sauce:

1 (10¾-ounce) can condensed cream of
    mushroom soup
1 cup commercial sour cream
1 tablespoon lemon juice
¼ teaspoon salt
¼ teaspoon paprika
1 teaspoon fresh chopped parsley

Heat all ingredients in top of a double boiler over rapidly boiling water. Do not let sauce boil. To hold heat, lower cooking temperature and keep over hot water until ready to serve. Yield: 16 servings.

CHICKEN BREASTS SUPREME

This delicious dish unites breast of chicken with heart of artichoke. Easy to prepare and excellent for company, it may be made a day ahead and reheated. Serve with fluffy rice or noodles and a tossed green salad for a complete meal.

6 chicken breasts, skinned
½ teaspoon salt
⅛ teaspoon white pepper
¼ teaspoon paprika
3 tablespoons butter
1 (3-ounce) can button mushrooms or ½
    pound large fresh mushrooms, trimmed,
    washed, and dried
2 cups hot chicken bouillon or 2 cups hot beef
    bouillon
3 tablespoons sifted all-purpose flour
4 tablespoons sherry (optional)
1 (14-ounce) can artichoke hearts, drained
    and rinsed

Sprinkle breasts with salt, white pepper, and paprika and sauté in butter over medium heat in a heavy skillet. Remove when lightly golden on both sides. Sauté mushrooms in same skillet. Add an additional tablespoon of butter if mushrooms tend to stick. Add hot chicken bouillon and stir in sifted flour. Add sherry, if desired. Place chicken breasts and artichoke hearts in a buttered 2-quart oblong baking dish and cover with mushroom mixture. Bake in a preheated 375° oven for 40 minutes. Yield: 6 servings.

COUNTRY CAPTAIN

Chicken Country Captain comes from Mildred Williams, food columnist for a Virginia newspaper. The original recipe came from Mrs. W. L. Bullard of Warms Springs, Georgia, who often served her famous dish to the late Franklin D. Roosevelt. And once, when there wasn't time for General George Patton to stay for dinner, he is said to have wired Mrs. Bullard to have the Country Captain waiting for him in a tin bucket at the train.

2 frying-size chickens
⅔ cup all-purpose flour
1 teaspoon salt
½ teaspoon black pepper
¼ teaspoon paprika
1 clove garlic, chopped
½ cup olive oil
1 cup finely chopped onion
1 bell pepper, sliced
4¾ cups canned tomatoes
2 teaspoons chopped parsley
1 teaspoon curry powder
½ teaspoon powdered thyme
⅛ teaspoon cayenne pepper
½ cup water
1 cup seedless raisins
½ cup toasted almonds
  Melted butter
2 cups hot cooked rice
  Fresh parsley (optional)

Cut chicken into frying-size pieces; split the breast, separate leg and thigh, and use the wings. Save bony pieces for stew. Flour chicken by shaking in a paper bag containing flour, salt, black pepper, and paprika. Make garlic oil by adding chopped garlic to olive oil and letting it stand until flavor is absorbed from garlic. Use ½ cup of hot garlic oil to brown chicken on both sides in a large skillet over high heat, turning pieces often so that it is golden but not dark. Remove chicken to roaster and cover. Add onion and bell pepper to drippings in skillet; cook over medium heat until they are limp but not brown, stirring constantly. Add tomatoes, parsley, curry, thyme, and cayenne pepper; cook slowly about 5 minutes until blended. Pour over chicken, rinsing out skillet with water. Cover and bake chicken in a preheated 325° oven for 45 minutes or until chicken is tender. Add raisins the last 15 minutes of cooking. Split blanched almonds in halves; brown lightly in a little melted butter. Arrange chicken in center of a large heated platter, pour sauce over it and pile cooked rice around edges. Sprinkle toasted almonds on top and garnish with fresh parsley, if desired. Yield: 8 to 10 servings.

CHICKEN VÉRONIQUE

A superb combination of chicken and white grapes with a marvelous sauce. Easy to prepare and economical when having guests.

1 (2½- to 3-pound) fryer chicken or 6 chicken
  breasts, skinned
1 teaspoon salt
¼ teaspoon paprika, divided
¼ teaspoon freshly ground white pepper
3 teaspoons dried green chives
1 celery rib, chopped
½ teaspoon dried tarragon
½ cup white wine or dry vermouth, divided
  Juice of 1 lemon
4 tablespoons butter, divided
½ cup whipping cream or undiluted
  evaporated milk
2 tablespoons all-purpose flour
½ pound white seedless grapes or 1 can white
  grapes, cut in half

Cut fryer into serving-size pieces and dry on paper towels. Sprinkle with salt, ⅛ teaspoon paprika, and white pepper and place in a large casserole or roasting pan. Cover with chives, celery, tarragon, ¼ cup wine or vermouth, lemon juice and dot with 2 tablespoons butter. Seal top of pan with aluminum foil and bake in a preheated 350° oven for 1 hour. Set timer at 20-minute intervals and gradually add remaining ¼ cup wine or vermouth, basting with juices formed. Test with a fork tine to be sure chicken is tender; then remove to a heated dish. Measure liquid left in baking dish. If more than 1 cup, reduce to about 1 cup by boiling rapidly; add cream, stirring constantly. Combine remaining 2 tablespoons butter and flour to form a paste and add to the hot sauce, stirring over a low heat until thickened and smooth. Taste to see if more salt is needed. Return chicken to sauce, add grape halves, and sprinkle chicken with remaining ⅛ teaspoon paprika. Allow chicken to sit in sauce at least 15 minutes before serving. Serve hot. Saffron rice makes an ideal accompaniment. Yield: 6 servings.

LIME BROILED CHICKEN

Unusual flavor.

3 broiler chickens or 1 (2½-pound) fryer
    chicken
½ cup fresh lime juice
½ cup vegetable oil
1 teaspoon seasoned salt
1 tablespoon grated onion
2 teaspoons crushed tarragon
¼ teaspoon freshly ground black pepper

Split broilers or cut fryers into whole legs and large breasts. Wash chicken and pat dry. Mix remaining ingredients in a small bowl. Brush generously over chicken pieces. Place chicken skin side down on rack pan in lowest part of broiler. Cook on broiler heat for 40 minutes or until tender and brown. Turn chickens every 10 minutes and brush with more lime juice mixture. Test with a fork in thigh; this should go in easily. Yield: 6 servings.

CHICKEN CHALUPAS FROM SANBORN'S

A zesty dish from Mexico City.

1 (3-pound) hen
1 large onion, finely chopped
5 cloves garlic, finely chopped
1 bell pepper, finely chopped
1 canned chili pepper, diced
2 pounds pasteurized process American
    cheese, shredded
2 pints commercial sour cream
    Reserved clear chicken stock
36 tortillas

Cook hen at a simmering boil for 2 hours; drain, reserving stock. Remove meat from bones and cut into small pieces as for hash. In a large bowl, combine diced chicken, onion, garlic, bell pepper, chili pepper, and shredded cheese. Dilute sour cream with a little of the reserved chicken stock to the consistency of thin cream. Spread chicken mixture on tortillas and roll as you would an enchilada.

Place tortillas side by side in a large shallow casserole and pour sour cream mixture over all. If there is some chicken mixture left over after spreading tortillas, spread on top before adding sour cream mixture. Let stand several hours in refrigerator. If tortillas seem dry, pour a little of the remaining chicken stock over them. Bake in a preheated 350° oven for 45 minutes. Mixture should be juicy with sauce running out and around tortillas. Serve with frijoles and a green salad. Yield: 12 servings.

SALLY C. WALKER'S CHICKEN SPAGHETTI

Step 1:

1 (3- to 4-pound) hen
  Water to cover
3 celery ribs with leaves, finely chopped
1 teaspoon dried green onion
1 teaspoon Mei-yen powder
¼ teaspoon salt

Place all ingredients in a large saucepan. Cover and bring to a simmering boil over high heat. Reduce heat and simmer about 2 hours or until tender. Test with fork in thick part of thigh. Cool for a few minutes; skin and cut off meat while chicken is still warm. Cut chicken into fair-sized pieces. Reserve broth.

Step 2:

¼ cup chicken broth
1 medium-size bell pepper, chopped
2 cloves garlic, chopped
1 large onion, chopped
  Chicken cut into fair-sized pieces
1 tablespoon chili powder
1 (8-ounce) can tomato sauce
1 (16-ounce) can tomatoes
14½ ounces reserved chicken broth
1 pound pasteurized process cheese spread,
    cut into chunks
1 (16-ounce) package spaghetti

In a large saucepan over medium heat cook chicken broth and chopped vegetables until transparent. Add remaining ingredients except cheese and spaghetti and simmer for 2 hours with pan covered. Add more broth if needed. The last 10 minutes of cooking add cheese and stir until melted. Cook spaghetti according to package directions; drain in colander. Stir cooked spaghetti into chicken-cheese sauce and serve. Flavor improves if dish is allowed to stand ½ hour or more before serving. This may be made ahead of time and refrigerated until reheated. Yield: 12 servings.

FRICASSEE DE POULET À L'AUGEVINE

Superb! A delicately flavored chicken cooked in dry white wine with tiny white onions and fresh mushrooms. Serve with its broth which has been elevated to a heavenly sauce by the addition of a pint of heavy cream. Serve with wild rice and a tossed green salad. A fruit sherbet, such as orange or raspberry, with macaroons makes an excellent dessert.

1 (3-pound) chicken fryer
2 teaspoons salt
½ teaspoon freshly ground white pepper
½ cup butter
12 very small white onions, peeled
½ quart dry white wine
½ pound fresh mushrooms, halved
1 pint whipping cream, warmed

Cut chicken into 8 pieces; wash and dry on paper towels. Sprinkle with salt and pepper. In a Dutch oven or large heavy casserole lightly brown chicken in hot sizzling butter. Use a high heat and adjust, turning pieces from side to side every minute for 3 or 4 minutes. Lower heat and cook 4 to 5 minutes longer. Add whole onions and cook about 20 minutes. Cover with wine, and continue cooking with pan covered at a simmering boil over low heat for 50 minutes or until chicken is very tender. Add mushrooms 15 minutes before end of cooking time. Test chicken thigh with fork tine to determine tenderness.

When chicken is done, remove to a hot platter and keep covered while making sauce. Add cream to chicken and wine broth. Cook slowly and stir often. When sauce attains more body, taste and adjust seasonings, if necessary. The desired consistency should resemble a thin custard or cream soup. To serve, cover chicken with sauce. Yield: 8 servings.

CHICKEN VIEUX CARRÉ

Picture yourself in a quaint courtyard of the French Quarter with the moon shining down, the air filled with the fragrance of Confederate jasmine, and your true love sitting across the wrought iron table as you enjoy this delightful repast.

12 large chicken breasts
 2 teaspoons salt, divided
½ teaspoon freshly ground white pepper
½ teaspoon paprika
 5 tablespoons butter, margarine, bacon drippings, or olive oil
½ cup chopped fresh or frozen onion
½ cup chopped celery
 2 cloves garlic, finely chopped or ¼ teaspoon garlic powder
½ cup chopped fresh or frozen bell pepper
 1 (16-ounce) can peeled tomatoes
 1 (12-ounce) can tomato juice
 1 cup beef bouillon or white wine
 1 tablespoon minced dried or fresh parsley
 2 teaspoons Worcestershire sauce
½ teaspoon ground mace

Skin chicken breasts and pat dry with paper towels. Sprinkle with 1 teaspoon salt, white pepper, and paprika; sauté in butter. Cook over medium heat in a large iron skillet. When breasts are lightly golden on both sides remove from skillet to two 13- x 9- x 2-inch casseroles for prettiest arrangement. Sauté onion, celery, garlic, and bell pepper and cook about 15 minutes. Add tomatoes, tomato juice, beef bouillon or wine, and remaining 1 teaspoon salt. Add parsley, Worcestershire sauce, and mace. Simmer sauce about 25 minutes, then pour over chicken breasts. Cover casseroles tightly with foil. Bake in a preheated 375° oven for 1 hour. Serve over cooked yellow rice with a tossed green salad and hot French bread. This dish freezes well. Yield: 12 servings.

Note: To serve 6, reduce tomato juice and all other ingredients by half with the exception of the canned tomatoes and bouillon or wine. They remain the same.

MARY HEIDELBERG'S CHICKEN DIVAN

A delicious casserole to prepare in advance for company. This takes only 15 or 20 minutes to heat before serving.

 1 (10-ounce) package frozen broccoli spears
 1 (3- to 4-pound) hen or 6 whole chicken breasts
 3 celery ribs with leaves
 1 teaspoon salt
 1 (10¾-ounce) can condensed cream of chicken soup
1½ tablespoons lemon juice
 1 heaping tablespoon mayonnaise
 1 tablespoon sherry
 1 clove garlic, pressed into soup or ⅛ teaspoon garlic powder
  Cracker crumbs
  Grated Parmesan cheese
 1 tablespoon butter

Cook broccoli spears according to package directions; drain well in colander. Cover chicken with water in a large saucepan; add celery and salt and simmer about 2 hours or until chicken cooks away from the bones. Cool and cut chicken into bite-size pieces. Place cooked and drained broccoli in a 1½-quart buttered casserole. Add chicken. In a small saucepan place soup, lemon juice, mayonnaise, sherry, and garlic. Warm oven medium heat; *do not let sauce boil.* When thoroughly warmed pour over chicken pieces. Sprinkle top with cracker crumbs and grated cheese. Dot with butter. Bake in a preheated 350° oven for 15 to 20 minutes or until bubbly and hot. If serving later or the following day, refrigerate. Reheat at 350° for 15 to 20 minutes. Yield: 6 to 8 servings.

KATHLEEN HUTCHINSON'S CHICKEN PIQUANTE

1 (2½-pound) chicken, cut up or 6 chicken
   breasts, skinned
3 tablespoons vegetable oil
1 large onion, chopped
2½ teaspoons all-purpose flour
3 tomatoes or 1 (16-ounce) can peeled whole
   tomatoes, chopped
2 celery ribs, chopped
2 cups water
2 teaspoons halved small stuffed olives
   Salt to taste
¼ teaspoon black pepper
10 drops Tabasco or ½ teaspoon cayenne
   pepper

In a large skillet over medium high heat brown unfloured chicken in vegetable oil; set chicken aside. Cook onions about 10 minutes or until tender; remove from skillet. Brown flour slowly in skillet, stirring constantly. Gradually add tomatoes, celery, and water. Cook a few minutes and put everything into a heavy pot. Add olives and season with salt, black pepper, and Tabasco. Simmer about 2½ hours, preferably until the chicken is almost falling off the bone and gravy has cooked down. Serve with cooked rice. Yield: 6 servings.

SWEET DAISY'S CHICKEN PIE

Taste perfection! The beauty of this pie lies in its marvelous pastry combined with delicious cooked chicken and mushrooms. I prefer to simmer chicken a day in advance so that I may remove all fat from the broth. Chill the pastry dough several hours in advance for a lighter pie.

1 (2- to 2½-pound) fryer or stewing chicken
   Water to cover
3 celery ribs with leaves
1 teaspoon dried green onion
1 teaspoon salt
1 teaspoon Mei-yen powder
1 (6-ounce) can button mushrooms or ½
   pound fresh mushrooms, sautéed in
   butter
   Pastry
1 cup reserved chicken broth
2 tablespoons butter

Place all ingredients except mushrooms and butter in a large saucepan. Bring to a simmering boil. Simmer about 2 hours or until done. Test with fork in thick part of thigh. Cool, remove skin and bones from chicken; cut into nice size pieces. Reserve chicken broth and prepare Pastry.

Fill pastry shell with chicken, drained canned or sautéed fresh mushrooms, and 1 cup reserved chicken broth or enough to make mixture moist. Sprinkle with remaining ½ teaspoon salt and dot with butter before adding top crust. Press down edges with a fork and prick top crust. Bake in a preheated 400° oven for 20 minutes; lower heat to 350° and continue cooking for 10 minutes longer or until golden brown on top. Yield: 6 to 8 servings.

Pastry:

2 cups all-purpose flour, measured after
   sifting
¾ cup vegetable shortening
1 teaspoon salt, divided
½ cup plus 1 tablespoon ice water

Have all ingredients as cold as possible. Combine flour, shortening, and ½ teaspoon salt; add water gradually and blend with a light touch. Use a fork or pastry blender. Chill dough for at least 20 minutes; 12 hours is preferable.

Divide dough in half and roll one half between two sheets of waxed paper, rolling in one direction only. Cut rolled dough 1-inch larger than a 10- x 6- x 2½-inch casserole. Line bottom and sides of greased casserole with pastry and prick all over with a fork.

CHICKEN LEGS SUPREME

An elegant dish that takes about 50 minutes to prepare and is less expensive than most gourmet creations. Fluffy, cooked yellow rice and a macédoine of fresh or frozen fruit with three or four tablespoons Cointreau added complete a superb meal.

 6 whole fryer chicken legs
 1 teaspoon salt
¼ teaspoon freshly ground black pepper
 3 tablespoons corn oil
 3 tablespoons brandy
½ pound fresh mushrooms
 3 tablespoons white or tawny port
 1 teaspoon dried green onion
 1 teaspoon cornstarch
 1 cup undiluted evaporated milk or whipping
     cream

Season chicken with salt and pepper. In a 12-inch skillet or large heavy pan brown chicken in very hot corn oil over high heat. When both sides are browned, pour off any leftover oil, add warmed brandy, and ignite it. Lower heat to medium, cover skillet, and cook 15 minutes. Lightly wash mushrooms and dry on paper towels. Cut large mushrooms into quarters. Add mushrooms, wine, and green onion to skillet. Cover and cook over medium heat for 15 to 20 minutes or until fork tine easily pierces the heavy part of thigh. Remove chicken to a hot serving platter. Raise heat to high and reduce liquid to about 2 tablespoons. Blend cornstarch and milk or cream, add to liquid, and cook over medium heat until slightly thickened, stirring constantly. Adjust season-ings. Spoon sauce over chicken as you serve it. Yield: 6 servings.

MISSISSIPPI FRIED CHICKEN

 1 (2½- to 3-pound) broiler-fryer chicken
½ cup all-purpose flour
 1 teaspoon salt
 1 teaspoon paprika
¼ teaspoon pepper
     Shortening, salad oil or bacon drippings

Cut chicken into serving-size pieces and rinse in cold running water; do not dry. Blend dry ingredients in a plastic or brown paper bag. Drop two or three pieces chicken at a time into floured mixture and shake until chicken is coated. In a large heavy skillet heat enough shortening to fill skillet ½ inch deep over high heat until a drop of water sizzles when added to grease. (I find that bacon drippings give the best and tastiest chicken.) Place chicken skin side down in hot fat; put in larger pieces, such as breasts and legs, first. You may need to adjust heat as chicken cooks, lowering to medium high. Turn pieces to brown evenly. Reduce heat to medium-low, cover, and cook about 30 minutes or until tender. Yield: 4 to 6 servings.

Variation: Add a teaspoon each of dry mus-tard and thyme to flour mixture, or add a teaspoon of curry powder for a zestier flavor.

227

ELSA KLAUS' BRUNSWICK STEW

North Carolina's best!

Step 1:

 1 (3- to 4-pound) hen
    Water to cover
 3 celery ribs with leaves, finely chopped
 1 teaspoon dried green onion
 1 teaspoon Mei-yen powder
 ¼ teaspoon salt

Combine all ingredients in a large saucepan. Cover and bring to simmering boil over high heat. Reduce and simmer about 2 hours or until tender. Test with fork in thick part of thigh. Cool for a few minutes and cut off meat while chicken is still warm. If skin is very tender, grind and use ½ cup. Cut chicken into small pieces as for hash.

Step 2:

    Diced chicken and broth
 4 (16-ounce) cans butter beans
 4 (16-ounce) cans tomatoes
 1 medium-size to large baking potato, peeled
    and diced
 ¼ teaspoon black pepper
 3 teaspoons sugar
 2 slices smoked bacon, diced
 4 (17-ounce) cans white cream-style corn
 1 tablespoon all-purpose flour
 1 cup cold water
    Salt to taste

In a large soup kettle or Dutch oven cook chicken and broth, butter beans, tomatoes, diced potato, black pepper, and sugar over medium-high heat until it comes to a simmering boil. Reduce heat to low and cook about 1½ hours, stirring often. In skillet fry bacon over medium heat until crisp; drain, and add with corn to chicken mixture and cook 1 hour, stirring almost constantly.

Dissolve flour in a cup of cold water and slowly stir into mixture. Add salt. Cook about 45 minutes longer, stirring constantly. Be sure to scrape bottom of pan often, for corn sticks easily. I put up in thoroughly washed quart or half-gallon plastic milk cartons. This freezes well. Yield: 6 quarts.

COQ AU VIN

"Délicieux," exclaimed Mademoiselle Tizon, my French teacher. "This is the way *Coq au Vin* tasted at home in Poitier. *Maman* served it with parslied potatoes, a green salad, crusty hot bread, and *un bon vin rouge.*"

 1 (2- to 3-pound) frying chicken, cut into
    serving-size pieces
 1 teaspoon salt
 ¼ teaspoon freshly ground black pepper
 3 tablespoons corn or olive oil
 1 cup finely chopped onion
 1 clove garlic, mashed
 ⅓ cup tomato paste
 1 bay leaf
 2 tablespoons all-purpose flour
 ¼ cup brandy
 3 cups red wine, Burgundy, Pinot Noir,
    Chianti, Beaujolais, or Chambertin
 1½ tablespoons butter
 12 small round onions, brown-braised
 1½ cups lean bacon, ham or Canadian bacon,
    cubed
 ½ pound fresh mushrooms, sautéed and
    sliced or 1 (3-ounce) can whole
    mushrooms, sliced

Dry chicken; sprinkle with salt and pepper. Pour oil into a skillet over medium heat. When oil is hot, brown chicken on both sides and place in a 13- x 9- x 2-inch oblong casserole. Brown chopped onions in same skillet and stir in garlic and tomato paste. Add to chicken in casserole. Add bay leaf, and sprinkle flour over top. Warm the brandy in a small saucepan and ignite with a match; when the flames subside pour the remaining liquid over chicken. If you prefer not to flame the brandy just pour it over the chicken. The alcohol will burn out during the cooking anyway. Add wine. Cover casserole and cook in a preheated 350° oven for 2 hours. Allow to cool. The flavor of *Coq au Vin* improves immeasurably if it is refrigerated overnight.

About 1 hour before serving, heat 1½ tablespoons butter in a 9-inch skillet and cook onions, bacon, and mushrooms over medium heat about 10 minutes, stirring so that all ingredients will brown evenly. Add these to chicken in casserole and stir sauce gently to blend. Reheat at 350° about 20 to 25 minutes or until mixture is hot and bubbling. This will freeze well. Yield: 6 servings.

CHICKEN OR TURKEY STICKS

Deliciously different!

5½ tablespoons butter or margarine
3 tablespoons all-purpose flour
1 cup milk
1 large egg, well beaten
2 teaspoons lemon juice
2 teaspoons grated onion or onion puree
1 teaspoon Worcestershire sauce
¼ teaspoon salt
⅛ teaspoon white pepper
¼ teaspoon paprika
2 tablespoon chopped dried, fresh, or frozen parsley
1 cup finely chopped celery
2 cups finely chopped, cooked turkey or chicken
2 egg whites
1½ cups cracker crumbs
2 cups vegetable oil

Melt butter in top of double boiler over rapidly boiling water. Add flour and blend with a wire whisk. Heat milk until hot and slowly add to mixture, stirring constantly. Cook until mixture begins to thicken; then add well-beaten egg, lemon juice, grated onion, and seasonings. Cook sauce until very thick. Add parsley, celery, and chopped turkey. Allow mixture to cool on a large platter. Take 1 tablespoonful of mixture and shape into a finger-length strip. Place on an ungreased cookie sheet, cover with foil, and chill overnight.

Thirty minutes before serving, dip strips in unbeaten egg whites and roll in cracker crumbs; cover completely. Put oil in a heavy skillet over high heat. When oil is bubbling hot, drop sticks in very gently; fry on each side 6 to 8 minutes or until golden brown. Watch carefully and adjust heat; drain on paper towels. These will keep on a hot platter in a warm oven for 30 to 40 minutes. One stick is adequate for a party serving. Yield: 12 sticks.

Variation: If you cannot eat fried food, bake sticks on an ungreased cookie sheet in a preheated 400° oven for 40 minutes or until golden brown. Prepared in this way, the sticks may need a sauce to complement them, for oven baking tends to dry them out a bit. The following sauce is delicious.

Sherry Cream Sauce:

2 tablespoons butter
2 tablespoons all-purpose flour
1 cup milk
½ teaspoon salt
⅛ teaspoon white pepper
⅛ teaspoon paprika
4 tablespoons grated Parmesan cheese
3 tablespoons sherry

Melt butter in top of double boiler over rapidly boiling water. Add flour and blend with a wire whisk. Heat milk until hot, and slowly add to mixture, stirring constantly. Add seasonings; cook and stir until mixture is smooth and boiling. Add Parmesan cheese and stir until melted. Add sherry just as you remove the sauce from heat. Serve over hot Turkey Sticks and put a sprig of parsley on top. Yield: about 1½ cups.

TURKEY IN A BAG

The easiest and most delicious way you will ever cook a turkey.

1 (12-pound or larger) turkey, room
    temperature
1 large onion
¼ teaspoon paprika (not hot variety)
2 tablespoons boiling water
1 cup corn or peanut oil
½ teaspoon salt per pound
1½ teaspoons freshly ground black pepper
2 celery ribs with leaves
1 large, heavy, brown paper bag with no
    breaks in it
  Salt
1 teaspoon dried green onion
2 hard-boiled eggs, diced

Scrub turkey inside and out with warm water to which you add 1 tablespoon baking soda. Remove outer onion skin and cut into about 8 pieces. Sprinkle paprika into boiling water and mix well; add oil and blend. Rub breast cavity with the proper amount of salt and pepper and place celery and onion in it. Massage outside of turkey with liquid mixture. Saturate interior sides and bottom of bag with remaining liquid and place the turkey breast side up in bag. Tie bag securely so that it is tightly sealed. Place bag in an open roasting pan. Bake in a preheated 325° oven for 10 minutes per pound. Time carefully. When tender, cut bag to remove steam, and place bird on platter.

While turkey is baking, cover giblets and neck with water in a separate saucepan; season with salt and 1 teaspoon dried green onion. Cook over a medium heat. The tine of a fork must go easily into the giblets when done. Dice meat from neck and giblets and add the diced, hardboiled eggs. These mixed with the broth they were cooked in make a tasty gravy. There is adequate turkey broth in the roasting pan to prepare dressing. You may cook a turkey breast in the same way, but allow 1 hour more

cooking time after bag has been cut for a 9½ to 10-pound breast. Also, tie breast with clean string to hold onion and celery in cavity. Yield: about 9 servings, allowing ¾ pound per serving.

LEFTOVER TURKEY SOUFFLÉ

The noble bird will never taste any better than it does prepared in this fashion. Easy to prepare, the soufflé must be made ahead of time. The time-consuming part of this recipe is assembling the ingredients. Chances are most of them are already on your pantry or refrigerator shelf. The soufflé may be cooked in three ways:

1. One 13- x 9- x 2-inch flat-bottomed baking dish serves 22.

2. Divided evenly between two smaller oblong casseroles, each serves 6.

3. Divided into an 8-inch square casserole, serves 8, and a 22-ounce smaller casserole serves 4. I prefer the third method because I freeze the small casserole for later.

This is such a rich casserole, serve a light green vegetable, green beans or English peas, a mixed fruit salad, and hot biscuits. A fruit sherbet or fresh lime pie completes a delightful repast.

4 tablespoons butter, divided
7 slices white bread, crust removed and cut
    into cubes
½ pound fresh mushrooms or 2 (4-ounce)
    cans sliced mushrooms
3 cups diced cooked turkey or chicken
½ cup homemade mayonnaise or commercial
    brand made with lemon juice
1 teaspoon dried green onion
¾ teaspoon salt
¼ teaspoon freshly ground white pepper
¼ teaspoon lemon bits or finely grated lemon
    rind
½ teaspoon monosodium glutamate
½ (12-ounce) can water chestnuts, drained
    and thinly sliced
1 (2-ounce) jar pimientos, drained and finely
    chopped
3 large eggs, well beaten
1½ cups milk
½ (10¾-ounce) can condensed cream of
    celery soup
1 (10¾-ounce) can condensed cream of
    mushroom soup
¼ teaspoon paprika
1 cup shredded sharp cheddar cheese

Grease baking dish with 1 tablespoon butter and line with most of the bread cubes. Sauté mushrooms in remaining 3 tablespoons butter for 7 to 10 minutes in a heavy skillet over medium heat. Drain on paper towel and slice. Combine the diced turkey, mayonnaise, onion, salt, white pepper, lemon bits, and monosodium glutamate in a large bowl. Spread mixture evenly over bread cubes. Place a layer of water chestnuts over this, then a layer of pimientos, a layer of mushrooms, and another layer of water chestnuts. Put remaining bread cubes over the mixture.

Add beaten eggs to milk and pour over entire dish. Cover and chill for several hours or overnight. Before placing in oven, spoon combined celery and mushroom soups over the top and sprinkle with paprika. Bake for 1 hour or until soufflé is set. Sprinkle grated cheese over top the last 10 minutes of cooking. Test with silver knife for doneness; it should come out clean if soufflé is done. The soufflé will hold in a warm oven for 30 minutes without affecting its consistency. Serve hot! The soufflé freezes well if the soup and cheese are added just before baking. When you do freeze, thaw completely at room temperature before cooking.

CORN BREAD DRESSING FOR TURKEY

One of the best!

1 cup finely chopped onion
1 finely chopped bell pepper
2 celery ribs with leaves, finely chopped
1 (9-inch) skillet corn bread, crumbled
6 slices fresh white bread
    Salt to taste
¼ teaspoon freshly ground black pepper
4 eggs, lightly beaten
    Turkey broth

In enough water to cover, boil onion, bell pepper, and celery for 10 minutes. Pour this into a very large mixing bowl and add crumbled corn bread and white bread which has been torn into small pieces. (Use your own recipe or mix for baked corn bread.) Add salt and pepper, and stir beaten eggs into bread mixture. Add enough turkey broth to make batter runny. Pour into a greased 13- x 9- x 2-inch baking dish and bake in a preheated 400° oven for 1 hour or until golden brown on top. This is also great for stuffing a turkey. In that case, boil giblets first in 3 cups water and use for broth. Yield: 12 servings.

TURKEY AMANDINE

Great for leftover turkey. Serve over individual cheese soufflés for a gourmet meal. Corn bread squares or toasted English muffins are second choice.

  1 pound fresh mushrooms, sliced
  6 tablespoons butter
  ⅔ cup all-purpose flour
2½ teaspoons salt
  ¼ teaspoon freshly ground white pepper
  2 tablespoons chopped fresh, frozen, or fried
    parsley
  ½ teaspoon Mei-yen powder
  2 quarts turkey or chicken broth, warmed
  5 cups diced cooked turkey
  ¾ cup sherry
  1 cup toasted almonds

Sauté mushrooms in butter over medium heat in a large iron skillet for about five minutes. Sift in flour, salt, pepper, parsley, and Mei-yen powder. Mix thoroughly. Add the warmed turkey broth gradually. Stir constantly until sauce thickens and allow to simmer for 5 minutes. Add turkey and sherry. Be sure turkey is well heated. Taste to adjust seasonings; you may wish more salt or pepper. If you wish, the dish may be prepared to this stage and frozen. Thaw and reheat. Add almonds and serve. Yield: 18 servings.

QUICKIE TURKEY À LA KING

The beauty of this recipe for leftover turkey is that you can make it, bake it, and have it on the table in 20 minutes. Keep a supply of cooked frozen turkey or chicken on hand and unexpected company will never catch you unaware. Buy turkey when it is cheap, cook it and cut into bite-size pieces and freeze in packages of 1½ to 2 cups each. You may dump frozen meat directly into double boiler and this adds only 10 minutes more to cooking time of Turkey à la King.

1½ cups cooked turkey or chicken chunks
  1 (2-ounce) jar pimientos, drained
  1 (10¾-ounce) can condensed cream of
    mushroom soup
  ½ teaspoon dried green onion
  ¼ teaspoon paprika
  ¼ teaspoon monosodium glutamate
  ⅛ teaspoon freshly ground white pepper
  1 tablespoon chopped dried or frozen parsley
  1 (4-ounce) can button or sliced mushrooms
    (optional)
  2 tablespoons sherry
    Melba toast, corn bread squares, or
      toasted English muffins
    Paprika
    Fresh Parsley

Cut chicken or turkey into bite-size pieces; chop pimientos finely. Place all ingredients except sherry in top of double boiler; have water boiling briskly in the bottom. Cook 10 to 15 minutes; taste to see if salt is needed. Add sherry and remove from heat. Serve over melba toast, corn bread squares or toasted English muffins. Sprinkle a little more paprika over top of each serving and add a sprig of fresh parsley if available. Yield: 4 servings.

TO PREPARE WILD RABBIT FOR COOKING

Wear rubber gloves for cleaning game; animals sometimes have tularemia. For dressing, cut rabbit with a sharp knife from ribs to anus. Remove intestines and allow blood to drain. Remove head and wipe body cavity with clean paper towels or cloth. Leave animal in its skin and wrap in clean paper until you reach home. To remove skin, make a crosswise incision about 3 inches along the back. Gently pull skin from hind legs and from incision toward tail. Small game is best when left in refrigerator for several days before cooking. Or you may hang game for two days.

RABBIT STEW WITH DUMPLINGS

Simply delicious and easy to prepare. Commercially grown rabbits are available in many cities and are ideal for people who must watch their cholesterol.

1 (2½- to 3-pound) rabbit
1 tablespoon all-purpose flour
    Water to cover
1 tablespoon salt
9 black peppercorns
2 celery ribs with leaves
2 medium-size onions, finely sliced
3 tablespoons butter or corn oil
    Dumplings

It is necessary to parboil a wild rabbit for at least 45 minutes to an hour; cook with enough water to cover and with pot covered. Discard this water and cook as follows; cut down on cooking time, and test with fork tine for tenderness.

Clean and cut rabbit into serving-size pieces; sprinkle with flour and cover with water. Add remaining ingredients except butter. Bring to a simmering boil over medium heat, cover, and cook for 1 hour. Fork tine should go into leg easily. Add butter and drop in Dumplings. Yield: 6 servings.

Dumplings:

1 cup all-purpose flour, measured after sifting
2 teaspoons baking powder
½ teaspoon salt
1 egg
    Milk

Combine flour with baking powder and salt and sift three times into a large bowl. Break egg into measuring cup and add enough milk to make ½ cup. Pour into a small bowl and beat well. Add egg-milk mixture slowly into flour mixture. Add more milk if necessary, but keep batter as stiff as possible; beat well. Drop by teaspoonfuls into thin hot gravy. Cover and cook for 2 or 3 minutes, turning dumplings over. To avoid heavy dumplings, cover skillet with a glass pie plate to see how they are cooking without lifting lid. After turning dumplings, re-cover and cook 4 minutes longer. These dumplings are so light they are even good reheated at the next meal, but do not refrigerate.

RABBIT SMOTHERED WITH ONIONS

A great dish, easy to prepare, and low in cholesterol.

1 (2½- to 3-pound) rabbit
1 teaspoon salt
¼ teaspoon freshly ground black pepper
½ cup plus 1 tablespoon all-purpose flour, divided
¼ cup vegetable oil
1 cube instant beef bouillon
3 cups hot water, divided
2 medium-size onions, finely sliced
¼ teaspoon lemon bits or grated lemon rind

Clean and cut rabbit into serving-size pieces. Season with salt and pepper, and dredge in ½ cup flour. In a large heavy skillet brown rabbit in oil over high heat, adding several pieces at a time and cooking until they are lightly browned. Continue until all rabbit is cooked, adding more oil if necessary. Remove rabbit to a platter. Add remaining 1 tablespoon flour to hot grease and brown over medium heat. Dissolve beef bouillon cube in 1 cup boiling water and add to browned flour, stirring constantly with wire whisk until smooth. Add remaining 2 cups hot water and return rabbit to skillet; cover with sliced onion and lemon bits. Cover skillet and simmer for 1½ to 2 hours or until done; do not boil at any time. Fork tine should go into leg easily. Serve hot with cooked rice or noodles. Yield: 6 servings.

RABBIT FRICASSEE

This tasty rabbit stew is very easy to prepare and its meat lacks the fat found in chicken, making it a perfect dish for people watching their cholesterol count.

1 (2½- to 3-pound) rabbit
1 teaspoon salt
¼ teaspoon freshly ground black pepper
½ cup all-purpose flour
¼ cup vegetable oil
¼ cup chopped white or green onions
1 cube instant beef or chicken bouillon,
    dissolved in 1 cup boiling water
¼ teaspoon lemon bits
1 teaspoon dried parsley
1 teaspoon celery seeds
   Rabbit Gravy

Clean and cut rabbit into serving-size pieces. Season with salt and pepper and dredge in flour. Heat oil in a large heavy skillet over a high heat; add several pieces of rabbit and cook until lightly browned. Continue until all rabbit is browned, adding more oil if necessary. Remove rabbit from skillet to a platter and brown onions in same skillet. Return rabbit to skillet and add remaining ingredients. (In making the stock, use either the instant or packaged beef or chicken bouillon.) Cover skillet and simmer for 1½ to 2 hours or until tender; do not boil at any time. Fork tine should go into leg easily. Remove rabbit from skillet and pour off all but 2 tablespoons of the drippings for making gravy. Yield: 6 servings.

Rabbit Gravy:

2 tablespoons drippings from cooked rabbit
2 tablespoons all-purpose flour
1 cube instant beef or chicken bouillon
   dissolved in 1 cup boiling water
  Salt and pepper to taste
  A few drops of Maggi seasoning

In a heavy skillet heat drippings over medium heat and blend in flour with wire whisk, cooking slowly and stirring constantly. Add 1 cup hot stock made by dissolving instant beef or chicken bouillon cube or package in boiling water. Taste to see if salt and pepper is needed; add Maggi seasoning. Strain gravy, reheat, and serve with hot cooked rabbit.

LINDA LACEFIELD'S HONEYED DUCK

1 mallard duck
2⅛ teaspoons salt, divided
1 teaspoon ground ginger
1 teaspoon ground basil
½ teaspoon pepper
¾ cup honey
¼ cup butter
3 tablespoons orange juice
2 teaspoons lemon juice
1 teaspoon orange peel
⅛ teaspoon dry mustard
1 to 2 oranges
½ teaspoon cornstarch

Parboil duck in 1½ to 2 quarts boiling, salted water for ½ hour. Dry duck thoroughly inside and out. Combine 2 teaspoons salt with ginger, basil, and pepper. Rub half of this mixture inside of duck. Heat honey, butter, orange and lemon juices, orange peel, mustard, and remaining ⅛ teaspoon salt together until butter melts. Rub 2 to 3 tablespoons inside of duck. Slice unpeeled oranges ½ inch thick. Stuff duck with as many as possible. Pour 4 to 5 tablespoons more honey mixture into duck. Truss duck. Rub remaining seasoning mixture on outside of duck. Place bird on a large piece of heavy-duty aluminum foil. Pour remaining honey mixture over duck and wrap. Roast in a preheated 325° oven for 1¾ hours. Unwrap, baste, and bake 25 minutes longer until brown. Combine cornstarch with cold water and add to drippings to make brown gravy. Yield: 2 to 3 servings.

LINDA LACEFIELD'S APRICOT STUFFING FOR DUCK

5 cups crumbled corn bread
6 cups soft bread crumbs
2 tablespoons salt
½ teaspoon pepper
½ teaspoon sage
2 cups chopped, cooked, dried apricots
2 tablespoons chopped onion
⅔ cup butter, melted
¾ cup milk

Lightly toss together all ingredients except melted butter and milk. Sprinkle butter and milk over dry ingredients, tossing lightly until combined. (Add a few more tablespoons milk if you prefer a very moist dressing.) Stuff lightly into body cavity and neck region of each duck. Place any leftover dressing in a buttered 1-quart casserole and bake in a preheated 325° oven about 40 minutes. Roast ducks uncovered in a 325° oven for 20 to 25 minutes per pound. Baste frequently with small amounts of hot water and place 4 to 5 slices bacon across breast of duck to prevent drying. Yield: stuffing for 2 medium-size wild ducks.

SUSAN GREEN'S PHEASANT WITH WILD RICE

A superb creation! For an elegant meal serve this with a fresh fruit salad, asparagus or green beans with almonds, hot rolls or biscuits, and a light dessert such as ice cream and cookies.

The secret to tender pheasant is using a slow, low temperature. You never know whether you are cooking a young tender bird or an old tough one. By using this method the pheasant falls away from the bone and is not dry.

4 pheasants, picked and cleaned
2 teaspoons salt
½ teaspoon freshly ground black pepper
¼ teaspoon paprika
¼ teaspoon poultry seasoning
1 cup butter
1 (10¾-ounce) can chicken broth
3 (6-ounce) cans button mushrooms, drained and liquid reserved
1 (6-ounce) box wild rice

After birds are picked and cleaned, remove oil sac at base of tail. Cut breast fillets from pheasants, sever leg-thigh all in one piece. I discard the neck and back. Sprinkle both sides of cut pieces with salt, black pepper, paprika, and poultry seasoning. In a Dutch oven or heavy skillet brown in butter over medium heat until both sides are golden. Set browned pieces aside until all are cooked. Return to Dutch oven after all excess fat has been removed. Combine chicken broth and reserved mushroom liquid and pour 1 cup mixture over pheasant pieces. Cover and simmer over low heat for 2½ to 3 hours. Keep adding more liquid as necessary; *do not allow pheasant to dry out.* When ready to serve put pheasant in covered dish and place in a warm, not hot, oven. Add remaining bouillon-mushroom liquid and all mushrooms to Dutch oven. Turn heat to medium or medium high for 5 minutes or less. Add more salt, pepper, or poultry seasoning to taste. Cook wild rice according to package directions; then arrange rice on a warm serving platter. Pour ¾ to 1 cup liquid from Dutch oven over rice; then add pheasant pieces on top and circle with mushrooms. Add a bit more liquid over bird. Serve with remaining meat juices and cranberry sauce. Freeze uncooked pheasant in water to prevent drying. Yield: 8 servings.

DOVES THE EASY WAY

Here's a simple and delicious way to prepare doves.

12 medium-size doves, cleaned
½ teaspoon seasoned salt
½ teaspoon salt
¼ teaspoon freshly ground black pepper
1 cup water, divided
½ cup butter or margarine
2 tablespoons lemon juice

Do not wash birds unless necessary, and then very quickly. Wipe with a clean damp cloth or paper towels. Blend seasonings and sprinkle generously on each dove. Place doves in a large iron skillet; add ¼ cup water, cover tightly, and steam over medium heat for 20 minutes. Remove lid and allow doves to continue cooking until water disappears. Slice butter evenly into 12 pieces and place one on each bird; sprinkle with lemon juice. Turn doves to brown on both sides; when golden brown remove from skillet and place in a hot oblong casserole. Increase heat slightly under skillet, add remaining ¾ cup water and cook about 2 minutes longer. Pour gravy over doves, and keep warm until serving time. Serve with wild rice. Unless doves are very large, allow two per serving. Yield: 6 servings.

QUAIL BAKED IN VERMOUTH

Marvelous to the last bite.

8 plump quail, dressed and split down the
**   back**
1 teaspoon salt
¼ teaspoon freshly ground black pepper
1 cup butter, divided
3 tablespoons corn oil
3 tablespoons lemon juice
1 tablespoon Worcestershire sauce
½ cup dry vermouth
8 slices melba toast
Cooked wild rice

Salt and pepper quail. Heat 3 tablespoons butter and corn oil in a 12-inch iron skillet over high heat; brown quail quickly, turning from one side to the other. I find long-handled tongs do the best job. When birds are brown, remove skillet from heat, pour lemon juice, Worcestershire sauce, and vermouth over the sides of each bird. Melt remaining butter. Place quail breast side down in skillet and pour melted butter over all. Cover with foil and bake in a preheated 325° oven for 1 hour and 15 minutes. Test with fork in thick part of breast to be sure birds are tender. Remove to a heated platter and place on melba toast. Serve hot with cooked wild rice. Yield: 6 to 8 servings.

Salads and Salad Dressings

SEYMOUR GORDON'S AVOCADO-GRAPEFRUIT SALAD

2 large pink grapefruit
12 fresh strawberries
1 Jonathan apple
2 large ripe avocadoes
  Boston lettuce
  Fresh Strawberries (optional)
  Poppy-Seed Dressing

Peel and section grapefruit and place in a colander to drain. Wash and remove stems from strawberries, dry on paper towel, and slice in half. Do not peel apple; core and slice wafer-thin lengthwise. Cut avocadoes in half, remove seeds, slice in ½-inch lengthwise sections and peel.

Place alternating sections of fruit on nest of Boston lettuce, garnish with strawberries, if desired. Dribble Poppy-Seed Dressing over top and serve immediately. Yield: 6 servings.

Poppy-Seed Dressing:

1½ cups sugar
  2 teaspoons dry mustard
  2 teaspoons salt
⅔ cup white or wine vinegar
  3 tablespoons onion juice
  2 cups salad oil
  3 tablespoons poppy seeds

Mix sugar, mustard, salt, and vinegar in a deep narrow bowl. Add onion juice and stir. Slowly add oil, beating constantly until thickened. If using an electric mixer, place on medium speed. Stir in poppy seeds and store in refrigerator until ready to use. Stir well and allow to reach room temperature before serving. Yield: 3½ cups.

ZOLLIE KIMBROUGH'S MANDARIN SALAD

A marvelous salad to serve with any meat, particularly ham, lamb, and pork. A dieter's delight, it is easy to make and inexpensive for the number it serves.

2 tea bags
2 cups boiling water
1 (6-ounce) package orange flavored gelatin
2 (11-ounce) cans mandarin oranges
2 (8-ounce) cans crushed pineapple
½ (12-ounce) can water chestnuts
4 tablespoons fresh lemon juice

Steep tea bags in boiling water for 10 minutes. Dissolve gelatin in the hot tea. Cool gelatin-tea mixture in pan of ice for expediency. When cold, add mandarin oranges and juice, crushed pineapple and juice, water chestnuts which have been sliced very thinly and cut into pieces, and lemon juice. Lightly oil two 1-quart flat casseroles or two 1-quart molds and pour in ingredients. Refrigerate. This keeps beautifully and makes a nice supper dish with cottage cheese for the dieters. Yield: 14 to 16 servings.

MAUDE LANE'S BEST EVER SALAD

Delightful with chicken or ham, this makes a beautiful Saint Patrick's Day salad.

1 (3-ounce) package lime flavored gelatin
1 (3-ounce) package lemon flavored gelatin
2 cups boiling water
1 cup mayonnaise
1 cup small curd cottage cheese
3 tablespoons prepared horseradish
1 cup well-drained, crushed pineapple
½ cup sliced pecans

In a saucepan dissolve gelatins in boiling water, cool, and add remaining ingredients. With a little mayonnaise, oil eight 4-ounce molds or a glass oblong casserole. Chill until set. Unmold on lettuce and top with mayonnaise. Yield: 8 servings.

MANGO DELIGHT

Cool and smooth. A colorful dessert or salad for company or a party. This is delicious at the end of a heavy meal to replace sherbet. It is easy to make, inexpensive, and may be prepared the day before serving.

1 (30-ounce) can sliced mangoes in light syrup
2 envelopes (2 tablespoons) unflavored gelatin
½ cup cold water
2 cups boiling water
¼ cup sugar
¼ teaspoon salt
½ cup plus 1 tablespoon strained lemon juice
1 (8-ounce) package cream cheese, softened

Drain mangoes and reserve 1 cup juice. After soaking gelatin in cold water about 5 minutes, dissolve in boiling water. Add sugar and salt, and stir until dissolved. Add mango and lemon juices. When gelatin is cool, add mangoes and

mashed softened cream cheese. I place in blender for just a minute. This leaves the stringy part of the mango in very small pieces. Place in an oblong, 2½-quart casserole, individual molds, or two 8-inch ring molds lightly greased with vegetable oil or mayonnaise. Chill for 3 to 4 hours to set properly. To serve as a salad, place on a lettuce leaf and top with mayonnaise. As a dessert, slice and serve it as it is. Yield: 14 to 16 servings.

AVOCADO MOUSSE

Beautiful and luscious, a perfect luncheon dish. This is ideal to serve with a cold lamb roast or baked ham.

4 (3-ounce) packages cream cheese
1 cup commercial mayonnaise made with lemon juice
2 medium-size to large avocadoes
2 tablespoons key lime juice or 3 tablespoons Persian lime juice
2 envelopes (2 tablespoons) unflavored gelatin
¼ cup cold water
2 cups boiling water
1 small onion, grated or 1 teaspoon onion puree
¼ teaspoon dried green onion
1 (16-ounce) can grapefruit sections, drained
1½ cups finely chopped celery
¼ teaspoon paprika
1 teaspoon salt
1 teaspoon Worcestershire sauce
½ teaspoon Beau Monde Seasoning
1 rounded tablespoon capers
½ teaspoon Tabasco
1 pound cooked shrimp

Allow cream cheese to reach room temperature, then beat together with mayonnaise until smooth and fluffy, using electric mixer on medium speed. Peel and finely mash avocadoes; add to cream cheese along with lime juice. Soften gelatin in cold water and dissolve in boiling water; cool. To cream cheese mixture add grated onion, dried green onion, grapefruit sections cut in halves, chopped celery, paprika, salt, Worcestershire sauce, Beau Monde seasoning, capers, Tabasco, and cooked shrimp, deveined and cut into thirds.

When gelatin is cool but not jelled, gently stir into cream cheese mixture. Taste to see if more salt is needed. Grease two 9-inch ring molds or two 9- x 5- x 3-inch loaf pans with salad oil or mayonnaise. Pour in mixture; chill. This mousse keeps beautifully in refrigerator for 3 or 4 days. Yield: 12 to 14 servings.

FAIRY APRICOT SALAD

This is filling but is as light and airy as food for the fairies. The salad is delightful with ham or chicken fixed in any way your taste dictates.

  1 (16-ounce) can peeled whole apricots,
      drained and juice reserved
  1 (3-ounce) package orange flavored gelatin
  ½ (3-ounce) package (4 tablespoons) lemon
      flavored gelatin
  1 cup orange juice
  ½ cup cold water
  ⅛ teaspoon salt
  1 (8-ounce) package cream cheese

The drained juice should make 1 cup; if not, add water. Remove apricot seeds. Dissolve gelatins according to package directions, but use apricot juice instead of cold water. Add orange juice, cold water, and salt to gelatin mixture. Divide mixture, putting 1½ cups into cream cheese; beat smooth by hand or electric mixer. Pour gelatin-cream cheese mixture into bottom of 4-ounce molds or pyrex cups. Refrigerate until congealed, usually less than an hour.

Puree apricots through sieve or in blender, add to remaining 1½ cup gelatin-fruit mixture. Pour over congealed cream cheese. Chill until set. Remove from molds and serve on lettuce with a dollop of mayonnaise. Yield: 4 servings.

BECKY VOGHT'S APPLE-MINT COOLER

Colorful and tasty.

  1 (3-ounce) package lime flavored gelatin
  ½ cup boiling water
  ½ cup chopped nuts
  ¼ teaspoon peppermint flavoring
  1 (16-ounce) can unsweetened applesauce
  ¼ cup mayonnaise
  ¼ cup commercial sour cream

In a small saucepan dissolve lime flavored gelatin in boiling water. Stir until completely dissolved; refrigerate until thickened but not firm. Add chopped nuts, flavoring, and applesauce to gelatin mixture and mix well. Pour into four 4-ounce oiled molds and chill until set. Unmold and serve on lettuce leaf with blended mayonnaise and sour cream as a dressing. Yield: 4 servings.

POLYNESIAN SALAD

  1 (15¼-ounce) can chunk or crushed
      pineapple, drained and juice reserved
  ¼ pound cheddar or pasteurized process
      American cheese, shredded
  ⅓ cup plus 1 tablespoon sugar
      Scant ¼ cup all-purpose flour
  ⅜ cup reserved pineapple juice

Combine pineapple and shredded cheese, and spoon into a small casserole. Mix sugar, flour, and pineapple juice. Pour over pineapple in casserole. Bake in a preheated 350° oven about 20 minutes. Serve warm. Yield: 2 or 3 servings.

CARROT-APPLE SALAD

  6 carrots
  3 Golden Delicious apples
  ½ cup diced nuts
  1 cup diced celery
     Enough mayonnaise to blend

Peel carrots and apples and put through a meat grinder. In a large bowl blend with remaining ingredients. Yield: 4 to 6 servings.

SUE HOUGH'S ORANGE SHERBET SALAD

Refreshing!

  2 (3-ounce) packages orange flavored gelatin
  1 cup boiling water
  1 pint orange sherbet
  1 (8-ounce) can crushed pineapple
  1 cup miniature marshmallows
  1 (11-ounce) can mandarin orange sections, drained
  ½ pint whipping cream, whipped

In a medium-size saucepan dissolve gelatin in boiling water. Cool for a short while; then add sherbet while gelatin is still warm. Pour into a 2-quart oblong casserole. When mixture is partially set, add remaining ingredients, folding in whipped cream last. Chill until firm. Yield: about 12 servings.

FRESH ORANGE JUICE GELATIN SALAD

Soothing, refreshing, and healthful, this is great for a person with a cold, flu, or any kind of throat condition. It also makes a delightful dessert topped with sweetened whipped cream. Frozen orange juice made according to directions will do a good job, but fresh does the best.

  1 envelope (1 tablespoon) unflavored gelatin
  ½ cup cold orange juice
  ¼ cup sugar
  ⅛ teaspoon salt
  1 tablespoon strained lemon juice
1½ cups orange juice

Sprinkle gelatin over ½ cup cold orange juice in a small saucepan. Place over low heat, stirring constantly until gelatin dissolves, about 3 minutes. Remove from heat and add remaining ingredients; stir until sugar dissolves. Pour into 4 individual molds or a 2-cup glass bowl. Chill until firm. Yield: 4 servings.

BETTY PIPER'S FROSTED CRANBERRY MOLD

  1 envelope (1 tablespoon) unflavored gelatin
  ½ cup water
  ½ cup mayonnaise
  1 teaspoon grated lemon rind
  6 tablespoons water
  1 (16-ounce) can whole cranberry sauce
  1 cup chopped celery
  ½ cup chopped bell pepper

Soften gelatin in ½ cup water and heat in small pan until dissolved; remove from heat. Measure 2 tablespoons gelatin mixture and stir into mayonnaise, lemon rind, and 6 tablespoons water. Let mixture cool. Divide mayonnaise mixture evenly into eight 4-ounce molds. Chill 30 minutes or until thickened and sticky, but not firm. Break up cranberry sauce; then stir in celery, pepper, and remaining gelatin mixture. Spoon over sticky layer in the molds, dividing mixture evenly. Chill and serve on lettuce. The mayonnaise layer is the dressing. Yield: 8 servings.

PINEAPPLE CREAM CHEESE SALAD

A lovely salad for a buffet luncheon. Good with baked ham.

4 (3-ounce) packages cream cheese, softened
1 (29½-ounce) can sliced pineapple, drained
    and juice reserved
2 tablespoons cold water
1 envelope (1 tablespoon) unflavored gelatin
1 cup mayonnaise
1 cup chopped blanched almonds
¼ teaspoon dried green onion
½ teaspoon Worcestershire sauce
½ teaspoon salt
¾ teaspoon Beau Monde seasoning
3 dashes cayenne pepper
1 cup whipping cream, whipped

In a large mixing bowl beat cream cheese until light and fluffy. Cut pineapple into bite-size pieces. Dissolve gelatin in cold water. Heat pineapple juice in saucepan and add dissolved gelatin to it; cool. Add mayonnaise to cream cheese along with pineapple juice and gelatin mixture. Add almonds and seasonings. Fold in whipped cream. Lightly grease 2 large oblong casseroles with mayonnaise and spoon mixture into them. Chill until set, cut into slices, and serve. Yield: 20 to 22 servings.

GRAPEFRUIT WEDGE SALAD

Attractive and tasty.

3 large grapefruits
1 (3-ounce) package lemon flavored gelatin
1 cup strained apricots (baby food)
1 cup chopped pecans
    Honey Lime Dressing

Cut grapefruits into halves. Remove pulp and cut enough sections to make 1 cup. Squeeze enough juice to make 2 cups, adding water if necessary. Heat grapefruit juice and dissolve lemon gelatin in it; cool. Add apricots and pecans to grapefruit pieces and mix into cooled gelatin. Pour into empty grapefruit halves and place in refrigerator to set. Serve as they are, or cut each half into two wedges. Top with Honey Lime Dressing. Yield: 6 to 12 servings.

Honey Lime Dressing:

½ cup whipping cream, whipped
¼ cup honey
½ cup mayonnaise
2 tablespoons lime juice

Fold cream and honey into mayonnaise. Add lime juice and mix gently but thoroughly. Pour over grapefruit wedges.

MARJORIE DRAKE'S CRANBERRY SALAD

A festive salad for a holiday meal.

1 pound cranberries
2 cups sugar
3 envelopes (3 tablespoons) unflavored
    gelatin
¼ cup cold water
2 (8-ounce) cans crushed pineapple, drained
    and juice reserved
1 cup boiling water
1 (3-ounce) package raspberry flavored
    gelatin
1 cup finely chopped nuts

Wash and drain cranberries; grind berries in a large glass or enamel bowl; cover with sugar, and let stand overnight. Soak unflavored gelatin in cold water for 5 minutes. In saucepan heat pineapple juice, add boiling water and dissolved gelatin along with raspberry gelatin, stirring constantly until dissolved. Add cranberries with juice, crushed pineapple, and nuts to gelatin mixture. Rinse twelve 4-ounce molds in cold water before filling them. Yield: 12 servings.

TART THREE FRUIT SALAD

A lovely salad to serve with cold sliced chicken, lamb, or ham.

1 (11-ounce) can mandarin oranges, drained
1 (16-ounce) can grapefruit segments, drained
1 (3-ounce) package lemon flavored gelatin
2 cups golden sweet ginger ale, divided
1 medium-size avocado, peeled and sliced

Cut fruit into small pieces. Dissolve gelatin in 1 cup hot ginger ale. Add 1 cup cold ginger ale. Pour a thin layer of gelatin into a 1-quart mold which has been lightly greased with vegetable oil or mayonnaise. Chill until firm. When firm, arrange fruit and avocado in a decorative pattern, add a little more gelatin, and chill until firm. When remaining gelatin thickens, add remaining fruit and avocado. Chill until firm. Unmold and serve on salad greens with mayonnaise. Yield: 6 to 8 servings.

PICKLED PEACH SALAD

A marvelous accompaniment for lamb or chicken.

½ cup sugar
½ cup light corn syrup
2 tablespoons cider vinegar
1 cup water
2 whole cloves
1 envelope (1 tablespoon) unflavored gelatin
½ cup cold water
2 cups sliced peaches, drained

In a saucepan bring sugar, corn syrup, vinegar, 1 cup water, and cloves to a boil over high heat; then lower heat and simmer 20 minutes. Dissolve gelatin in ½ cup cold water. Remove cloves from syrup mixture and add gelatin; stir until dissolved. Add peaches. Spoon into 4-ounce oiled molds; dividing fruit evenly. Refrigerate until set. Unmold and serve on lettuce leaf. Yield: 4 servings.

COLESLAW WITH COOKED DRESSING

This tasty dish comes from the lovely old town of Tarboro, North Carolina. Served with barbecue or Brunswick stew, it is a combination hard to beat and ideal for picnics or church suppers.

1 (7-inch diameter) head green cabbage
    (about 8 cups shredded)
1 large onion
1 bell pepper
1 cup sugar
1 cup cider vinegar
¾ cup olive or salad oil
1 teaspoon prepared mustard
1 teaspoon celery seeds
1 teaspoon salt

Finely shred cabbage, onion, and bell pepper into a large glass or stainless steel bowl. Sprinkle with sugar; do not stir. Blend remaining ingredients in a saucepan and bring to a boil; pour over cabbage, do not stir. Refrigerate overnight. This will keep for a week or more if refrigerated. Yield: 16 (½-cup) servings.

QUILTER'S POTATO SALAD

Try quilter's choice for a picnic lunch or a family supper on the patio.

2½ pounds red potatoes
 ⅓ cup chopped green onions or an equal
    amount of white onions
 ½ cup chopped celery
1½ teaspoons salt
 4 hard-boiled eggs, finely chopped
 ¼ teaspoon paprika
 ¼ cup cider vinegar
 ⅓ cup vegetable oil
 ¼ teaspoon Tabasco sauce
 ½ cup homemade mayonnaise
 ⅓ cup chopped sweet pickle
 4 tablespoons chopped parsley

Wash potatoes and boil in their jackets in a covered saucepan until tender. Set aside to cool. When the potatoes are cool, peel, cube, and add onion, celery, salt, eggs, and paprika. Blend vinegar, oil, and Tabasco, and pour over potato mixture. Toss lightly with a fork, making sure the dressing coats the whole salad. Let cool completely and stand for about an hour. Add mayonnaise, pickle, and chopped parsley; toss well. Refrigerate until ready to serve. Yield: 12 servings.

DELICIOUS TOMATO ASPIC

A highly seasoned salad marvelous with seafood or any full-bodied meat such as lamb, pork, or ham.

3 cups tomato juice
2 envelopes (2 tablespoons) unflavored
    gelatin
¼ cup cold water
1 teaspoon salt
1 teaspoon sugar
½ teaspoon dried green onion
½ teaspoon dried parsley
2 teaspoons Worcestershire sauce
1 tablespoon onion juice or 1 teaspoon onion
    puree
4 drops Tabasco
2 teaspoons lemon juice
1 tablespoon prepared horseradish
½ cup finely chopped celery
½ cup sliced stuffed olives
1 avocado, cut into chunks, or 1 (14-ounce)
    can artichoke hearts, drained and washed

Lightly wipe an oblong or square 2-quart baking dish with vegetable oil or mayonnaise. Heat tomato juice in a saucepan until it begins to boil. Dissolve gelatin in cold water and add to tomato juice with salt, sugar, dried green onion, and parsley. Allow mixture to cool and add Worcestershire sauce, onion juice, Tabasco, lemon juice, and horseradish. Taste to see if more salt is needed. Add celery, olives, and avocado chunks. Spoon mixture into baking dish and chill. Yield: 8 servings.

Variations: For extra special company, use both avocado chunks and artichoke hearts. One 4-ounce can button mushrooms is excellent used alone or with avocado or artichoke hearts. If using the artichoke hearts or mushrooms, marinate overnight in a good French dressing for a gourmet touch, if desired.

Also, you may use this as a main dish for a luncheon or for a cold supper by adding 2 cups cooked shrimp. Cut each shrimp into three pieces.

Another attractive way to serve this is to omit avocado and artichoke hearts and to add 2-inch wedges of cream cheese to aspic when it is cold but not congealed.

To make 12 servings of tomato aspic, use the following ingredients, with the above method:

4 cups tomato juice
2 envelopes (2 tablespoons) unflavored
    gelatin
¼ cup cold water
1 teaspoon salt
1 teaspoon sugar
1 teaspoon dried green onion
1 teaspoon dried parsley
1 tablespoon Worcestershire sauce
1 tablespoon onion juice or 1 teaspoon onion
    puree
5 drops Tabasco
1 tablespoon lemon juice
1 tablespoon prepared horseradish
¾ cup finely chopped celery
¾ cup sliced stuffed olives
1 avocado, cut into chunks, or 1 (14-ounce)
    can artichoke hearts, drained and washed

MRS. SAM HOUSTON'S MOLDED TOMATO SALAD

A different taste delight, serve this with chicken or ham for a great combination.

1 (3-ounce) package raspberry flavored gelatin
⅓ cup boiling water
1 (16-ounce) can stewed tomatoes
Salt to taste
⅛ teaspoon Tabasco for zest, ¼ teaspoon for more zest
3 tablespoons mayonnaise made with lemon juice
1 cup commercial sour cream

In a saucepan dissolve gelatin in boiling water. Puree tomatoes in blender or put through a sieve. Add tomatoes to gelatin mixture; salt to taste. Stir in Tabasco. Oil four 6-ounce molds with a little mayonnaise and pour in mixture. Chill until set. Unmold on fresh lettuce leaves. Blend sour cream with mayonnaise and spoon over top of each mold. Yield: 4 (6-ounce) servings.

SALAD NIÇOISE

6 medium-size potatoes
1 (16-ounce) can French-style green beans, drained
2 (4½-ounce) cans French tuna fillets
⅓ cup French virgin olive oil
⅓ cup white wine vinegar
1 teaspoon salt
¼ teaspoon white pepper
2 teaspoons Dijon mustard
Romaine lettuce leaves
2 tomatoes, sliced
Black olives
Capers
Tarragon leaves (optional)

Wash potatoes, cover with water in a saucepan and boil in their jackets over high heat until done. When a fork tine goes in easily they are ready. Peel and slice ¼ inch thick. Mix potatoes with green beans. Drain tuna fillets, reserving juice and 8 fillets for garnish. Mix fillets with potatoes.

To make salad dressing, combine fillet juice with olive oil, vinegar, salt, pepper, and mustard. Pour dressing over salad and toss lightly until well blended. On a salad plate arrange a circle of romaine lettuce leaves. Make a mound of the salad on the leaves. Garnish top of salad with reserved tuna fillets. Put half tomato slices around bottom of salad. Top with black olives. Put a few capers on top of salad and garnish with sprig of fresh tarragon, if desired. Yield: 6 to 8 servings.

MARGARET GUNN'S VEGETABLE MOUSSE

Serve this marvelous sweet and sour medley with smoked ham, lamb, or turkey. Good with crabmeat or shrimp dishes, it makes a colorful holiday accompaniment and substitutes for a cooked vegetable.

1½ envelopes (1½ tablespoons) unflavored gelatin
½ cup cold water
½ cup boiling water
2 teaspoons salt
½ cup sugar
½ cup white or rice vinegar
2 tablespoons strained lemon juice
1 (14-ounce) can artichoke hearts
2 (10½-ounce) cans tender cut green asparagus tips
½ (12-ounce) can water chestnuts, drained
2 tablespoons diced pimientos

Grease a ring mold, an oblong casserole, or individual molds with vegetable oil. Soak gelatin in cold water, add to boiling water and stir until dissolved. Add salt, sugar, vinegar, and lemon juice. Cut artichoke hearts in half and arrange in bottom of mold or casserole; cover with a little gelatin mixture. When it begins to thicken, add asparagus, a layer of water chestnuts, diced pimientos, and remaining gelatin. Chill until set. Serve on lettuce and top with a dollop of mayonnaise and a dash of paprika. Yield: 10 servings.

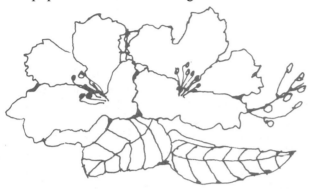

SALADE SUPREME

Savor the taste of fresh tender mushrooms on a bed of escarole lying between hearts of artichoke and palm. Garnish with sliced ripe olives and a strip of pimiento and dress with seasoned oil and vinegar. A dieter's treat or, when served with hot French bread and a dessert, this salad completes a very satisfying meal.

½ head escarole
6 medium-size fresh white mushrooms
1 (14-ounce) can artichoke hearts, drained
1 (14-ounce) can hearts of palm, drained
⅓ cup red wine vinegar
⅔ cup virgin olive oil
¼ teaspoon salt
6 pitted ripe olives, sliced
1 strip pimiento
⅛ teaspoon freshly ground black pepper

Wash escarole leaves separately and toss in clean kitchen towel; dry on paper towel or whirl dry in wire salad basket. Rinse mushrooms under cool running water and dry on paper towels. Rinse hearts of artichoke and palm. Place vinegar, olive oil, and salt in a screw-top jar and shake vigorously for a minute to blend thoroughly.

On a large, flat salad plate arrange several escarole leaves down the center. Slice mushrooms thinly lengthwise and place on top. On one side place three artichoke hearts and on other side two hearts of palm, garnish with several ripe olive slices and complete with pimiento strip across center of mushrooms. Keep chilled in refrigerator until serving time. Grind black pepper over top and douse generously with oil and vinegar dressing. Yield: 4 servings.

PINK VEGETABLE SALAD

Appealing to eye, this congealed cream cheese salad is easy to make and will keep refrigerated for days. Delicious with baked ham. This will make a party entrée with shrimp or crabmeat added.

2 envelopes (2 tablespoons) unflavored gelatin
½ cup cold water
1 (10¾-ounce) can tomato soup
3 (3-ounce) packages cream cheese, softened and thoroughly mashed
1 cup finely chopped celery
1 cup finely chopped bell pepper
1 cup mayonnaise
1 teaspoon grated onion or onion puree

Dissolve gelatin in cold water. Bring tomato soup to a boil in a saucepan and add gelatin. Allow mixture to cool. Test with a drop on the inside of the wrist; when it is barely warm, add mashed cream cheese. Blend well and add celery, bell pepper, mayonnaise, and onion. Taste to see if salt is needed. Yield: 12 to 14 servings.

Variation: To make a party entrée, add ½ pound cooked shrimp, each sliced into 3 pieces or ½ pound fresh or canned Japanese crabmeat. Add shrimp or crabmeat last.

245

ARTICHOKE ASPIC

A gourmet delicacy, this is marvelous with lamb. There are two easy steps.

Step 1:

3 artichokes
3 tablespoons salt
1 lemon, sliced
1 tablespoon vegetable or olive oil
2 celery ribs with leaves or 1 teaspoon celery seeds
1 teaspoon instant crab and shrimp boil
1 tablespoon Worcestershire sauce
1 bay leaf
1 tablespoon dried parsley

Cut off artichoke stems and soak artichokes in enough cold water to cover for 30 minutes; drain. In a large soup kettle or Dutch oven, cover artichokes with fresh water. Add remaining ingredients and bring to a boil over a high heat. Boil for 45 minutes to 1 hour depending on size of artichokes. Drain and cool. Scrape the soft edible part from each leaf onto a plate. Remove the chokes and hearts. Mash the meat from leaves and hearts well.

Step 2:

1 envelope (1 tablespoon) unflavored gelatin
½ cup cold water
1 (10½-ounce) can consommé or same amount beef broth, divided
¼ teaspoon Tabasco
1 tablespoon Worcestershire sauce
2 tablespoons plus 1 teaspoon lemon juice
⅛ teaspoon cayenne pepper
Salt to taste
1 tablespoon grated onion or onion puree
¼ pound cooked shrimp, diced

Dissolve gelatin in cold water for 5 minutes. Heat half of consommé or beef broth. Add gelatin and remaining consommé, Tabasco, Worcestershire sauce, lemon juice, cayenne pepper, and salt; cool. Oil a ring mold. Combine artichoke mixture from Step 1, grated onion, and diced shrimp. Pour into an 8½-inch mold and chill. Serve with mayonnaise. Yield: 8 servings.

JOANNE BELLENGER'S ORIENTAL SALAD

1 (10½-ounce) package frozen English peas
½ cup plus 2 teaspoons quick-cooking rice
2½ pounds cooked peeled shrimp
1½ cups diced celery
¼ cup chopped onion
½ pound fresh mushrooms, washed and sliced
1 tablespoon soy sauce
1 teaspoon sugar
2 teaspoons curry powder
¼ cup sliced almonds
½ teaspoon celery seeds
½ cup salad oil
3 tablespoons cider vinegar
½ teaspoon monosodium glutamate
1 (14-ounce) can artichoke hearts, drained
6 cocktail tomatoes, washed

Cook English peas and rice in separate pans according to package directions; drain. In a large glass or enamel bowl mix English peas, shrimp, rice, celery, onion, and mushrooms. In another bowl combine soy sauce, sugar, curry powder, almonds, celery seeds, salad oil, cider vinegar, and monosodium glutamate and pour over other ingredients. Chill overnight. Serve salad surrounded by artichoke hearts and cocktail tomatoes. Yield: 10 to 12 servings.

Family reunions are always happy occasions, especially if the table is piled high with favorite, home-cooked foods. Winifred's Golden Fried Chicken recipe is on page 227, her Plantation Pecan Pie on page 212, and her delicious baked beans are on page 91.

CUCUMBER ASPIC

A delightful treat with cold meat.

2 envelopes (2 tablespoons) unflavored
   gelatin
½ cup cold water
2 cups boiling water
4 small cucumbers, washed and ground
1 small onion, peeled and ground
½ cup cider vinegar
⅛ teaspoon pepper
¼ teaspoon sugar
   Salt to taste

Soak gelatin in cold water; then dissolve in boiling water in a saucepan. Cool slightly and add remaining ingredients. Rinse eight 4-ounce molds in cold water and fill with aspic. Refrigerate until set. Serve on lettuce with a dollop of mayonnaise. Yield: 8 servings.

LILLIAN DUKE'S FROZEN TOMATO SALAD

Tasty and economical, it's a perfect salad to serve for a bridge luncheon or patio meal for the family. Corned beef, baked ham, lamb roast, barbecued beef, or chicken make an ideal accompaniment.

3 (8-ounce) cans tomato sauce
1 cup mayonnaise made with lemon juice
3 tablespoons strained lemon juice
4 drops Tabasco (optional)
1 tablespoon grated onion
1 tablespoon celery seeds
   Salt to taste

Dress up an otherwise ordinary meal by serving fluffy hot rice. A scrumptious recipe for baked eggplant with shrimp is located on page 97 in the Casseroles chapter.

Mix all ingredients with electric beater or wire whisk and pour into an oiled 9- x 5- x 3-inch pan or a 9-inch square pan. Freeze. This will keep in the freezer for a month. When ready to serve, remove from freezer and cut into servings; place on lettuce leaves and top with mayonnaise. Yield: 6 to 8 servings.

FRESH VEGETABLE SANDWICH

Zesty with the crunchy flavor of celery, cucumber, bell pepper, red onion, and tart tomato. This may be cut in slices that exactly fit between two slices of bread or cut in bite-size pieces for a marvelous hors d'oeuvre. It makes a delicious salad served alone or on lettuce.

1 medium-size bell pepper
1 (4- to 5-inch) cucumber
2 medium-size tomatoes
¾ cup (1 medium-size) finely chopped red
   onion
1 cup finely chopped celery
1½ teaspoons unflavored gelatin
2 tablespoons cold water
2 tablespoons boiling water
2 cups commercial mayonnaise
1 teaspoon salt
¼ teaspoon Tabasco
1 tablespoon lemon juice

Wash bell pepper, remove seeds and hard white fiber, and chop finely. Wash cucumber and chop finely; wash tomatoes, remove stem ends and cut into 1-inch pieces. Add onion and celery to vegetables. Dissolve gelatin in cold water, then add boiling water and allow to cool. Combine mixture with mayonnaise in a large bowl; mix well. Add salt, Tabasco, lemon juice and vegetables. Pour into a 9- x 5- x 3-inch oblong casserole. Chill until set, about 2 hours. There is nothing to spoil and could be used easily in a lunchbox for husband or child. Yield: 8 servings.

SPRINGTIME VEGETABLE SALAD

A beautiful congealed vegetable salad with a tangy flavor and low in calories. This makes a colorful luncheon dish.

> 4 envelopes (4 tablespoons) unflavored gelatin
> 1 cup cold water
> 1 quart boiling water
> 1 cup white vinegar
> 2 teaspoons salt
> 4½ tablespoons lemon juice
> ¼ cup sugar
> 4 cups finely chopped celery
> 1 (2-ounce) jar sliced pimientos, finely cut
> 4 shallots or spring onions, minced
> 2 (10½-ounce) cans green asparagus tips
> ½ (8-ounce) can water chestnuts, finely sliced, or ½ cup finely sliced pecans

Grease a very large shallow pan with mayonnaise or vegetable oil. Soak gelatin in cold water until dissolved. Add boiling water, vinegar, salt, lemon juice, and sugar; stir well. When mixture is cool, add celery, pimientos, and minced shallots. If pecans are used, add with the celery, etc. Arrange asparagus in bottom of pan and pour mixture over all. Space the sliced water chestnuts on top. Refrigerate until congealed. Cut into oblong servings and place on lettuce leaves with French dressing. Yield: 16 servings.

SPINACH-COTTAGE CHEESE MOUSSE

Zesty and lovely to look at, this dish is ideal for a luncheon or buffet supper with cold sliced lamb, ham, or pork. It is filling for a complete luncheon when served with a hot corn pudding or baked stuffed tomatoes, hot rolls or biscuits, and dessert.

> 1 (10-ounce) package frozen chopped spinach
> 1 envelope (1 tablespoon) unflavored gelatin
> ½ cup cold water
> 2 teaspoons sugar
> ½ teaspoon salt
> ⅓ cup strained lemon juice
> ½ cup finely chopped celery
> ½ cup finely chopped onion
> ½ cup mayonnaise
> 1 (12-ounce) carton small curd cottage cheese
> ½ teaspoon Tabasco
> 1 teaspoon Worcestershire sauce
>   Salt to taste

Thaw spinach; drain and chop finely. Sprinkle gelatin over cold water in small saucepan; heat over low heat, stirring constantly, until gelatin dissolves. Add sugar and salt and stir until completely dissolved. Remove from heat. Place lemon juice in ½ cup measure and add enough water to fill cup. Add to gelatin mixture and stir in remaining ingredients. Taste to see if more salt is needed. Chill until firm. Refrigerated this will keep for a week. Yield: 8 servings.

ASPARAGUS VINAIGRETTE

This is excellent served as a vegetable or salad.

> 6 tablespoons olive oil
> 1 teaspoon dry mustard
> 1 teaspoon parsley flakes
> 1 teaspoon chopped chives, fresh or frozen
> 1 teaspoon chopped capers
> 1 hard-boiled egg, finely chopped
> 3 tablespoons wine vinegar
> ½ teaspoon freshly ground black pepper
> ½ teaspoon tarragon leaves
> 1 teaspoon garlic salt
> 1 cup water
> 2½ pounds fresh asparagus or 2 (12-ounce) packages frozen asparagus
> ¼ teaspoon lemon bits or grated lemon rind
> ½ teaspoon salt

Combine all ingredients except asparagus, lemon bits, and salt in a bowl and chill for at least 1 hour. This allows flavors to blend properly. Cook asparagus in boiling water. Use 1 cup water to ¼ teaspoon lemon bits, and ½ teaspoon salt. Cook until just tender, about 10 minutes. Drain and chill. A half hour before serving, pour vinaigrette sauce over asparagus and chill until served. Yield: 8 to 10 servings.

FAMOUS CRABMEAT SALAD OF MRS. HUGH WHITE

Mrs. White, one of Mississippi's former first ladies, was a gracious hostess and often served her own creations at elegant state dinners. The historical governor's mansion carries the mark of her valuable assistance in its restoration. You will enjoy this zesty and colorful sample from her marvelous collection of recipes.

3 envelopes (3 tablespoons) unflavored gelatin
½ cup cold water
2 cups boiling water
1 (16-ounce) can crabmeat, Japanese or Alaskan, or 2½ cups fresh crabmeat
⅓ cup sweet pickle, finely chopped
1 cup celery, finely chopped
2 hard-boiled eggs, chopped
½ cup chili sauce
3 tablespoons lemon juice
1 teaspoon salt
3 tablespoons pimientos, chopped

After soaking gelatin in cold water, dissolve in boiling water and allow to cool. Fold in remaining ingredients and pour into an 11- x 5- x 3-inch oblong casserole lightly greased with vegetable oil. Chill; cut into squares and serve with homemade mayonnaise on bibb or romaine lettuce. Yield: 10 servings if used as an entrée, 12 servings if used as a salad.

CRABMEAT LOUIS

A light and tasty salad for a summer luncheon or supper.

1 pound lump or white crabmeat
1 cup homemade mayonnaise or commercial mayonnaise with an extra tablespoon of lemon juice
1 tablespoon lemon juice
1 tablespoon finely chopped chives
1 tablespoon finely chopped green onion
1 tablespoon minced green pepper
1 teaspoon chow chow pickle
½ cup chili sauce
¼ teaspoon Tabasco
1 teaspoon Worcestershire sauce
⅛ teaspoon cayenne pepper
Salt to taste
Tomato
Lettuce
Hard-boiled egg, finely grated
½ cup whipping cream, whipped (optional)

Wash hands and pick through the crabmeat, removing any bits of shell. Make sauce ahead of time and chill to allow the seasonings to meld properly. In a large bowl combine mayonnaise, lemon juice, chives, onion, green pepper, pickle, chili sauce, Tabasco, Worcestershire sauce, cayenne pepper, and salt. Place a sliced or quartered tomato on a bed of lettuce and mound with a nice serving of crabmeat. Spread generously with the Louis dressing and add finely grated hard-boiled egg over top of each. For the ultimate taste touch, just before serving fold ½ cup whipped cream into dressing. Yield: 6 servings.

FROZEN CHICKEN SALAD

Delicious summertime treat for family or party fare.

 2 cups diced cooked chicken
¾ cup drained crushed pineapple
½ cup broken pecans, almonds or walnuts
 1 cup whipping cream
 1 cup mayonnaise

In a large mixing bowl, toss together chicken, pineapple, and nuts. Whip cream and fold in mayonnaise. Fold into chicken mixture. Pour into a 4-cup ring mold or a medium-size loaf pan lightly greased with a little mayonnaise. Freeze at least 3 hours. Unmold about 30 minutes before serving and keep in refrigerator. Slice and serve on lettuce with cheese straws or biscuits. Yield: 8 to 10 servings.

SUMMERTIME CHICKEN MOUSSE

Take the heat off the cook and prepare this tempting main dish. Make in the morning or even the day before. With either spiced peaches or quartered tomatoes and hot biscuits, this is fine for a party luncheon or as supper for guests. Corn on the cob or a corn pudding complete a delicious meal.

Step 1:

1 (2½- to 3-pound) fryer
  Water to cover
1 teaspoon Mei-yen powder
1 celery rib
1 teaspoon chopped dried green onion
1 teaspoon salt

Cover chicken with water in a medium-size kettle and add remaining ingredients. Cook until tender. Test with fork in thigh of chicken. The tines should go in easily. Do not overcook. Cool and reserve broth. Cut chicken into very small pieces, but do not mince. Yield: About 2 cups.

Step 2:

 1 envelope (1 tablespoon) unflavored gelatin
¼ cup cold water
1½ cups boiling chicken stock
¼ cup chopped celery
¼ cup chopped sweet pickle
½ teaspoon Mei-yen powder
 1 teaspoon Worcestershire sauce
¼ teaspoon paprika
 1 tablespoon lemon juice
⅛ teaspoon ground nutmeg
¼ teaspoon freshly ground black pepper
½ tablespoon grated onion or commercial
    puree
½ teaspoon salt
 2 cups cut up chicken
½ cup mayonnaise

Dissolve gelatin in cold water, then add to boiling chicken stock and stir well. Add remaining ingredients except mayonnaise. Taste to see if more salt is needed. Allow mixture to cool and add mayonnaise. Pour into a 9- x 5- x 3-inch loaf pan greased with a little of the mayonnaise. Chill; the mousse sets very quickly, 45 minutes to 1 hour. Unmold on a bed of garden lettuce. Top with a dollop of mayonnaise and sprinkle lightly with paprika. Mousse slices nicely. The recipe is easily doubled. Yield: 6 servings.

PARTY CHICKEN SALAD

A congealed chicken salad, easy to prepare, boasts a lot of zing. A sharp pair of kitchen scissors comes in handy because a lot of cutting is required. Recipe may be made in two parts: cook the chicken and cut celery one day, and mix ingredients the next. Fine for a party luncheon or supper for guests. Serve with either spiced peaches or quartered tomatoes and hot biscuits. For dessert serve half a cantaloupe with orange sherbet and a sprig of mint.

Step 1:

3 chicken bouillon cubes
3 cups boiling water
1 (6-pound) hen or 3 pounds chicken breasts
2 whole green onions or 1 large white onion
1 teaspoon salt
¼ teaspoon lemon pepper marinade
1 tablespoon dried parsley
 Juice of ½ lemon and rind
2 celery ribs with leaves
6 peppercorns

Dissolve bouillon cubes in boiling water. Place hen in Dutch oven or heavy soup kettle with dissolved chicken bouillon and remaining ingredients. Add enough water to cover chicken. Bring to a boil and simmer for 45 minutes to 1 hour. Test with fork for doneness. Remove from stove and allow hen to cool in broth. Yield: About 7 cups finely diced chicken.

Step 2:

 2 envelopes (2 tablespoons) unflavored
 gelatin
½ cup water
 2 cups hot chicken broth
 7 cups finely diced chicken
1½ cups celery hearts, finely chopped
 1 cup tiny sweet peas
½ cup slivered almonds or thinly sliced water
 chestnuts
 2 tablespoons strained lemon juice
¾ teaspoon Tabasco
⅛ teaspoon ground nutmeg
¼ teaspoon paprika
 1 teaspoon Worcestershire sauce
½ teaspoon Beau Monde seasoning
 1 teaspoon onion puree
 2 cups mayonnaise made with lemon juice
 4 hard-boiled eggs, sliced or diced

Dissolve gelatin in water and add to hot broth; cool. Add remaining ingredients. With a little mayonnaise lightly grease a 13- x 9- x 2-inch glass or stainless steel pan or two medium-size pans. Pour in the mixture; chill. It will set in an hour's time. Yield: 14 to 16 servings.

EXOTIC TURKEY SALAD

Almonds are the toast of an exotic turkey salad. If accompanied by a cheese soufflé and hot rolls, it is a delightful repast. You'll need a (4- to 6-pound) cooked turkey breast.

2 quarts coarsely cut cooked turkey
1 pound fresh seedless grapes or 1 (16-ounce)
 can seedless grapes, drained
2 (12-ounce) cans water chestnuts, drained
2 cups finely chopped celery
3 cups toasted slivered almonds, divided
3 cups mayonnaise
2 tablespoons lemon juice
1 tablespoon curry powder
2 tablespoons soy sauce
1 (20-ounce) can pineapple chunks

Cut cooked turkey into bite-size pieces. Wash grapes and dry on paper towel. Dice water chestnuts and mix with turkey. Add celery, grapes, and 2 cups toasted almonds to turkey mixture. Blend mayonnaise with lemon juice, curry powder, and soy sauce. Combine with turkey mixture. Chill for several hours in large glass or stainless steel bowl. Place a generous serving on a crisp lettuce leaf, sprinkle each mound with remaining almonds and garnish with pineapple chunks. Yield: 12 servings.

MY CHICKEN SALAD

Perfect for a luncheon or buffet supper. Serve salad in a large, chilled, ripe tomato or on a lettuce leaf.

1 (4-pound) hen or stewing chicken
1 small onion, chopped
1 chicken bouillon cube
3 celery ribs with leaves
1 teaspoon salt
1 teaspoon Mei-yen powder
1 teaspoon black pepper
2 tablespoons lemon juice
5 tender celery hearts, finely chopped
¾ to 1 cup mayonnaise made with lemon juice
    Dash Cayenne pepper
    Dash ground nutmeg
    Salt to taste
    Paprika

In a large saucepan cover chicken with water seasoned with onion, dissolved bouillon, celery ribs, salt, Mei-yen powder, and black pepper; bring to a boil over high heat. Lower heat, cover, and allow chicken to simmer for 1½ to 2 hours or until done. Test with fork in thick part of thigh. Cool, remove skin and bones from chicken; cut meat into very small pieces. (I use scissors.) Place chicken in a large mixing bowl and pour lemon juice over all, toss with spoon to be sure lemon juice is evenly distributed. Add chopped celery and enough mayonnaise to bind mixture together. (Use more than 1 cup if needed.) Add seasonings, mix well, and refrigerate until serving. Garnish each serving with paprika. Yield: 14 to 16 servings.

Note: Salad will serve more if served in tomatoes.

WINIFRED'S SALAD DRESSING

This sauce has a superb flavor—ideal for whole peeled tomatoes, shrimp, boiled or poached fish, or crabmeat. Pour over broccoli, cauliflower, or artichoke hearts. The sauce will keep for at least three weeks in the refrigerator.

1 cup commercial sour cream
1 cup mayonnaise
3 tablespoons Persian lime juice or 2
    tablespoons key lime juice
¼ teaspoon Mei-yen powder
¼ teaspoon dried green onion
3 tablespoons any good creamy commercial
    roquefort or blue cheese dressing
¼ teaspoon salt
¼ teaspoon paprika
¼ teaspoon Tabasco
½ teaspoon onion puree or 1 teaspoon grated
    onion

Blend sour cream and mayonnaise in a large bowl. Add remaining ingredients and mix well with a spatula. Pour into a glass jar with a tight-fitting lid; refrigerate. Yield: about 2 cups.

MARIE ELLIOT'S SHRIMP DRESSING

Use over tomato aspic for a gourmet treat.

½ pound boiled shrimp
1 clove garlic
1 pint commercial sour cream
½ cup catsup
2 tablespoons Worcestershire sauce
1½ tablespoons grated onion
1 teaspoon salt
2 tablespoons prepared horseradish
1 tablespoon lemon juice
1 teaspoon paprika
¼ teaspoon dry mustard

Cut each shrimp into two or three pieces; leave small shrimp whole. Rub a small bowl with garlic and discard clove. Add remaining ingredients except shrimp; stir and blend well but do not beat. Add shrimp. Chill and serve. Keep under refrigeration. Yield: about 3½ cups.

CUCUMBER CREAM DRESSING

2 tablespoons vinegar
2 tablespoons sugar
1 cup peeled and diced cucumber
1 cup whipping cream, whipped

Add vinegar and sugar to diced cucumber and fold into whipped cream. Yield: 2 cups.

RAMON'S CAESAR SALAD DRESSING

This is a twin sister to the original found at Ramon's Restaurant in Cocoa Beach, Florida. It is marvelous and will keep two months or more in the refrigerator.

1 quart commercial mayonnaise made with
    lemon juice
½ to 1 teaspoon curry powder
½ teaspoon garlic powder
6 eggs
1¼ cups grated Parmesan cheese
4 rounded tablespoons anchovy paste
1 (1⅜-ounce) package onion soup mix

Combine all ingredients in a large pyrex, plastic, or crockery bowl. Keep salad dressing in sealed glass jar in refrigerator; if mixture becomes too thick, thin with a little mayonnaise. Yield: 1½ quarts.

Note: Serve with romaine or iceberg lettuce torn into small pieces; add croutons and toss thoroughly. To serve 4 to 6, use 1 medium head romaine, 1 cup croutons, and enough salad dressing to blend well.

VINAIGRETTE DRESSING

Excellent on tossed green salad or on cold vegetables. Blanch and chill vegetables before pouring dressing over them. For that wonderful dressing you find in France use virgin oil, preferably from Provence. The can is always marked and denotes oil from the first pressing.

6 tablespoons virgin olive oil
2 tablespoons wine vinegar
1 teaspoon salt
⅛ teaspoon freshly ground black pepper
    Pinch dry mustard

Stir well all ingredients, do not use an electric mixer for it will emulsify the mixture. Yield: about ½ cup.

FRUIT SALAD DRESSING

A delightful, special dressing to serve with a fruit salad.

½ cup sugar
1 teaspoon dry mustard
1 teaspoon paprika
¼ teaspoon salt
⅓ cup honey
1 tablespoon lemon juice
4 tablespoons white or champagne vinegar
1 teaspoon grated onion
1 cup vegetable oil, not olive
1 teaspoon celery seeds
1 teaspoon poppy seeds
1 teaspoon mango chutney

Mix dry ingrdients in a bowl. Add honey, lemon juice, vinegar, and grated onion; blend well. Pour oil slowly into mixture, beating constantly with a dover or electric beater. Stir in celery and poppy seeds, and mango chutney. This will keep under refrigeration, but stir well and allow to reach room temperature before using. Yield: 2 cups.

TASTY MAYONNAISE

Bright yellow and zesty, a fitting companion to improve any sandwich or recipe where mayonnaise is needed.

 2 large egg yolks
 1 pint vegetable oil, chilled
   Juice of 2 lemons, strained
 1 teaspoon salt
 ¾ teaspoon dry mustard
 ¾ teaspoon paprika
 3 drops Tabasco

In a deep, narrow-necked bowl beat egg yolks at high speed of electric mixer until thick and lemon colored. Slowly add oil, 1 tablespoon at a time. When mixture begins to be very thick, add small amount of lemon juice. Add salt, mustard, paprika, and Tabasco. Spoon mayonnaise into a glass or plastic container, seal, and refrigerate. Do not store in a metal container. This will keep for several weeks. Yield: 2 to 3 cups.
   Note: If mayonnaise curdles in making, add the curdled mixture a teaspoonful at a time to a fresh cold egg yolk, and continue adding oil slowly.

RECTOR'S FRENCH DRESSING

An excellent dressing from the famous old New York restaurant.

   Salt to taste
 ⅛ teaspoon cayenne pepper
 1 teaspoon freshly ground black pepper
 1 teaspoon dry mustard
 1 teaspoon paprika
 ¼ cup vinegar
 1 cup olive or corn oil
 6 drops Worcestershire sauce
 1 whole clove garlic, finely chopped

In a cruet mix salt, cayenne and black pepper, mustard, and paprika. Add vinegar, oil, Worcestershire sauce, and garlic. Shake well and chill. Delicious with crumbled blue cheese added. Yield: 1¼ cup.

BEAUTY LUCKETT'S POPPY-SEED DRESSING

Poppy seeds add a just-right crunch to this tart-sweet dressing.

 ½ cup sugar
 1 teaspoon poppy seeds
 1 teaspoon salt
 1 teaspoon dry mustard
 1 teaspoon paprika
 ⅓ cup lemon juice, fresh, frozen, or canned
 ¾ cup salad oil

Combine all ingredients except salad oil. Gradually add salad oil, beating with an electric mixer or dover beater until thickened. Yield: about 1½ cups.

KUM BAK-LIKE DRESSING

 ½ cup salad oil
 ½ cup mayonnaise
 1 clove garlic, finely chopped
 ¼ cup chili sauce
 ¼ cup catsup
 1 teaspoon horseradish mustard
 1 teaspoon Worcestershire sauce
 1 teaspoon pepper
   Dash paprika
   Dash Tabasco
   Juice of 1 lemon mixed with 1 tablespoon
     water
 1 medium-size onion, grated
   Salt to taste

Blend all ingredients. Spoon into a glass jar and refrigerate. Allow to reach room temperature before using. Yield: 1½ cups.

SHRIMP-SOUR CREAM DRESSING

A zesty dressing for fish cooked in any fashion, for raw vegetables, or for tomatoes. Use half an avocado as a boat for lump crabmeat and pour this sauce over top for a superb meal. Ideal for a summer luncheon or buffet.

½ pound shrimp
1 clove garlic
1 pint commercial sour cream
½ cup catsup
2 tablespoons Worcestershire sauce
1½ tablespoons grated onion
2 tablespoons prepared horseradish
1 teaspoon paprika
1 tablespoon lemon juice
¼ teaspoon dry mustard

Cook and devein shrimp. Cut finely. Rub bowl with cut garlic and discard clove. Add remaining ingredients. This sauce is best made the day before using. Surround bowl with ripe olives and raw carrots that have been marinated overnight in wine vinegar. Delicious on raw cauliflower. The dressing is quite tasty without shrimp. Yield: about 3 cups.

NO CHOLESTEROL SALAD DRESSING

1 cup tomato juice
4 tablespoons lemon juice
2 teaspoons minced onion
1 teaspoon Worcestershire sauce
1 teaspoon seasoned salt
Salt and pepper to taste

In a deep bowl mix all ingredients with a dover egg beater or electric mixer. Refrigerate. Yield: about 1½ cups.

DOROTHY TARTT'S FROZEN FRUIT SALAD DRESSING

An excellent topping for almost any combination of fresh fruits: peaches, green grapes, cherries, and blueberries.

1 (3-ounce) package cream cheese, softened
1 (10-ounce) jar currant jelly
1 cup mayonnaise
½ pint whipping cream

Beat cream cheese with electric mixer on high speed. Add jelly and beat well. Add mayonnaise and beat until blended. Whip cream and fold into mixture. Put in freezer tray and let freeze. (It takes a long time for it to get firm and it never gets really hard.) Yield: about 3½ cups.

FRENCH DRESSING DELUXE

This delicious dressing is easily made, economical, and keeps well refrigerated in a sealed jar.

2 cups vegetable oil
½ cup wine vinegar
½ cup powdered sugar
¾ tablespoon paprika
½ tablespoon dry mustard
¾ tablespoon salt
¼ cup lemon juice (about 1½ lemons)
½ cup orange juice (about 1½ oranges)
½ tablespoon Worcestershire sauce
½ clove garlic or ⅛ teaspoon garlic powder

In a deep narrow bowl beat oil and vinegar with egg beater or electric mixer. Combine dry ingredients and add to oil mixture; beat well. Add fruit juices and seasonings and beat until thoroughly blended. Pour into a clean 1-quart jar. Keep refrigerated. Allow to reach room temperature and stir well before using. Yield: about 1 quart.

Sauces

SAUCE RAVIGOTE

Serve on cold roast beef, boiled chicken, or fish.

6 tablespoons virgin olive oil
2 tablespoons wine vinegar
1 teaspoon salt
⅛ teaspoon freshly ground black pepper
   Pinch dry mustard
2 tablespoons finely chopped herb mixture
    (chives, chervil, and parsley)
1 teaspoon capers
1 teaspoon chopped onion

Combine first five ingredients in a glass bowl; stir well. Add remaining three ingredients and mix well. Yield: about 1 cup.

RÉMOULADE SAUCE

3 teaspoons finely chopped anchovies
1 cup commercial mayonnaise with lemon
   juice
1 tablespoon tarragon vinegar
1 tablespoon white wine vinegar
2 tablespoons dry sherry
¼ teaspoon garlic powder
½ cup chopped parsley, fresh or frozen
4 tablespoons small capers, well drained
1 tablespoon onion juice or onion puree
½ teaspoon Tabasco

Combine all ingredients and blend well. Refrigerate. Yield: 1¼ cups.

CORINNE MORRIS' BARBECUE SAUCE FOR CHICKEN

Tasty and very hot. You may omit some of the pepper if desired.

½ cup butter
1 tablespoon vinegar
1 teaspoon prepared mustard
1 teaspoon sugar
½ teaspoon salt
¼ teaspoon chili powder
1 tablespoon steak sauce
¼ teaspoon Tabasco
½ teaspoon black pepper
1 teaspoon paprika
1 teaspoon scraped onion
¼ clove garlic, crushed
   Dash of cayenne pepper
2 broiler chickens, cleaned and halved

Simmer first four ingredients in a saucepan for 20 minutes over medium heat. Add remaining ingredients and simmer about 5 minutes longer. Baste chickens with sauce, and place in a pan skin side down. Broil until brown, turning often. Baste every time you turn. After 15 minutes cover pan and bake in a preheated 275° oven about 30 minutes or until tender, basting every 10 minutes. A very young broiler may be broiled in about 20 minutes and needs no baking. Yield: about ¾ cup sauce (basting for 4 servings chicken).

ROSE GERANIUM SAUCE

This delicately flavored sauce is superb over peaches, ambrosia, other fruits, and berries.

6 rose geranium leaves, divided
1 cup whipping cream
¼ cup sugar
1 (8-ounce) package cream cheese, softened

Use leaves as large as your plant will provide (mine were the size of a small saucer). Have water in bottom of a double boiler very hot but not boiling. Place cream, four leaves, and sugar in top pan. Stir occasionally; when cream feels hot to the finger and the leaves are drawn and shriveled, remove leaves and cool mixture. Mash softened cream cheese. When a drop of cream feels warm on inside of wrist, add mashed cream cheese. Blend well. Add two fresh leaves and chill. Pour a generous amount over each dessert serving. Yield: About 2 cups.

NEVER FAIL HOLLANDAISE SAUCE

The beauty of this sauce is that it can be prepared well in advance. Hollandaise can be held warm for an hour in top of a double boiler or in a saucepan over hot water. To store, chill and reheat over hot water when needed; place sauce in a small saucepan and stir constantly with wire whisk until it is fully warm. It should be served warm, not hot.

½ cup butter, divided
2 egg yolks
1 tablespoon strained lemon juice
Pinch salt
Dash cayenne pepper

Divide butter in half, and put half in a small saucepan with slightly beaten egg yolks. Hold saucepan over hot water; do not allow water to boil. Beat constantly with a wire whisk until butter melts; then gradually add remaining butter and warmed lemon juice with salt, and beat until mixture thickens. Remove and add cayenne pepper. Serve at once or remove from heat until needed. For reheating, use directions given above. Yield: 1 cup (enough for 4 servings).

Note: If your sauce refuses to thicken, rinse out saucepan with hot water, and put in 1 teaspoon lemon juice and a tablespoon of the sauce and beat with wire whisk until sauce creams; add remaining sauce ½ tablespoon at a time. Should sauce separate or curdle, beat in 1 tablespoon of cream or undiluted canned milk. If this happens again, add cream and beat again. The sauce may be made in top of a double boiler. Hold the top pan over the steam; never permit it to touch the boiling water. A teaspoon of cornstarch added to egg yolks before they are beaten will help hold sauce that is to be kept warm for a long time.

DATE AND WHITE WINE SAUCE

Marvelous over pound cake or plain white or yellow cake. Does wonders for gingerbread.

½ cup butter
1 cup firmly packed dark brown sugar
1 (8-ounce) package seedless dried or fresh dates
2 cups dry white wine, preferably Rhine variety

Melt butter slowly in a saucepan over medium heat and add sugar, stirring occasionally. Dice dates or cut up whole dates very finely. Add to melted butter and blend well. Add wine, stirring constantly. Bring to a boil and remove from heat. Place sauce in blender, and puree or put through ricer. Serve warm over cake. Yield: 3½ to 4 cups.

FIDELIA'S JEZEBEL SAUCE FOR PORK

Some of this sauce would have made King Ahab's wife a better woman.

1 (16-ounce) jar pineapple preserves
1 (6-ounce) jar prepared mustard
1 (5-ounce) jar fresh light horseradish
1 (12-ounce) jar apple jelly
  Salt to taste

Blend all ingredients with an electric mixer. This sauce keeps well refrigerated in a sealed glass jar. Yield: 3 cups.

MOUSSELINE SAUCE

Great with fish, particularly salmon, and with asparagus and artichoke hearts.

 ½ cup chilled whipping cream
1½ cups Never Fail Hollandaise sauce

Beat chilled whipping cream in a chilled bowl with a wire whisk or electric mixer until it is light and stands in peaks. Fold into Hollandaise Sauce just before serving. The Hollandaise should be barely warm. Yield: 2½ cups.

MRS. PAINE LENOIR'S HAM SAUCE

This sauce is excellent with seafood and is superb with ham.

1 pint commercial mayonnaise made with
    lemon juice
1 clove garlic, crushed
  Creole mustard to taste

Blend all ingredients in a small mixing bowl. The more Creole mustard used, the zestier the sauce. Yield: 1¼ to 1½ cups.

CURRY SAUCE

A quick dressing to serve on raw cauliflower, fresh mushrooms, or seafood cocktail.

 1 whole lemon
 ½ cup homemade mayonnaise or commercial
    mayonnaise made with lemon juice
 ½ cup chili sauce
 ¼ teaspoon curry powder

Cut lemon in half lengthwise and scoop out pulp; retain lemon shell and use juice for dressing (lemon should yield at least 2 tablespoons juice). In a small bowl combine all ingredients. Serve sauce in lemon boats. Yield: 1 cup.

SAUCE MOUTARDE

Serve on cold beef or anything you like.

6 tablespoons virgin olive oil or finest quality
    cottonseed or corn oil
2 tablespoons wine vinegar
1 teaspoon salt
⅛ teaspoon freshly ground black pepper
  Pinch dry mustard
1 tablespoon Dijon mustard
2 tablespoons boiling water
  A squeeze of lemon juice
1 teaspoon chopped parsley, fresh or frozen

Combine all ingredients in a narrow deep glass bowl; beat thoroughly. Yield: 1 cup.

BUTTERSCOTCH SAUCE

 1 cup sugar
 1 cup dark corn syrup
 ½ cup whipping cream
 1 tablespoon butter

Combine ingredients in top of a double boiler, and cook for 1 hour over low heat. Stir occasionally. Yield: 2 cups.

Soups

FRENCH ONION SOUP

A lovely soup, delicately flavored and ideal for lunch or supper. Served with a salad and dessert, it makes a filling meal.

2 pounds thinly sliced yellow onions
1 tablespoon olive or corn oil
3 tablespoons butter
1 teaspoon firmly packed brown sugar
1 teaspoon molasses
1 teaspoon salt
1 teaspoon white pepper
3 tablespoons all-purpose flour
8 cups beef stock or consommé
¾ cup dry white wine or vermouth
   Salt and black pepper to taste
   Toasted French bread
1 to 2 cups shredded Port Salut, St. Paulin,
   or Bonbel cheese

In a heavy-bottomed, covered saucepan cook onions in oil and butter over medium heat for 15 minutes. Uncover and add brown sugar, molasses, salt, and white pepper; stir well. Continue cooking for 35 to 40 minutes or until onions have turned golden brown, stirring often. Sprinkle in flour, blend well, and cook for a few minutes while you bring beef stock to a boil in a separate saucepan. Remove onion mixture from heat and stir in boiling beef stock. (For best results use Beef Stock recipe in this chapter rather than commercial beef stock.) Allow mixture to simmer 20 minutes. Add white wine and cook 20 minutes longer. Skim off foam if necessary and add salt and pepper. Pour soup into oven-proof bowls. Place slice of toasted French bread on each and sprinkle with shredded cheese. Brown under preheated broiler. Serve immediately. Soup may be frozen before adding toasted bread. Yield: 8 servings.

MULLIGATAWNY SOUP

This is the Greenbriers' own delectable version of the East Indian curry soup.

1 cup finely chopped onion
3 tablespoons butter
1 cup all-purpose flour
½ tablespoon curry powder
2 quarts chicken broth
2 apples
½ cup shredded coconut
1 cup whipping cream
1 cup diced eggplant
1 tablespoon butter
   Salt and pepper to taste

In a heavy skillet sauté onion in 3 tablespoons butter over medium heat until brown. Add flour and simmer 20 minutes. Add curry powder, mixing well. (Some people like hot food; if you do not, use ¼ to ½ teaspoon curry powder.) Add broth and bring to a boil. Peel and dice apples, reserve the peelings. Add coconut and apple peelings to broth and allow soup to simmer for 1 hour. Strain. Bring to a boil again and add cream and diced apples. Sauté eggplant in 1 tablespoon butter over medium heat and add to cooked broth; add salt and pepper. Yield: 10 to 12 servings.

ANTOINETTE W. MILLER'S TOMATO CHEESE SOUP

Cold, colorful, and delicious—a good weight-watcher's treat.

1 (10¾-ounce) can condensed cream of
  tomato soup
2 cups whole or skimmed milk
1 tablespoon strained lemon juice
3 or 4 dashes Tabasco
1 teaspoon prepared horseradish
  Salt to taste
½ cup small curd cottage cheese
2 tablespoons finely chopped green onion

In large bowl combine undiluted tomato soup, milk, lemon juice, Tabasco, and horseradish; beat until blended and add salt. Add cottage cheese and green onion and blend well. Chill. This keeps well in a glass jar in the refrigerator. Yield: 1 quart.

VICHYSSOISE

Delightfully refreshing and always a big hit with my guests. This vichyssoise will freeze nicely. Chicken broth may be prepared a day or two ahead.

4 tablespoons butter
4 leeks or shallots, finely sliced
1 large white onion, finely sliced
4 cups Chicken Broth
4 medium-size potatoes, diced
1 teaspoon dried green onion
¼ teaspoon freshly ground white pepper
¼ teaspoon Tabasco
½ teaspoon salt
1 cup half-and-half, divided
1 cup whipping cream, divided
1 tablespoon chopped fresh or frozen chives

Melt butter in a saucepan over medium heat; add leeks or shallots using only white part. Add onion and simmer gently over low heat for 10 to 15 minutes, stirring occasionally with wooden spoon until nearly cooked and clear. (This is very important to produce proper flavor.) Add chicken broth, potatoes, dried green onion, white pepper, Tabasco, and salt. Simmer for 15 to 20 minutes. Pass through a very fine sieve or put into blender. Since a blender holds only 48 ounces, it will be necessary to divide broth mixture into two parts and add ½ cup half-and-half and ½ cup whipping cream to each part. Be sure broth is cold before adding cream. Blend thoroughly and taste. Add more salt if needed. Pour into bowl and refrigerate until ready to serve. Chill soup cups, pour in vichyssoise, sprinkle with chives, and serve. Yield: 10 servings.

Chicken Broth:

1 (2½- to 3-pound) chicken, large fryer or
  young hen
6 cups water
1 teaspoon Bovril
1 chicken bouillon cube
1 teaspoon dried green onion
3 celery ribs with leaves
1 teaspoon salt
1 teaspoon Mei-yen powder

Cover chicken with water in a large saucepan and add remaining ingredients. Bring to boil over high heat. Lower heat and simmer, covered, for about 2 hours. Allow broth to cool, then refrigerate overnight. Remove congealed fat from top of broth and measure out 4 cups broth.

GRANDMA'S VEGETABLE SOUP

Here is a hearty meal in itself with a definite appeal for children who will not eat vegetables. More economical if made when vegetables are plentiful and cheap. A morning's work makes a winter supply.

1 pound boneless chuck roast cut into 1-inch
 squares
3 tablespoons butter
1 (1- to 1½-pound) beef shank or knuckle
 bone or 1 leftover rump bone of rare
 roast beef or 1 leg of lamb bone or bone
 from a large sirloin steak
5 quarts water
3 red or green hot peppers
3 medium-size white onions, each cut into
 tenths
4 celery ribs, finely chopped
3 carrots, cut into small rings
1 teaspoon dried green onion
6 ripe tomatoes
1 (16-ounce) can tomatoes
1 tablespoon plus two teaspoons salt
2 teaspoons seasoned salt
1 medium-size Irish potato, diced
1 quart fresh butterbeans or 1 quart small
 frozen green limas
8 ears fresh corn cut from the cob or 1 quart
 frozen corn
1 quart fresh okra, cut up, or 1 (10-ounce)
 package frozen cut-up okra
1 tablespoon Worcestershire sauce
½ tablespoon salt (optional)

Brown boneless beef chuck in butter in a heavy skillet over medium heat. Rinse out skillet with some of the water, and pour rinsings into large Dutch oven or soup kettle. Add bone, browned beef, water, seasonings, and vegetables listed up through the diced potato. Bring to a boil and let cook for 1 hour on medium heat. Arrange cover so that steam may escape. If cholesterol is a problem in your diet, cook these first ingredients, cool and refrigerate. The next morning, remove the congealed fat with a spoon. Resume preparation by adding butterbeans and cooking for 30 minutes. Add corn and let soup simmer 30 minutes more. Add okra and Worcestershire sauce and cook an additional 30 minutes. Taste and gradually add ½ tablespoon salt, if desired. Remove hot peppers when desired zip pleases your palate.

Soup requires no thickening, it has plenty of body. Should you like it even thicker, add 2 tablespoons flour to 1 cup cold water and stir gradually into soup. Allow soup to cool completely before freezing. Yield 3½ gallons.

CREAM OF BROCCOLI SOUP

A full-bodied soup with a delicate flavor. Served with a salad and dessert it makes a complete meal, ideal for a winter day. Freezing improves its quality.

1 pound fresh broccoli or 2 (10-ounce)
 packages frozen whole broccoli
3 cups chicken broth
¼ teaspoon salt
¼ teaspoon lemon bits or grated lemon rind
½ teaspoon dried green onion
1½ teaspoons powdered mushrooms
⅛ teaspoon freshly ground black pepper
¼ teaspoon Tabasco
1 tablespoon butter
3 tablespoons all-purpose flour
2 cups half-and-half or milk

Soak fresh broccoli in cold water for 15 minutes; drain well. Remove large leaves and tough part of stalks. Cut deep gashes in bottom of stalks. Bring chicken broth to a boil over high heat in a medium-size saucepan and add broccoli, salt, lemon bits, dried green onion, powdered mushrooms, pepper, and Tabasco. Cover pan, lower heat to a simmering boil, and cook for 30 to 35 minutes until stalks are tender when tested with a fork. Puree mixture in blender or put through sieve or ricer.

In large skillet melt butter over medium heat, stir in flour with wire whisk. When smooth, add broccoli puree and continue stirring. As soon as mixture thickens, taste and adjust seasonings if desired. Warm milk in separate pan and add to broccoli mixture. When thoroughly mixed, turn off heat. This will hold for hours on the stove. Reheat slowly. Yield: 6 to 8 servings.

261

CHILLED LEMON SOUP

A refreshing Bajan favorite.

**1 (10¾-ounce) can condensed cream of
    chicken soup**
1 cup half-and-half
**⅛ to 2 teaspoons curry powder, depending on
    taste**
1 tablespoon water
7 tablespoons strained lemon juice, chilled
4 slices lemon

Pour soup and cream into a blender and mix
well. Dissolve curry powder in water and add
to soup mixture. Cover blender and blend for
1 minute. Chill several hours. Stir in chilled
lemon juice just before serving and garnish
with sliced lemon. Chill soup cups before
adding soup. Yield: 4 servings.
Note: On Barbados the islanders like very
hot food and use 2 teaspoons curry powder;
use the amount your taste dictates.

COLD CREAM OF AVOCADO SOUP

Cool and colorful! Ideal to serve at a luncheon
from a crystal punch bowl. This soup is rich
and filling, served with a salad it makes a
complete meal. For a special picnic take it in
a large thermos.

3 large ripe avocadoes, peeled and seeded
**4 cups chicken broth, well seasoned, or 2½
    (13¾-ounce) cans broth**
1 teaspoon salt
⅛ teaspoon cayenne pepper
½ teaspoon Tabasco
2 tablespoons strained lemon juice
2 tablespoons strained lime juice
**2 tablespoons fresh minced onion or 2
    teaspoons dried green onion**
¼ cup dry white wine
3 cups commercial sour cream
¼ teaspoon paprika
1 tablespoon chopped fresh or dried chives

Puree avocado in blender or put through a
sieve; pour into a large bowl. In a saucepan
heat chicken broth, salt, cayenne pepper,
Tabasco, lime and lemon juices, and onion.
When mixture becomes very hot but not boiling, stir in pureed avocado. Add wine and sour
cream; blend well. Divide mixture, return to
blender, and mix well. Chill and garnish with
a sprinkling of paprika and chopped chives.
Yield: 12 servings.
Variation: Any leftover soup may be used
as sauce over a whole chilled tomato. Add a
little more lemon juice, seasoned salt, and
Worcestershire sauce to taste. The combination is colorful and the taste is superb.

CREAMY PEANUT SOUP

Golden rich and very filling, very nutritious.
A quickie!

¼ cup finely chopped onion
1 tablespoon butter
½ cup creamy peanut butter
**1 (10¾-ounce) can condensed cream of
    chicken soup**
**1 (10¾-ounce) can condensed cream of
    celery soup**
1 chicken bouillon cube
2¼ cups milk
¼ cup chopped salted peanuts
⅛ teaspoon paprika
**   Sprigs of parsley**

Sauté onion in butter in a skillet over medium
heat until onion is clear and transparent; do
not brown. Add peanut butter and cook for
3 or 4 minutes, stirring constantly. In a saucepan blend soups, bouillon cube, and milk and
add peanut butter mixture. Sprinkle in
chopped peanuts, and cook until soup is very
hot but not boiling. Serve at once in preheated
soup bowls. Garnish with paprika and a sprig
of parsley for each serving. Yield: 6 to 8 servings.

A QUICK CONGEALED BORSCH

Serve this piquant dish as an appetizer on a hot summer evening. Filling and tasty, it is excellent for those on low-calorie diets.

1½ teaspoons unflavored gelatin
  ¼ cup cold water
  1 (10½-ounce) can beef consommé
  3 (4½-ounce) jars strained beets (use any baby food)
  1 bay leaf
  4 whole cloves
  4 peppercorns
  ½ teaspoon salt
  ¼ teaspoon lemon bits or grated lemon rind
  ⅛ teaspoon freshly ground black pepper
  3 tablespoons strained lemon juice
    Commercial sour cream

Soften gelatin in cold water. In a covered saucepan, combine beef consommé, strained beets, and seasonings; simmer over medium heat for 30 minutes. Remove bay leaf, cloves, and peppercorns. Add dissolved gelatin and stir until thoroughly blended. Add lemon juice, and pour into small glasses or pyrex cups; chill. Top with a dollop of sour cream. Yield: 4 (6-ounce) servings.

BEEF STOCK

  2 pounds beef brisket
  4 quarts cold water
  4 celery ribs, finely chopped
  2 medium-size onions, peeled
  3 scraped carrots, cut into small rings
12 peppercorns
  1 teaspoon dried parsley
  1 bay leaf
  2 whole cloves
  ¼ teaspoon lemon bits or grated lemon rind
  2 teaspoons seasoned salt
  2 teaspoons salt
  2 beef bouillon cubes

In a large kettle combine brisket and 4 quarts cold water, and bring to a boil over medium heat. When water comes to a boil, remove foam as it starts to rise. A sharp pointed spoon does the best job. This foam may appear for several minutes. Add chopped celery and peeled onions which have been cut into tenths. Add remaining ingredients and bring mixture to a simmering boil with kettle partially covered. Turn heat to low and cook for 3½ to 4 hours. Skim off any foam. If liquid evaporates below the level of vegetables, add more boiling water. Taste to see if the stock has obtained the flavor of your ingredients. Chill stock. When fat has set, scrape it off. Reheat and strain for use in onion soup. Yield: 2 quarts or more.

SPLIT PEA SOUP

A taste treat and economical.

1 pound split peas
5 cups water
1 medium-size onion, chopped
2 peppercorns
1 clove garlic
2 carrots
1 ham bone or hock with trimmings
1 bay leaf
3 celery ribs or ¼ cup chopped celery tops
1 tablespoon butter
  Salt to taste
1 (5-ounce) can Vienna sausage (optional)

Wash peas, cover with water, and let stand overnight; drain. Add 5 cups water and remaining ingredients except butter, salt, and Vienna sausage. Bring to a boil, cover, and let simmer about 2 hours or more until peas are tender and mixture is thick. Remove bone and bay leaf and press mixture through a sieve. Before serving add butter and salt. For a sumptuous repast garnish with sliced Vienna sausage when ready to serve. Serve hot. Yield: 6 servings.

BAYOU LEMON SOUP

Exotic and very similar to Greek lemon soup. It's a quickie.

  3 (13¾-ounce) cans chicken broth or 1½
      quarts homemade chicken broth
  2 tablespoons cold water
  ¼ cup regular long grain rice
  ½ teaspoon white pepper
  1 teaspoon dried green onion
5½ tablespoons strained lemon juice
  3 large eggs

In a saucepan bring chicken broth and water to a boil over high heat; add rice, pepper, and onion. Reduce heat to low and simmer about 15 minutes or until rice is tender. In a small bowl beat lemon juice and eggs until light and frothy. Pour small amount into hot broth, beating rapidly with a wire whisk; gradually add remaining egg mixture, beating constantly with whisk. Cook over low heat until broth reaches the boiling point. Remove at once; *do not allow to boil.* Serve hot. Yield: 6 servings.

SALMON-CORN CHOWDER

Easy to prepare, this delicious chowder makes an ideal Lenten meal. For a lovely lunch serve with a tart congealed fruit salad and hot biscuits.

  1 (16-ounce) can salmon
  1 quart water
  1 (12-ounce) can whole kernel corn
  1 (11-ounce) can condensed tomato bisque
  ¼ teaspoon lemon bits or grated lemon rind
  ¼ teaspoon Mei-yen powder
  ¼ teaspoon freshly ground white pepper
1½ teaspoons salt
  1 bay leaf, broken in two
  4 dashes Tabasco
  ¼ cup finely chopped celery leaves
  1 cup half-and-half or milk

Combine all ingredients except half-and-half in a large soup kettle or saucepan; blend thoroughly. Bring to boil over medium heat; cover and simmer for 40 minutes, stirring occasionally. Add half-and-half slowly and cook 15 minutes longer keeping vessel covered. Yield: 6 servings.

MARIAH MITCHELL'S FAMOUS SEAFOOD GUMBO

Mother Mitchell was known along the Mississippi Gulf Coast for her Christian deeds and fabulous seafood cooking. She truly excelled in both. This gumbo is typical of southern Louisiana Bayou cookery and very similar to that of the Carolina Low Country. True gumbo results from slow cooking which allows ingredients to blend perfectly. You will never taste any better. There are 3 easy steps.

To Prepare Crabs for Soup:

  Water to cover
 2 teaspoons salt
½ teaspoon cayenne pepper
 6 big hard shell crabs

In a large kettle bring enough water to cover crabs to a boil; add salt and pepper and drop in live crabs. Cover and allow crabs to boil for 10 to 15 minutes or until they turn red. Pour off boiling water and cover with cold water. As soon as crabs are cool enough to handle, remove small legs and crack claws. Pull off back shell or apron and remove spongy membranes or "deadmen's fingers" that adhere to the shell, scraping from the inside out. (These can make you ill if they are not removed.) The yellow eggs may be removed if you wish, but many people consider them a delicacy. Break the crabs in half along the natural ridge, and with a sharp knife cut in half. You may pick out the meat or leave for each guest to pick out his own. To prepare cold boiled crabs, use the above directions, but add 1 teaspoon crab and shrimp boil to the first water.

Soup Stock:

3½ quarts water
 ½ pound veal, cubed
  1 pound ham (preferably with bone), cubed
  2 teaspoons salt

Combine all ingredients in a very large kettle or stock pot, and bring to a boil over high heat. Reduce to medium heat, cover, and simmer for 2 hours. To save time, prepare the soup stock the day before you make the gumbo.

Gumbo:

½ cup bacon drippings or corn oil, divided
½ cup all-purpose flour
 1 pound fresh okra or 2 (10-ounce) packages frozen okra, cut into ½-inch pieces
 1 large onion, finely chopped (1 cup or more)
 1 cup finely chopped celery
 2 cloves garlic, finely chopped
 1 pound fresh tomatoes or 1 (16-ounce) can tomatoes
 4 large ears fresh corn, shucked and corn cut from cob or 2 (10-ounce) packages frozen corn
 6 large hard shell crabs, cleaned and broken in half or 1 pound claw or white crabmeat
 1 pound fresh butterbeans or 2 (10-ounce) packages frozen tiny butterbeans
 1 tablespoon Worcestershire sauce
 2 teaspoons salt
 1 teaspoon dried thyme
 1 hot pepper or ½ teaspoon Tabasco
 1 pound fresh shrimp
 1 quart water
 2 tablespoons gumbo filé powder

Make a roux by heating ¼ cup bacon drippings in a heavy skillet over medium heat. Add flour and stir until absorbed by oil. Cook over low heat, stirring constantly until flour is fairly brown; do not let flour burn, it will ruin the roux. This takes about 30 minutes.

In another skillet, fry okra in remaining ¼ cup bacon drippings over medium high heat until soft and ropy texture is gone. Add more oil if okra sticks. Add onion, celery, and garlic to roux and cook until onions are wilted, not brown. Add tomatoes and stir constantly for several minutes. Add this mixture to veal-ham Soup Stock in a very large kettle and stir until mixture is completely blended. Add cooked okra and all remaining ingredients except shrimp, water, and gumbo filé. Allow mixture to simmer for 1 hour.

Cook shrimp in 1 quart water over medium heat for 7 minutes. Drain, reserving liquid; clean and devein shrimp. If shrimp are very large, cut each into 3 pieces. Add shrimp, cooked, cleaned crabs, and 1 cup shrimp liquid. Allow to simmer 30 minutes. Just before you are ready to serve, add gumbo filé while soup is still boiling. Stir well and remove from heat; filé becomes bitter if cooked. Serve hot. To freeze, cool gumbo, refrigerate, and freeze. Never leave gumbo on the stove overnight to cool. The gumbo's marvelous flavor improves even more with reheating; the seasonings have had time to meld fully and ripen. Serve in hot bowls over a mound of fluffy cooked rice with a tossed green salad and hot French bread for a meal beyond compare. True gumbo results from slow cooking which allows ingredients to blend perfectly. Yield: 1¾ gallons. If serving nothing but gumbo, I would count on 20 to 22 servings.

Note: Use only 1 hot pepper if you do not like your food very zesty. Let your taste buds dictate.

TURTLE BEAN SOUP

This delectable soup, a favorite of my grandmother's, ranked high on the list of soups to serve special company. A treat for a late supper or after a football game. Serve it with tossed green salad and hot French bread for a very satisfying meal.

 1 pound black beans
 3 quarts water
 1 ham bone with meat
 ½ pound lean beef, chopped
 2 medium-size onions, thinly sliced
 ¾ cup julienne-sliced celery
 ¾ cup sliced carrots
 6 black peppercorns
 2 cloves
 ⅛ teaspoon ground mace
 4 teaspoons salt
 ¼ teaspoon lemon-pepper marinade
 ½ cup chopped parsley
 1 bay leaf
 4 tablespoons butter or olive oil
 ¼ cup sherry
 1 lemon, sliced
 2 hard-boiled eggs, sliced

Cover beans with water and soak overnight. Drain and add 3 quarts fresh water to beans in a large saucepan or soup kettle. Add remaining ingredients except butter, sherry, sliced lemon, and eggs. Bring to a boil over high heat, cover, lower to a simmering boil, and cook for 3 hours or until beans are soft. Remove ham bone and bay leaf and run through a sieve or puree in blender. Reheat soup, add butter, taste to see if more salt is needed. When ready to serve, put 1 tablespoon sherry in each soup bowl, add 1 thin slice lemon and 2 slices egg. Yield: 8 to 10 servings.

SHE-CRAB SOUP

Superb! Serve with a lovely fresh fruit salad and hot French bread for a very filling meal.

 1 pound white crabmeat and roe
 6 tablespoons butter
 1 tablespoon all-purpose flour
 1 pint milk
 1 pint half-and-half
 ½ teaspoon Worcestershire sauce
 1 teaspoon grated lemon rind
 ¼ teaspoon ground mace
 1 teaspoon salt
 ¼ teaspoon freshly ground white pepper
 3 crackers, rolled into crumbs
 3 tablespoons dry sherry
 ½ cup whipping cream, whipped
   Paprika

With clean hands, check crabmeat for bits of shell or cartilage. Melt butter in top of a double boiler over rapidly boiling water and blend in flour. Add milk and half-and-half, stirring constantly. Add Worcestershire sauce, grated lemon rind, mace, and crabmeat and roe. Stir well and cook slowly for 20 minutes. Season with salt and white pepper and add cracker crumbs. Allow to stand over hot water on back of stove for 10 or 15 minutes. Serve in heated soup bowls, add ½ tablespoon sherry to each bowl, top with a dollop of whipped cream, and sprinkle with paprika. Yield: 6 to 8 servings.

Note: If you live inland, have a butcher open a can of fresh crabmeat and see whether it has the small yellow particles or roe. Lump crabmeat usually does.

SHRIMP SOUP SUPREME

This superb soup comes from Beau Fort, historical plantation of Mrs. C. Vernon Cloutier near Nachitoches, Louisiana. The soup is very filling and makes a complete meal when served with a scoop of rice in each bowl.

½ cup finely chopped celery
½ cup butter
3½ pounds shrimp
3 (10¾-ounce) cans condensed cream of
    mushroom soup
½ cup finely chopped green onion tops
1 cup water
¼ cup finely chopped parsley
½ cup dry sherry
¼ teaspoon Tabasco
   Salt to taste
   Cooked Rice

In a large saucepan or soup kettle sauté celery in butter over very low heat for 15 minutes, stirring occasionally. Wash, peel, and devein shrimp. In separate saucepan combine mushroom soup, green onions, and water. Heat slowly over low heat; do not allow to boil. When celery is cooked, add shrimp, mushroom mixture, parsley, sherry, Tabasco, and salt. Cook over medium heat for 20 to 25 minutes until soup comes to a simmering boil. Serve with cooked rice. This will freeze. Yield: 8 servings.

CREOLE OYSTER SOUP

During the Lenten season add variety to your menus with this superb soup. Guaranteed to make your task lighter and your family's enjoyment brighter.

2 tablespoons vegetable shortening
¼ cup butter
4 tablespoons all-purpose flour
2 small onions, finely chopped
1 clove garlic, minced
1 celery rib, finely chopped
⅛ teaspoon pepper
1 beef bouillon cube
1 cup boiling water
¼ teaspoon ground mace
1 pint oysters and juice
1 quart milk
   Salt to taste
   Croutons, crackers, or French bread

In a heavy skillet melt shortening and butter over medium heat. Add flour, stirring constantly until blended. Add onion, garlic, celery, and pepper and cook for about 7 minutes. Add beef cube which has been dissolved in boiling water. Add mace and oysters with juice after checking oysters for bits of shell. Cook until oysters plump up and are ruffled around the edges. In a separate saucepan heat milk but do not boil; add milk to oyster mixture and serve at once. If the oysters are salty, no salt need be added to the soup. Taste after milk has been added, and add salt accordingly. The oyster base may be prepared ahead of time, but be sure to refrigerate until it is used. Serve with croutons, crackers, or French bread. Yield: 6 servings.

Vegetable Varieties

SOUR CREAMED GREEN BEANS

A delightful quickie!

2 (16-ounce) cans Blue Lake cut green beans
2 tablespoons butter or margarine
2 tablespoons all-purpose flour
1 cup milk
3 tablespoons minced or grated onion
½ teaspoon salt
5 tablespoons fresh lemon juice
1 (16-ounce) carton commercial sour cream

In a saucepan heat green beans slowly over low heat and keep warm. In a teflon skillet melt butter over medium heat, add flour and blend well with wire whisk. Stirring constantly, add warmed milk gradually; then add onion, salt, and lemon juice. Cook until thickened, add sour cream, and stir about 2 minutes—just long enough to heat thoroughly. Drain beans and place in a hot serving dish and pour sauce over all. Yield: 6 to 8 servings.

GREEN GODDESS BEANS

My little granddaughter likes these beans so much that she asked me to have them at every meal during her visit. Easily prepared, it's a quickie.

1 (16-ounce) can Blue Lake whole green beans
1 bottle 1890 French salad dressing
5 slices bacon

Drain beans and marinate in dressing and refrigerate overnight. Divide beans into 5 even stacks and roll each stack in a slice of bacon. Secure with a toothpick. Place in an oblong pan or casserole and bake in a preheated 350° oven for 25 to 30 minutes or until bacon is crispy brown. Serve hot. Yield: 5 servings.

CAROTTES COINTREAU

Carrots at their party best—tart and different.

1 (16-ounce) can small Belgian carrots
1 tablespoon tart sweet orange instant breakfast drink
¼ teaspoon salt
1 tablespoon cornstarch
⅛ teaspoon ground nutmeg
2 tablespoons butter
1 teaspoon chopped fresh or dried parsley
1 tablespoon sugar
2 tablespoons Cointreau

Drain carrots; reserve liquor. Place carrot liquor, orange breakfast drink, salt, cornstarch, and nutmeg in a medium-size saucepan and bring to boil over medium heat, stirring constantly until mixture thickens. Add butter, dried parsley, sugar, Cointreau, and carrots. Cook 3 or 4 more minutes over low heat, serve hot. If fresh parsley is used, sprinkle on top just before serving. Yield: 4 servings.

Note: To serve 8, use 2 cans of carrots and above quantities of sauce. To serve 16, use 4 cans of carrots and double the quantities given for the sauce.

STUFFED BAKED TOMATOES

The shocking red tomato has always graced our table on such special occasions as Thanksgiving and Christmas as an exciting accompaniment to roast turkey. Served on my mother's giant Chinese blue platter and wearing a golden hat topped with a sprig of parsley, a tomato never ceases to be a conversation piece.

  8 large ripe tomatoes
  ⅓ stick butter (reserve 1 tablespoon for top of
      tomatoes)
  ½ cup finely chopped onion
  ½ cup finely chopped celery
  4 slices white bread, soaked in water and
      squeezed out in colander
  9 soda crackers, finely crushed, divided
  1 egg, well beaten
  1 (4½-ounce) can deviled ham
  ¼ teaspoon dried green onion
  1 teaspoon salt
  ⅛ teaspoon freshly ground black pepper
  1 tablespoon Worcestershire sauce
  ⅛ teaspoon baking powder
  8 sprigs parsley (optional)

Remove core and tops of tomatoes. Scoop out pulp with a measuring spoon. Place pulp in a large skillet over medium heat and cook about 20 minutes until pulp is cooked to pieces and there is very little moisture left. Use potato masher if tomatoes are firm. At the same time place butter in another skillet over medium heat and add chopped onion and celery. Cover and stir occasionally. Cook about 15 minutes or until vegetables are tender. In a large mixing bowl put softened bread, 4 crushed crackers, and beaten egg. Pulverize this mixture with a potato masher; add cooked tomato pulp, deviled ham, celery, onion, and dried green onion. Blend well and return to large skillet. Add salt, pepper, Worcestershire sauce, and baking powder. Cook slowly until mixture thickens and moisture evaporates, stirring often. Fill and mound tomato cups with stuffing and cover with remaining 5 crushed crackers and reserved tablespoon of butter, melted. Place tomato cups in a shallow pan and barely cover bottom of pan with water. Bake at 400° for 10 to 15 minutes or until golden on top. Add sprig of parsley before serving. You may prepare stuffing in morning and wait until last minute to fill tomato cups and bake. Yield: 8 tomatoes.

BAKED COCKTAIL TOMATOES

A quick and easy dish to prepare and serve with steak.

  ¼ cup vegetable oil
  1 teaspoon salt
  ⅛ teaspoon freshly ground black pepper
  1 pint ripe cocktail tomatoes
  ¼ teaspoon fresh or dried basil
  ¼ cup grated Parmesan cheese (optional)

Combine oil and seasonings and swish tomatoes around in mixture in baking dish; sprinkle with basil. Bake in a preheated 400° oven for 3 minutes on one side; turn over and cook 2 minutes on the other side. Serve hot with broiled steak. For an extra fillip sprinkle generously with grated Parmesan cheese after tomatoes are turned. Yield: 3 or 4 servings.

DANNIE HELUM'S TOMATOES STUFFED WITH ARTICHOKE HEARTS

A tangy quickie with a party flair. The tomatoes, cut into neat squares, make a delicious companion for roast beef or a broiled steak.

  2 (16-ounce) cans whole peeled tomatoes, drained
  1 teaspoon salt
  ¼ teaspoon freshly ground black pepper
  ⅛ teaspoon sugar
1¼ teaspoons sweet basil
  1 (14-ounce) can artichoke hearts, drained and rinsed
  4 tablespoons butter or margarine
  1 cup toasted bread crumbs (about 3 slices bread, buttered and toasted)
  ½ cup grated Parmesan cheese

Butter a 10- x 6½- x 2-inch casserole. Cross cut tomatoes so they can hold an artichoke heart. Place tomatoes, properly spaced, in the casserole. Blend salt, black pepper, sugar, and basil; sprinkle over top and sides of tomatoes. Allow tomatoes to stand 15 minutes. Place one artichoke heart in the center of each tomato and top with pat of butter.

Combine bread crumbs and Parmesan cheese. Sprinkle half of crumb-cheese mixture over tops and sides of tomatoes; bake in a preheated 400° oven for 10 minutes; then sprinkle remaining crumb-cheese mixture over top and turn dial to broil. Cook on middle oven shelf for 2 or 3 minutes or until golden brown. Serve hot. Yield: 6 to 8 servings.

SPINACH TART

A superlative dish that is easy to prepare, does not drip and can be reheated. It is ideal for ringing a ham, roast, or whole baked fish. It may be served as a separate course for luncheon or buffet supper and is marvelous with cold roast and potato salad.

  1 (10-ounce) package frozen spinach
  1 teaspoon salt
  ¼ teaspoon dried lemon bits or grated lemon peel
  2 tablespoons minced onion
  1 tablespoon butter
  ⅛ teaspoon ground oregano
  1 cup commercial sour cream, divided
  1 egg, well beaten
  1 teaspoon lemon juice
  6 (3-inch) unbaked pastry shells
  ⅓ cup chopped ripe olives

Cook spinach according to package directions, but use 1 teaspoon salt and ¼ teaspoon lemon bits. Drain, pressing out as much water as possible. Cook onion with butter and oregano until soft but not browned. Combine spinach, onion, ½ cup sour cream, egg, additional salt if needed, and lemon juice. Spoon into unbaked pastry shells and bake in a preheated 375° oven for 25 to 30 minutes or until golden. Spoon remaining sour cream over tarts and top with olive slices. Yield: 6 servings.

SPINACH LOAF

You might expect to find this loaf with its delicious Creole Sauce in one of the restaurants in New Orleans' French Quarter.

  2 cups chopped frozen or fresh spinach, uncooked
  2 eggs, well beaten
  ¾ cup diced pasteurized process cheese loaf
  2 tablespoons bacon drippings
  1 cup toasted bread crumbs
  1 tablespoon vinegar
  ½ teaspoon pepper
    Creole Sauce

Combine all ingredients except Creole Sauce; stir gently to mix well. Place in a greased 9- x 5- x 3-inch glass loaf pan, and bake in a preheated 400° oven for approximately 30 minutes. The mixture will set and can be turned out to slice. Serve hot with Creole Sauce. Yield: 6 to 8 servings.

Creole Sauce:

4 slices bacon, diced
2 tablespoons chopped onion
2 tablespoons chopped green pepper
2 tablespoons all-purpose flour
1 cup strained tomatoes or tomato sauce
1 teaspoon Worcestershire sauce
¼ teaspoon salt
   Pinch pepper
⅛ teaspoon ground mace

Fry bacon with onion and green pepper until lightly browned. Add flour and tomatoes and cook until thickened, stirring constantly. Add remaining ingredients; cook for 5 minutes and serve over sliced Spinach Loaf. Yield: 6 to 8 servings.

MARY WAGNER'S CREOLE EGGPLANT

This makes an excellent vegetable to serve with barbecued food on the patio. Garlic bread makes an ideal accompaniment.

1 medium-size eggplant
1 medium-size white onion
1 bell pepper, cut into small pieces
3 medium-size tomatoes, sliced
½ cup olive oil
1 hot pepper, finely chopped (optional)
1 teaspoon salt
4 drops Tabasco

Peel and cube eggplant. Peel and chop onion coarsely. Remove seeds and hard core of bell pepper and cut into small pieces. Place vegetables in a saucepan over medium heat and add olive oil. Stir mixture occasionally. For a spicy hot dish, add hot pepper. Cook 30 minutes until vegetables are tender when tested with a fork. Add salt about 10 minutes before

removing from heat. Taste to see if adequate. For just a little zing, add 4 drops Tabasco when dish is done. Serve hot or cold. Yield: 6 to 8 servings.

JO NICHOLSON'S EGGPLANT JALAPEÑOS

Marvelous and better if made a day in advance.

2 large eggplants
6 ounces jalapeño cheese
1 (10¾-ounce) can condensed cream of
   mushroom soup
1 bell pepper, finely chopped
4 green onions, finely chopped
½ cup butter
3 slices white bread, broken into small pieces
1 pound fresh mushrooms
   Salt to taste
1 teaspoon monosodium glutamate
1 teaspoon Tabasco
1 teaspoon Worcestershire sauce
1 teaspoon ground marjoram
   Dash oregano
   Toasted French bread crumbs
2 tablespoons butter

Peel and cube eggplant and cook in a saucepan in a small amount of water over medium heat about 20 minutes or until tender. Drain off liquid. In a double boiler melt jalapeño cheese in cream of mushroom soup. In a skillet sauté bell pepper and green onions in butter until tender. Add bread, drained eggplant, cheese-soup mixture, and mushrooms which have been washed, dried, and sliced. Add seasonings.

To prepare French bread crumbs, cut loaf of bread in half lengthwise, butter, and toast at 250° until very crisp; then grate. Reserve any leftover bread crumbs to use at a later time. Pour eggplant mixture into a buttered 2-quart oblong casserole, cover with toasted buttered bread crumbs and bake at 350° about 25 to 30 minutes or until bubbly. Yield: 8 servings.

ARTICHOKE DELIGHT

Try these artichoke hearts with roquefort cheese. Delicious with roast or steaks.

 1 (3-ounce) package roquefort cheese
 ½ cup butter
 1 tablespoon lemon juice
 1 (14-ounce) can artichoke hearts, drained
 ¼ teaspoon paprika
   Salt

Crumble cheese into small pieces. Melt butter in top of a double boiler; add cheese and lemon juice. Add artichoke hearts and paprika. Taste to see if salt is needed. Serve hot. Yield: 2 to 4 servings.

ARTICHOKE HEARTS WITH SAUCE WINIFRED

A zesty treat anytime of the year.

 2 tablespoons finely chopped onion
 3 tablespoons pureed or finely diced carrots
 2 tablespoons butter or corn oil margarine
 2 cups chicken stock
 6 peppercorns
 3 sprigs parsley
 1 bay leaf
 4 tablespoons butter or corn oil margarine
 4 tablespoons all-purpose flour
 1½ cups scalded milk
 ¼ teaspoon salt
 ⅛ teaspoon white pepper
 2 cups cubed cooked chicken or turkey
 ½ (2-ounce) jar pimientos, drained and finely
   chopped
 1 teaspoon dried green parsley
 1 pound large fresh mushrooms or 1
   (8-ounce) can button mushrooms
 6 fresh artichoke hearts, cooked

Sauté onion and carrots in 2 tablespoons butter using a heavy iron skillet. When onion is clear and golden, add chicken stock, peppercorns, parsley, and bay leaf. Simmer for 30 minutes, uncovered. Strain and place broth in refrigerator until ready to complete the sauce.

To complete sauce, melt 4 tablespoons butter in top of a double boiler; add flour slowly and stir with wooden spoon until mixture is bubbly. Slowly add scalded milk using a wire whisk for blending. When sauce is the consistency of thick cream, stir in salt, pepper, and reserved broth; heat. Then stir in hot chicken chunks, pimientos, parsley, and mushrooms. Cook for 10 minutes; then taste to see if more salt is needed. Serve over very hot artichoke hearts. Yield: 6 servings.

FONDS D'ARTICHAUTS AUX ÉPINARDS (Atichoke Hearts with Spinach)

Snowy mounds of souffléed spinach atop artichoke hearts make a spectacular and tasty dish for company. These may be made hours ahead and heated 15 minutes before serving.

 2 (10-ounce) packages frozen spinach
 1 (4-ounce) can mushroom pieces
 6 tablespoons butter, divided
 1 tablespoon all-purpose flour
 ½ cup milk
 ½ teaspoon salt
 ⅛ teaspoon garlic powder
 1 (14-ounce) can artichoke hearts (8 to 10
   hearts), drained
   Sour Cream Hollandaise

Cook spinach according to package directions. Sauté mushrooms in 4 tablespoons butter for 4 or 5 minutes. Melt remaining 2 tablespoons butter in a skillet over medium heat. Add flour and milk and stir until smooth. Add salt, garlic powder, and sautéed mushrooms. Drain spinach and puree in blender; then add to sauce. Cut off bottom end of hearts so they will stand evenly. Rinse artichoke hearts with cold water. Prepare Sour Cream Hollandaise to go with spinach. Put 1 tablespoon Sour Cream Hollandaise on each bottom; top with a mound of spinach and cover with an additional tablespoon of sauce. Yield: 8 to 10 servings.

Note: Quickie way: use a commercial spinach soufflé, one package for 6 artichoke bottoms. Cook the frozen spinach soufflé according to package directions and proceed as directed above. Save the extra sauce to serve over asparagus or broccoli.

Sour Cream Hollandaise:

1 cup commercial sour cream
1 cup mayonnaise
¼ cup lemon juice
½ teaspoon salt
¼ teaspoon Tabasco

Combine ingredients in a saucepan and warm slowly over low heat.

FRESH ARTICHOKE RING

A delectable luncheon dish. Fill ring center with creamed chicken, crabmeat, oysters or shrimp and serve hot with cream sauce on round silver tray or chop dish.

Step 1:

7 artichokes
  Water to cover
7 tablespoons salt
1 lemon, sliced
1 tablespoon vegetable or olive oil
1 bay leaf
1 teaspoon celery seed or 2 celery ribs
1 teaspoon concentrated instant crab and
    shrimp boil
1 tablespoon Worcestershire sauce

Cut off artichoke stems or bases, and soak artichokes in cold water for 30 minutes. Bring enough water to cover artichokes to a boil in a large soup kettle or Dutch oven. Add artichokes and remaining ingredients and bring water back to a boil as rapidly as possible, and boil slowly for 45 minutes to 1 hour. Artichokes are done when leaves pull out easily. Drain and cool. Remove leaves and scrape soft tender flesh from bottom of each leaf onto a plate. Remove choke and cut up the hearts. This preparation may be done the day before and refrigerated.

Step 2:

  Artichoke flesh and hearts
⅓ cup saltine cracker crumbs
½ pint whipping cream
4 large eggs, beaten
1½ tablespoons grated onion
⅛ teaspoon garlic powder
1 (10¾-ounce) can condensed cream of
    mushroom soup
1 teaspoon salt
½ teaspoon Tabasco
1 tablespoon butter

Whip artichoke flesh and hearts with an electric mixer until light; remove strings from beaters. Add cracker crumbs, whipping cream, and beaten eggs. Add onion, garlic powder, undiluted mushroom soup, salt, and Tabasco. Taste to see if more salt is needed. Butter a 9-inch ring mold and fill with mixture. Set mold in pan of warm water and bake in a preheated 350° oven for 35 to 40 minutes. Gently go around edges with spatula and turn out on tray. Serve hot, fill center with your favorite creamed chicken or seafood and plenty of cream sauce. Yield: 8 to 10 servings.

HEARTS OF ARTICHOKE SUPREME

This unusual recipe from southern France is delicious with a Cajun fish stew or Creole shrimp. Alone, it's great with a cocktail. Artichoke hearts cooked in this manner provide a tasty cup for hot chicken à la king or cold shrimp salad.

  6 fresh artichoke hearts
    Lemon juice
  2 quarts water
  2 tablespoons salt
  ½ teaspoon lemon-pepper marinade
    Juice and rind of 1 lemon
  4 cups Madeira, or enough to cover hearts
  3 to 4 drops green food coloring (optional)
  1 (2¾-ounce) can pâté de foie gras

To prepare the artichoke hearts: begin with the outermost leaves of the artichoke and bend each back until it snaps; then pull off and discard. Continue to do this until the bottom of the leaves reaches the curve of the base. Cut off the top of the remaining leaves a full ½ inch from their base. Cut off the stem even with the base. This leaves the choke and the base with a rim. Then trim base portion of leaves until only white is showing. Rub with lemon juice as you cut to prevent discoloration of artichoke.

Combine the water, salt, lemon-pepper marinade, and lemon juice and rind in a large pan. Bring to boil and add fresh artichoke hearts. Place the hearts in seasoned boiling water as soon as possible. Cook 20 minutes; then drain in colander. Place the hearts, Madeira, and food coloring, if desired, in a smaller saucepan. Simmer another 20 minutes or until tender. Test with fork. Take from pan and gently remove choke with small spoon. These hearts may be prepared several days in advance and refrigerated; reheat before serving. Place the hot artichoke hearts on a warm serving platter and spread the cold pâté de foie gras on each heart. Yield: 6 servings.

Note: To serve 12, double the ingredients with the exception of the wine (use 6 cups). Canned hearts may be used, but they will not make as flavorful a dish. Do not cook these, but soak them in hot Madeira for 30 minutes before using.

BEETS IN ORANGE CUPS

A colorful, fresh and tasty way to serve beets.

  1 cup fresh orange juice (4 small to
    medium-size oranges)
  1 (16-ounce) can shoestring beets, drained
  2 tablespoons lemon juice
  ½ teaspoon powdered ginger
  1 tablespoon vegetable oil
  2 teaspoons sugar
  2 tablespoons grated orange peel

After squeezing juice, remove inner skin from orange and cut outer peel in a saw-tooth design around top of each half. In a saucepan combine all ingredients except orange cups and peel. Cook over medium heat for 15 to 20 minutes. Place in warmed orange cups and sprinkle grated orange peel over top. This makes 4 to 6 servings without use of cups. Yield: 8 cups.

MUSTARD OR TURNIP GREENS

  3 ½ to 4 pounds (3-ounces) mustard and
    turnip greens mixed
  ½ cup water
  2 tablespoons corn oil
    Ham bone or a 3-inch thick slice of ham,
    diced
  1 hot pepper
  1 teaspoon sugar
  1 teaspoon salt
    Vinegar (optional)

Wash greens in five or six changes of water until water is clear. Pick and discard leaves from heavy stalks. Place small tender leaves in a large saucepan with remaining ingredients except salt and bring to a boil over high heat with pan covered. Lower heat and cook at a simmering boil for about 2 hours. When greens cook down, add salt. Taste to see if more is needed. Remove ham bone and hot pepper before serving. Drain greens and cut up finely with two knives. Serve vinegar with greens, if desired. Hot corn bread is always served in the South with turnip greens. These will freeze. Yield: 8 to 10 servings.

ZUCCHINI SOUFFLÉ

A palate teaser and light as a summer breeze. The zucchini base makes enough for four soufflés. Freeze each cup separately. Serve with broiled ham steak and hot biscuits for an unforgettable meal.

    3 cups sliced zucchini (about 1 pound)
    1 cup water
    2 chicken bouillon cubes
    1 tablespoon instant minced onion
    1 tablespoon dried parsley flakes
    1 teaspoon Season-All
 2½ tablespoons butter
    2 tablespoons all-purpose flour
    1 cup beef bouillon
    4 egg yolks
    ¼ teaspoon Tabasco
    ¼ teaspoon dried green onion
    ½ teaspoon salt
    4 egg whites
    ¼ teaspoon cream of tartar
    ⅛ teaspoon paprika

Wash zucchini, slice and place in a large saucepan with water, chicken cubes, instant minced onion, parsley flakes, and Season-All. Bring mixture to a boil over medium-high heat. Cover and cook until zucchini is tender, about 20 minutes. Put through a sieve or puree in a blender; if using blender, put half of mixture in at a time.

Melt butter in a saucepan over low heat. Add and blend in flour, stirring constantly with wire whisk. Stir hot bouillon in slowly. Raise heat to medium and cook until sauce is smooth and boiling. This will be very thick. Remove from heat and add egg yolks; beat well. Add one cup zucchini mixture, Tabasco, dried green onion, and salt.

Preheat oven to 400°. Beat egg whites until very frothy using high speed of electric mixer. Add cream of tartar and continue beating until the whites are very stiff, stand in peaks, and hold. Stir in a fourth of the beaten egg whites into soufflé mixture to lighten it. With a spatula fold in remaining egg whites. This does not take more than a minute or two. Pour soufflé into a 6-cup charlotte mold or a 1½ quart casserole of the bowl type. Sprinkle top of soufflé with paprika. Lower heat to 375° and place mold on middle rack of oven. Bake at 375° for 25 to 30 minutes. A well-cooked soufflé will hold 5 to 10 minutes in a turned off hot oven. Yield: 6 servings.

ZUCCHINI FRITTERS

    1 pound zucchini
    1 teaspoon finely chopped dried or fresh
        green chives
    1 tablespoon finely chopped dried or fresh
        parsley
    1 cup buttermilk pancake mix
    ¼ teaspoon salt
    ¼ teaspoon freshly ground black pepper
    1 egg, beaten
    ½ cup corn or olive oil

Wash zucchini and grate in blender or by hand. Place in a large bowl and add remaining ingredients except oil. Mix well. Heat oil in a large skillet over a medium-high heat. Drop mixture by heaping tablespoonfuls onto skillet. As soon as fritter browns on one side, about 3 minutes, turn with pancake turner and brown the other side. This recipe will serve 6 to 8. Yield: 14 fritters— 6 to 8 servings.

CARROTS SUPREME

Carrots with glamour. They are superb—be sure there are enough for second helpings.

8 large carrots or 1 (16-ounce) can sliced carrots
¼ teaspoon salt
½ cup cherry preserves
¼ cup apricot preserves
¼ cup pineapple preserves
1 teaspoon strong or spicy prepared mustard
1 tablespoon sherry or 2 teaspoons lemon juice

Wash, scrape, and dice raw carrots into 1-inch bias slices. Cover with cold water. Add salt and cook until tender, allowing carrots to absorb the water. Drain off any excess. Combine cherry, apricot, and pineapple preserves with mustard and sherry; add carrots to mixture. Taste to see whether a dash of salt is needed. Yield: 4 to 6 servings.

MARTY HEDERMAN'S CARROT COPPER PENNIES

Carrots in a delicious marinade.

2 pounds carrots
1 medium-size white onion
1 small bell pepper
2 cups water
1 (10¾-ounce) can condensed cream of tomato soup
½ cup vegetable oil
1 cup sugar
¾ cup vinegar
1 teaspoon salt
1 teaspoon freshly ground black pepper
1 teaspoon Worcestershire sauce
1 teaspoon prepared mustard

Wash and scrape carrots and cut into rounds, ⅛ to ¼ inch thick. Remove outer skin and cut onions into thin round slices. Remove seeds and white pithy part of bell pepper; cut into thin round slices. Add carrots to 2 cups water in covered saucepan and cook over very high heat for 10 minutes. Drain, cool, and add to sliced rounds of onion and bell pepper in a large glass or stainless steel bowl. Blend tomato soup, vegetable oil, sugar, vinegar, salt, black pepper, Worcestershire sauce, and mustard in another bowl. Pour over vegetables and stir well. Cover bowl and marinate overnight in refrigerator. Drain to serve. These will keep two weeks or more refrigerated. Yield: 12 servings.

BLACK-EYED PEA SOUFFLÉ

Zesty! Serve with broiled ham steak and hot biscuits for an unforgettable meal.

2½ tablespoons butter
2 tablespoons all-purpose flour
1 beef bouillon cube dissolved in 1 cup boiling water
4 egg yolks
1 cup Gourmet Black-Eyed Pea Dip (see Appetizers and Hors d'Oeuvres)
¼ teaspoon Tabasco
¼ teaspoon dried green onion
4 egg whites
¼ teaspoon cream of tartar

In a saucepan melt butter over low heat; add and blend in flour, stirring constantly with wire whisk. Slowly stir in hot bouillon, raise heat to medium and cook sauce until smooth and boiling. This will be very thick. Remove from heat and add egg yolks; beat well. Add Black-Eyed Pea Dip, Tabasco, and dried green onion. Adjust seasoning; taste to see if salt or more Tabasco is needed.

Preheat oven to 400°. Beat egg whites until very frothy using high speed of electric mixer; add cream of tartar and continue beating until

276

whites are very stiff, standing in peaks and holding. Stir a fourth of the beaten egg whites into soufflé mixture to lighten it. With spatula fold in remaining whites. Pour soufflé into a 6-cup charlotte mold or a 1½-quart pyrex casserole of the bowl type. Lower heat to 375°, place casserole on middle rack of oven, and bake for 25 to 30 minutes. A well-cooked soufflé will hold 5 to 10 minutes in a turned off hot oven. Yield: 6 servings.

SOUFFLÉED SQUASH

The tastiest!

2 pounds small tender squash, white or yellow
4 tablespoons butter or margarine, divided
½ teaspoon salt
1 teaspoon dried green onion
¼ teaspoon freshly ground black pepper
⅓ cup celery, finely chopped
¼ cup onion, finely chopped
¼ cup green pepper, finely chopped
2 large eggs, room temperature
1 tablespoon milk
1 tablespoon honey
Salt to taste
1 teaspoon baking powder
⅛ teaspoon Tabasco
1 teaspoon Worcestershire sauce
1 teaspoon all-purpose flour
2 tablespoons fine cracker crumbs or 2 tablespoons finely shredded sharp cheddar cheese

Wash unpeeled squash and slice as thinly as possible; place slices in saucepan with 3 tablespoons butter, salt, dried green onion, and freshly ground pepper. Cover and simmer over low heat for about 25 minutes or until squash is tender when tested with a fork. Mash squash in a large bowl and add celery, onion, and green pepper. Combine lightly beaten eggs with milk, honey, salt, baking powder, Tabasco, Worcestershire sauce, and flour; fold into squash mixture. Taste to see if more salt is needed. Grease soufflé cups with butter or margarine and fill with mixture. Top with cracker crumbs and brush with remaining 1 tablespoon melted butter. Place in a pan of hot water which is at least 1-inch deep. Bake in a preheated 350° oven for 30 minutes or until light brown and bubbling. Yield: 6 servings.

ACORN SQUASH WITH RUM AND NUTS

Miss Eudora Welty, one of my favorite tasters, answered in reply to my question about adding more brown sugar to the dish, "I would not change it. It has a subtle, mysterious flavor. It's lovely; you know it came from the earth."

1 medium-size acorn squash, cut into halves
2 teaspoons firmly packed dark brown sugar
¼ teaspoon salt
2 tablespoons butter
4 teaspoons dark rum
¼ teaspoon freshly ground black pepper
2 teaspoons butter
2 teaspoons chopped almonds, pecans, walnuts or filberts

Remove pith and seed from squash, score cut squash deeply and place in each half 1 teaspoon brown sugar, ⅛ teaspoon salt, 1 tablespoon butter, 1 teaspoon rum and ⅛ teaspoon pepper. Place pan containing water on the lower shelf of oven. Cover squash with foil and bake on middle shelf in a preheated 375° oven about 45 minutes or until tender. Test with fork for tenderness.

Scoop out squash meat taking care not to spill the succulent juice. Blend well with fork or spoon and return to shell, add another teaspoon butter with 1 teaspoon rum to each half and sprinkle with 1 teaspoon chopped nuts. Continue baking until nuts are golden brown. Serve hot for best results. This may be reheated. Yield: 4 to 6 servings.

277

MIXED VEGETABLES AND SAUCE

A marvelous *bouquetière* of vegetables to serve with a roast or meat loaf.

1 (10-ounce) package frozen English peas
1 (10-ounce) package frozen baby lima beans
1 (10-ounce) package French-cut green beans
1 teaspoon salt
2 cups boiling water
1 cup mayonnaise
3 hard-boiled eggs
3 tablespoons lemon juice
2 tablespoons minced onion
1 teaspoon Worcestershire sauce
1 teaspoon prepared mustard
¼ teaspoon garlic salt
3 to 4 dashes Tabasco

Cook vegetables in boiling salted water according to package directions; drain. Combine remaining ingredients in a saucepan over low heat and cook until warm, not too hot because mayonnaise will separate. Pour over well-drained vegetables; mix well. Yield: 8 to 10 servings.

CORN FRITTERS

An excellent accompaniment to chicken or ham.

1 cup milk
2 large eggs, slightly beaten
2 cups all-purpose flour, spooned into cup
2 teaspoons baking powder
1 teaspoon salt
2 tablespoons melted butter
1 (17-ounce) can whole kernel corn
Vegetable oil

In a large bowl add milk to slightly beaten eggs. Add dry ingredients, butter, and corn and beat until well mixed. Heat ⅛-inch deep oil in a large skillet on high heat and drop batter by tablespoonfuls into hot grease. These cook quickly in 2 or 3 minutes, turn with pancake turner and let other side turn golden brown. If you use a deep fat fryer, cook at 350° and fry 3 or 4 minutes until golden. Drain on absorbent paper and place on warmed platter in oven until ready to serve. The batter will hold refrigerated until the next day. Yield: 16 to 18 fritters.

SOUL FOOD—SWEET POTATO PONE

Something different from Lonestar Plantation in the heart of the Mississippi Delta. Serve hot with chicken, turkey, or pork.

4 large sweet potatoes
1 cup butter or margarine, softened
1 cup firmly packed dark brown sugar
2 large eggs, well beaten
½ teaspoon ground nutmeg
½ teaspoon ground cinnamon
½ teaspoon ground cloves
¼ teaspoon salt
1½ cups half-and-half or undiluted evaporated milk
1 teaspoon vanilla extract
½ cup Blue Ribbon molasses
Grated rind of ½ orange
Grated rind of 1 lemon

Peel sweet potatoes and grate medium finely. Cream butter and brown sugar by hand or with electric mixer on medium speed. Add beaten eggs to creamed mixture. Add grated potatoes, spices, salt, half-and-half, and vanilla. Stir in molasses and grated orange and lemon rinds. Beat all together and pour mixture into a well-buttered, 13- x 9- x 2-inch oblong pan. The mixture should not be very thick but on the runny side. Bake in a preheated 300° oven for 1 hour. Yield: 14 to 15 servings.

Hints and Measures

HELPFUL HINTS FOR COOKING SUCCESS

Every cook has her own tricks of the trade—special tips on how to make cakes more moist or how to make fluffy, light biscuits or how to keep gravy smooth and rich. I have learned many such helpful hints throughout my years of cooking experience, a few of which I'd like to share with you here.

Baking	Unless otherwise specified, always preheat the oven at least 20 minutes before baking.
Browning	For best results in browning food in a skillet, dry the food first on paper towels.
Measuring	Always measure accurately. Level dry ingredients with top of a cup or a knife edge or a spoon handle. Measure liquids in a cup so that the fluid is level with the top of the measuring line. Measure solid shortening by packing it firmly in a graduated measuring cup.
Freezing	Milk cartons make splendid freezing containers for stocks, soups, etc. They also serve well for freezing fish or shrimp, foods that should be frozen in water.
Baking Powder	Always use double-acting baking powder.
Breads and Cakes	To test for doneness in baking a butter or margarine cake, insert a straw or wire cake tester into the center of the cake in at least two places. The tester should come out perfectly clean if the cake is done. The cake should be lightly browned and should be beginning to shrink from the sides of the pan.

ORIENTAL VEGETABLES KABUKI

From the well-known Kabuki restaurant in Cincinnati, Ohio.

½ pound fresh mushrooms
½ pound white onion (1 large onion)
½ pound zucchini squash
⅓ cup olive oil
1 teaspoon salt
½ teaspoon coarsely ground black pepper
¼ teaspoon sugar
3 tablespoons soy sauce

Wipe mushrooms with a damp cloth. If they are very dirty, rinse in a colander under cold running water; then dry thoroughly on paper towels. Slice fine, lengthwise. Peel onion and cut into very fine rings. Wash zucchini and cut into very narrow strips, lengthwise. In a large skillet heat olive oil over medium heat and toss in the vegetables. Using a pancake turner, constantly toss the mixture. Add salt, pepper, and sugar and continue cooking for 15 minutes. Add soy sauce and cook 5 minutes longer. Serve alone as a vegetable or over cooked rice for a main dish. Yield: 4 servings.

Variation: For a fancier entrée add ½ pound cleaned and deveined shrimp the last 5 minutes of cooking.

SAFFRON RICE

Exotic and colorful! Serve with seafood dishes and highly seasoned meat.

2 tablespoons olive or vegetable oil
2 tablespoons butter or margarine
¼ teaspoon crumbled saffron
1 tablespoon boiling water
3 cups water
1½ teaspoons salt
1½ cups regular white rice, uncooked

Blend oil and butter in a medium-size saucepan and cook over medium heat 5 minutes,

stirring occasionally. Mix saff
spoon boiling water and allov
minutes. Add 3 cups water an
butter mixture and bring to a
water and rice. When mixture
reduce heat, cover, and simn
minutes until liquid is absc
colander with cold water and s
a fork. Place colander over ho
until rice is fluffy and grains st
hot. Yield: 10 servings.

TASTY CANNED GREEN B

As flavorful as fresh beans.

1 slice country ham about 3 i
diameter of 1 slice ½-incl
or small ham hock
2 tablespoons bacon dripping
salt pork only)
½ medium-size onion, coarsel
1 cup water
2 (16-ounce) cans Blue Lake
beans, drained and liquid
1 hot pepper or ¼ teaspoon T
Salt to taste

In a heavy skillet cook ham ov
brown on both sides. If using
and brown in bacon drippin
heat. With both meats lowe
onion until clear. Add water
to prevent spattering. Add be
liquid with hot pepper and br
ing boil. Cook for 25 minut
from heat and allow beans to
more. Season with salt. Yield

HE
CO
Eve
or
ma
to s

Bal

Brc

Me

Sto

Bal

Bre

Breads and Cakes *Continued*	If the cake is pressed with a finger in the center, it should come back into shape at once.
	If cake tests done, remove from oven, invert cakepan for 5 minutes (or time specified in the instructions), then loosen the cake from the sides and bottom of the pan. Invert it onto a plate or cake rack and turn it right side up on another cake rack so that air may circulate around it. This prevents sogginess.
	A sponge cake should be tested for doneness in the same manner as a butter cake, but keep the sponge cake inverted until it is thoroughly cold. Then run a knife around the sides and across the bottom and remove from pan. Trim off any hard edges.
	To test bread made with fruit or nuts, thump the crust and if it sounds hollow, remove the bread from the oven and cool on a wire rack.
	Bread cooked with fruit or nuts should be tested with a straw in the center. The straw should come out perfectly clean if the bread is done.
Butter	When a recipe says "greased pan," grease the pan with solid shortening or an oil, unless butter is specified.
	Do not use commercial whipped margarine in place of butter unless the recipe calls for melting it.
Candies	The weather is a big factor in candymaking. On a hot, humid day it is advisable to cook candy 2° higher than in cold, dry weather.
Eggs	Unused or extra egg whites may be frozen and used as needed. Make Meringues or Angel Pies with the whites later. Egg whites freeze well and do not need to be defrosted.
	When boiling eggs, add 1 teaspoon salt to the water. This prevents a cracked egg from draining out.
Fruit	A whole lemon heated in hot water for 5 minutes will yield 1 or 2 tablespoons more juice than an unheated lemon.
Sauces	When a sauce curdles, remove pan from heat and plunge into a pan of cold water to stop cooking process. Beat sauce vigorously or pour into a blender and beat.
	When making a cream or white sauce, melt butter, add flour, and blend well. Remove from heat before adding warmed milk. It should never lump.

Seafood	For improved texture and flavor when using canned shrimp, soak shrimp for 1 hour in ice water and drain.
	One pound raw shrimp yields about 2 cups cooked and peeled shrimp.
Vegetables	Cooking such vegetables as green peppers and cucumbers briefly in boiling water makes them more digestible than raw vegetables.
	All strings can be easily removed from string beans after washing if they are plunged into boiling water for 5 minutes. Drain in colander and string.
	New potatoes should be cooked in boiling water. Old potatoes should start in cold water and be brought to a boil.
	When vegetables or other foods scorch in cooking, immediately remove the pan's cover and the contents and plunge the saucepan into cold water for 20 to 30 minutes. Wash saucepan and return contents and resume cooking.
	When cooking cabbage, shrimp, or other foods that cause unpleasant odors, put a dozen cloves in a small pan of boiling water and let simmer. The odor of the cloves will counteract the unpleasant odor with a delightful fragrance. (It's cheaper than commercial deodorant sprays.)
	Rub hands with parsley to remove any odors after chopping garlic or onions.
Whipping Cream	Day-old, heavy cream whips stiffer than new cream. If cream is too thin to whip, add an egg white and see the result.

COOKING MEASURE EQUIVALENTS

Metric Cup	Volume (Liquid)	Liquid Solids (Butter)	Fine Powder (Flour)	Granular (Sugar)	Grain (Rice)
1	250 ml	200 g	140 g	190 g	150 g
¾	188 ml	150 g	105 g	143 g	113 g
⅔	167 ml	133 g	93 g	127 g	100 g
½	125 ml	100 g	70 g	95 g	75 g
⅓	83 ml	67 g	47 g	63 g	50 g
¼	63 ml	50 g	35 g	48 g	38 g
⅛	31 ml	25 g	18 g	24 g	19 g

APPROXIMATE CONVERSION TO METRIC MEASURES

When you know . . .	Multiply by . . .	To find . . .	Symbol
	Mass (weight)		
ounces	28	grams	g
pounds	0.45	kilograms	kg
	Volume		
teaspoons	5	milliliters	ml
tablespoons	15	milliliters	ml
fluid ounces	30	milliliters	ml
cups	0.24	liters	l
pints	0.47	liters	l
quarts	0.95	liters	l
gallons	3.8	liters	l

HANDY SUBSTITUTIONS

It is always best to use the ingredient called for in the recipe, but occasionally it is necessary to make a substitution. For best results, use this table only when you do not have the ingredient called for in the recipe.

If Recipe Calls For	You May Use
1 square unsweetened chocolate	3 tablespoons cocoa plus 1 tablespoon butter or margarine
2 large eggs	3 small eggs
1 egg	2 egg yolks (for custards)
1 egg	2 egg yolks plus 1 tablespoon water (for cookies)
1 cup sifted all-purpose flour	1 cup sifted cake flour plus 2 tablespoons
1 cup sifted cake flour	1 cup sifted all-purpose flour minus 2 tablespoons
1 cup honey	¾ cup sugar plus ¼ cup liquid
1 cup fresh milk	½ cup evaporated milk plus ½ cup water
1 cup fresh milk	3 to 5 tablespoons nonfat dry milk powder in 1 cup water
1 cup fresh milk	1 cup sour milk plus ½ teaspoon soda (decrease baking powder 2 teaspoons)
1 cup sour milk or buttermilk	1 or 2 tablespoons lemon juice or vinegar with milk to fill cup (let stand for five minutes)
1 cup brown sugar (firmly packed)	1 cup granulated sugar
Thickening	1 tablespoon quick-cooking tapioca or 1 tablespoon cornstarch or 2 tablespoons all-purpose flour

283

CANNED FOOD GUIDE

Can Size	Number of Cups	Number of Servings	Foods
8-ounce	1 cup	2 servings	fruits, vegetables
10½- to 12-ounce (picnic)	1¼ cups	3 servings	condensed soups, fruits and vegetables, meats and fish, specialties
12-ounce (vacuum)	1½ cups	3 to 4 servings	vacuum-packed corn
14- to 16-ounce (No. 300)	1¾ cups	3 to 4 servings	pork and beans, meat products, cranberry sauce
16- to 17-ounce (No. 303)	2 cups	4 servings	principal size for fruits and vegetables, some meat products
1 pound, 4 ounce (No. 2)	2½ cups	5 servings	juices, pineapple, apple slices
27- to 29-ounce (No. 2½)	3½ cups	7 servings	fruits, some vegetables (pumpkin, sauerkraut, greens, tomatoes)
46-ounce (No. 3 cyl.)	5¾ cups	10 to 12 servings	fruit and vegetable juices
6½-pound (No. 10)	12 to 13 cups	25 servings	institutional size for fruits and vegetables

EQUIVALENT WEIGHTS AND MEASURES

Food	Weight	Measure
Apples	1 pound (3 medium-size)	3 cups, sliced
Bananas	1 pound (3 medium-size)	2½ cups, sliced about 2 cups, mashed
Bread	1 pound	12 to 16 slices
Butter or margarine	1 pound	2 cups
Butter or margarine	¼-pound (1 stick)	½ cup
Butter or margarine	size of an egg	about ¼ cup

Food	Weight	Measure
Candied fruit or peels	½ pound	1¼ cups, cut
Cheese, American	1 pound	4 to 5 cups, shredded
cottage	1 pound	2 cups
cream	3-ounce package	6 tablespoons
Cocoa	1 pound	4 cups
Coconut, flaked or shredded	1 pound	5 cups
Coffee	1 pound	80 tablespoons
Cornmeal	1 pound	3 cups
Cream, heavy	½ pint	2 cups, whipped
Dates, pitted	1 pound	2 to 3 cups, chopped
Dates, pitted	7¼-ounce package	1¼ cups, chopped
Flour		
all-purpose	1 pound	4 cups, sifted
cake	1 pound	4¾ to 5 cups, sifted
whole wheat	1 pound	3½ cups, unsifted
Lemon juice	1 medium-size	2 to 3 tablespoons
Lemon rind	1 medium-size	2 teaspoons, grated
Macaroni	1 pound	4 cups dry
Milk		
evaporated	6-ounce can	¾ cup
evaporated	14½-ounce can	1⅔ cups
sweetened condensed	14-ounce can	1¼ cups
sweetened condensed	15-ounce can	1⅓ cups
Nuts, in shell		
almonds	1 pound	1 to 1¾ cups nutmeats
peanuts	1 pound	2 cups nutmeats
pecans	1 pound	2¼ cups nutmeats
walnuts	1 pound	1⅔ cups nutmeats
Nuts, shelled		
almonds	1 pound, 2 ounces	4 cups coarsely chopped
peanuts	1 pound	4 cups coarsely chopped
pecans	1 pound	4 cups coarsely chopped
walnuts	1 pound	3 cups coarsely chopped
Onion	1 small	¼ cup, chopped
	1 medium-size	½ cup, chopped
	1 large	1 cup, chopped
Orange, juice	1 medium-size	⅓ cup
Orange, rind	1 medium-size	2 tablespoons, grated
Raisins, seedless	1 pound	3 cups
Sugar		
brown	1 pound	2¼ cups firmly packed
powdered	1 pound	3½ cups unsifted
granulated	1 pound	2 cups

EQUIVALENT MEASUREMENTS

Use standard measuring cups (both dry and liquid measure) and measuring spoons when measuring ingredients. All measurements given below are level.

3 teaspoons	1 tablespoon
2 tablespoons	1 fluid ounce
4 tablespoons	¼ cup
5 tablespoons plus 1 teaspoon	⅓ cup
8 tablespoons	½ cup
16 tablespoons	1 cup
1 cup	8 fluid ounces
2 cups	1 pint (16 fluid ounces)
⅛ cup	2 tablespoons
⅓ cup	5 tablespoons plus 1 teaspoon
⅔ cup	10 tablespoons plus 2 teaspoons
¾ cup	12 tablespoons
Few grains (or dash)	less than ⅛ teaspoon
Pinch	as much as can be taken between tip of finger and thumb

APPROXIMATE TEMPERATURE CONVERSIONS—FAHRENHEIT TO CELSIUS

	Fahrenheit (°F)	*Celsius (°C)*
Freezer		
coldest area	–10°	–23°
overall	0°	–17°
Water		
freezes	32°	0°
simmers	115°	46°
scalds	130°	56°
boils (sea level)	212°	100°
Soft Ball	234°-238°	112°-114°
Firm Ball	240°-242°	115°-116°
Hard Ball	248°-250°	120°-121°
Slow Oven	268°	131°
Moderate Oven	350°	177°
Deep Fat	375°-400°	190°-204°
Hot Oven	450°-500°	232°-260°
Broil	550°	288°

To convert Fahrenheit to Celsius:
  subtract 32
  multiply by 5
  divide by 9.

To convert Celsius to Fahrenheit:
  multiply by 9
  divide by 5
  add 32

Index